NINIAN SMART ON WORLD RELIGIONS (VOLUMES 1–2)

John Shepherd has achieved a mammoth task in gathering this extraordinarily rich and diverse collection of Ninian Smart's papers. Carefully selected, skilfully arranged and, most valuable, complemented by a substantial introduction and a complete bibliography of his writings, this work bears witness to Smart's wide-ranging studies on world religions, philosophies and cultures, always set within a larger global vision. A real landmark, this publication reveals like no other Smart's numerous achievements and proves his lasting importance for the contemporary study of religions. It also provides the foundations for a critical reassessment by the next generation of scholars. Exceeding mere academic interest, it has much to offer to all students, teachers and readers interested in world religions or in Ninian Smart as scholar and human being. Surprises will await them on both accounts.

Ursula King, Professor Emerita, University of Bristol, UK

Ninian Smart was a seminal figure in the emerging discipline of Religious Studies and this book of wide-ranging, incisive and often witty essays helps us to understand why. Ranging from ancient Buddhism to contemporary Californian culture, and from ethics to worldview analysis, these essays show how Smart's agile and inventive mind helped to create a new academic discipline. This useful book deserves to be on the shelf of every serious scholar of Religious Studies as a reference, inspiration, and testimony to one of the intellectual giants of the twentieth century.

Mark Juergensmeyer, Professor, University of California, Santa Barbara, author of *Terror in the Mind of God* and *Global Rebellion* and President, American Academy of Religion.

Ninian Smart was arguably one of the most gifted and tough-minded thinkers in the field of Religious Studies of the past generation. This collection of writings – many difficult to find – will make available a wide range of remarkable work, displaying in full the best qualities of Smart's thinking. As such, it will be a valuable resource for future work in the study of religion.

Ivan Strenski, Professor, UC Riverside, USA

It is very clear that Shepherd has done a masterful job in collecting the only complete bibliography of Smart's enormous contributions to the study of religion in the last half of the twentieth century. This is a work which will be definitive and authoritative and will contribute much at three levels. First, Smart was the heir of a long tradition of scholarship on religion. How he assimilated that tradition and at the same time made major advances in how we might study religion is fully documented in this collection. So much of Smart's way of doing the study of religion has become so commonplace that we often overlook how we achieved the present state of the discipline. Shepherd's collection of Smart's work should lead a new generation of scholars to consider the powers of comparison and to execute an intellectual agenda with the same boldness of spirit which is present in the corpus of Smart's work. As a marker of where we have been and where we might go, this collection will be indispensable. Third, Smart's contribution to the pedagogy of the study of religion is equally remarkable and is fully present for the first time in this collection. This collection by Shepherd will thus help to train new generations of teachers who will make their contributions not only in their published research, but also in how they enact and carry forward the study of religion in their classrooms and lecture halls. This will be a very important contribution to scholarship and I urge you to think boldly about how it might be realized in its entirety.

Richard Hecht, Professor, University of California, Santa Barbara, USA

Ninian Smart will surely remain best known for his philosophically informed analyses of religion as a cultural phenomenon, but his numerous occasional writings provided entertainment and stimulation, for some disturbing and for others liberating. He was unstoppably creative.

Michael Pye, Professor, University of Marburg, Germany. President of the International Association for the History of Religions 1995–2000

John Shepherd, a student of Ninian Smart's at Lancaster Unversity and the organizer of the Ninian Smart Archive at Lancaster, knows the Smart corpus better than anyone else. For Ninian Smart on World Religions *he has chosen writings that evince the extraordinary range of Smart's work on religion. Smart wrote about religion generally and about specific religions, both Western and Eastern. He contributed to the philosophy of religion, to the sociology of religion, to the comparison of religions, to mysticism, to religious ethics, and to religious dialogue. He linked up traditional religions with new ones and with secular ones. His approach, like his character, was inclusivist and irenic rather than exclusivist and dogmatic. He knew multiple religions firsthand, not just in the abstract. Living religions, not just texts, grabbed him. He was as much an ethnographer as a theorist, and even his theorizing focused more on the identification of elements, or 'dimensions', of religion than on the explanation of them. No contemporary scholar was a finer ambassador for Religious Studies than Ninian, as the writings chosen by Shepherd evince. With its comprehensive overview of Smart's multifarious writings on religion, this excellent volume, better than any other, shows what made Ninian Ninian.*

Robert A. Segal, Professor, University of Aberdeen, UK

Ninian Smart was the Dean of Religious Studies in the Anglophone world and a major influence on the discipline in the last half of the twentieth century, author of many books and founder of one of the excellent, independent journals of Religious Studies, Religion.

It is high time there was a collection of Smart's essays that reflects the development of his thought on world religions – something which deserves to be an object of study, in its own right. This is that collection. Here, under one cover is a snapshot of Smart's intellectual legacy. John Shepherd is to be commended for his assembly of a rich and representative set of essays, spanning Ninian Smart's long career. This collection, edited by Shepherd, is a must-have for anyone interested in the study of world religions or the history of the study of religion. Certainly, no library should be without it.

Thomas Ryba, Adjunct Professor, Purdue University,
North American editor of *Religion*

Ninian Smart, the past master of Religious Studies, whose influence today is as a source for critical reflection and the sounding out of new directions in research and pedagogy. The carefully selected and themed essays of the volume range from the well-known to those which are hard to track down. John Shepherd, who has previously established the Ninian Smart Archive in the Library of Lancaster University, provides an outstanding critical analysis, teasing out the tensions in Smart's thought which are very much alive today. A marvellous volume to mark the forty years anniversary of Ninian's founding of Religious Studies in Britain.

Paul Heelas, Professor, Department of Religious Studies, Lancaster University, UK

Few of us interested in the study of religion during the second half of the twentieth century could fail to have been influenced directly or indirectly by Ninian Smart; and even fewer of us could fail to be stimulated and learn much from this invaluable collection of his papers. A truly Renaissance man, Smart belonged to and fostered a tradition in which learning spanned both space and time. The breadth of his comparative knowledge has rarely been equalled, but there was also a sensitivity and depth to his understanding of religions. Those who are acquainted with Smart's work will need no encouragement to turn to this volume. Those who are acquainted are strongly recommended to do so to gain both erudition and sheer pleasure.

Eileen Barker, Professor Emeritus, London School of Economics, UK

ASHGATE CONTEMPORARY THINKERS ON RELIGION: COLLECTED WORKS

General Editor: John R. Hinnells

Ninian Smart on World Religions

ASHGATE CONTEMPORARY THINKERS ON RELIGION: COLLECTED WORKS

General Editor: John Hinnells

Other titles in this series:

ASHGATE CONTEMPORARY THINKERS ON RELIGION: COLLECTED WORKS

General Editor: John R. Hinnells

Ninian Smart on World Religions

Volume 1: Religious Experience and Philosophical Analysis

Edited by
John J. Shepherd
University of Cumbria, UK

ASHGATE

Published in the series **Ashgate Contemporary Thinkers on Religion: Collected Works** by

Ashgate Publishing Limited
Wey Court East
Union Road
Farnham
Surrey, GU9 7PT
England

Ashgate Publishing Company
Suite 420
101 Cherry Street
Burlington
VT 05401-4405
USA

www.ashgate.com

British Library Cataloguing in Publication Data
Smart, Ninian, 1927–2001
    Ninian Smart on world religions : selected papers
    Vol. 1: Religious experience and philosophical analysis. –
    (Ashgate contemporary thinkers on religion : collected works)
    1. Religions
    I. Title II. Shepherd, John J.
    200

Library of Congress Cataloging-in-Publication Data
Smart, Ninian, 1927–2001
    Ninian Smart on world religions : selected works / edited by John J. Shepherd.
        p. cm. — (Ashgate contemporary thinkers on religion)
    Includes bibliographical references.
    ISBN 978-0-7546-4080-6 (v. 1 : alk. paper) – ISBN 978-0-7546-6638-7 (v. 2 : alk. paper)
    – ISBN 978-0-7546-6639-4 (set : alk. paper) 1. Religions. 2. Religion.
    I. Shepherd, John J. II. Title. III. Title: On world religions.

BL80.3.S63 2007
200 – dc22

2007026160

ISBN 978 0 7546 4080 6

Mixed Sources
Product group from well-managed
forests and other controlled sources
www.fsc.org Cert no. SGS-COC-2482
© 1996 Forest Stewardship Council

Printed and bound in Great Britain by
TJ International Ltd, Padstow, Cornwall

For Libushka and family

Contents

IV: COMPARATIVE STUDIES

V: RELIGIOUS STUDIES AND RELIGIOUS EDUCATION: METHOD AND THEORY IN THE STUDY OF RELIGIONS

Ninian Smart

Ninian Smart (1927–2001)

One of the best known and, certainly in the UK, one of the most influential scholars of religion of the latter half of the twentieth century, Ninian Smart shot to national prominence as founding professor of the new Department of Religious Studies in the University of Lancaster, opened in 1967. The first department of its kind in the country, it aroused considerable controversy with the announcement that the holder of the chair might be 'of any faith or none'.

Smart was in fact a committed Christian, moving to Lancaster from the position of H.G. Wood Professor of Theology at the University of Birmingham, but was already known in academic circles, through his research work and various publications, as a lucid and thought-provoking practitioner of comparative religion. From his new base in Lancaster he now worked at giving fresh shape to this field methodologically, and also at cementing its place at all levels in the education system. Publishing widely, both at an advanced academic and also at a more popular level, he achieved an international reputation as a skilled analyst and exponent of religions (and related worldviews).

From 1976 to 1982 Smart divided his time between Lancaster and the Department of Religious Studies at the University of California, Santa Barbara, where from 1986 to his retirement in 1998 he was the J.F. Rowny Professor in the Comparative Study of Religion. From 1998 to 2000 he was President of the American Academy of Religion. Widely travelled, Smart was a popular guest lecturer in many parts of the world, combining a sharp intellect and a keen sense of humour. He was honoured with a number of awards.

Smart advocated a distinctive multidisciplinary method in the study of religion, although in some earlier publications he perhaps overemphasized a so-called phenomenological approach, leading some commentators (and critics) to place him in an unduly confined pigeon-hole. His overall aim was to minimize confessional bias and maximise open-mindedness – the study of religion being too important to be anything other than appropriate for people 'of any faith or none'.

In the UK this stance became central to debates about the changing shape of religious education in schools. Smart was a key figure in the move that gathered momentum from the late sixties onwards from a Christian confessional to a multi-religious non-confessional approach, and he helped set up the influential Shap Working Party on World Religions in Education. Many would regard his impact on education as central to his legacy.

Smart returned to Lancaster in order to spend his last years, still full of fresh ideas and projects. Sadly, the years were to be only weeks. He is buried in Lancaster.

(For a fuller account, see the entry on Smart in *Encyclopedia of Religion*, 2nd edition, 2005, vol. 12, New York: Macmillan Reference Books.)

Preface

Ninian Smart published nearly three hundred papers in scholarly books and journals, and the task of selecting from them is a daunting one. My approach has been to attempt an analytical framework within which the choice can be made, and which facilitates an overall understanding of Smart's wide-ranging and varied output. A mix of earlier and later papers has been included, giving at least some sense of developments in his interests and thought, and some less severely academic items have also been included, so that there is a mix here for the kind of wide audience that he himself was adept at addressing. The aim has been to provide representative coverage of main themes and topics in Smart's work, while also attempting a balance between papers that are little-known because they are difficult to access, and some that have already appeared more than once, but are too important to omit. The latter, though, have been kept to a minimum, especially where they have already reappeared in the two edited collections *Concept and Empathy*, ed. Don Wiebe (1986), and *Reflections in the Mirror of Religion*, ed. John P. Burris (1997) – hence there are a number of cross-references to these two publications in the Introduction, 'A Critical Analysis'.

In the Introduction I have sought to convey a sense of the shape of the work overall, and thus to contextualize the papers that follow. Additional papers are referred to from time to time, as are some of the forty plus books that Smart authored or co-edited, by way of reinforcing the overall analysis. (Papers included in the present volumes are indicated by their chapter and page numbers herein.)

The allocation of papers to the different categories is no doubt sometimes rather artificial, but it is preferable to providing an undifferentiated list. With this in mind, I have, in an appendix, added a bibliography of further publications relevant to each section (reference to some of them in the introductory analysis will, perhaps, whet appetites). Here too the allocation to the various categories can only be indicative. The lists are intended for judicious use, not unreflecting acceptance; but as such, I hope that they may be found helpful.

Full bibliographical details of all Smart's papers appear in the Ninian Smart Bibliography which appears as an appendix to Volume 2, and is also available on the Ashgate website. It was first published in the journal *Religion*, which Smart was instrumental in launching, and it appears with permission. The Bibliography is divided into sections (A, books by Smart, and also the two edited collections of Smart's papers mentioned above; B, papers in other edited collections; C, papers in academic journals, and pamphlets), with publications in order of date of publication within each section. The combination of date and letter – for example, 1998, B – after the title of a paper referred to permits location of the full publishing details accordingly. (However, in the case of books by Smart where the actual title is quoted, addition of the letter A is otiose, and therefore omitted.)

Dividing the papers into two relatively independent volumes is also a somewhat artificial task: despite the extraordinary range of Smart's work, the numerous themes do in fact knit together into an integrated whole. Yet a rough logic can be claimed for division in terms of the sub-titles to each volume.

In Volume 1, *Religious Experience and Philosophical Analysis*, the emphasis is on delineating the foundations of Smart's oeuvre. What emerges, at the most fundamental level, is what might almost be dubbed a 'fundamentalist' appeal to religious experience (and distinctive patterns thereof) as authenticating the phenomenon of religion in general, and as essential to any properly rounded conception of human fulfilment and wisdom.

The distinctive patterns consist of varied interweavings of two strands of religious experience in particular, identified as the numinous and the mystical respectively. Empathetic understanding of these permits the disclosure of an internal logic of religious discourse, philosophical analysis of which conduces to a deeper and more sensitive understanding of religion in its essence and manifestations (Smart much admired G. van der Leeuw's *Religion in Essence and Manifestation*, 1938, and provided a Foreword when it was reissued in 1986).

Integral to this joint appeal to religious experience and philosophical analysis, as conceived by Smart, was the importance of comparative studies in religion. Yet these in turn generated an increasingly complex mix of elements whose nature and interconnections called for careful mapping. This Smart proceeded to undertake with enthusiasm, providing an ambitious model of religious studies in universities and colleges, and launching a revolution in religious education in schools in Britain and elsewhere. Both the concern with comparative studies, and Smart's distinctive contribution to theory, are reflected in the papers that follow.

In Volume 2, *Traditions and the Challenges of Modernity*, the focus shifts on the one hand to Smart's study of individual religious traditions, and on the other to questions surrounding the fate (and the future) of these traditions in the world today.

In several of his books, such as the frequently revised *The Religious Experience* (1st edition 1969, 5th edition 1996), or *The World's Religions: Old Traditions and Modern Transformations* (1st edition 1989, 2nd edition 1998), Smart dealt with the full range of religions, and this outstanding breadth of knowledge is apparent too in a number of his papers. Yet his fondness for Buddhism in particular, along with (aspects of) Hinduism, is also apparent from the disproportionate number of occasions on which he returned to these topics.

·Analysis of specific religious traditions, though, began to give way to, or to be complemented by, exploration of similarities with quasi-religions, especially nationalism and Marxism. This task he dubbed 'worldview analysis' – commenting, a little ruefully, what a pity it was that 'Weltanschauung' happened not to be an English term (a judgement with which one may feel free to disagree). This fresh focus led to numerous publications, including *Worldviews* (1983) and his Gifford Lectures, *Beyond Ideology* (1981, 1982). A selection of his papers on this theme is included alongside ones dealing with religions as traditionally understood.

Comparative studies, though, remained a topic to which he attached great significance (and to which he brought great skill). The final groups of papers explore different aspects of the relationship of religions to each other in the modern world (including interfaith dialogue), and also of their relationship to the liberal pluralism by which they are increasingly surrounded (and challenged). Several of the most thought-provoking of these papers appeared relatively late in Smart's career, and can be seen as teasing out lessons from his accumulated experience and learning.

Finally, scrutiny of the Bibliography will reveal that the papers included or referred to in the present two volumes do not quite exhaust Smart's academic output. However, apart from book reviews and contributions to the press, the main papers omitted either deal with topics other than those relevant to the present publication, or consist of contributions to reference handbooks such as dictionaries and encyclopaedias.

The Table of Contents for *Ninian Smart on World Religions: Volume 2, Traditions and the Challenges of Modernity* can be found in Appendix 2.

Acknowledgements

In the case of material that is out of print, copyright permission has not needed to be sought posthumously. In all other cases, grateful acknowledgement is made to the copyright holders of these papers for their permission to reproduce them in this volume.

1   'Methods in My Life', Jon R. Stone, ed., *The Craft of Religious Studies* (London: Macmillan; New York: St. Martin's Press, 1998), pp. 18–35. Copyright © 1998 Jon R. Stone. Reprinted with permission of Palgrave Macmillan.

23   'The Political Implications of Religious Studies', Ninian Smart, *Religion and the Western Mind* (London: Macmillan; Albany, NY: State University of New York Press, 1987), pp. 25–46. Reproduced with permission of Palgrave Macmillan. Reprinted by permission of the State University of New York Press © 1987 State University of New York. All rights reserved.

26   'Clarity and Imagination as Buddhist Means to Virtue', Barbara Darling-Smith, ed., *Can Virtue Be Taught?* (Notre Dame, IN: University of Notre Dame Press, 1993), pp. 125–136. Copyright © 1993 University of Notre Dame Press.

29   'A Global Ethic Arising from the Epistemology of Religious and Similar Value-Systems', Ninian Smart, *Religion and the Western Mind* (London: Macmillan; Albany, NY: State University of New York Press, 1987), pp. 120–131. Reproduced with permission of Palgrave Macmillan. Reprinted by permission of the State University of New York Press © 1987 State University of New York. All rights reserved.

Every effort has been made to trace all the copyright holders, but if any have been inadvertently overlooked the publishers will be pleased to make the necessary arrangement at the first opportunity.

A Critical Analysis

'What is the difference between Ninian Smart and God?'
'God is everywhere. Ninian Smart is everywhere but here!'

The joke emerged in Lancaster in the 1970s as Smart was ever more frequently invited to address groups nationally, and indeed internationally (in 1976, in fact, he began to divide his time between the universities of Lancaster and California, Santa Barbara – his opening gambit in seeking to set up this arrangement having been to ask the Vice-Chancellor of Lancaster whether he preferred to have half of him or none – he knew his worth!). He had shot to particular prominence as Professor of the very first university Department of Religious Studies in Britain in 1967 – a post advertised (at his own suggestion, as it transpired) as open to members 'of any faith or none', thus provoking letters to the national press, and a wave of public controversy. The air of controversy was, if anything, heightened by his eloquent and considered promotion of an ambitious agenda for radical reform of religious education in schools, involving a change from a primarily Bible-centred and Christian confessional approach to a non-confessional world religions approach. All of this was backed up by an influential range of publications (including the early highly influential Schools Council Working Paper 36, *Religious Education in Secondary Schools* (1971), product of a project under Smart's direction (and inspiration) at the University of Lancaster). Indeed it was to be a hallmark of his career that he combined mastery of an impressive range of knowledge with sustained skill in thought-provoking analytical exposition and exploration at a variety of levels.

Yet a figure influential in his day may in later days, and sometimes quite soon, come to be regarded as somewhat passé. It is necessary to ask, therefore, in the context of a publication such as this, what reasons there may be for continuing to read Smart. There seem to me to be at least two.

First, of course, is the very fact of his having been such an influential figure in the field of the academic study of religion. For such an influence there needs to be an appropriate record, and there has not hitherto been a systematic analytical and representative anthology of his work.

Second, though, and for many perhaps more importantly, are the benefits to be derived for one's own understanding of religions and their place in the world. For although the field of the academic study of religion continues to change apace, the result is not always an increase in wisdom, and much of the body of Smart's analyses and arguments is both widely accessible and also invites continued reflection and evaluation.

Smart brought to his scholarly tasks a bifocal vision – that of a deeply committed Christian, and that of a philosopher. This was reflected in his early academic career, which began with posts in the philosophy of religion, and was followed by his appointment as the first H.G. Wood Professor of Theology in the University of Birmingham. Both aspects of this vision were to remain constant throughout his work, and both came to be interrelated with his ever more prominent advocacy of, and involvement with, the burgeoning field of multidisciplinary religious studies – in ways which will become apparent in due course.

Wearing the hat of a theologian, Smart vigorously rejected the type of Christianity labelled exclusivism, according to which salvation is through Christ alone, and possible only through Christian faith and explicit Christian commitment. This stance he regarded as myopic in its understanding of Christianity, and parochial in its insensitivity to the range of insights and (in particular) of genuine religious experience apparent, in his view, right across the spectrum of religions.

In place of this theological exclusivism he advocated a kind of Christian inclusivism, according to which the Holy Spirit is at work in religions other than Christianity, and these accordingly contain some measure of religious truth, and engender some measure of experience of the true God (as revealed in Christianity). Admittedly, while his rejection of exclusivism is explicit, 'inclusivism' is not a label he claims as such, and we shall find him coming to claim a kind of 'pluralism'. The deeper issues that arise in this connection will be considered later (see Section 2.III).

Wearing the hat of a philosopher, Smart consistently advocated a reshaping of philosophy of religion, as traditionally understood and practised in Western academic circles, to incorporate both analysis of, and reflection upon, a full spectrum of religions rather than just Christianity – and typically an etiolated version of Christianity at that.

Comparative religion was thus essential to Smart both as a Christian theologian and as a religiously neutral (or, as he came to call it, methodologically agnostic) philosopher. Yet it was clear to him that each of these two stances involved a different way of engaging with religions.

Given the fact of religious plurality, Christians need an account of other religions which places them in an encompassing theological framework. This account, if it is to be done properly, requires an accurate understanding of other religions. This accurate understanding may be aimed for in two different but sometimes interrelated ways. One is through sensitive and empathetic interreligious dialogue; the other is through empathetic phenomenology of religion, in which theologians (or more generally Christians) seek temporarily to suspend their Christian convictions in order to enter, as best they may, into the mindset of alternative religious convictions. Once the understanding, to the best degree possible, has been achieved, it is then grist to the theological mill, to be evaluated according as one sees fit from one's Christian perspective.

The philosopher's task is different, for it eschews theological judgement in favour of as dispassionate and neutral a treatment of religions as possible, at least in the first instance; and any subsequent evaluation will be in terms of such criteria as intelligibility and logical consistency, rather than coherence with Christian presuppositions. As a philosopher of religion, Smart accordingly addressed two rather different issues. The first was philosophical analysis of types of religious discourse, and of the types of religious experience which, in his view, engendered them and gave them point. The second was the exploration and evaluation of rival religious truth-claims. Now clearly, conclusions reached philosophically in this second task may cohere with, or indeed be invoked as reinforcement for, conclusions drawn in the specifically theological endeavour. Yet Smart energetically defended the propriety in principle of the same person proceeding in either a religiously neutral or in a religiously committed way provided the distinction was always clearly upheld and consistently applied. Some might argue, as we shall see, that he did not entirely succeed in this, but the principle is surely sound, and it is certainly the case that in much of his work Smart is very clearly identifiable as wearing the hat now of a Christian theologian, now of a religiously neutral philosopher.

From both directions, then, Smart was impelled into ever deeper engagement with comparative religion, resulting in due course in a distinctive vision of 'religious studies' (to use the title given to the innovative Lancaster department) which was distinguished from theology by its non-confessionalism, while incorporating philosophy along with phenomenology of religion as part of a more complex polymethodic study of religions. This rich and varied approach he advocated not only as appropriate for higher education but, with relevant modifications for particular age ranges, as appropriate too for education at all levels.

At the same time, its fruits could be incorporated into interreligious dialogue, and used to enhance Christian theology. Thus the three salient strands of his overall project – philosophy of religion, Christian theology, and religious studies/comparative religion – can be seen to be in principle separate yet also mutually interrelated.

With this bird's eye view of the field – which illuminates perhaps both the internal logic of Smart's work and also something of its development – we can now turn to a closer scrutiny of the various components. This is something of a challenge, given the astonishing range of Smart's writings, and no little complexity in their overall substance. Just what the components may be is no doubt susceptible of differing judgements. Still, let us begin more or less where Smart did, and explore where it leads. What will become apparent is that themes developed in the earlier stages of his thinking often remain as leitmotifs throughout.

The Introduction is in numbered sections (for example, 1.III or 2.IV) corresponding to the numbered sections of Volumes 1 and 2 respectively. Cross-references generally apply both to the papers in a given section and also to the corresponding discussion in the text.

1.I Autobiographical

The original impetus for Smart's involvement with non-Christian religions came from his being sent by the army to Ceylon (as it then was) after the war. Immediately prior to this, also through the army, he had gone to the University of London School of Oriental and African Studies to learn Chinese, followed by a brief posting in Singapore. It was during his stay as a British serviceman in Ceylon, though, that he experienced his first major encounter with Buddhism, a religion which was to continue in many ways to inspire him from then on – indeed he would come to enjoy describing himself, playfully, as a Buddhist Episcopalian.

Through his study of Buddhism he was led into the much broader field of Indian religions in general, and the complex world of Hinduism in particular. Although he subsequently extended his interests to virtually the full panoply of religions, at least in the modern world, by far the greater emphasis, in his work as a whole, remains on the Indian religious traditions. He commented that, while he had tried to write empathetically about many religions, he had found it much easier in regard to some than to others, and his affection for the Indian religious heritage – or certain oft-discussed aspects of it in particular – shines through.

Following his untimely death, fragments of a projected autobiography were found among his papers, and it is much to be regretted that he was unable to bring this to proper fruition. He did, though, publish some smaller, partly overlapping, autobiographical accounts, and one of these, 'Methods in My Life' (Chapter 1), is included here to illustrate the interaction between developments in his life and developments in his thought.

1.II Religious Experience and the Logic of Religious Discourse

Following demobilization Smart went up to Oxford to study classics, ancient history, and philosophy. He had won a Classics Scholarship before being called up into the army, and decided to proceed with this even though there was the option of taking Chinese, and thus extending his SOAS studies. 'But the syllabus in those days was absurd: it involved no spoken Chinese (it being, for the purposes of Oxford, a dead language pronounced in English). And the whole study was of literature up to the 13th century C.E.' Smart rejected the opportunity to continue with Chinese, given this curriculum. 'It was an extreme expression', he continues, 'of a tendency in those days (to be found even now) of treating the literature of a tradition or country separately without regard to history, sociology, art history and philosophy, not to mention religion' ('Smart Ivory', unpublished fragment of autobiography, unpaginated, section entitled 'Oxford', in the Ninian Smart Archive at Lancaster University).

By the same token, of course, studying a religion through ancient texts separately from all its other aspects was to be deplored, and Smart would go on to develop and emphasize a multi-dimensional analysis of religion as a corrective. This was of intrinsic value, but also of instrumental value in attracting students who, as he later noted, 'did not just want theology', and 'in particular … did not want the kind of theology which I had encountered when I first went to the H.G. Wood Chair in Birmingham's theology department [in 1961] … : there 93% of students' time was taken up with texts, events and languages up to the mid-5th century A.D. (i.e. C.E.) and the remaining 7% with Reformation history or a study of the 39 Articles of the Church of England – this at a secular university' ('Religious Studies in the United Kingdom', 1988 [C] p. 6; see too *Secular Education and the Logic of Religion*, 1968, pp.101–102, 'no sociology, no philosophy of religion, no comparative study of religion, no modern theology, nothing about Marxism or Humanism, no Barth, no Bonhoeffer, no Existentialist theology, no A.J. Ayer, no discussion of the relation between modern science and religious belief, nothing about the psychology of religion, no modern church history, no Christian ethics – need I go on?').

Graduating with First Class Honours, Smart remained in Oxford for postgraduate studies. Working with the noted linguistic philosopher, J.L. Austin, and the comparative religionist, R.C. Zaehner, Smart presented the first post-war Oxford dissertation in philosophy of religion. Its flavour is reflected in the title of his very first academic publication in 1956, 'The Comparative Logical Analysis of Religious Doctrines' (Chapter 2), and it subsequently appeared as his first book, *Reasons and Faiths: An Investigation of Religious Discourse, Christian and Non-Christian* (1958) (hereafter *Reasons and Faiths*). Here he established what were to become consistent keynote themes throughout his work.

The relevance of Smart's two supervisors is immediately apparent, with the ingredients of comparative religion and linguistic analysis respectively – though in line with what was noted above, the non-Christian religions invoked are overwhelmingly Buddhism and Hinduism. Also apparent are prime elements of a distinctive Smartian perspective, which was both a personal worldview and a professional analysis, and was to be sustained throughout his career.

Prominent among these elements, and arguably foundational to this perspective, is an emphasis on religious experience – an emphasis worked out in several ways.

One notable way is as a major qualification of the analysis given by Rudolf Otto in his influential *The Idea of the Holy* (1917). Otto famously coined the term 'numinous' to refer to experience of the *mysterium tremendum* and *fascinans* which he saw as being at the heart of religion. For Smart this was, so to speak, only half the story. There was another half which Otto had overlooked – or rather, which he had unconvincingly attempted to assimilate to the numinous – namely the mystical. For Smart, both strands were central to an understanding of religions, although they could be interrelated in different ways, or emphasized to different degrees, in the various traditions. (They could also, we shall see, mesh with a third significant aspect, the incarnation strand.)

In later writings, Smart does refer to a rather greater variety of religious experience than this, including, for example, visions and conversion experiences, and shamanic experience. With the latter we see the influence of Mircea Eliade's 1964 study, *Shamanism*, and Smart sought to incorporate this into his analysis by envisaging shamanic experience as prefiguring in important ways both numinous and mystical experience. Yet one is left with the impression that this is something of an addendum, for the central emphasis on the dual strand of the mystical and the numinous does not change from the first to the very last of his writings.

There is, though, a third important strand, centred on incarnation, which makes its appearance in *Reasons and Faiths*, and reappears still, for example, in the much later *Christian Systematic Theology in a World Context* (1993). The latter was co-written with Steven Konstantine, but the analysis there of the incarnation strand of religious experience and discourse matches that in *Reasons and Faiths* exactly.

What is striking here, of course, is on the one hand the continuity of analysis over the years, and on the other hand that in *Reasons and Faiths* Smart is wearing the hat of a philosopher, while in the later work he is wearing that of a Christian theologian. Inevitably, therefore, the suspicion arises that the supposedly dispassionate and neutral philosophical analysis has been covertly influenced by central theological convictions. Certainly the philosophical conclusions are theologically convenient. It is a point to which we shall return.

Meanwhile the key contrast between the numinous and mystical strands – also labelled the prophetic and contemplative strands – is that the former gives rise to worship, and an associated pronounced sense of distance between worshipper and object of worship (see *The Concept of Worship*, 1972), whereas the latter is associated with claims of closeness or indeed unity.

Such claims, despite important aspects of similarity between them, occur in otherwise often strikingly different religions (Christianity and Hinduism, for example), or different 'doctrinal schemes', and the same is true of the numinous type of experience. Thus an important distinction is generated between experience and interpretation, and this emerges as crucial to Smart's analysis of mysticism in particular (see Section 1.III).

Before moving on to this thorny topic, though, let us identify further key facets of Smart's analysis of religious experience, for arguably it is this that underpins his whole work; and fundamental to it all is his claim that at its core religious experience is to be trusted.

From one point of view, of course, this could be worked up into some kind of 'argument from religious experience' to the existence of God, in the manner of natural theology; and we shall see that Smart does feel able to work with some kind of related natural theology project (in which philosophy and theology are able to go public in holding hands). Yet in the first instance, as exemplified in *Reasons and Faiths*, the thrust of his analysis is rather different. He proposes a theory of religious reasons, in which a non-reductionist, non-deflationary account of religious experience is used to generate certain 'internal' criteria of religious truth.

The burden of this argument is somewhat complex. The constantly recurring twofold pattern of numinous and mystical experiences should be regarded as something of a given (otherwise one would be exercising an undue scepticism in respect of whole swathes of valuable human experience). These two types of experience, whether severally or jointly, both give rise to, and give point to, a range of doctrinal propositions (so that, for example, the experience of religious awe generates propositions about the Creator, and in a sense explains both their meaning and their force – or similarly, say, with mystical experiences and propositions concerning the Atman or Self). This Smart calls *basic* justification. There is also *formal* justification, where appeal is made to such considerations as simplicity (so that monotheism and monism both have a formal advantage over polytheism, for example). Third there is *organic* justification, where various weavings together of doctrines can be seen to rest on analogies between doctrines and experience (so that the 'timelessness' inherent in a mystical experience can serve to link propositions about Atman and Brahman). Fourth there is *preferential* justification, involving the making of priority decisions as between the different strands (*Reasons and Faiths*, p. 127, and so on). It is primarily here that the issue of theologically convenient conclusions arises.

Simplifying somewhat, the argument is that a religion which features only one strand of experience is deficient as compared to a religion which features both – the latter is more comprehensive; and a religion which further incorporates the incarnation strand is open to being regarded as more comprehensive still, and thus preferable overall.

This over-simple summary is misleading not least in implying that being comprehensive is the only criterion of preference. Smart's analysis is far more intricate and subtle than that. Still, he argues that a religion with a virtually exclusive emphasis on the mystical strand, such as Theravada Buddhism or Jainism (or the Samkhya version of Hinduism) in effect excludes most people, for mysticism is undoubtedly for the few (this is to ignore, of course, the rich realities of Theravada as practised by the many – a point to which we shall need to return). Conversely, a religion with a virtually exclusive emphasis on the numinous strand, such as early Islam, fails, unless it changes, to do justice to what are surely valid mystical experiences when they occur – hence the crisis over Sufi mysticism. Thus an interrelating, an interweaving, of the two strands is to be preferred. Further, though, in the numinous strand such is the awful majesty of the holy that it engenders in the worshipper a strong sense of unworthiness, and indeed sin, from which emerges in turn the felt propriety of the principle that sin requires expiation, with the corollaries that expiation requires sacrifice, and that a divine incarnation is the most appropriate form of sacrifice. Thus there are reasons internal to religion – persuasive without being probative – for preferring an incarnational religion.

It would seem at this point that a somewhat fine line is being trod between philosophical analysis and theological advocacy. Smart is clear, though, that what he is claiming to present, as a philosopher, is a neutral analysis of 'reasons and faiths', of the logic of religious discourse (analogous, no doubt, to the would-be neutral meta-ethical analyses of the logic of moral discourse, such as that produced, for example, by R.M. Hare, also working in the post-war Oxford linguistic analytic tradition – see his *The Language of Morals*, 1952; see too the influential paper, 'Language Strata', by F. Waismann, 1946, with its thesis about each stratum – including that of mysticism – having its own logic, and whose influence on Smart is apparent, see, for example, *Reasons and Faiths*, p. 10). Hence his assertion that what he is about is 'an investigation of religious concepts in a spirit of higher-order neutrality' and that it is necessary to distinguish between 'the question as to how one *would* justify a belief and the question whether *in fact* the belief *is* justified' (*Reasons and Faiths*, pp. 4 and 5). Philosophical analysis addresses the former, theological advocacy (or alternatively, metaphysics) the latter. The distinction is perfectly sound, and once granted, suspicions regarding Smart's possible confusion of analysis and advocacy largely evaporate, at least as an issue of principle. Nevertheless, the flow of argument linking sin, expiation, sacrifice, and divine sacrifice, undoubtedly reflects Christian predispositions (see also Section 2.III).

A final point to which attention should be drawn, although it has already been referred to in passing, is that doctrines become etiolated, Smart urges, if they are wrenched out of the experiential context that furnishes their prime point and force. They may then be debated as metaphysical, but not illuminated as religious. Moreover, treating as purely metaphysical propositions that are in fact 'disguised religious claims' (*Reasons and Faiths* p. 4) is to fail to do them justice. Thus the task of philosophy of religion should be conceived differently from what has been traditional, and reshaped to incorporate comparative religion. Smart would later comment that he had anticipated *Reasons and Faiths* giving rise to a new wave of comparative philosophy of religion, and had been disappointed when this had not occurred. (An exception of which Smart much approved was the work of William A. Christian, Sr., for example his *Doctrines of Religious Communities*, 1987.)

This analysis, then, with which Smart in effect launched his career, was to remain a hallmark of his work throughout. It recurs, with appropriate changes of register, in work that is now theological, now philosophical (either independently, or as integral to the much more broadly conceived enterprise of religious studies). It is rooted in an intimate understanding of Christianity, Buddhism and Hinduism in particular, but functions in effect as a kind of grid into whose compartments relevant material from religions in general can be slotted. There is a question, however, of the extent to which this is plausible – a question which becomes particularly acute, perhaps, with regard to mysticism (to which we turn shortly). Even apart from this, though, the sustained preference for a primarily dual analysis of the varieties of religious experience (with the incarnational strand as a key modification) is at least open to question. For Smart, though, the numinous and the mystical remained broadly valid categories of religious experience capable of accommodating (or in the case of shamanism perhaps illuminating – see Section 2.Ivi) what he regarded as in effect experiential variations of one or the other of them.

Smart's very first publication to deal with these matters appeared even before *Reasons and Faiths*. It consists of a report of a short presentation in Rome to the eighth congress of the International Association of the History of Religions, but despite its brevity, 'The Comparative Logical Analysis of Religious Doctrines' (Chapter 2) sets out Smart's opening gambit in the study of religion in illuminating conciseness.

Another early paper reflecting many of his initial – and indeed lasting – basic concerns is 'Empiricism and Religions' (Chapter 3). An emphasis on empirical verification as a necessary criterion of intelligibility (never mind plausibility) had gained widespread currency among philosophers, under the influence of the Vienna School and the enthusiastic advocacy of the Verification Principle by A.J. Ayer in his *Language, Truth and Logic* (1936). The challenge presented to theologians by this development had led some to seek to recast their religious commitments quite radically. Thus R.B. Braithwaite argued that religious assertions should be construed primarily as moral assertions (*An Empiricist's View of the Nature of Religious Belief*, 1955); and later would come, for example, Paul M. van Buren's *The Secular Meaning of the Gospel* (1963). Smart's work needs to be seen in this overall context, and as marking a stance of radical opposition to it, despite his allegiance to a certain kind of linguistic philosophy.

Some of the grounds of this opposition are worked out in 'Empiricism and Religions', addressed initially to an audience of Indian philosophers. Many of the current critiques of religion, he notes, are severely limited, for many philosophers, including the contributors (amongst them, incidentally, his brother J.J.C. Smart) to the influential collection *New Essays in Philosophical Theology* (A. Flew and A. MacIntyre, eds, 1955), 'show a total unawareness of the fact that some of the points they adduce only apply to Christianity, so that the arguments are parochial. Nevertheless', he continues, 'the notion that there is a transcendent Reality or state apprehended through revelation or religious experience needs to be defended in the face of modern empiricism and anti-metaphysics if it is to be acceptable to intelligent persons' (p. 27).

The anti-metaphysics he proceeds to consider is in effect a form of fideism. There is warrant, he claims, both for the view 'that it is by revelation that we know the truth', and also for the view 'that it is by faith and spiritual experience, rather than by ratiocination, that the truth is to be apprehended' (pp. 28–29). Nevertheless, a simple appeal, in faith, to revelation is untenable, given the diversity of putative revelations.

Yet perhaps the diversity is only apparent? Might there be a fundamental unity of religions? This is a view with much support in modern Hindu apologetics, but Smart finds it unsatisfactory. The argument can be made to work, perhaps, from within a particular religious perspective (for example Advaita Vedanta), but not if the different religions are viewed 'from a "neutral" and sympathetic point of view'. Unity perceived from within one religion is bought 'at the expense of misinterpreting other faiths when these are considered *from their own point of view*' (p. 32). It is an argument Smart went on to advance on numerous occasions throughout his career, including against the variant of the unity thesis that came to be advanced by John Hick (see Section 2.IV).

Smart's more positive proposals are merely sketched, but match the analysis given above. Some kind of natural theology or metaphysics in a very broad sense is necessary 'to vindicate the truth-claims of religious experience; but it is parasitical upon the latter in so far as without living experience religion is pointless and empty' (p. 35). Moreover, it is essential to recognize that 'different realms of discourse have different methodologies', and given that religious 'truth' (*sic*) is 'not the same sort of thing as scientific truth … it must further be shown what the rules of religious argument are' (ibid., p. 195). These tasks require both linguistic analysis and comparative studies – in short, just what was attempted in *Reasons and Faiths*, along with the more direct attempts at a 'soft' natural theology that come later (see Section 2.III).

While emphasizing once again the importance of religious experience, Smart also urges, without developing the point, that in contrast to the thesis of religious unity, which implies a spurious uniformity of religious experience, 'the richness and variety of patterns of religious experience must be kept in view' (p. 32) – a view underlined still in the much later paper, 'Understanding Religious Experience' (Chapter 4). This brings us back to his essentially dual typology, and questions surrounding his treatment of the mystical strand in particular.

1.III Mystical Experience

Smart's understanding of mysticism is clearly of major importance in his overall analysis. Unlike the equally important emphasis on the numinous, it has attracted a fair amount of criticism. Perhaps discussion of the numinous has gravitated in the main towards Otto. Or perhaps Smart's account of the mystical is simply less plausible. Certainly there are grounds for powerful challenge.

Smart's account was worked out early on – see 'Mystical Experience' (1962) [C], and especially the classic 'Interpretation and Mystical Experience' (Chapter 5); and he held to it with great tenacity. Indeed, it is itself a criticism that he seems not to have responded to criticism, or only in a relatively perfunctory way. Be that as it may, let us consider the nature of Smart's account, and the nature of the charges brought by his critics.

Smart bases his account on a crucial distinction between experience and interpretation, arguing that divergence in the latter is compatible with convergence in the former. Thus while there are conflicting, or indeed mutually contradictory, doctrinal accounts of mystical experiences (so that, for example, in theistic interpretation the mystic is seen as having been 'one' with God while remaining ultimately distinct, while in monistic mysticism an actual merging of, say, Atman and Brahman, is held to have been effected – or, so to speak, perceived), these doctrinal accounts are in fact essentially separable from the shared type of experience which underlies them.

The importance of this claim for Smart's general analytical and interpretative framework is apparent from the exposition given above in Section 1.II. For if mystical experiences fall into mutually contradictory categories, this does not simply mean that Smart's basic dual typology needs to become more complex (a superficial problem), but implies further that his deeper epistemological claim concerning the essential reliability of religious experience is called into question (a serious problem). It is called into question because one type of mystic's claim cancels out the other's – or requires a commitment to one at the expense (perhaps relative, cf. Sankara's two-level theory) of the other, and hence the adoption of a non-neutral stance inimical to Smart's project of higher-level neutrality. It is perhaps not surprising, therefore, that Smart should have held out with such determination against rival views of mystical experience. Yet certainly there are major considerations which count against his own.

In developing his view Smart took issue with previous scholars of mysticism, not least his own supervisor, R.C. Zaehner. Zaehner (1957) advocated a threefold typology of nature mysticism, monistic mysticism and theistic mysticism. The first of these, also referred to as panenhenic mysticism, involves a profound sense of unity or harmony with nature (expressed, for example, in some of Wordsworth's poetry, or in Richard Jefferies' *The Story of My Heart*, 1883). It is, Smart agrees, to be differentiated from other forms of mysticism (it does not involve the same kind of emptying of consciousness), but he comes to classify it as akin to the numinous. This does, of course, clear the ground for his collapsing of the distinction between the other two types (as far as the core experiences are concerned); but an assimilation of the panenhenic and the numinous is very far from immediately plausible, given the sense of fusion pervading the one, and the sense of humble distance inherent in the other. To this part of the analysis, though, he devotes far less attention than to discussion of the key categories of theistic and monistic mysticism respectively.

He points out that Zaehner's monistic category is something of a muddle, since it is used to lump together the radically different claims of Advaita (unity of the Atman and Brahman), Yoga (liberation as soul-isolation), and Theravada (no-soul). The differences between all of these are as great as the difference between any of them and theism.

Logically, therefore, Zaehner should either lump them all together, or multiply his categories considerably.

This critique, correct in itself, leads Smart to advocate the possibility of regarding all mystical experiences as essentially similar at heart, despite dissimilarities in expression. Distinguishing between descriptions given by mystics themselves and those given by others (auto- and hetero-interpretation), and descriptions which bear a higher or lower degree of doctrinal weight (high and low degrees of ramification), Smart argues that a 'low hetero-interpretation' matching a 'low auto-interpretation' will yield an agreed phenomenological account of mystical experience. To this agreed account may, indeed often will, be added different doctrinal accounts (as when al-Ghazali reinterprets al-Hallaj's apparently blasphemous monistic utterances in an orthodox theistic way); yet the conflicts or contradictions between these more highly ramified doctrinal descriptions need not impugn the validity of what is essentially a shared basic experience.

There are, of course, good paradigms for making the distinction between experience and interpretation work – think of the parable of the blind men and the elephant. It is not clear, though, that the analogy holds when we turn to mystical experiences. The blind men may all be described in one sense as having had the shared experience of touching an elephant, but in a more immediate sense there is no shared phenomenological experience at all ('it' was rough, smooth, thick, thin, and so on). On this analogy, therefore, we should be led to argue (in the spirit of Smart's would-be higher-order neutrality) that while it remains an entirely open question whether some kind of higher synthesis of mystics' conflicting claims may in principle be possible, meanwhile, on the basis of their actual accounts mystical experiences should be accepted as being radically varied.

Smart's argument rests, then, crucially, on the claim that there is, at a kind of lowest common denominator level, a deep similarity of experience, and this is urged partly by comparison of mystics' utterances, and partly by an argument from analogy.

The comparison of mystics' utterances is subtle, but one cannot readily infer shared experiences from shared elements of experiences, especially where – as typically with mystics – intentionality is involved. Thus if one person is deliberately walking up a mountain for the pleasure of reaching the summit, it hardly does to claim, on the basis of a common negotiation of angled grass, that this is essentially the same experience as that of another person who is deliberately walking up in order to obey an army training command, and hating every minute of it; while to add that one person's description of basking in sunshine, and the other's of experiencing numbing sleet, are adventitious accretions to the core experience would be palpably absurd. Yet this is very like the implication surely to be drawn from Smart's analysis, that the Theravadin aiming for tranquil nibbanic detachment is experiencing at root much the same as al-Hallaj's numinous ecstasy, or that the latter may indeed, without realizing it, have been halfway to nibbana. (The substance of this implication is in fact made explicit in *Buddhism and Christianity: Rivals and Allies*, 1993, where Smart urges that 'from the Christian angle, it is possible for people in other faiths to have an experience of God without knowing that it is God … There is nothing absurd in this supposition, especially given the elusive, difficult and paradoxical nature of mystical states'. Conversely, 'from the Buddhist perspective, the Christian mystic has a glimpse of *Tathata* or Suchness, perhaps, but deludedly wraps that vision in the clothes of faith of a personal God' (p. 54). The 'perhaps' is surely instructive.)

In terms of an argument from analogy, as we have already seen, it all depends on the analogy. Smart more than once uses the analogy of a visitor to Rome seeing a figure in a white surplice passing in a chauffeur-driven limousine. Here contrasting descriptions are indeed possible. 'It was the Pope', and 'You thought it was the Pope, but he's in Timbuktu, so it must have been that actor in the film they're shooting', do both make sense. On the other hand, there are limits. 'Actually it was Sophia Loren' stretches credulity somewhat (although there are cases – the story is told of Labour politician George Brown, inebriated at a reception in South America, accosting an attractive figure in a shimmering long red dress to request a dance, only to incur the frosty response: 'Sir, I am the Cardinal Archbishop of Rio de Janeiro'!). True, there could be a shared phenomenological account, 'I saw someone in white'; but this would be such an eviscerated description as to have omitted elements integral to the experience itself – 'But it was a *man*', say; or, 'He had a beard' (or whatever).

It would not be implausible to conclude, therefore, that such common features as can be identified between the accounts of mystics in widely divergent religious traditions justify us in classing these figures together as *mystics*, but that there are too many deeply embedded differences to permit a claim to essential unity. Rather, indeed, it may be prudent to appeal to the notion which Smart makes much of elsewhere, namely that of family resemblances. Mystical experiences lack a shared essence, but a sequence of overlapping characteristics functions as a set of markers of close kinship.

Criticisms along these lines have been advanced by several writers, and Smart does to an extent, mainly in 'The Purification of Consciousness and the Negative Path' (Chapter 6), take up the challenge posed by such as Steven Katz and Peter Moore ('Language, Epistemology, and Mysticism', and 'Mystical Experience, Mystical Doctrine, Mystical Technique', respectively, in Katz, ed., 1978, pp. 22–74, 101–131; cf. too Peter G. Moore, 'Recent Surveys of Mysticism: A Critical Survey', 1973). Yet while this paper is very useful as an elucidation of Smart's understanding of the language of mysticism, it does not really get to grips with objections to his general account of mysticism with anything remotely like the kind of detailed rebuttal he accorded to Zaehner; and nor did he attempt such a rebuttal elsewhere. A suspicion therefore remains that he unconsciously persisted in trimming the luxuriant diversity of mystical experiences to fit a much-desired theory. Be that as it may, he did insist that we are in the early stages of an agreed phenomenological account of religious experiences, so that in a sense the jury should be regarded as still being out. He was committed to his theory, but it remained a hypothesis. The hypothesis has proved fruitful, not least in putative rebuttal; and his critics might well say of Smart's analysis, as Smart did of Zaehner's, that in the end 'interestingly false propositions are worth far more than a whole lot of boringly true ones' (Chapter 5, p. 65).

The notion of a hypothesis, of course, does imply a measure of uncertainty and lack of dogmatism, and these qualities are, we should note, characteristic of Smart's work. Indeed in a later paper, 'What Would Buddhaghosa Have Made of *The Cloud of Unknowing*?' (Chapter 7), Smart admits in conclusion that while some forms of mystical experience seem to be compatible with both Christian theism and 'Buddhist nirvanism', it may be that others 'have a personal quality that suggests the language of God rather than that of *nirvāna*' (p. 97). So mysticism may in the end be, so to speak, one or many. 'Do we indeed need to decide which?', he asks. Yet clearly his preference remains, as always, for the former option; and he continues to rely on the principle that an account in 'less ramified language is likely to be closer to immediate experience because more ramified language – like the above references to the Buddha and to Jesus – suggests a wider epistemological context' (p. 81). Yet while doctrinally more ramified language does indeed invoke wider epistemological considerations (for example in respect of the historicity of various sayings and actions attributed to Jesus), it does not necessarily follow that less ramified accounts will be 'closer to immediate experience'. If I went to a book-signing by Sophia Loren (wider epistemological considerations – did she write a book?), the less ramified account, 'I went to this store and a woman in white signed this book', would not in any obvious sense count as being closer to the immediate experience. Indeed, the experience would have been eviscerated

At this point, though, it is perhaps time to move on to the next aspect of Smart's work, and having introduced the example of the comparative study of Buddhaghosa and *The Cloud of Unknowing*, it is convenient to indicate other such comparative studies.

1.IV Comparative Studies

Comparative studies are to be found to a greater or lesser extent throughout Smart's work, so to single this theme out for separate mention is in a way somewhat artificial. Still, suggesting that certain of his discussions can be juxtaposed to form a particular strand may not be unhelpful.

Mention was made above of Smart's invoking the Wittgensteinian notion of family resemblances as a tool for marking identity, as an alternative to the more traditional view (going back to Aristotle) of seeking a defining essence shared by a group of things. The idea makes a brief appearance in *Philosophers and Religious Truth* (1964), for example, as a way of introducing patterned interrelationships between 'the great religions' (paragraph 5.12). In an earlier paper, 'Numen, Nirvana, and the Definition of Religion' (Chapter 8), it is used – admittedly also, despite the title, rather briefly – to illuminate the concept of 'religion', as opposed to talk about 'religions' in particular. The paper is of considerably wider interest, for much of it is an exploration of the need to amend Otto's account in order to accommodate the mystical or contemplative strand of religious experience alongside the numinous. Thus it complements or reaffirms much of the argument of *Reasons and Faiths* and, setting the tone of a great deal of Smart's work, takes Theravada Buddhism as the litmus test of the adequacy or otherwise of given analyses. In this sense it points forward as well as back.

The issue of the definition of religion is one that Smart does return to quite often, for example in 'What is Religion?' (Chapter 9). Here the issue of developing appropriate policies for religious education draws attention to the 'need to come to an intellectual understanding of what religion is and what the main dimensions of belief, feeling and practice are' (p. 111). In outlining his dimensional analysis (first expounded in *Secular Education and the Logic of Religion*,1968, pp. 15–19), Smart focuses more on what counts as 'a religion' than on how to understand the concept 'religion', but both issues are tackled. The dimensional analysis, of course, continues to permeate his subsequent work, leading both to a refinement of the dimensions, and a broadening of their application to cover non-religious 'worldviews'. Both aspects feature in the much later paper, 'Theravada Buddhism and the Definition of Religion' (Chapter 10). Here the original six dimensions (mythical, doctrinal, ethical, ritual, social and experiential) have been extended to seven, described now as ritual-practical, legal-ethical, emotional-experiential, doctrinal-philosophical, narrative-mythic, social-organizational, and material-artistic; the notion of family resemblances is invoked; and there is the extension of 'religion' to cover 'secular symbolic systems' (p. 122), namely secular worldviews. This last move in particular is open to some question (see Section 2.I(iii), below).

(The dimensional analysis, incidentally, appears initially to have been borrowed in good measure, albeit without due acknowledgement, it has to be said, from Raimundo Panikkar, as Ursula King has spotted – see King, 2006, pp. 14–15: a point subsequently confirmed by Panikkar himself.)

Returning more directly to the topic of comparative studies, 'The Work of the Buddha and the Work of Christ' (Chapter 11) is in many ways a model of clear and concise analysis, with the discussion of Buddhism being broadened, as would become common in Smart's overall scheme, to include the Mahayana. 'The Logos Doctrine and Eastern Beliefs' (Chapter 12) considers Hinduism, Buddhism, and Taoism: clearly Smart's interest in China had not disappeared. It would in due course, as we shall see, give rise to a number of papers on Chinese religions (and Maoism). This particular paper was published in a theological journal, yet while Smart makes clear at the outset its relevance to inter-faith dialogue, and in conclusion its relevance for theology, he is also quite clear that his intention is a neutral analytical comparison – an illustration of his generally scrupulous approach to the wearing of appropriate hats.

Smart's fondness for comparisons involving Hinduism and Buddhism in particular extends from *Reasons and Faiths* onwards. Examples include 'Consciousness: Permanent or Fleeting? Reflections on Indian Views of Consciousness and Self' (1989 [B], repr. Smart, 1997 [A]), 'Transcendence in a Pluralistic Context' (1997) [B], where there is also some reference to Jain cosmology, and 'The Comparative View of the Person: East and West' (Chapter 13). Despite the rather severely philosophical flavour of these titles, the discussions draw deeply on the relevant religious traditions, recalling the observation, noted earlier, that 'many metaphysical claims are disguised religious claims' (*Reasons and Faiths*, p. 4).

At times Smart turned from comparisons with Hinduism to comparisons between Buddhism and Western worldviews. An early example of this is 'Buddhism and Religious Belief' (1961) [C], which explores similarities and differences between the teachings of Buddhism, particularly in its more 'rationalist' Theravada form, and the views of secular humanists (the article was written specifically for the journal of the British Humanist

Association). The discussion here is clearly pertinent to the question of how religion should be defined, though it is not cast directly in those terms. Indeed, the difficulty posed by Theravada Buddhism for virtually all proposed definitions of religion is a recurrent theme in Smart's thought.

It surfaces again, briefly, in 'Buddhism and the Death of God' (Chapter 14), though the main focus here is that of similarities and differences between central ideas of the Theravada and those of certain radical Christian theologians concerned to cast Christian theology in a new mould by 'modifying or even scrapping belief in God as previously understood by the traditional worshipper' (p. 151). Clearly there is a degree, at least, of kinship between any 'death of God' theology and secular humanism, and Theravada does lend itself to illuminating comparisons in both directions. This particular theological trend appears in retrospect to have been something of a short-lived fashion, perhaps, but Smart's discussion contains comparisons of lasting interest.

The same may be said of 'Western Society and Buddhism' (1989 [C], repr. Smart, 1997 [A]), which explores developments set in train by the 1960s vogue for the writings of such as Aldous Huxley, Alan Watts and D.T. Suzuki. As with the previous two papers, Theravada emerges as a possible relevant alternative to Christianity, given its ultimate non-theism, and its teachings regarding 'salvation without God' (p. 46), but aspects of a wider appeal are also brought out (Smart mentions, for example, E.F. Schumacher, *Small Is Beautiful*, 1973, with its advocacy of 'Buddhist economics', and the strong similarities between aspects of modern physics and traditional Buddhist metaphysics). The discussion is not densely academic, and this is true of a fair amount of Smart's writing (including the two previously mentioned papers), but this does not prevent it from being illuminating. Indeed, Smart's facility with writing that is clear, informative, yet also analytic and thought-provoking, while being pitched at different levels, was undoubtedly a key to his influence and popularity.

In addition to dual comparisons of this kind, there is a body of work involving a whole range of comparisons. In 'Attitudes towards Death in Eastern Religions' (1968) [B], for example, Smart ranges across Buddhism, Jainism, and Hinduism to Taoism, Confucianism and Shinto. In later work this wide-ranging approach is frequently extended to scrutiny of relationships between religions and politics in the modern world, and a paper such as 'Types of Religious Liberation: An Implicit Critique of Modern Politics' (Chapter 15) can be seen (as, this time, the title indicates) as something of a bridge between the earlier comparative philosophy of religion and the later comparative worldview analysis (see Sections 2.V and 2.VI).

As a coda to this section it is of interest to note that in a paper co-written with Knut A. Jacobsen, and only recently published ('Is Hinduism an Offshoot of Buddhism?', 2006 [B]), the argument is made that, contrary to what is typically assumed, the gradually emerging identity of Hinduism was significantly shaped by Buddhism, rather than the reverse: these two major products of the Indian religious world continued to attract his attention to the very end.

1.V Religious Studies and Religious Education: Method and Theory in the Study of Religions

Arguably a consideration of Smart's views on method should properly have been considered earlier in this analysis. It is a topic on which he wrote extensively, and in at least some respects influentially, given their contribution to the changing nature of religious education in British schools, for example. On the other hand, he did not first devise a method for the study of religions, and then apply it. The process was a gradual, cumulative one, emerging from reflection on different aspects of the task at different times. It seemed adequate, therefore, simply to provide an introductory sample early on (Chapter 1), and reserve discussion until later.

Of course, there have been, inevitably, glimpses of his thoughts on theory and method in the substantive studies considered so far – despite the desire to categorize the main strands of his thinking, few of his publications, or at any rate of his published papers, fall neatly into the categories identified. Thus reference has been made to his early emphasis on linguistic analysis; his theory of the relative autonomy of religion rooted in religious experience; the associated typology of religious experience; the theory of internal religious reasoning; his dimensional analysis of religions; and theories regarding the definition of religion. This is already much. In the late 1960s and especially in the 1970s, though, Smart set out to construct a wide-ranging, systematic account of how best to conceptualize the study of religion in what was, as he insists, a new field of study 'scarcely formed until the 1960s' (Chapter 1, p. 3).

Its formation intellectually was connected with its institutionalization educationally, and in Britain most especially with the launch of a new-style Department of Religious Studies in Lancaster in 1967, with Smart at its head. Not unnaturally, therefore, discussion of academic theory and of educational policy are often interwoven.

The early paper, 'Religion as a Discipline?' (Chapter 16), is primarily a plea for institutionalization – and a remarkably successful one in that, as he tells elsewhere, it led Smart to Lancaster (Chapter 1, p. 4). Yet already two aspects of the study of religion are identified as jointly necessary, which in some of Smart's later work are prised apart. The consequence can be a misunderstanding of Smart, and an undermining of part of the project of religious studies.

The two aspects, emphasized throughout, are religion as a significant phenomenon with numerous ramifications, and 'its validity or otherwise in claiming to give us an insight into reality' (Chapter 16., p. 178). Thus exploration of religion as a phenomenon, and exploration of religious truth-claims, are both highlighted as central to religion as a discipline.

Later, though, Smart's name came to be associated in particular, certainly in Britain, with the 'phenomenological' approach to the study of religion, in which a 'bracketing' or temporary suspension of one's own views, combined with the exercise of empathy, leads (to varying degrees in different people, according to their relative ability to practise these skills) to a sensitively informed understanding of religion as experienced by religious people – or members of another religion – themselves. This is a largely uncritical approach, except in so far as the insiders' views under consideration may not be wholly consistent with each other, so that some critical comparison is called for. Yet internal adjustment is different from external criticism; and though the propriety of the latter is not denied, Smart sometimes argues for its somewhat indefinite postponement on the ground that sound critical evaluation presupposes sound understanding, and in respect of religion this is in all kinds of ways still some way off (see for example *Religion and the Western Mind*, p. 13). Hence we find such remarks as 'what we as students of religion are concerned with is the power (not the truth) of religious experience, etc.' ('Foreword', to G. van der Leeuw, *Religion in Essence and Manifestation*, 1986, p. xv), remarks which imply a radical disjunction between the exploration of religion as a phenomenon, and the exploration of religious truth-claims.

The roots of this apparent disjunction lie in part in the way that Smart in the early 1970s focused on articulating a 'science of religion'. This, in addition to being phenomenological, was also plural or cross-cultural, historical, theoretical (involving the kind of intra-religious explanations advanced in *Reasons and Faiths*, but not reductionist-type external explanations), and multidisciplinary or polymethodic ('in the early days of the Lancaster Department … we used to say that we polymethodoodled all the day', 'Religious Studies and Theology', 1997 [C], p. 67). Clearly this is a vastly broader canvas than just phenomenology, yet the bounds of the latter are not transcended to include critical evaluation as part of the 'science of religion' (a topic explored at some length in *The Science of Religion and the Sociology of Knowledge*, 1973). It is against this background, then, that remarks about prescinding from critical evaluation are to be construed.

Yet wide-ranging as the science of religion is in comparison with 'the phenomenological approach', it is still not the whole story. For in that very book Smart also draws 'a distinction between religious studies and the scientific study of religion, as I am trying to expound it. The latter is part of the former, but religious studies legitimately can include aims other than the scientific study of religion. For example, much of the philosophy of religion is concerned with probing questions of truth, directly or indirectly, and is a legitimate part of religious studies' (pp. 41–42).

Despite, then, a number of comments emphasizing the importance of non-evaluation in the study of religion, and much emphasis on the importance of descriptive-historical studies, in the full picture critical evaluation is both appropriate and indeed ineluctable, given the plural nature of religions and worldviews, and given that 'propaganda is not the aim of teaching, but the production of a ripe capacity to judge the truth of what is propagated' (*Secular Education and the Logic of Religion*, p. 97). The dual concern with the exploration of religion as a phenomenon and the exploration of religious truth-claims recurs, from 'Religion as a Discipline' right through. If this has often been overlooked, it is because it is at times obscured by the way in which his key distinctions between phenomenology of religion, science of religion, and religious studies are sometimes allowed to fade into the background (or have not yet been clearly drawn), permitting some of his statements to be taken rather too easily out of context, as we shall see.

An unusually large number of Smart's published papers focus on theory and method, often as such, sometimes linked to education (see Volume 1, Appendix 1). On this basis, a subdivision of the present section into two, one on religious studies, the other on religious education, could no doubt be attempted. Yet Smart himself was keen to emphasize that the two enterprises should be construed as resting on shared core principles, and that theme of continuity is perhaps better served by placing what is in any case often overlapping material together in one section. There is, in fact, a fair amount of repetition on the topic, since Smart in effect conducted a tireless campaign to persuade a variety of audiences of the virtues of his vision of religious studies.

'What is Comparative Religion?' (Chapter 17) dates from just before Smart's move to Lancaster, and builds on the argument of 'Religion as a Discipline?' by marking off comparative religion from related fields such as Christian theology of other faiths, missiology, interfaith dialogue, and history of religions. The subsequent emphasis on phenomenology is anticipated: 'the descriptive side of comparative religion is not just a recording of data: it is the attempt at a warmly dispassionate delineation of the outer shape and inner meaning of religious phenomena' (p. 185) – what Smart would later call the need to 'transcend the informative' (*Secular Education and the Logic of Religion*, p. 105). The possibility of 'correlations within the various dimensions or levels of religion' is mentioned (pp. 185–186) – there is as yet no list of dimensions, but interestingly passing reference is made to 'mythological correspondences', and also doctrinal and experiential ones (p. 186): the dimensional analysis is already forming. The by now familiar dual typology of 'bhakti-yoga', 'devotionalism and contemplation' (Section 1.II, above), is invoked (p. 187), and the putative primacy of experience in the correlation of types of experience and of doctrine is proposed. At the same time, 'as to truth, that is another argument (and not one incidentally which lies within the province of the comparative study of religion proper')' (ibid., pp. 186–187) – the later apparent equivocation regarding the proper scope of study is already apparent.

'The Principles and Meaning of the Study of Religion' (1970 [C], repr. Smart, 1986 [A]) was Smart's Lancaster Inaugural Lecture, and here we find one of the earliest formulations of his famous list of six key dimensions of religion, though they are not emphasized in the way that occurs in subsequent writings, or in the somewhat earlier 1966 York Haslington Lectures (see *Secular Education and the Logic of Religion*, pp. 15–19). The themes of 'structural description' and transcending the informative recur (the latter now dubbed 'the principle of inwardness'), with the clear statement that insiders' views, however necessary and informative, may need supplementation from outside (so phenomenology cannot be the whole story) (pp. 3–4). Summing up, Smart lists history of religions as a necessary ingredient of the study of religion – whereas in the previous paper he had explicitly marked history of religions off as distinct from comparative religion; so the study of religion is broader in scope than comparative religion. This is not actually spelled out here, though; and indeed even when relevant distinctions are made clear, as between religious studies and the science of religion, they may well not be underlined, and hence, as noted above, may well be overlooked (or readily forgotten or neglected). Admittedly, labels for the study of religion are several, and their use often imprecise. Yet despite Smart's concern for methodological clarity, and his facility for conceptual distinctions, he at times veered from one label to another in a less than immaculate manner. (In the brief paper 'History of Religions', (1979) [C], for example, he writes almost cavalierly of the need to 'pay attention to theoretical issues, or putting it another way, to what goes on under the name of phenomenology of religion' – as if the two were identical (p. 73), and elides history of religions and comparative religion in a way contrary to the need, expressed elsewhere, to distinguish carefully between them.)

Alongside history of religions, Smart lists phenomenology, sociology, psychology, and philosophy of religion. In connection with the latter, its being strongly conceptual and analytic is emphasized rather than its exploration of truth-claims. Yet he does refer to the need for 'a realistic evaluation of religious and atheistic positions' (p. 8), and adds modern religious and atheistic thought as a further ingredient to his list, as a sort of penumbra to religious studies (a course on precisely this did in fact feature in the opening offerings of the Lancaster department). Later, as we shall see, he would argue that religious studies should become worldview analysis, and urge that, say, Maoism be construed as a religion. Here, though, he adopts the very different stance – consonant with the critique of his views on Maoism outlined in Section 2.I(iii) – that religion be defined 'in such a way that it does not include anti-religious atheism', for otherwise 'the atheist is deprived of his anti-religion' (p. 8).

We have here, then, something of a transitional position. Earlier concerns with conceptual analysis of religious discourse and structured empathy are carried over into broader concerns with multidisciplinary as well as comparative studies, reflecting a burgeoning concern to map out a whole new field of study rather than just deal with some of what may be regarded as its traditional components or predecessors.

A further step in this direction is marked by 'The Structure of the Comparative Study of Religion' (Chapter 18), where the programme outlined in his inaugural lecture is developed both somewhat more systematically and also in a little more detail. A label that is new for Smart at this time makes an appearance, 'the scientific study of religion' (p. 198), for the neutral, descriptive part of the study of religions, while philosophy of religion is grouped with theology and dialogue of religions in the second, committed or evaluative, part. Here Smart discriminates carefully between the various enterprises and types of enterprise, concluding in respect of the latter that 'it is unlikely that the study of religion can ever be fully rich without including both sorts of approaches' (p 202). Still, 'religious studies' includes, we see, philosophy of religion, but excludes theology and dialogue of religions. The different maps on offer do not unambiguously mark out quite the same territory.

Hints of ambiguity in Smart's own understanding are perhaps clarified in the very much later paper, 'Some Thoughts on the Science of Religion' (1996) [B]. He begins with 'one or two clarificatory observations' about 'Religious Studies', and writes: 'It is the name of a discipline which was institutionalized primarily in the Sixties. It had precursors, such as Comparative (Study of) Religion, *Religionswissenschaft*, History of Religion(s), etc. It comprises three elements. First, there is what may be called the Science of Religion, which includes both the histories of religion and the social scientific approaches to religion. Second, there is the Science of Religion, with philosophy of religion and the like added. Third, it comprises the former elements plus sundry other miscellaneous pursuits, including reflections on theologies, religious ethics, etc.' (p.15). His various accounts over the years can be seen as hovering over (and at times perhaps wavering between) these three possible categories. He does subsequently conclude, though, that at present 'it is probably best to confine Religious Studies to a combination of the Science of Religion and Reflective Studies connected therewith, ranging from methodology and philosophy of religion to broad-based thinking about the roles of religion and ideology' (p. 19).

Still from the early period, and leading up to the publication of *The Science of Religion and the Sociology of Knowledge* (1973), is 'Scientific Studies of Religion' (Chapter 19). Here many of the items mentioned earlier are developed still further (for example we now have a distinction between descriptive phenomenology and speculative phenomenology – yet the latter is in effect a new label for what Smart was about in *Reasons and Faiths*), and brought to fruition. The paper is a good summary of Smart's thought at this stage. Of interest, in the light of later discussion in Section 2.I(iii), is the view expressed regarding Maoism, that while it exemplifies the six dimensions of religion, 'these as it happens are not focused on a transcendent being or state', and Maoism is therefore better characterized as a 'quasi-religion' (p. 207).

About this, though, Smart was to change his mind, and there emerges an emphasis on extending the study of religions to incorporate study of secular worldviews. Such study already occurs, of course, 'among historians of philosophy, sociologists, anthropologists, classicists, orientalists, Africanists, political scientists and so forth' ('Worldview Analysis: A Way of Looking at Our Field', 1982 [C], p. 2), but religious studies provides an excellent base too. (On worldview analysis see also Section 2.II.)

Worldview analysis appears, then, in some later papers, several of which reflect, in overlapping but partly distinct ways, Smart's mature views on methodology. 'Religious Studies and the Comparative Perspective' (Chapter 20) is very systematically analytical, and includes discussion of the interface between religious studies and theology. It also contains a strong statement that 'Religious Studies must engage with truth and criteria questions … It cannot just remain at the descriptive and theoretical level' (p. 225). In 'The Study of Religion as a Multidisciplinary and Cross-Cultural Presence Among the Human Sciences' (Chapter 21), Smart's University of California, Santa Barbara inaugural lecture, on the other hand, we are back with the other emphasis, that 'it is the power of religion, rather than its truth, that primarily concerns us' (p. 232), and that 'generally speaking, religious studies in its modern form does not want to make judgments about the truth of religion, since we explore its power, rather' (p. 237). Still, philosophy of religion does form part of religious studies, so 'we rightly cannot escape some consideration about criteria of truth' (p. 237). Even here, though, there is perhaps a certain coyness in the implied distinction – or at any rate difference of emphasis – between 'consideration about' criteria, and their application. 'The Philosophy of Worldviews, or The Philosophy of Religion Transformed' (1995 [C], repr. Smart, 1986 [A]) introduces issues that will be addressed below in Sections 2.IV and 2.V, and concludes that 'the philosophy of religion should be extended to be the philosophy of worldviews, and that it should be the upper storey of a building which has as its middle floor the comparative and historical analysis of religions and ideologies, and as a ground floor the phenomenology not just of religious experience and action but of the symbolic life of human beings as a whole' (p. 31). (See also 'Does the Philosophy of Religion Rest on Two Mistakes?', 1997 [C].)

The connection between conceptualization of religious studies as a field of study, and discussion of its proper implementation in the education system, is a recurrent theme. Smart's role in respect of the latter was pivotal in the UK, not only through his publications and frequent public lectures, but also as director of major Lancaster-based projects on religious education in schools, and as co-founder of the Shap Working Party on World Religions in Education. Yet although his involvement in helping to change the curriculum in schools led to a number of publications (mention has already been made of *Secular Education and the Logic of Religion*, which took a lot further the argument and implications of his earlier *The Teacher and Christian Belief* (1966)), the published papers on education overlap substantially in content with material already covered here – see, for example, 'A Curricular Paradigm for Religious Education' (1981) [B], or 'The Exploration of Religion in Public Education' (1979–1980) [C].

That there should be this overlap is not surprising, given Smart's view that religion as a subject is like history or maths etc., in that a core understanding of the subject applies throughout the different levels of the education system. This view, though, is no doubt open to challenge, given the sensitivities of many parents and teachers in respect of how religion should be handled with often vulnerable younger people. The present section may therefore be usefully rounded off with the pithy 'Comparative Religion Clichés (Chapter 22), written for teachers, which continues to provide much food for thought; and the trenchantly argued 'The Political Implications of Religious Studies' (Chapter 23) (which could also be placed in Section 11), which urges the necessity of educating young people to become 'religiate', so that they are better placed to make up their minds about what is good and about what is bad in religions. (The notion of religiacy, involving skills in respect of religion analogous to skills in respect of reading and mathematics involved in literacy and numeracy, appears to have been borrowed from Brian Gates' Lancaster doctoral dissertation on religious education, which Smart supervised.) Exploration of what is bad has, of course, tended to be somewhat eclipsed by a concern to emphasize what is good ('learning from religion', as a prime aim in the English education system, for example). Yet given the public profile of religion in the global village today, it is surely time to pay due attention to both sides of the picture: religiacy is not adequately nurtured on a diet of unduly sanitized religion. 'The bad side of a religion should not be ignored' (Chapter 22, p. 244).

1.VI Religious Ethics

The ethical dimension was one of Smart's original six, and one of his earliest papers, 'Gods, Bliss and Morality' (Chapter 24), dealt in some detail, and with considerable subtlety, with the relations between religious and moral discourse. It was a topic to which he returned in *Reasons and Faiths*, yet with a few exceptions his views on this remained relatively low key although fairly constant. Partly this was because of a suspicion that, in discussions of religion and morality, people all too easily focus on morality at the relative expense of religion; so the earlier concern to establish the study of religion as a subject led to a tacit demotion of religious ethics. With the established vigour of religious studies, though, greater attention to ethics began to emerge, and Smart warmly welcomed the gradual burgeoning of 'comparative religious ethics', for example, as well as addressing ethical aspects of religion and politics.

The chapter on moral discourse in *Reasons and Faiths* establishes certain parameters which remained more or less axiomatic throughout Smart's career. First, he sided in many ways with philosophical advocates of the thesis of the autonomy of ethics. Moral rules and duties can be justified very generally in terms of 'the prevention of suffering and the enhancement of natural goods' (p. 180); proscriptions against stealing and lying etc. function more or less as socially necessary rules (see Alasdair MacIntyre, *A Short History of Ethics*, 1967, pp. 95–96); and some kind of utilitarian ethic seems to underpin our social conduct. Therefore 'it seems not inappropriate to treat moral propositions as logically independent of religious ones, except in the sense that by becoming incorporated into doctrinal schemes they acquire the status also of being religious propositions' (*Reasons and Faiths*, p. 182).

This is, of course, a minimalist account of morality which raises as many questions as it answers. Smart in effect raises some of them himself, adverting in passing to both negative utilitarianism as an option (with 'prevent suffering' rather than 'promote happiness' as overall aim), and the distinction between rule- and act-utilitarianism – about which his brother held strong views (J.J.C. Smart and Bernard Williams, *Utilitarianism For and Against*, 1973; see also Smart, 'Negative Utilitarianism', 1958 [C]). Other questions which would need to be raised include the apparent need to balance utilitarian considerations against those of distributive justice (see, for example, D.D. Raphael, *Moral Philosophy*, 1981, ch. 7). Nevertheless, the thesis of the logical autonomy of at least a basic human morality is well-nigh universal in modern ethical theory, and that thesis is Smart's initial basic point.

Second comes the notion of 'superimposition', which remains a standard part of his repertoire of basic ideas. At its simplest this is the idea that a secular activity is reinterpreted in religious terms ('work shall be prayer', he quotes from a Christian hymn), so that 'the performance of a duty is regarded in a new light, but yet also remains a duty justifiable in the ordinary way, and this is the ground for saying ... that spiritual concepts are, in this sort of case, *superimposed* upon moral ones' (*Reasons and Faiths*, p. 183). Hence, for example, 'moral rules are viewed under the guise of commandments' (ibid.).

Smart notes at the outset of this discussion that to separate out moral discourse as a strand of religious discourse is somewhat artificial, and the drawback with the notion of superimposition as (re)interpretation is that it may be thought to imply that spiritual interpretation is an optional extra. Logically this may be so (basic moral duties remain even if religious commitment disappears); psychologically it is often not like that at all, for to religious people moral duties are likely to be felt to be also intrinsically religious. Smart's notion of superimposition, therefore, might usefully be seen as an early version of John Hick's notion of 'experiencing-as' (Hick, 1969). Admittedly, he expresses a preference at one point for the 'intuitionist' approach of H.D. Lewis and Rudolf Otto over that of Hick ('Our Experience of the Ultimate', 1984 [C], p. 19); yet in his final published interview he notes explicitly, in respect of the interpretation of religious experience, 'I follow the lead given by Hick', and proceeds to illustrate the point with reference to superimposition (while still insisting that, for him, Hick's notion is 'secondary' – to, one assumes, the primary numinous and contemplative 'intuitions') ('Another Conversation with Ninian Smart', 2004 [B], p. 287; see also 'Transcendental Humanism', 1982 [B], p. 392, 'a religion indeed makes us experience the world *as*').

There are cases, though, where religious morality differs in actual moral substance from secular morality, as in the wrongness of blasphemy, or the duty to become a martyr for one's faith; and notoriously tensions can arise over an issue like euthanasia. These, though, are not matters that Smart sought to pursue.

The above remarks apply to the interweaving of the moral with the numinous strand. In connection with the mystical strand, the independent claims of morality rein in a tendency to turn one's back on the world in complete withdrawal, Smart urges, yet pursuit of the contemplative ideal in its turn introduces the idea of morality as part of 'good training in self-control', and the latter introduces the virtue of some degree of asceticism. The overall quietistic ideal 'will conduce towards such principles as *ahimsa* or non-injury' (*Reasons and Faiths*, p. 192).

This early general analysis was one that Smart maintained, and it is reflected at various points in his writings, but rarely in detail or in depth. Thus, for example, in 'Religious Studies and the Comparative Perspective' (1986) [C] the notion of superimposition is still being used, 'so that doing good is seen as a form of worship or humility is seen as a form of reverence towards God or as a sacrifice – and so on', as part of looking to the way 'differing types of religious experience and practice shape different kinds of ethics: thus the yogic techniques of pacification of the passions tend towards a prudential and gentle ethic of self-control and harmlessness, while the numinous dynamism of prophetic religion is more activist and authoritarian. So there is here one side to the whole enterprise of comparative religious ethics' (p. 10).

Of course, in a programmatic paper like the one just quoted, one does not expect a detailed discussion, but the topic is one that Smart tended to deal with only fairly sketchily. In *Dimensions of the Sacred* (1996) there is a chapter on the ethical-legal dimension, with a fuller treatment. The question of different kinds of moral motivation deriving from different religions is introduced, and there is a section on the virtues encouraged in Buddhism, Christianity and Confucianism respectively. Yet there is also a section on the effect of the Enlightenment and colonialism on religious ethics, and it was to this more political dimension that Smart came to devote closer attention (see Section 2.II, below). *Worldviews: Crosscultural Explorations of Human Beliefs* (1983) is also structured in terms of his dimensional analysis, and in the chapter on the ethical dimension we now have a section on 'Comparative Religious Ethics'. Once again, though, the comments, though neither uninformative nor uninteresting, remain fairly general. The thesis of the autonomy of ethics is discussed in connection with Kant, but is left hanging in the paragraph where cursory criticisms of Kant are outlined, for these deal with separate issues.

Unlike his output on methodology, then, there are relatively few published papers on religious ethics from which to choose. As noted above, though, 'Gods, Bliss and Morality' (Chapter 24) offers a substantial and indeed highly original kind of analysis. Written at the time of working on *Reasons and Faiths*, it covers more or less the ground outlined above, although the conclusion presses home the lesson that 'an analysis of religious moral language requires an investigation of such concepts as *atonement, worship, sacrifice, sin, grace, holiness*, and so on: it is not just that religious people, while sharing principles, have different factual or metaphysical beliefs' (p. 288). This meshes with our earlier comment about superimposition as experiencing-as, and Smart's persistent theme of the often complex ramification of doctrinal schemes.

'The Ethics of Chinese Communism' (Chapter 25) is very different in style, and reflects both Smart's engagement with Maoism in the 1970s (see Section 2.I(iii), below) – he would later quip that he'd visited the 'Maosoleum' in Beijing – and also his advocacy of worldview analysis as a broader version of religious studies. In the first part we find the kind of broadly sociological analysis that he applied elsewhere to India, for example, as well as to China, after which he focuses on the distinctively 'spiritual' and ethical character of Maoism. There is, of course, much about Mao of a negative character that has now gained general acceptance, and may be thought to undermine Smart's analysis in important ways. Yet looked at closely, there is not here an idealization of Mao, but rather a thesis about the apparent match between, on the one hand, Maoism as a movement and the idealism it engendered, and on the other hand, the social and political conditions of ideological success in China at the time. A one-sided vilification of Mao the person (as in Jung Chang and Jon Halliday, *Mao: The Unknown Story*, 2005), however well founded as far as it goes (and this is much debated), should not be allowed to derogate either from the practical successes of Maoism the movement, or the ethical impulse to be found in Mao's writings (see for example the review of Chang and Halliday by Delia Davin, *The Times Higher*, August 12, 2005, pp. 22–23, or R.L. Whitehead, *Love and Struggle in Mao's Thought*, 1977.) Viewed against this broader canvas, Smart's account still merits serious attention.

In later writings, though, he did sometimes strike a cooler note. Thus while he once wrote 'I admire the Chinese ideology greatly having recently written a book on Mao' ('Discussion' [of 'Does a Universal Standard of Value Need to be Higher-Order?'], 1974 [B], p. 606), he would later comment that while Mao and Maoism 'became for a time strong forces in the lives of millions of Chinese', it was ('of course') 'the phenomenological Mao that had this power, as he was presented to and occurred in the imagination of his followers. The actual Mao was an orgiastic and corrupt man, who abused his position. But that only came out later than the Chinese age of faith' (*Religion and Nationalism: The Urgency of Transnational Spirituality and Toleration*, 1994, p. 41). Elsewhere he urged that Maoism had been 'a bad deal, as far as the restoration of cultural identity went' ('Old Religions and New Religions: The Lessons of the Colonial Era', 1991 [B], p. 72), and that in comparison with India, 'China under Maoism, by contrast, was much less effective, since so much of Chinese tradition had to be sacrificed in the course of a social reconstruction which was supposed to make China strong. It was powerful militarily; but in economics and politics it was long in a state of rigidity and oppression' ('Tradition, Retrospective Perception, Nationalism and Modernism', 1998 [B], p. 80). One is left with the impression of a certain ambivalence – or perhaps simply of a gradually waning enthusiasm.

Smart begins 'Clarity and Imagination as Buddhist Means to Virtue' (Chapter 26) with the disclaimer that 'this paper is not intended as an analytic or descriptive one. In it I wish to commend certain ideas drawn from the Buddhist tradition and freely adapted to a global view of ethics' (p. 294). It would have been more accurate, perhaps, to say that it was not intended to be 'only' analytic or descriptive, since it does offer a mini-survey of Buddhist ethics. In effect we have here in respect of Buddhism what Smart had in earlier work illustrated in respect of Christianity, namely the way in which moral virtues (like the four *brahmaviharas*) are embedded in a broader doctrinal scheme (where 'clarity' is linked to the need to overcome 'delusion' about the true nature of reality as 'impermanent', and morality needs to incorporate the attendant doctrine of *anatta*, or no-self).

At one point there is a reminder of his analysis of morality in *Reasons and Faiths*, when we read that 'Theravadin ethics, while generally speaking predicated upon a utilitarian schema, differs from its typical Western counterparts in its conception of happiness and the means of getting there' (p. 304). Smart's understanding of ethical theory here is rather limited. Admittedly, he is not by any means alone in likening Buddhist ethics to Utilitarianism (see for example David Kalupahana, *Buddhist Philosophy: A Historical Analysis*, 1976), but the two parts of the above quotation lend themselves to a major disjunction and a significantly different interpretation. The different conception of happiness, and the different means of getting there, jointly imply an ethic that is 'teleological' (aiming at a goal, *telos*) but not 'consequentialist' (judging the rightness and wrongness of an act or policy in terms of its consequences) – in other words that is broadly Aristotelian, with an overall goal of 'flourishing' (eudaimonia), not Utilitarian, with its more immediate goal of 'pleasure/ happiness'. These latter terms are indeed slippery, but the broad contrast between an Aristotelian and a Utilitarian understanding of morality runs deep, as recent work in moral philosophy has emphasized; and in part drawing on this, a very plausible case has been made for the affinity (though not the identity) between Buddhist ethics and the Aristotelian rather than the Utilitarian approach (see Damien Keown, *The Nature of Buddhist Ethics*, 1992, passim; Peter Harvey, *An Introduction to Buddhist Ethics*, 2000, pp. 49–51). It seems a more apt interpretation than Smart's 'a critical, transcendental utilitarianism' (p. 304): this does reflect his awareness of the essential need for qualification, but not of the advantage of a change of paradigm. (The same applies, as it happens, to Christianity. 'In so far as ethical and spiritual discipline has a meaning it is because it is directed towards a transcendent goal. The Christian's utilitarianism is transcendental utilitarianism', 'Measuring the Ideal: Christian Faith and the World's Worldviews', 1997 [B], p. 49.)

An interesting variation on the theme of Buddhist ethics is provided by 'Religious Values and the University' (Chapter 27), the Presentation Speech given on the occasion of his receiving an Honorary Doctorate from the University of Kelaniya in Sri Lanka. It picks up some of the same values discussed above, though viewing them now as contributing to the ethos of a university, and hence to the wider community: 'all in all the study of religions links in with the values of the modern university and the modern world', he urges, and 'Buddhist values', he concludes, 'course through my veins as well as Christian and liberal ones!' (p. 313) – we recall his self-designation as a Buddhist Episcopalian.

Lessons to be learnt from comparative ethics form the theme of 'Sacred Civilities' (Chapter 28), which starts off with the remark that 'we have a fairly narrow conception of what counts as a moral issue or a moral rule in Western society', and 'perhaps virtues extend further in scope than moral behaviour' (p. 314) – a comment that can be linked, of course, with the suggestion made above that the eudaimonistic model of virtue ethics might be preferable to the utilitarian model of ethics. The notion of superimposition is still being used, we may note: 'a piously Christian person may see her actions as occurring in praise of God. This is where praise is superimposed upon moral, civil, or polite action to give it a deeper sense. But this does not subtract from its other meanings' (p. 315). Smart then moves on from Christianity to Confucianism, where we have perhaps 'the most vital fusing of the notions of the ethical and civility ... through the ideas of *jen* and *li'* (p. 316), roughly benevolence and the rules of propriety, and concludes with brief remarks on Buddhism. Like some other papers, this one illustrates Smart's penchant for explorations that are thought-provokingly fresh at the expense of being worked out in detail.

Most of these papers are relatively late, and none of the later ones really matches the early 'Gods, Bliss and Morality' (Chapter 24) in terms of sophistication and originality. Even so, they are not without interest – Smart was consistently able to spark fresh thoughts on virtually any topic.

One other paper, though, may usefully be added, 'A Global Ethic Arising from the Epistemology of Religious and Similar Value-Systems (Chapter 29). Here we find adumbrated a position that informs many of Smart's other analyses.

The comparative study of religions reveals many mutually incompatible doctrines and prescriptions between different religions (and other worldviews), yet rooted severally in authoritative traditions each transmitted as certain. They are, in Smart's terms, based on 'hard epistemologies'. How, then, to resolve such oppositions? Any attempt to do so has the unintended consequence that 'crosscultural or crosstraditional arguments on behalf of my hard epistemology over yours are soft' (invoking, say, aesthetic judgements, or judgements of historical (or other) probability). Moreover, there is the further unintended consequence that any worldview epistemology is soft: 'for soft arguments for the validity of a hard proof render the proof soft' (pp. 326–327). Yet soft arguments can still be cogent, so there is no further implication of subjectivism or relativism. The conclusion to be drawn, rather, is the propriety of 'soft non-relativism'; and this in turn implies an impetus to toleration, recognition of basic human rights, and the desirability of a pluralistic society consciously determined to promote and practise non-dogmatic forms of religious education, for soft non-relativism does not license a right to teach one's own religion or worldview 'as though it alone could be true' (p. 326).

To the possible objection that this all sounds like typical Western liberalism, Smart replies that while the liberalism may be inherent, its Westernness is not; and in any case, the liberalism advocated arises not from a prior ideological commitment, but from the logic of the situation. Members of 'conservative seminaries and prestigious mosques ... sacred temples or totalitarian academies' (p. 325) may not see things this way, but that does not alter the logic of the situation, and 'the logic of the one world will have its slow effects, despite frontiers and visas of the mind' (p. 326). We shall find extensive use of such arguments in Sections 2.III, 2.IV and 2.V.

2.I Individual Traditions

In addition to the specifically comparative studies, Smart also published on individual religions, not least from his beloved Indian traditions. Admittedly, here too comparative comments occur, yet the prime focus is on an individual religious tradition, or on some aspect or thinker drawn from it.

Notable, in a sense, by their virtual absence in this context are studies of Islam. Of course, in major texts like *The Religious Experience of Mankind* (1969, 1976, 1984, subsequently entitled simply *The Religious Experience*, 1991, 1996), *The World's Religions* (1989, 1998), and *World Philosophies* (1999), Islam is covered too. Still, Smart commented that he found some religions harder to write about than others, and this may well have been the case with Islam. The seemingly instinctive empathy that he brought to so many aspects of the South Asian traditions is not immediately apparent in respect of Islam, except perhaps to an extent with the subtradition of Sufism. For 'epistemologically and in the light of the study of religions and worldviews, those religious forms which have fanatic certitude are unsound. I believe that the spirit of modern science, of humanistic enquiry, and of critical education is not truly compatible with monistic orthodoxies … . This is where, frankly, I find Islam as having greater difficulty coming to terms with open modernity than many other religious traditions' ('Buddhism, Christianity, and the Critique of Ideology', 1984 [B], p. 153 – the argument of this paper is expanded in Smart's Gifford Lectures, *Beyond Ideology: Religion and the Future of Western Civilization*, 1981).

The case of Christianity is rather different. *The Phenomenon of Christianity* (1979) is an attempt to consider his own religion through the same kind of 'warm distance' (p. 8) that he brought to others, in order to take a fresh look at a religion 'whose familiarity can breed distortion' (p. 9). In the first half of the book he investigates important varieties of Christianity, such as Orthodoxy and Roman Catholicism, but also Copts, Lutherans, Baptists and African Christianity, through a selective focus on individual examples (for example, Romanian Orthodoxy, Italian Catholicism), while in the second half he applies his by now well established dimensional analysis. Yet his published papers on Christianity as such tend to be written less from this generally phenomenological perspective and more from that of a committed believer (and often with a primarily Christian audience in mind). They will therefore be introduced in the context of Christian theology and inter-faith dialogue (Sections 2.III and 2.IV). There are, though, one or two papers which do belong here, and they are introduced below in Section 2.I(iv).

(i) Buddhism

As seen in Section 1.I, the encounter with Theravada Buddhism was a prime impetus to Smart's engagement with comparative religion, and it features again and again in his writings, from the earliest onwards, as began to be apparent in Section 1.IV. Moreover, it was always a pleasure to introduce Buddhism to a new audience, especially a Christian one: the thesis that Christianity and Buddhism might profitably be regarded as in many ways mutually complementary became indeed very pronounced – see, for example, *Buddhism and Christianity: Rivals and Allies* (1993), and *Lights of the World: Buddha and Christ* (1997).

'Learning from Other Faiths: II, Buddhism' (1972) [C] was one such introduction, offering a dispassionately descriptive analytical survey, even though intended for a Christian readership. Still, elements of his theory of religious reasons, as outlined in Section 1.II, are also discernible, as when he notes that people develop 'radically diverse interpretations of the world *on the basis of religious experience* (p. 213, italics added), and in his comment, vis-á-vis the Mahayana, that 'from this we can doubtless learn something about the tendency of religions to enrich themselves with the differing types of religious experience' (p. 214).

A feature of many religions, of course, is the existence of sacred texts. In some religions, notably Judaism and Islam, we find a highly elevated view of scripture as divine revelation, while in Hinduism there is the analogous understanding of Vedic *śruti*. In 'Mysticism and Scripture in Theravada Buddhism' (Volume 2, Chapter 1) Smart examines reasons why, despite the respect accorded the Pali canon, its status is notably different, so that, indeed, in the Theravada, the scriptures are in a sense 'a bit of a disappointment ... compared to the "high" views of scripture elsewhere' (p. 12).

Both of these papers are accessible to the non-specialist, as too, despite a somewhat forbidding title, is 'Problems of the Application of Western Terminology to Theravada Buddhism, With Special Reference to the Relationship between the Buddha and the Gods' (1972 [C], repr. Smart, 1986 [A]). An important thrust of the argument here is an elucidation of the claim, which Smart also advances elsewhere, that 'the Buddha, so to say, did not launch a direct assault upon current beliefs; but retained something of their outer form, while sucking away their inner substance', thereby building 'a bridge to popular religion' (p. 445). Thus, for example, the gods too, like humans, suffer from impermanence, that key mark of *dukkha* characterizing all existence; and worship is not a means to liberation. The Theravada of the Pali canon is 'Janus-faced' (p. 448), with on the one hand the rather austere path of contemplation, and on the other hand gods, spirits, heavens, purgatories, miracles, and so forth. Yet the two facets may be seen as in a sense complementary rather than in mutual conflict with each other.

Here, it has to be said, a rather important critical question arises. Despite the passing reference above to 'popular religion', Smart's accounts of the Theravada rarely venture into this territory, and do therefore lend themselves to the criticism that they convey a predominantly intellectualist picture that is in significant respects a distortion of

Theravada Buddhism as a lived religion. This is all the more remarkable in that major anthropological studies have sought precisely to correct this kind of impression.

Smart was, of course, well aware of this literature, but the findings of the anthropologists are not incorporated to the extent one might expect. Indeed, at times Smart is even rather dismissive: 'Generally, the Sangha has survived in unison with surrounding religions; but it is wrong to identify Buddhism with those peripheral religious forces. There is a tendency in anthropology to do this' (Volume 2, Chapter 1, p. 5).

This is, perhaps, an oblique reference to a work like Stanley J. Tambiah, *Buddhism and the Spirit Cults in North-East Thailand* (1970), but in any case anthropologists of Buddhism have produced a wide range of material. Smart did write an appreciative review article (1973) [D] of Richard Gombrich's important study, *Precept and Practice: Traditional Buddhism in the Rural Highlands of Ceylon* (1971) – a topic close, of course, to Smart's heart, given his formative post-war experiences in Ceylon. There is also an unpublished lecture on Buddhism as a popular religion (partly handwritten and perhaps incomplete) among his papers in the Ninian Smart Archive. Yet the major findings of Melford Spiro in Burma (and matched elsewhere), that merit-accumulation has largely replaced the contemplative pursuit of nirvana as the immediate goal of Theravadins – that nibbanic Buddhism has given way to kammatic Buddhism, and that 'there has been an important shift ... from salvation through knowledge to salvation through works' – is not something that Smart's readers would become aware of much, if indeed at all (Melford E. Spiro, *Buddhism and Society*, 1970, p. 93. See also, for example, Winston L. King, *In the Hope of Nibbana*, 1964). Even in his major surveys of religions the topic is neglected – no mention at all in *The World's Religions* (2nd edition, 1998), and one perfunctory reference in *Dimensions of the Sacred* (1996, pp. 86–87). Spiro's book does get one mention in the latter, but only to the effect that 'it has usually been the case in Asia that Buddhism has had an interface with peasant cults of a miscellany of gods and spirits, and has sometimes incorporated elements of Brahmanism in court ceremonial and the like' (p. 196): 'has had an interface with' is, to say the least, an understatement.

In 'Action and Suffering in the Theravadin Tradition' (1984 [C], repr. Smart, 1997 [A]) we read that 'while it is important to look to intellectual analysis ... that should in turn be seen as embedded in the practical life' (p. 371), yet despite their promise these remarks do not lead, as might be thought, in the direction identified above. The emphasis, rather, is on the distinction between action and intention, with no mention of merit-making as integral to the practical life. At one point, admittedly, the question is asked 'how it comes about that the cosmos responds to merit', with the answer that 'like attracts like', and merit 'attracts a reward somewhere and somewhen', so that in effect 'there is a solidarity between compassion and ultimate self-interest', and, for example, 'a person who has attained some of the higher stages of *jhana* is apt to be reborn in a higher realm within the cosmos' (p. 375). This, though, is (as Smart in effect says) more the description of an assumption than the offering of an explanation; and its implied description of 'the practical life' is at best somewhat tenuously connected with that described by such as Spiro.

Given his general emphasis on nibbanic as opposed to kammatic Buddhism, along with his philosophical bent for conceptual analysis, it was virtually inevitable that Smart should seek to elucidate the ever-elusive notion of nirvana. In 'Buddhism and the Death of God' (Chapter 14) he referred to 'one of the intellectually most intractable features of Buddhist eschatology – the thesis that we cannot talk of individual existence after death in nirvana'. The Buddha is famously – or notoriously – credited with the view that 'it is neither correct to say that the saint survives after death nor that he does not nor that he both does and doesn't nor that he neither does nor doesn't' (p. 153). These are the so-called 'undetermined questions'. Then there is the distinction between nirvana/nibbana and parinibbana, nirvana 'with substrate', and nirvana 'without substrate'. A hornet's nest of issues is raised.

A somewhat sceptical view might be that nibbana 'originally' meant a state of equanimity or detachment achieved, for the most part, through practice of the contemplative path, and that when the Buddha died, his followers, loath to lose him completely, postulated a condition for him which could not properly be accommodated in their (his) metaphysics. The undetermined questions could then be seen as constituting the theoretically necessary stonewalling that Buddhists' ultimately incoherent theory requires by way of respectable camouflage.

Smart, by contrast, offers, as one would expect, empathetic non-sceptical analyses. In 'Living Liberation, *Jīvanmukti and Nirvāṇa*' (1973 [B], repr. Smart, 1986 [A]) he seeks to illumine the nexus of issues through an exploration of the two aspects of liberation of his title in early Buddhism, seeking to redress an alleged imbalance created by treatment of nirvana without due consideration of 'living liberation', and the discussion is certainly substantial. Still, difficulties remain, and as he admits in 'Nirvana and Timelessness' (1976 [C], repr. Smart, 1986 [A]), there is the very real risk of explaining *obscurum per obscurius* when it is claimed that 'mysteriously nirvana can be both timeless and given a date', and is that prima facie self-contradictory thing, a 'timeless Event' (p. 320), or indeed 'the permanent event' (p. 322).

Returning to the subject several years later, in '*Theravāda* and Processes: *Nirvāṇa* as a Meta-process' (Volume 2, Chapter 2), Smart is still forced to rely on paradox: 'in such a way one might begin to think of a timeless process' (p. 18). Nirvana, it seems, remains ineluctably mysterious (or, could it be, incoherent?).

The challenge posed by the Theravada, at least in its normative nibbanic mode, to traditional definitions of religion is a recurring theme in Smart's writing. As noted above in Section 1.IV, it is implicit in his early paper comparing similarities and differences between Buddhism and secular humanism, and explicit in the much later 'Theravada Buddhism and the Definition of Religion' (1995) [C].

In 'The Dramatic Effect of the Buddha on Western Theories of Religion' (Volume 2, Chapter 3), Smart argues, amongst other things, against John Hick's view of all (major) religions pointing to a single Reality, on the ground that Buddhist nirvana is 'not a being or Being itself'. A very early version of this argument occurred, we saw, in 'Empiricism and Religions' (see Section 1.II). Smart proposes instead a form of 'complementarism', 'in which the differing religions may share an undefined transcendental level and in which they present complementary foci' (p. 30). The issues raised by these remarks will receive closer consideration in Section 2.IV.

(ii) Hinduism

There are those who argue that 'Hinduism' is a label which distorts by implying a degree of cohesion that is in fact notable by its absence. Smart, on the other hand, while more than commonly aware of the diversities encompassed by the term, preferred to retain it, arguing that it made good sense of dominant trends, certainly in modern times, not least under the continuing influence of the integrative vision of Vivekananda.

Smart wrote extensively about many of the more rarified aspects of Hindu thought in *Doctrine and Argument in Indian Philosophy* (1964, 1992) – a story he enjoyed telling was of Gilbert Ryle asking him why he was wasting his time on all that stuff, to which he replied: Why, you've been reading a lot lately, Gilbert! He contributed the sections on 'The Making of Early Hinduism' and 'Classical Hindu Philosophy and Theology' to the Open University's *Hindu Patterns of Liberation* course (1978) [B], as well as a number of related entries to the *Encyclopedia of Philosophy* (1967) [B], and an astonishing range of entries to S.G.F. Brandon's *Dictionary of Comparative Religion* (1970) [B]. Arguably his treatment of Hinduism was often quite selective, with its emphasis on the intellectual rather than the popular, yet his awareness of the dynamisms of the local and less intellectual does also shine through as and when appropriate.

'Indian Arguments About the Existence of God' (Volume 2, Chapter 4) appeared in the same year as *Doctrine and Argument in Indian Philosophy*, and clearly draws on the same research – Smart acknowledged his debt to the magisterial five volumes of Surendranath Dasgupta, *A History of Indian Philosophy* (1922 onwards). Both in this paper and also in his book Smart experimented with asterisks as an indication of where English translations of Sanskrit terms might be misleading; yet the gain in awareness of possible imprecision could be held to be outweighed by the extra demands on the reader of an additionally cluttered text. The experiment was not repeated. The paper's conclusion, though, is as apt an indicator of Smart's own position as it is a comment on Indian philosophy: 'it became fairly clear that arguments for God's existence could at best be a subsidiary means of persuasion, as Madhva held. Of greater importance has been the appeal to, and interpretation of, religious experience' (p. 40).

That Indian philosophy is typically embedded in some way in religion is the theme of 'The Analogy of Meaning and the Tasks of Comparative Philosophy' (Volume 2, Chapter 5), a nicely analytical survey leading into the notion of worldview analysis or even 'cross-cultural world-view construction' (p. 49) undertaken by members of 'the new para-tribe, Humanity' (p. 50). This is a task which, while resting on a solid basis of comparative philosophy (and religion) of a descriptive and analytical nature, moves beyond this. The extent to which Smart himself ventured in this direction is something to be considered later (see especially Sections 2.IV and 2.V).

Meanwhile, though, initial steps in that direction crop up in various contexts. Thus in 'Reflections on the Sources of Knowledge in the Indian Tradition' (1989 [B], repr. Smart, 1997 [A]), for example, we find the notion of 'soft non-relativism' (already encountered briefly above, at the end of Section 6) – a twin, in a sense, of the notion of a 'soft natural theology' (encountered above, at the end of Section 2), and to both of which we shall return. Otherwise we find here the familiar theme, say, of the duality of yoga and bhakti – with an intriguing aside, in respect of Otto on the numinous and Katz on the mystical, that 'the Jain query as to whether experience of God is brought about by the belief or the belief by the experience is pertinent here' (p. 122). It is indeed – but not just here! The 'Jain query' is fundamental to Smart's whole project, as noted in Sections 1.II and 1.III; yet his objections to the more sceptical of these two alternatives are as perfunctory as those he directed towards criticisms of his views on mysticism.

Not all of Smart's writing on Hinduism operated at an advanced analytical level, of course. 'The Meaning of Hinduism' (1972) [C] is a good example of clear descriptive compression, as is the rather more nuanced 'An Analysis of Hinduism in the Modern World' (1986 [B], repr. Smart, 1997 [A]) – the first paragraph of the 'Ingredients of the Hindu Tradition' section of the latter constitutes in its own right a rich condensed curriculum on which students new to the subject could profitably cut their teeth!

Two leading Hindu thinkers much referred to by Smart are Sankara and Vivekananda, and from time to time he wrote about them individually. There are related articles of his in reference works – mention has already been made of those in the *Encyclopedia of Philosophy* (1967) [B], and of S.G.F. Brandon's *Dictionary of Comparative Religion* (1970) [B] – and he also co-authored (with Swami Purnanda) a rather different individual study, *Prophet of a New Hindu Age: The Life and Times of Acharya Pranavananda* (1985). Yet he also contributed to volumes celebrating particular thinkers, and often aimed in the first instance at a predominantly Indian audience.

A relatively early, though sadly brief, piece in this category is 'Sankara and the West' (1969/1970) [B]. Smart's conclusion, that Sankara 'will remain a central human exponent of religious ideas and will thus play a vital role in the dialogue of religions and ideologies', is not a mere rhetorical flourish, as the recurrent references to Sankara throughout Smart's work over many years adequately testify. Rudolf Otto, be it noted, had also written about Sankara in his *Mysticism East and West* (1937), a comparative study of Sankara and Eckhart which Smart much admired (a 'fine comparison', *Reasons and Faiths*, p. 145), though he had serious reservations about its understanding of nirvana (for example 'Numen, Nirvana and the Definition of Religion', 1959 [C], pp. 219–221). Otto's work here, as in *The Idea of the Holy*, was undoubtedly influential on Smart, who nevertheless went on to study Sankara independently, and was clearly intrigued, amongst other things, by his doctrine of differing levels of truth, 'a principle which can naturally be applied to the problem of seeing differing religious formulations as lying on a continuum from popular cults, through theism, to the absolutism expressed in Sankara's idealism' ('Sankara and the West', unpaginated). It was not a principle that Smart went on to share, but his frequent references to it indicate that he saw it as a serious alternative.

The ecumenism found here in Sankara was developed to embrace all religions by Vivekananda in what Smart saw as a new Hindu synthesis, and one brilliantly tailored to respond to the challenges presented by British rule and so on (see Section 2.II). A more rounded consideration of this thinker is to be found in 'Swami Vivekananda as a Philosopher' (Volume 2, Chapter 6), where Smart also notes certain similarities with both Aurobindo and Teilhard de Chardin. The latter's ideas had, notoriously, been savaged by

Peter Medawar in his review of *The Phenomenon of Man* (1959) in *Mind* (1961) (as Smart was fully aware, see 'What is Wrong with Teilhard de Chardin?', 1964 [C]), but continued to be taken very seriously by Smart in certain respects (for example *Christian Systematic Theology in a World Context*, 1991, p. 143, 'We are not uninfluenced by the image depicted by Teilhard de Chardin. His concept of the noosphere daily becomes more relevant, as the various parts of the world are in virtually instant communication').

Vivekananda's philosophical views were linked, as typically in Indian philosophy, with religion – Smart never tires of making the point – but also helped to shape Indian nationalism. This nationalism, taking now the irredentist form of 'Hindu fundamentalism', has become a feature of Indian politics in recent times, and Indian politics, perhaps not unnaturally, given his emerging advocacy of worldview analysis, was a topic to which Smart turned his attention (see, for example, *Ethical and Political Dilemmas of Modern India*, 1993). From roughly the same time we have 'Swami Vivekananda: Where Are You When We Need You?' (1994) [B], outlining Vivekananda's influence on Indian nationalism, while at the same time urging, in the spirit of Vivekananda, opposition to the 'disgraceful groupism' that is on the upsurge in the world today (p. 556). 'What we need', Smart concludes, 'is a recognition of a transcendental humanism, and a deep recognition that every one of us has as his or her community of ultimate concern the human race (and no doubt beyond that the animal kingdom)' (p. 557). These too are notions that will be developed in later work (see Section 2.V).

Finally there is the figure of Sri Aurobindo, who left behind his earlier strong political nationalism to develop a partly original spiritual vision – a Hindu worldview for the world. In 'Integral Knowledge and the Four Theories of Existence' (Volume 2, Chapter 7) Smart offers a critical appreciation of Aurobindo's major work, *The Life Divine*, while in 'Sri Aurobindo and History' (1961) [C] he develops the kind of comparison between Aurobindo and Teilhard de Chardin referred to a moment ago.

(iii) Chinese Religions/Worldviews

Despite his early encounter with Chinese studies, Smart seems never to have been attracted to Chinese religious traditions in the way that he clearly was to Buddhist and South Asian traditions. He did incorporate the Confucian notion of *li* into his thinking (see for example *Christian Systematic Theology in a World Context*, pp. 375–376), and he wrote about the Chinese traditions in his books on world religions, but there are few papers on the subject, and they are more about the transition to Maoism than studies of the religions/philosophies in their own right (with the exception, perhaps, of 'The Ethics of Chinese Communism', Volume 1, Chapter 25). They belong, therefore, to subsequent sections on worldview analysis or religions in the modern world as much as here. Still, with this caveat, there is some point in considering them together.

'Reflections on Chinese Religious and Other Worldviews in Regard to Modernization' (Volume 2, Chapter 8) maps the challenges China faced ideologically, identifies the in many ways limited potential of the traditional religions to respond to these (in contrast, as he argues elsewhere, to the potential available in Hinduism for the challenges facing India), and indicates some of the ways in which Maoism remedied their deficiencies.

Smart's consideration of Maoism was by this time at least two decades old – his little book, *Mao*, dates from 1974, and from the same period come 'Maoism and Religion' (Volume 2, Chapter 9), and 'The Bounds of Religion and the Transition from the Tao to Mao' (Volume 2, Chapter 10). Both contain the kind of analysis noted above in connection with China and modernization (as does 'Discontinuities and Continuities Between Mao Zedong Thought and the Traditional Religions of China', 1990 [C], repr. Smart, 1997 [A]), though with somewhat more detail – the second of the two includes, for example, the Taipings, and introduces the idea of Maoism as 'an ideology *or* religion' (p. 93, italics added). This is something addressed in greater detail in the first of the two ('Maoism and Religion'), and links with 'worldview analysis', as later advocated by Smart (see Section 2.II).

The issue of what counts as a religion is one that crops up regularly, as noted already (Section 2.I(i), above, see also Section 1.IV), and Smart's sometimes somewhat equivocal views are open to challenge (but then, on this topic in particular, so are everyone's). In 'Maoism and Religion' he suggests that there are roughly three main approaches to defining religion. 'One is by content, another by formal characteristics or as I call them dimensions, and the third is by existential significance' (Volume 2, Chapter 9, p. 83). The first is vulnerable to having to accommodate the typologically rather deviant views of Theravada Buddhism, and the third ends up succumbing to the charge of vagueness – yes, religions address, for example, the fact and meaning of death, but 'the direction of concern is not necessarily or at all the focus of definition' (p. 84). We are left, therefore, with the second, dimensional approach.

This move enables Smart to argue that what Mao in fact offered China was a religion; for the phenomenon of Maoism yields to the same kind of dimensional analysis as religion. Yet against this, clearly it is arguable that it involves a blurring of the vital distinction between a religion and a non-religious ideology, philosophy, or worldview.

One notable way of resisting such equivocation is to hold that religion involves some kind of transcendent referent, and that it is precisely this that non-religious outlooks are particularly keen to deny. Elsewhere, in fact, Smart does refer quite frequently to belief in 'a transcendent being or state' as the hallmark of the religious – in other words, this aspect of the content of religions marks them off as distinct (the first of the three possible approaches canvassed a moment ago). Indeed at times, for example, he can state forcefully 'I regard attempts to have religion without the transcendent as doomed' ('Measuring the Ideal: Christian Faith and the World's Worldviews', 1997 [B], p. 42; and see also, from over thirty years earlier, 'I shall argue that it is misleading to count Marxism as a religion; and atheistic humanism likewise. The typical religious belief involves the conception either of a being or of a state of existence which lies beyond the universe as we ordinarily perceive it', 'The Nature of Religion', 1964 [E1], p. 835). Now, though – prompted perhaps in part by the thought that in fact 'our problems break out again in trying to define the key term "transcendent"' (*The World's Religions*, 1998, p. 12) – in response to this anticipated criticism, Smart comments: 'But I think here what we need to say is only this: that

Maoism's vision of the world differs from that of the religious, including Christianity, but it still functions greatly as a religion. And we should not lose sight of what might be called the "spiritual" aspect of Mao's thought' (Volume 2, Chapter 9, p. 86) – by which Smart seems to have meant the importance of socialization in the 'right' attitudes and values (see also Section 1.VI).

Yet 'functioning as' a religion is not the same as 'being' a religion; and even a justified claim to the former does not license a valid claim to the latter. Smart's concluding summary, that 'it is by no means foolish to see Maoism *in the company of* the religions' (p. 97, italics added), can indeed be read as implying the weaker rather than the stronger of these two divergent claims.

(iv) Christianity

Although the majority of Smart's papers on Christianity belong in Sections 2.III and 2.IV, two early papers, written largely for teachers, do typify the neutral descriptive-analytical perspective used in his general approach to other religions. In 'The Uniqueness of Christianity' (1974) [C] his account begins with the familiar devotion-contemplation polarity, while incorporating throughout comparisons with several other religions. It is all done very briefly, but with exemplary clarity, and reflects a great deal in a short compass of his wider work in the comparative study of religions.

The mythological dimension of religion is one to which Smart repeatedly draws attention, yet it is also one that can be difficult to enter empathetically – hence, indeed, the famous project of 'demythologization' associated with Rudolf Bultmann (*Jesus Christ and Mythology*, 1960), and the related impetus generated by *The Myth of God Incarnate* (John Hick, ed., 1977). Smart himself states the difficulty rather forcefully at one point in connection with the latter. Having noted that, despite its title, the book lacks a proper account of the concept of myth, Smart goes on, with reference to Hick's own contribution (the details of Hick's position to which Smart is objecting need not concern us here): 'His picture is psychologically untenable … because he states a splitting paradox: that we can worship God with one side of our brain using mythological and liturgical language, while not worrying about what the other side of our brain tells us, that from the analytical and intellectual perspective the language is literally false.' 'If the language is analogical', he continues, 'its literal falsity would not matter: but Hick seems to think that we can in an emotional stance take what we know not to be the case to be true' (*Christian Systematic Theology in a World Context*, p. 182).

The difficulty identified here is generalizable to many aspects of the mythological dimension, and it may not be altogether fanciful to detect an element of unease in this connection when the earlier dimensional label 'mythological' later becomes the 'mythological-narrative' – the criteria by which a narrative counts as myth are not altogether clear. Indeed, already in *Secular Education and the Logic of Religion* (1968) we read that 'such stories of the gods, of God, of God's activities in history, of the career of the sacred teacher – these can, *by a generous extension of the term*, be called myths' (p. 16, italics added). Still, in 'How to Understand Myth: A Christian Case' (1974) [C], and elsewhere, Smart advances the very different case (compared with his criticism of Hick) that 'in trying to understand myth we should forget the credibility or otherwise of the material under consideration'. Rather, indeed, 'we need to work at myth in its original luxuriance: we must wander in the bush, not seek to alter it to our wishes'. The way to do this is 'to explore as far as possible the principles which lie within the mythic mode' (p. 144). These include 'the principle of numinous polarization', according to which 'the Holy is experienced as other'; and, since 'like inheres in like … because if A inheres in B, B becomes like A; or because if A is like B, it inheres in B', 'the principles of inherent power and of similarity' (pp. 141–142).

These principles are applied to a passage from Irenaeus which builds on a certain parallelism or possible analogies between the Cross and the tree in the Garden of Eden, and between Eve and the Virgin Mary. Not everyone would necessarily find their application convincing. Still, the overall approach is instructive.

Very different in approach is 'Myth and Transcendence' (Volume 2, Chapter 11). Taking as its starting-point Bultmann's project of demythologizing the message of the New Testament, Smart proposes, as an alternative to Bultmann's strategy of relying on a particular philosophical system (in his case that of Heidegger), seeking 'to analyse transcendence in such a way that demythologizing is possible without prior commitment to a metaphysical system'. For 'religious concepts do not have their principal roots in philosophizing, so that an analysis of transcendence should not depend on some particular philosophical viewpoint' (p. 98).

Making it clear that his analysis is of the concept of transcendence in theism in general, and Christianity in particular (and thus not, for example, of nirvana), Smart articulates a set of distinctions in a subtle and cumulatively persuasive way. It is a classic example of Smart's skill in conceptual analysis applied successfully to a key religious doctrine.

(v) Islam

The relative absence of individual studies of Islam was noted earlier. A separate lecture on Islam, 'Islamic Responses to the West'(Volume 2, Chapter 12) does feature, though, in a typescript of lectures on the response of world religions to modernity located in the Ninian Smart Archive (see Volume 2, Appendix 2), and it is included here, although it could equally well feature in Section 2.II. Smart applies, in respect of the range of options available to Islam as possible responses to modernity, the 'position theory' he works out elsewhere in respect of Hinduism and Buddhism (see 'A Theory of Religious and Ideological Change' (1984) [C]. A second unpublished typescript, 'Salman Rushdie in a Plural World' (Volume 2, Chapter 13), is also included. Here Smart argues that the 'supposed crime' of blasphemy should not be recognized, for 'it is too easy for groups to inflate their sense of outrage' (p. 122). Yet a deeper issue, in a sense, is the issue of certainty (and doubt) in matters religious – an issue around which Smart develops crucial theses, as will be seen in Section 2.V.

(vi) Shamanism

The dual dynamic of the numinous and the mystical runs, as has been emphasized, like a brightly embroidered thread through Smart's work, with other types of experience such as conversion experiences basically incorporated into this pattern. A partial exception, though, is provided by shamanic experience (see Section 1.II, above). It is interesting to speculate whether Smart's overall analytical framework would have been significantly affected had he come across this during his original postgraduate research. Be that as it may, it does feature in later work, in a way that is exemplified in 'The Twenty-first Century and Small Peoples' (Volume 2, Chapter 14).

Partly Smart is concerned here with the fate of small-scale indigenous societies and their 'spiritist' religious beliefs and practices, advocating that where possible they might seek strength through forming loose alliances to promote their values and help them to resist gradual absorption or elimination by 'the great traditions' (p. 128). He notes too the presence of shamanistic elements in some of the major traditions, for example in Tibetan Buddhism, or in the Hebrew Bible among the Prophets. Indeed, he suggests, shamanism 'is ancient and preceded the foundation of cities and the creation of the major religions'. Pursuing this line of thought, he continues: 'The question which I am inclined to ask is whether shamanism is as it were the ancestor of two notable (and sometimes contrasting) kinds of religious experience, those of the numinous and the mystical or contemplative kinds' (p. 132). He argues, here as elsewhere (for example *Worldviews*, 1983, pp. 68–69), that it is plausible to think that it was.

The suggestion is intriguing. Still, it could be argued that even so the shamanic still stands out as identifiably different from the numinous and the mystical, so that Smart's longstanding dual schema stands in need of significant modification. There is, admittedly, belated recognition of shamanic experience, but its allocated role as in effect an adjunct of the prime dual schema could be argued to be doing it less than full justice.

(vii) New Religious Movements

Counting New Religious Movements (NRMs) as an 'individual tradition' is to cheat, rather. Moreover, NRMs are not something that Smart wrote much about. Yet one paper is of sufficient interest to warrant inclusion. 'Distinctively Californian Spiritual Movements' (Volume 2, Chapter 15) arose out of a project at the University of California, Santa Barbara that in due course issued in a series of books on the Religious Contours of California. It provides a fascinating insight into the plethora of different forms of spirituality, often of Eastern origin or influence, that characterize that most mixed and pluralist of societies.

2.II Worldview Analysis: Religions in the Modern World

Attempts to describe and analyse the place of religions in the modern world from a global perspective became an increasingly frequent part of Smart's publications from the 1980s onwards. 'Religions in the Contemporary World' (1992) [B], for example, is something of a descriptive tour de force in this respect. At the same time, the interplay between religions and non-religious ideologies, especially between religions and political outlooks centred on Marxism and nationalism, came to be an important focus of Smart's attention. This links with, indeed fuses into, his advocacy of expanding the study of religions into worldview analysis.

A criticism of one way of making the case for worldview analysis was voiced above in Section 2.I(iii) – it seems odd to count anti-religious Maoism as a religion (and hence a proper component of an expanded religious studies). At times, though, Smart adopts from Tillich the term 'quasi-religions', which is perhaps preferable in that it does not collapse the ordinary language distinction between what counts as religious and what counts as secular, while on the other hand analogies between typical religions and non-religious movements can be highlighted and teased out. Moreover, the way in which, in the modern world, there has been significant blending between religions and such ideologies (as, for example, in Christian liberation theology, or Sri Lankan Buddhist nationalism) does give some purchase to the broader notion of worldview analysis. It was, in any event, a notion that Smart keenly espoused (on the grounds, mainly, of analogies and blendings).

The analogy between religion and nationalism is one that Smart came particularly to favour – nationalism is, he says at one point, 'the most powerful new religion' ('Nationalism, Identity, and a More Secure World Order', 1979 [C], p. 11). An instructive early exploration of the theme is 'Religion, Myth, and Nationalism' (1980 [C], repr. Merkl and Smart, 1983 [A] and Smart, 1986 [A]), where he deploys the concept of a 'performative act' (note the continued influence of his postgraduate research supervisor, J.L. Austin, whose *How to Do Things With Words*, 1962, introduced the concept) as a more general category than ritual, of 'charged story' as a more general category than myth, and of 'a certain sort of charge' as a more general category than 'sacred'. The application to nationalism of the dimensional analysis worked out in connection with religion becomes indeed a recurrent theme, and a particularly clear statement of the theme is to be found in 'Religion and Polity' (Volume 2, Chapter 16), in which he sketches 'some patterns of relationship between traditional religions and nationalisms' (p. 156). This leads in due course to proposals for a 'dynamic worldview analysis'.

Yet as well as, indeed more than, rather theoretical analysis of this kind, Smart develops a kind of applied practical analysis with reference to the various ways in which religious and non-religious worldviews interact and blend in different circumstances in different parts of the world in modern times. 'In modern times' entails, of course, consideration of colonialism and the various burgeoning imperialisms – Smart refers at times to Immanuel Wallerstein and his world-systems theory (I. Wallerstein, *The Modern World-System*, 1974, 1980), with which he seems broadly to have sympathized – but it is the general historical background rather than anything like 'theories of imperialism' which actually features in his analyses. For, as he puts it in *The World's Religions*, 'nothing ultimately has matched the effects of European conquest, for it introduced a whole variety of challenges across the world and spread ideas as heady as democracy, liberation, modernity, and the need for higher education in the Western mode' (p. 28).

This can be seen in what is, for this section, a relatively early paper, 'Religions and Changing Values' (1979) [B]. Despite its title, according to which it belongs in Section 1.VI, it offers a good introduction to the kind of survey of religions and regions which forms much of Smart's work in this particular field, moving from Hinduism and Buddhism to Maoism and Japanese developments, then Islam, tribal societies, new religious movements, and aspects of Christianity. At the end he suggests in passing that the pluralism he has surveyed may give rise to a 'meta-value' of peaceful coexistence (p. 28), a higher-order principle of toleration. This notion comes to receive a good deal of attention elsewhere, as we shall see in Section 2.V.

Unsurprisingly, despite his ability to negotiate a path through virtually any religion or region, it was above all the modern fate of Hinduism and Buddhism that absorbed Smart's attention most, and he published a number of papers on this, some already available quite readily elsewhere, for example 'The Dynamics of Religious and Political Change: Illustrations from South Asia' (1984 [C], repr. Smart, 1987 [A]) and 'Asian Cultures and the Impact of the West: India and China' (1982 [B], repr. Smart, 1997 [A]).

In 'Religion and Nationalism in India and Sri Lanka' (Volume 2, Chapter 17) Smart introduces an interesting analysis of a religious tradition as falling into four phases: a primordial, an early, a classical, and a modern (in *The World's Religions*, 1989, the four are reduced to three: roots, formation, and reformation, see pp. 26–28). Both here and in the rather similar 'A Theory of Religious and Ideological Change: Illustrated from Modern South Asian and Other Religious Nationalisms' (1984) [C] the focus is more on Hinduism than Buddhism: the case of modern Hinduism is one that Smart returns to often, and the imbalance in treatment is due, no doubt, to the fact that there is no real Buddhist counterpart to the neo-Hindu synthesis worked out by Vivekananda – one of the points made in the complementary 'Buddhism, Sri Lanka, and the Prospects for Peace' (Volume 2, Chapter 18).

'Old Religions and New Religions: The Lessons of the Colonial Era' (1991) [B] examines 'the experience of China, Japan, India, and Islam during the period of the formation and elaboration of the modern world order' (p. 67). The discussion of China takes us back to Maoism in due course, but against the background of a developed historical perspective. With regard to Islam, Smart urges the need of a Sufi revival, but although Sufism is described as one of Islam's 'most creative' aspects (p. 75), the question of what counts as Sufism is not raised – is Smart referring to mysticism again, for example, or to the popular veneration of 'saints'? From a Muslim perspective (and not only a Muslim one) the issue is crucial, since 'Sufism' covers a whole spectrum of phenomena, including mystics, established fraternities or orders, and often local shrine cults, the creativity of at least some of which would be open to question. Smart's relative lack of enthusiasm for Islam, though, is fairly apparent. 'Of all the cultures we have looked at briefly, Islamic culture remains the most unproductive, on average', due in part to 'a failure of the intellectuals of Islam' (p. 75).

One of the highly significant consequences of colonialism (and neo-colonialism) has been fresh patterns of the international movement of labour; and one of the consequences of this, in turn, has been the transplanting of religious groupings (or 'faith communities' as they are tendentiously referred to in Britain) from their traditional sites into new and often alien contexts. Numerous studies of aspects of this phenomenon have appeared – it is very convenient (though also very worthwhile) to be able to conduct one's anthropological fieldwork from home – but in 'The Importance of Diasporas' (Volume 2, Chapter 19) Smart surveys more generally some of the kinds of changes that have occurred and may be expected to occur. He cites, for example, a new 'consciousness of belonging to a world community' (p. 184) among Hindus, and the 'tendency toward the consolidation of world religions, however dispersed. Thus we have the formation of such institutions as the World Fellowship of Buddhists' (p. 185). Other trends instanced are a blurring between traditionally missionary and non-missionary groups, and the encouragement of 'a pluralistic *modus vivendi*' among diasporas which may in due course have lessons for the mainstream religions as they come to terms with the fact that globally they are all minorities: 'It is an attitude of "Islam within the wider framework of sincere religion". That already is a modification of traditional Islam which, where it is dominant in a society, leaves only a limited place for alternative religions' (p. 188).

A certain amount of this is admittedly speculative, and speculation features prominently in several papers regarding the future of religion or religions. Inevitably in some ways parts of these are already dated, not least in respect of developments in the former Soviet Union, and the waning appeal of Marxism. Even so, a certain fallibility is often offset by considerable perspicacity – a comment applicable too, perhaps, to Smart's Gifford Lectures, *Beyond Ideology: Religion and the Future of Western Civilization* (1981), which provide a wide-ranging background to the present section.

2.III Christian Theology of Religions and Interfaith Dialogue

Smart's Christian commitment never wavered, finding some expression in earlier books like *The Teacher and Christian Belief* (1966) and *Philosophers and Religious Truth* (1964), and coming to full expression in *Christian Systematic Theology in a World Context* (1991). A few published papers, like 'Towards a Systematic Future for Theology' (1966) [B], focus on Christian concerns without invoking dialogue with other religions, but more typically the importance to Christians of thinking theologically in a comparative religion context is emphasized, as in the very early 'Revelation and Reasons' (1958) [C], and it is around this theme that the present section is built.

'Revelation and Reasons' is a response to a paper by Austin Farrer, and as its date suggests, it draws very much on the thinking that went into *Reasons and Faiths*, as does the important 'Revelation, Reason and Religions' (Volume 2, Chapter 20), which appeared in *Prospect for Metaphysics* (Ian T. Ramsey, ed., 1961), a collection much discussed at the time. This paper, indeed, is in many ways a summary of the key themes of *Reasons and Faiths* as outlined in Section 1.II above. Thus Smart expounds his theory of religious reasons for holding doctrines: 'For I believe on the one hand, with the revelationists, that one cannot excogitate religious truth: one has to judge what is given, in the form of revelations and teachings – since ordinary philosophers and theologians are neither prophets nor Buddhas.

But I believe on the other hand, with the rationalistically inclined, that one can still detect considerations favouring one position rather than another' (p. 193). These considerations are then developed in respect of the two basic strands of religious experience, the numinous and the mystical (the sceptic's questioning of the validity of either being dealt with, as is typical with Smart, quite summarily – religion's 'truth-suggesting fascination in daily life and the testimony of many profound and holy men is [sic] not lightly to be disregarded', p. 193). The upshot is an endorsement of monotheism as against polytheism, pantheism and monism: 'since' (as he puts it elsewhere) 'from the point of view of experience there is no special reason to cast doubt on either form of religious perception as worthless, it would seem reasonable to hold that a doctrine which made sense of both forms was to be accepted. Theism – though not extreme forms which are hostile to mysticism – can do this' ('Christianity amid the Great Religions', 1965 [C], p. 14).

Smart then argues further in support of the specifically Christian doctrine of the incarnation as a solution to the problem of the need, arising from the numinous strand, for a satisfactory expiation of human sinfulness vis-à-vis the holy. (See also Otto, *The Idea of the Holy*, chapter 6.) That there is such a problem would not, of course, be accepted by all believers in the holy – Muslims, for example. Its importance, indeed its existence, cannot therefore be regarded as particularly plausibly established on the basis of numinous experience. Yet Smart takes it as axiomatic in a way that his theory of religious reasons itself calls in question; for it is said, as noted, to arise out of the numinous strand – yet of this Islam is a prime exemplar.

The argument in support of the need for a historical divine incarnation such as is found (uniquely) in Christianity is reproduced from *Reasons and Faiths* (chapter 4), and here we return to the issue of the conveniently Christian character of that analysis. Still, there is no reason in principle why a neutral philosophical analysis should not be consonant with Christianity in particular. One cannot equate fortuitous agreement with bias. The point here is not that, but the questionable nature of the grounds of the alleged agreement.

Irrespective of the question of whether or not the original allegedly neutral analysis sprang unconsciously from prior Christian commitments, it is deployed here in a consciously Christian way, as part of a new 'soft' natural theology. 'Natural theology is the Sick Man of Europe', the paper begins (p. 193); 'I do not profess to have cured him. But at least I have tried to give advice on how to live with one's coronary', it concludes (p. 205). The old-style natural theology of 'proofs' does not work; fideistic appeals to revelation are 'utterly self-defeating'; so 'our only choice is to work with the notion of religious reasons of the kind which I have sketched' (p. 205). Thus Smart the philosopher dons the theologian's hat. And why not? 'The purism of thinking that philosophical analysis is the only proper employment for philosophers is excessive. Intellectual compartmentalization, though often good at the start, may be sterile at the finish' (p. 194).

'The Relation Between Christianity and the Other Great Religions' (Volume 2, Chapter 21) appeared just a year later in yet another collection that was much discussed at the time, especially in church circles, namely *Soundings: Essays Concerning Christian Understanding* (A.R. Vidler, ed., 1962). Smart begins by noting that popular appeals by Christians to notions of revelation, religious experiences, and history as a way of grounding their faith are invariably couched in a culturally parochial way that ignores the claims of Eastern religions. Investigation of these claims, though, leads, he urges, to an exploration of the claims and counter-claims of two main kinds of religious experience – and the second section of the paper proceeds to rehearse the analysis of religious reasons with which we are now familiar. The third and final section then discusses Christ, and the logic of incarnation and atonement, emphasizing the need for Christians to appreciate that talk about sin only makes sense against the background of belief in 'a Holy One'. 'Remove the holiness of God, and all we can speak about is moral badness, not sin in the proper sense. First God, then sin: not vice versa' (p. 221).

Both of these first two papers are in their way classics, and they undoubtedly contributed enormously to Smart's growing reputation as a Christian thinker who was both unusually well versed in Eastern religions, and also skilled in deploying a subtle and wideranging analysis with great clarity and to good theological effect.

Describing himself as a Buddhist Episcopalian, Smart's particular Christian affiliation was Anglican, and in 'The Anglican Contribution to the Dialogue of Religions' (1967) [C] he propounded ten theses in the hope 'that they represent something of the spirit and circumstances of Anglicanism as it affects me', for 'I have imbibed something, I hope, from my Church' (p. 303). Dialogue, of course, is not the same as apologetics (in the previous paper Smart describes himself as 'descending into the dusty arena of general apologetic', Volume 2, Chapter 20, p, 194), though it may function as an important prelude. For 'a trouble with apologetics is that it tends furiously to leap into the fray, without wondering what the rules of combat are', while a prime purpose of dialogue can be 'to show the kinds of considerations – the reasons – which are relevant in religious discussions' – comments taken from the Introduction of that early tour de force, *A Dialogue of Religions* (1960) (pp. 12–13). It is interesting, then, to read Smart's account of his particular indebtedness to the formative influence of his own denomination. The possibility that the account is in effect a retrospective 'superimposition' cannot, of course, be excluded.

'Theology and Other Religions' (1965) [B], like his *Soundings* paper, links comparative religion more explicitly with Christian theology than with philosophy or metaphysics. The opening claim that 'there are two distinct reasons for studying religion' (p. 253) takes us back to earlier discussions of methodology (Section 1.V), and the necessity of comparative work is then brought to bear on the theologies of Thomists, Bultmann, and Barth and Kraemer. The latter two feature again and again in Smart's work. Representing the position diametrically opposed to his own, clearly he felt the need for sustained rebuttal – he had great admiration for what he felt was in many ways their profundity, while at the same time finding himself in major disagreement with their stance of theological exclusiveness. There follows discussion of the benefits of re-evaluating one's own faith in the light of others', and of the 'more practical and mundane way' (p. 265) in which comparative study of religion can be theologically beneficial, in missiology.

In connection with missiology, of course, a major theme generally has been the issue of whether, and if so to what extent, Christians should pursue 'indigenization', in other words expressing their message both verbally and ritually in local cultural and religious terms. The Vatican, for example, moved decisively in 1975 to curb what it regarded as excesses in this direction on the part of some Catholics in India. Smart's position, argued at length in *The Yogi and the Devotee: The Interplay between the Upanishads and Catholic Theology* (1968) and elsewhere, was that 'the Christian experience as hitherto understood can be enriched by the insights of the multitudinous traditions of India' (p. 168), especially in the Hindu theology of Ramanuja, which 'may serve as a means of appropriating Christianity to the Indian tradition' (p. 129) as part of a much needed move to 'express a truly Indian Christianity' (p. 125).

Very different in tone is 'Truth and Religions' (1974 [B], repr. 1982, 1991), which revolves around the question of whether there is in fact a problem about how the truth-claims of Christianity can be reconciled with those of other religions. The paper is perhaps more philosophical than theological, though one conclusion is that problems about the criteria of religious truth are not seen in sharp focus partly because 'there is still unclarity about the threefold distinction between Christian theology, philosophy, and the scientific study of religion' (p. 58). Still, Smart declares himself sympathetic to 'lowering Christian-theological (missiological) temperatures in relation to truth-questions – being convinced on philosophical-historical grounds that theologians and missiologists miss the main truth-issues, for the reason of the neglect of criteria, and also being convinced on Christian grounds of the necessity to combat arrogance' (p. 45). The said lowering of temperatures involves some impressively concentrated analysis, including a tilt at two targets that surface with some regularity in Smart's work, namely the appeal to faith as deployed by W. Cantwell Smith, and its very different role in the Wittgensteinian-type 'conceptual fideism' urged by such as D.Z. Phillips (see for example W.C. Smith, *The Meaning and End of Religion*, 1962; D.Z. Phillips, *The Concept of Prayer*, 1965). Both feature in the related, brief but intriguing, 'Truth, Criteria and Dialogue between Religions' (1995) [B].

Smart could at times be combative about the importance of Christians taking other world religions seriously, and 'Eight Propositions against the Prevailing Narrowness in Theology' (1960) [C] is an early pithy and pungent wake-up call. Much substance is crammed into a small space, and the piece is notable too for the adoption of a rigorous neo-scholastic style of argument.

'Theology, Philosophy and the Natural Sciences' (1962) [C] was Smart's Inaugural Lecture as H. G. Wood Professor of Theology in the University of Birmingham. He declares his task to be 'philosophy of religion', taking this to embrace, as required of the first occupant of this Chair, the three enterprises listed in the lecture title. Some reference to the challenge of the natural sciences occurs regularly in Smart's work, at times with reference to substantive issues (cosmology, evolution etc.), often with reference to methodology – science is in principle incurably self-critical, he argued, hence its great capacity to progress; Christianity has likewise made great progress through the impetus derived from self-critical liberal Protestantism (Biblical scholarship, for example); and 'I believe that self-criticism is vital to social health, scientific rectitude and spiritual development' ('Measuring the Ideal: Christian Faith and the World's Worldviews', 1997 [B], p. 42). All flourish in an open society: the oft-acknowledged influence on Smart of Karl Popper (1945) was very considerable.

In 'What are the Dimensions of Belief in the Resurrection?' (1967) [C] Smart adopts his neutral dimensional analysis as a tool to be used theologically on a key aspect of his own faith. What emerges clearly is how very traditionally orthodox Smart was. This should not necessarily be at all surprising, but is likely to seem so to many in view of his endorsement of the merits of liberal Protestantism, combined with his indefatigable enthusiasm for learning from other faiths. Yet here we read, for example, that 'the Incarnation is the warrant, so to say, for the liturgical reverence for Christ, which has its logic in the recognition that the fuller Jesus is indeed the transcendent God and Creator of the world ... . In addition, binding these dimensions together even more firmly, the sacrament of the Lord's Supper is a kind of extension of the Incarnation, in which the risen Christ is present to us within the elements and in the community' (p. 118). That these views were profoundly and persistently held is unmistakably clear from their extensive elaboration in the much later *Christian Systematic Theology in a World Context* (1991). Smart indeed advocates and in part practises cross-cultural Christian theology, but the conclusions, even though clothed in different discourse, can still be very conservative (see for example 'The threefold Divine Being has three centers of consciousness, one being the *Iśvara*, another the *avatara*, and the third the *antaryamin*', 'A Speculation About the Trinity Doctrine', 1990 [B], p. 134).

'Global Christian Theology and Education' (1996) [B] explores issues dealt with extensively in Sections 2.IV and 2.V below, but this time from an explicitly Christian perspective. The question is whether there is a possible basis for a world-view for the world which members of different religions can share without feeling that their own religious commitments are being seriously compromised. To this we shall return.

The theme of learning from other faiths is central to Smart's outlook, and Hinduism and Buddhism remain the two upon which he draws most. In the Hindu tradition Smart was particularly taken with Ramanuja, and especially with his notion of the world as God's body. Smart refers to this quite often, from earlier works through to much later ones. It is explored in some detail in 'God's Body' (Volume 2, Chapter 22), while in 'The Inner Controller: Learning from Ramanuja' (1996) [B] it is also linked to the Christian doctrine of the Holy Spirit. Meanwhile 'Learning from One Another: Buddhism and Christianity' (2000) [C] reviews the kind of comparisons that led him to think of himself as a 'Buddhist Episcopalian', and which are delved into in far greater detail in *Buddhism and Christianity: Rivals and Allies* (1993), and *Lights of the World: Buddha and Christ* (1997). (See also 'Buddhism, Christianity, and the Critique of Ideology', 1984 [B].)

In the previous section we saw something of Smart's thesis of worldview analysis being applied to nationalism. Nationalism was an issue which greatly concerned him, as is apparent in a number of papers, and at greater length in *Religion and Nationalism: The Urgency of Transnational Spirituality and Toleration* (1994). In 'Christianity and Nationalism' (1984 [C], repr. Smart, 1987 [A]), as well as applying his dimensional analysis to the phenomenon, he sketches 'a possible Christian evaluation of nationalism' (p. 45). 'The nation is at best a secondary haven' and should not be allowed to be 'the group of ultimate concern'; 'combining religion and State ... is a way of doing just that: giving ultimacy to the State' (p. 50). 'The Christian's ultimate group is humanity, seen of course as possessing the imprint of the divine image', and 'religions as transnational groups, and Christianity in particular with its myth of neither-Jew-nor-Greek, etc.,' can help to dilute the divisive appeal of nationalism (p. 48).

Having begun this section with Smart's diagnosis of natural theology as the sick man of Europe, it seems appropriate to end it with his cautious judgement that since then 'there have been signs of his recovery' ('Soft Natural Theology', Volume 2, Chapter 23, p. 233). The theme of 'at least two major categories of religious experience…, one numinous and the other mystical or contemplative' recurs, as one would expect – with, now, the rider that 'actually, one can add other forms, too' (p. 236). There is also the theme of the traditional cosmological and teleological arguments 'as having an affective or experiential side' (p. 237), and not being entirely without value in a soft natural theology – a theme found already, for example in *Philosophers and Religious Truth* and *The Philosophy of Religion*. Yet a natural theology that relies exclusively on the affective or experiential side of these arguments (combined with his theory of religious reasons), at the expense of construing them as having some explanatory force over and above this experiential side, may still be thought to be too soft (see for example John J. Shepherd, *Experience, Inference and God*, 1975, based on a thesis supervised by Smart).

Towards the end of this paper he notes: 'it seems therefore to me that the directions of natural theology lie towards a world-wide discussion issuing in a soft non-relativism' (p. 240). It was very much in this direction that his later thought moved, as we see in the next section.

2.IV Plurality of Religions: Religious Interpretations

The notion of soft non-relativism has surfaced briefly before and is one of a number that recur in the material featured in this section and the next. Against any kind of relativism Smart urged that there were always reasons (perhaps mainly 'religious reasons') in support of particular positions; these could always be debated; and such debate implied the possibility in principle of one set of reasons being right, even if they continued to be debated. Yet the reasons never amounted to proofs, and so were always 'soft' rather than 'hard'.

From this, various conclusions followed. Because of their softness, reasons were persuasive rather than probative, and hence while they might legitimately be held to warrant personal, private certitude, they could not support public certainty. Since religions lacked public certainty, social policies of toleration and pluralism were required. Meanwhile, private certitude should engender personal attitudes of open-minded non-dogmatism, and a readiness to learn from others in a spirit of critical self-evaluation. Such readiness, though, was universalizable, so different religions could be encouraged to engage in mutual constructive criticism as part of an ongoing informed dialogue. Further, such readiness implied the possibility of a degree of change in, or reinterpretation of, one's own views in the light of others', breeding a measure of (thoroughly legitimate) eclecticism. To this extent different religions could be regarded as mutually complementary – and possibly even ultimately converging.

This family of ideas fed into two rather different stances. One involved the issue of how different religions might legitimately view each other. The second involved the issue of how the different religions might legitimately (from both an internal and an external perspective) be treated by their encompassing societies and world. To the first of these issues we turn in this section; to the second we turn in the next.

A recurrent theme in many of Smart's writings is a distancing of himself from the position of John Hick. The latter's Copernican revolution in theology saw the different religions as revolving around God, who subsequently became more ecumenically (or agnostically) 'the Real'. Smart rejected this as a version of the neo-Vedanta synthesis developed by Vivekananda (see Section 2.II). A major ground of disagreement was Smart's view that 'the Real', as in some sense personal, is simply incompatible with the Theravada, or with Jainism, which recognize no personal ultimate, so that the theory necessitates a distortion of the facts. (Arguably, of course, this very criticism might be directed at key aspects of his own analysis of mysticism – as in Section 1.III, above.) Yet he could still at times express a strong sympathy for Hick's position, as will be seen shortly.

In opposition to Hick's thesis of a kind of religious unity, Smart proposed a theory of complementarity and future convergence, a view set out, for example, in 'The Convergence of Religions' (Volume 2, Chapter 24). This had the advantage, he claimed, of allowing each religion to be seen for what it is (or what it sees itself as being) without being pressed into an alien mould.

The disagreement with Hick was explored in considerably greater detail in 'A Contemplation of Absolutes' (Volume 2, Chapter 25), Smart's contribution to a set of essays in honour of Hick. The argument is addressed in part to apparent drawbacks in Hick's espousal of the Kantian distinction between the noumenal (the Real) and the phenomenal (actual religious foci). For example, 'the abstractness of the idea of the noumenon means that we can infer no resemblance between what lies behind and what is phenomenal' (p. 256). Thus the Real might be neither singular nor substantial, neither being nor becoming. The concept is an empty placeholder. This, though, could have a positive function according to an alternative view. 'This is to hold that the differing traditions point at a placeholder. That is, we can talk of the ultimate as lying beyond them, but that placeholder is a space for alternatives, not the point at which differing paths meet (though it might *per accidens* be that)' (p. 260). These alternatives overlap in various ways, and may be seen as complementary. From the hoped-for ensuing dialogue, a degree of convergence may occur. Indeed, the outcome could be a degree of unity about the ultimate much as postulated by Hick's theory. So 'in the long run, perhaps, not too much difference is generated by the alternative models' (p. 261). Meanwhile, from a Christian point of view, there is the thought that the Holy Spirit might be at work in all religions, and that 'the rivalry of religions is designed by the Divine to keep them honest so far as possible' (p. 266). This is a view that Smart reiterates in a number of places, but it is a theological interpretation superimposed on an independent analysis that is not based on Christian premises and that merits assessment in its own right.

Smart's views on how religious pluralism might best be construed religiously are set out in two further papers of some significance. Yet although they appeared within a year of each other, there is no consistency of terminology, and they do not provide an immediately clear picture. Still, perhaps a relatively clear picture may emerge.

'Models for Understanding the Relations between Religions' (Volume 2, Chapter 26) begins with the neo-Advaita view of Vivekananda and others, according to which all religions are 'so many diverse paths towards the one Reality, operating at different levels of sophistication' (p. 268). This Smart rejects, as already noted, not least because of Buddhism. He then turns to exclusivism – 'we have the revelation and all others are benighted' (p. 269) – which is a theoretical possibility, but which fails properly to address the issue of criteria of truth, and their relative softness – a conclusion to which, of course, his whole work stands as eloquent testimony.

Curiously, though, Smart also characterizes exclusivism differently as 'my tradition contains more of the truth, and all others less', and he quotes J.N. Farquhar's idea (1913) of Christianity being 'the crown of Hinduism'. Yet this 'relatively kindly doctrine', as he calls it (p. 269), normally counts not as exclusivism but as the very significantly different inclusivism. The relevance of this will become apparent shortly.

Moving then past versions of relativism and Wittgensteinian fideism, both declared unsatisfactory, he outlines what he rather laboriously labels 'Dialogical Convergentism': 'all religions do not point to the same truth but might by changing come to agree on the same truth, of which the traditions become bearers of localized variations' (p. 271). This is the position he favoured in the previous two papers above, and so far, so clear.

Here, though, he embarks on a complex discussion of whether using the noumenal-phenomenal distinction makes any difference, and there follows a renewed critique of Hick, but one which locates him closer to Smart's position in some ways than to the neo-Vedanta with which Smart usually associates him. Hick now emerges as a proponent of 'Noumenal Realism', and Smart of 'Noumenal Indeterminism' (p. 273), with the comment that 'maybe the divergence is not great, but it is still there, subtly' (p. 272).

Following this, Smart advances his theses of religious complementarity and soft non-relativism, emphasizes that neither of them 'block[s] out thoroughgoing commitment to one's tradition' (p. 276), and concludes that 'there is plausibility in combining Noumenal Realism or Indeterminism with Soft Non-Relativism and the Complementarity Thesis. That at any rate is my position' (pp. 276–277). 'His' position is actually one of these two options, the one invoking Noumenal Indeterminism (Noumenal Realism being associated with Hick).

The question raised by this is how Smart's (or anyone's) profound Christian (etc.) commitment is reconcilable with noumenal indeterminism. Indeed the whole burden of his work over the years in respect of his understanding of the powerful numinous strand of religious experience was to the effect that it precipitates worship of a holy deity, rather than pointing to an indefinite something-or-other (see too *The Concept of Worship*, 1972). His theory of the numinous clashes with his theory of the noumenal. Yet still he stands by thoroughgoing commitment to one's own tradition.

A possible resolution of this paradox may be inferred from, and is perhaps encouraged by, the related paper, 'Pluralism' (Volume 2, Chapter 27). Here Smart briefly outlines five models for theorizing religious pluralism. 'The positions are (1) absolute exclusivism, (2) absolute relativism, (3) hegemonistic inclusivism, (4) realistic pluralism, and (5) regulative pluralism' (p. 280). Positions 1, 2, and 4 are each criticized (position 4 is associated with Vivekananda and Hick, who are once more conjoined), on grounds familiar from previous papers. Position 5 represents Smart's own theory of future convergence. Once again, so far, so clear.

Intriguingly, though, the one position not criticized is that of inclusivism – this time correctly distinguished from exclusivism (but still linked with the example of Farquhar, as well as, now, Vatican II and Karl Rahner). And Smart concludes that inclusivism 'will remain the principal motif among theologians in the more liberal forms of the various religious traditions' (p. 282).

To the paradox of commitment and noumenal indeterminism a possible resolution may now be suggested. Given the absence, on his part, of criticism of inclusiveness, it seems reasonable to infer that Smart found it broadly acceptable. Indeed he writes that the discernible trend towards inclusivism 'is reinforced, and in practice presupposed, by the rise of interreligious dialogue' (p. 281) – the dialogue that he consistently advocated and conducted. Perhaps, then, he may be construed as holding inclusivism as a practical normative theory, and noumenal indeterminism/regulative pluralism as a meta-theory (a distinction paralleling that between normative ethics and meta-ethics). In other words, in practical terms one can be a committed Christian (Buddhist, Hindu etc.), yet see a measure of religious truth (by one's own standards) in other faiths, while at the same time being able to stand back from this commitment and admit its fallibility in principle – in line with the Jain tenet of *syadvada*, 'May-be-ism', which he commends elsewhere: 'In other words any claim about the ultimate nature of the world has to be prefaced by the prefix "May-be"!, namely that in matters of ultimate truth the best you can do is a certain plausibility. But no proof is possible' (*Religion and Nationalism*, p. 80; see also *Choosing a Faith*, p. 12, and passim).

This interpretation seems to be coherent internally, and also to cohere with the full range of Smart's work. Thus on the one hand he insists that, from within his 'vision as a Christian', he considers it 'absurd to suppose that as Christians we cannot learn from Jews, Muslims, Buddhists, Hindus and many others. Moreover, it seems an all-too-sad fact that Christianity unchallenged slides deep into human vices: dogmatism, heresy-hunting, concubinage of clergy, money-making, power-plays, uncharitableness and so on'. Thus critical dissent is healthy, and it may come from other faiths, as they manifest 'the Holy Spirit's riches. I cannot believe that the Spirit does not move within the other faiths' (*Religion and Nationalism*, 1994, p. 92). Meanwhile, on the other hand, certainly an appeal to 'higher-order' utterances is one that he made from time to time from *Reasons and Faiths* onwards. It also features prominently in his proposals concerning how religions might legitimately view, and be viewed by, their encompassing local and global societies. To this we turn next.

2.V Plurality of Religions: Ethico-Political Implications

Smart's views on what might be dubbed a world worldview were outlined in a little cluster of papers dealing with lessons to be drawn from the jockeying for position of a number – indeed, given the explosion of new religious movements, a growing number – of divergent and in part mutually incompatible worldviews in a plural world. His aim was to explore what might be acceptable 'from the perspective of the global community' ('Pluralism, Religions, and the Virtues of Uncertainty', 1989 [B], p. 31). His conclusion was that from this perspective 'the toleration of all worldviews should so far as possible be practised' (ibid.), and that to a very large extent this view from the perspective of the global community should be acceptable from the perspective of individual religions.

'The Truth of Religions and the Coming World Order' (1990) [C] highlights one of Smart's basic premises, that worldviews are matters of faith, not knowledge. This is true even of non-religious worldviews, for of any worldview it can, indeed must, be said that 'it cannot be proved or made evident by clinching public evidence' (p. 86). From this, much follows – for example, 'what cannot be proved should not be taken as a basis for disadvantaging citizens who do not believe it' (ibid.), by nurturing, say (often through faith-based education), 'groupism', 'the unreasonable treatment of, and attitudes towards, people of other groups' (ibid.). Yet there are, Smart acknowledges, 'religious obstacles' here, for 'sometimes there are elements within a religious tradition that favour discrimination against unbelievers and outsiders' (ibid.). Still, such discrimination, being based not on knowledge but uncertainty, is 'unreasonable' and should logically yield to pluralistic toleration and minority rights. Private certitude may license commitment and legitimately motivate mission and attempted conversion, but public uncertainty proscribes political privileging of any particular group or religion.

The distinction between private certitude and public certainty is basic to Smart's 'soft non-relativism', but there are issues here which require deeper discussion, and perhaps a little more care. In the present instance, for example, the distinction is virtually synonymous with that between faith and knowledge, yet elsewhere it is drawn somewhat differently. Thus in 'On Knowing What is Uncertain' (Volume 2, Chapter 28) appeal is made to the alleged universality of numinous and mystical experiences as a ground for a community's claiming 'a sort of wisdom *and knowledge*', just 'a less ramified knowledge' than doctrinal schemes typically claim (p. 292). Still, admittedly 'what can be known is rather limited, on my argument, and is largely confined to what immediately concerns religious encounter and various [for example moral] fruits and effects' (p. 294).

There is still, then, a reluctance to sacrifice claims to knowledge of religious truth altogether, even by Smart. Others would argue robustly against the faith-knowledge dichotomy anyway; and the relation between certainty and truth-claims also requires scrutiny. (See, for example, the complex discussion by Smart's former King's College colleague, H.P. Owen, in his *The Christian Knowledge of God*, 1969.) Thus the epistemological premise on which Smart bases his argument is less secure than many would be willing to admit. Nevertheless, it is not without a good measure of prima facie plausibility, and deserves to be taken seriously.

It is explored at greater length in 'The Epistemology of Pluralism: The Basis of Liberal Philosophy' (Volume 2, Chapter 29). 'Worldviews cannot be refuted and they cannot be proved' (p. 299), and 'if no worldview is certain, it follows that it is not right to teach a worldview as if it is certain' (p. 300). Yet education should enable people to reach an informed judgement, so should incorporate 'descriptive pluralism' (ibid.) in a spirit of 'openness and criticism' (p. 301). Thus a form of liberal society seems to be called for. (Smart calls it 'Popperish', but the argument also strongly reflects parts of J.S. Mill's *On Liberty*.)

Still, accommodating diversity of religious belief is easier than accommodating diversity of religious morals. Yet ironically 'liberalism has often accompanied the homogeneous impulse' (p. 302), seeking to mould minority cultures in the direction of conformity. This, though, is unnecessary. A society such as Britain could allow Muslims, for example, (Smart here anticipating recent debates by a quarter of a century) to 'have the benefit of Islamic divorce laws or property regulations' (ibid.). This would be less than the full implementation of Shari'a, 'but the Muslim could get let us say eighty per cent of what he [*sic*] might want' (ibid.). Every community, though, would need in effect to become a voluntary community, with individuals free to leave.

Would this still not mean that one worldview, liberalism, was being imposed on all others? Yet, Smart urges, 'the only values entrenched in the State would be higher-order ones – about procedures and structures' (p. 304), with the apparent implication that there is then no unacceptable clash. This, however, is open to question, as Smart elsewhere acknowledges.

However, before turning to this it is helpful to turn to a much earlier paper on the key idea, 'Does a Universal Standard of Value Need to be Higher-Order?' (Volume 2, Chapter 30). Given the deep pluralism of our world, 'we would seem to be driven to seek a common value-agreement at a higher logical level'. In other words, 'we might agree on how we establish and recognize values, even if we may not agree about the values themselves. In other words we might agree on higher-order values without agreeing on lower-order ones. This would be akin to the situation in science: we may agree about methods of verification and falsification while disagreeing about actual theories' (p. 308).

Now given the softness of criteria of truth in religion, 'it is idle to pretend that any certain way exists to demonstrate the superiority of one over the rest' (p. 310), so logically 'the proper attitude to adopt towards belief-systems one does not believe would be one of open-mindedness' including a desire to understand alternatives (p. 311); and 'the practical outflow of openmindedness and the desire to understand' is tolerance (p. 312). Moreover, some aspects of a rival system might come to seem worthy of acceptance (for example, Christian acceptance of Buddhist serenity as a value), so eclecticism may be added as a further higher-order value. 'Tolerance, openmindedness and eclecticism – these seem to be the values to be promoted, and all compatibly with the objectivity of truth and morals' (p. 313).

'If all this follows from the nature and situation of belief-systems in a plural world, these values themselves come to be criteria of the worth and truth of the systems themselves.

So though our common values may be higher level they have lower level consequences' (ibid.).

The nature of such lower level consequences could, though, it has to be said, lead some to call in question the higher level values, if, say, they felt they were being required to betray some of their key beliefs and values (for example, regarding the social status of women, the moral status of homosexuals, or the religious status of unbelievers); and the concept of tolerance, certainly, can be elucidated in terms of different conceptions, with differing degrees of acceptability from different perspectives (see, for example, Susan Mendus, *Justifying Toleration: Conceptual and Historical Perspectives*, 1988; John Horton and Susan Mendus (eds), *Aspects of Toleration*, 1985; Susan Mendus, *Toleration and the Limits of Liberalism*, 1989). So, again, an attractive line of argument faces sterner challenges when looked at a little more closely.

A degree of closer scrutiny emerges in the final paper of this section, 'Worldview-Pluralism: An Important Paradox and Its Possible Solution' (Volume 2, Chapter 31). Here the issue of higher-level values having lower-level consequences is faced very squarely. 'Worldview-pluralism' is the doctrine of the separation of worldview from State, so that religions are bereft of political support while blessed with political freedom. Clearly this would thwart the goals of, say, political Islam. So the liberalism envisaged is Janus-faced: on the one hand 'as a higher-order position it does not properly compete among the ideologies', is not itself one of the competing worldviews; but on the other hand it has to 'descend into the dusty plain and fight it out with the camels of Islam, the horses of Christianity, the elephants of Hinduism and the rest' (p. 317). Moreover, worldview-pluralism tends to have 'a liberal extension' (p. 323) in the form of general liberal values which may conflict with aspects of religions – values such as the full social equality of men and women, for example.

In respect of the latter, Smart again urges that communities should be allowed their religious law provided they are voluntary communities, yet admits that some restrictions may be necessary. He instances the case of animal rights, but others readily come to mind, for example children's rights in the event of Christian Science parents refraining from life-saving medical treatment for their child. In such cases higher-order liberalism is insufficient on its own to justify interference in religion. It needs the additional strength drawn from its 'liberal extension'. 'Let us concede', then, Smart concludes, that liberalism 'is up to a point a rival to worldviews' (p. 324).

Still, it is 'a minimalist adversary' (p. 325), and thus 'the best sort you could have' (p. 324), for each group in society could get 'most if not all of what it wants' (p. 325) – a judgement many would regard as sanguine in the extreme. Moreover, how would the restrictions on allowing groups what they want be decided? Would they be permitted to practise capital punishment? If not, why not? Liberalism may, arguably, be receptive to the case for minority group rights, but cannot prescind from their being set certain limits; and in doing so, it is hard to see how it can fail to rely on values which form part of a substantive ethic which is at odds with aspects of many religious moralities. The plain can get very dusty indeed.

We do not need to 'homogenize moralities', Smart argues (p. 329). Yet between the extremes of homogenization and radical pluralism some kind of practical compromise is ineluctable, and some kind of moral judgement in fashioning its contours inescapable. Smart recognizes this, but there is needed a fuller exploration than he provides of the knotty issues involved. Their complexity is, as it happens, a feature of much recent work in moral and political philosophy – see for example the debates surrounding the work of Will Kymlicka (1989, 1995, 1995), and more recently Tariq Modood (2007). Indeed, sooner or later, arguably, there will need to be a full recognition of the issue of moral criteria of religious truth (consider again the case of Christian Science, for example). Their possibility, and indeed propriety, is implicit in Smart's theory of superimposition, but this is as close as he gets to addressing the issue, and its contentious heart is not adequately explored. Admittedly, 'these [higher-order] values themselves come to be criteria of the worth and truth of the systems themselves', he concludes (Volume 2, Chapter 30, p. 313). Yet the 'eirenic realism' he advocates (ibid.) requires in the end stronger moral foundations than he provides.

Finally, the proposal for introducing minority group religious law sits uneasily against the background of concerns which became vocal in Britain following the Archbishop of Canterbury's (basically Smartian) support (in 2008) for introducing aspects of Shari'a law in British society. Smart's emphasis at times on the advantages of the Indian model, which allows, say, the operation of Muslim family law, as opposed to the American model, which emphasizes integration, runs directly counter to what many uphold as socially beneficial policies in a pluralist society, or ethically defensible ones in respect of safeguarding the rights of women (see, for example, the Shah Bano controversy in India, which highlighted the confusion generated by having a Muslim religious law and a secular state law in unstable coexistence). (See Asghar Ali Engineer, *The Shah Bano Controversy*, 1987; see also Sebastian Poulter, 'The Claim to a Separate Islamic System of Personal Law for British Muslims', 1990.)

2.VI Conclusion

Smart's vision continually expanded in scope and developed in complexity, yet certain features also remained remarkably constant.

On the Christian side, his commitment remained unequivocal, and although he incorporated elements from Buddhism (the diagnosis of greed, hatred and delusion as the source of our woes), and from Hinduism (the world as God's body), and castigated much Christian theological closed-mindedness, so that he could be regarded by some as unduly liberal, he saw what was good in other religions as the work of the Holy Spirit (helping to keep religions honest by the self-scrutiny necessitated by dialogue and plurality), and held 'conservative' views on the Trinity, the Incarnation, the Atonement, and the Eucharist. His belief that religious truth was not confined to Christianity was vigorously maintained throughout, although in later years his practical inclusivism sat, at times not altogether comfortably, alongside a theoretical ultimate metaphysical agnosticism. This, though, was tempered by an inveterate (and almost certainly theologically grounded) optimism regarding a present complementarity and future convergence of religions. 'My vision then is of several things: a view of religious complementarity; a hope that religions as transnational spiritual corporations can build bridges between ethnicities; the hope that saints of the world may meet each other; a vision of the Trinity as helping with dialogue, and a fine sense of May-be-ism. All this also rests on the notion that in Christianity the best is yet to come. Hope, rather than despair (however justified through analysis) is the note of the future' (*Religion and Nationalism*, 1994, pp. 93–94).

On the philosophical side, his typology of religious experience in terms primarily of the numinous and the mystical runs like a golden thread through all his work, as does his emphasis on the key role of religious experience in rendering religion credible. In this he stands, perhaps, in something of a modern theological tradition going back to Schleiermacher (see, for example, his comments in support of 'the move to experience' made by H.D. Lewis and others 'in the line of Schleiermacher, Rudolf Otto and Martin Buber', 'Our Experience of the Ultimate', 1984 [C] repr. Smart, 1997, p. 19). Philosophically, the position is worked out as a form of 'soft' natural theology, and soft nonrelativism, engendering attitudes of open-minded tolerance whose true home is the open society, and whose true seed-bed is a system of religious education in which an empathetic descriptive pluralism holds pride of place.

Some of the later papers are rather more discursive than the early ones (compare, for example, 'Revelation, Reason and Religions' (Volume 2, Chapter 20) and 'Soft Natural Theology' (Volume 2, Chapter 23), both about natural theology as the sick man of Europe – Section 2.III, above). Yet in general there is another constant to be noted, namely skill in dissection of issues (marred, though, on occasion, by a disposition to a surfeit of novel nomenclature).

Smart's thought is open to criticism in a number of respects, as has been illustrated; and there will doubtless be a number of critical reassessments. Yet his publications remained thought-provoking to the end; and he was pivotal in establishing religious studies on a firm footing, certainly in Britain, both institutionally and theoretically. As he put it in a paper which makes a fitting conclusion to this selection ('An Ultimate Vision', Volume 2, Chapter 32, p. 343), 'So it came to be that my major achievement in academic life from an organizational point of view was founding the Department of Religious Studies in Lancaster, which helped to revolutionize religious education at university and school levels. I was attacked in my church for this, alas. But I am sure that the Church too has benefited from religious studies. There is for me no conflict between faith and openness'. That combination, of faith and openness, is one that he would have cherished as a lasting legacy.

References

Austin, J.L. (1962), *How to Do Things With Words*, Oxford: Clarendon Press

Ayer, A.J. (1936), *Language, Truth and Logic*, London: Victor Gollancz

Braithwaite, R.B. (1955), *An Empiricist's View of the Nature of Religious Belief*, Cambridge: Cambridge University Press

Bultmann, Rudolf (1960), *Jesus Christ and Mythology*, London: SCM Press

Chang, Jung and Halliday, Jon (2005), *Mao: The Unknown Story*, London: Jonathan Cape; Westminster, MD: Alfred A. Knopf

Christian, William A., Sr. (1987), *Doctrines of Religious Communities: A Philosophical Study*, New Haven and London: Yale University Press

Dasgupta, Surendranath (1922–), *A History of Indian Philosophy*, 5 vols, Cambridge: Cambridge University Press

Davin, Delia (2005), 'Dark Tales of Mao the Merciless', *The Times Higher Education Supplement*, August 12, pp. 22–23

Eliade, Mircea (1965), *Shamanism*, Princeton: Princeton University Press

Engineer, Asghar Ali (1987), *The Shah Bano Controversy*, Hyderabad: Orient Longman; London: Sangam Books

Farquhar, J.N. (1913), *The Crown of Hinduism*, London: Humphrey Milford

Flew, Antony and MacIntyre, Alasdair (eds) (1955), *New Essays in Philosophical Theology*, London: SCM Press

Gombrich, Richard (1971), *Precept and Practice: Traditional Buddhism in the Rural Highlands of Ceylon*, Oxford: Clarendon

Hare, R.M. (1952), *The Language of Morals*, Oxford: Oxford University Press

Harvey, Peter (2000), *An Introduction to Buddhist Ethics*, Cambridge: Cambridge University Press

Hick, John (1969), 'Religious Faith as Experiencing-as', in G.N.A. Vesey (ed.), *Talk of God*, London: Macmillan; New York: St Martin's Press, pp. 20–35

Hick, John (ed.) (1977), *The Myth of God Incarnate*, London: SCM Press

Horton, John and Mendus, Susan (eds) (1985), *Aspects of Toleration*, London: Methuen

Kalupahana, David (1976), *Buddhist Philosophy: A Historical Analysis*, Honolulu: University of Hawaii Press

Katz, Steven T. (ed.) (1978), *Mysticism and Philosophical Analysis*, New York: Oxford University Press; London: Sheldon Press

Keown, Damien (1992), *The Nature of Buddhist Ethics*, Basingstoke: Palgrave Macmillan

King, Ursula (2006), *Cherished Memories, Fractured Identities and New Subjectivities: Celebrating Fifty Years of British Scholarship in Religious Studies*, British Association for the Study of Religions, Occasional Paper No. 27

King, Winston, L. (1964), *In the Hope of Nibbana: An Essay on Theravada Buddhist Ethics*, LaSalle: Open Court

Kymlicka, Will (1989), *Liberalism, Community and Culture*, Oxford: Oxford University Press

Kymlicka, Will (1995), *Multicultural Citizenship: A Liberal Theory of Minority Rights*, Oxford: Oxford University Press

Kymlicka, Will (ed.) (1995), *The Rights of Minority Cultures*, (Oxford: Oxford University Press

MacIntyre, Alasdair (1967), *A Short History of Ethics*, London: Routledge and Kegan Paul

Medawar, Peter B. (1961), Book review: Teilhard de Chardin, *The Phenomenon of Man*, *Mind*, **70** (277): 99–106

Mendus, Susan (1988), *Justifying Toleration: Conceptual and Historical Perspectives*, Cambridge: Cambridge University Press

Mendus, Susan (1989), *Toleration and the Limits of Liberalism*, Basingstoke: Macmillan

Modood, Tariq (2007), *Multiculturalism: A Civic Idea*, Cambridge and Malden, MA: Polity

Moore, Peter G. (1973), 'Recent Surveys of Mysticism: A Critical Survey', *Religion*, **3** (2): 146–156

Otto, Rudolf (1923), *The Idea of the Holy*, Oxford: Oxford University Press; original German edition, *Das Heilige* (1917)

Otto, Rudolf (1937), *Mysticism East and West*, London: Macmillan

Owen H.P. (1969), *The Christian Knowledge of God*, London: Athlone Press

Phillips, D.Z. (1965), *The Concept of Prayer*, London: Routledge and Kegan Paul

Popper, Karl (1945), *The Open Society and Its Enemies*, London: Routledge and Kegan Paul

Poulter, Sebastian (1990), 'The Claim to a Separate Islamic System of Personal Law for British Muslims', in Chibli Mallat and Jane Connors (eds), *Islamic Family Law*, London and Boston: Graham and Trotman

Ramsey, Ian T. (ed.) (1961), *Prospect for Metaphysics*, London: George Allen and Unwin

Raphael, D.D. (1981), *Moral Philosophy*, Oxford and New York: Oxford University Press

Schools Council (1971), *Religious Education in Secondary Schools*, Working Paper 36, London: Evans/Methuen Educational

Schumacher, E.F. (1973), *Small Is Beautiful*, London: Blond and Briggs

Shepherd, John J. (1975), *Experience, Inference and God*, Basingstoke: Macmillan; New York: Barnes and Noble

Smart, J.J.C. and Williams, Bernard (1973), *Utilitarianism: For and Against*, Cambridge: Cambridge University Press

Smart, Ninian, 'Smart Ivory', unpublished typescript, The Ninian Smart Archive, Appendix

Smith, Wilfred Cantwell (1962), *The Meaning and End of Religion*, New York: Macmillan

Spiro, Melford E. (1970), *Buddhism and Society: A Great Tradition and Its Burmese Vicissitudes*, New York: Harper and Row; London: Allen and Unwin(1971)

Tambiah, Stanley J. (1970), *Buddhism and the Spirit Cults in North-East Thailand*, Cambridge: Cambridge University Press

Van Buren, Paul M. (1963), *The Secular Meaning of the Gospel Based on an Analysis of its Language*, New York: Macmillan; London: SCM Press

Vidler, A.R. (ed.) (1962), *Soundings: Essays Concerning Christian Understanding*, Cambridge: Cambridge University Press

Waismann, Friedrich (1955), 'Language Strata', in A.G.N. Flew (ed.), *Logic and Language*, Second Series, Oxford: Blackwell

Wallerstein, Immanuel (1974, 1980, 1989), *The Modern World-System*, 3 vols, New York: Academic Press

Whitehead, Raymond L. (1977), *Love and Struggle in Mao's Thought*, Maryknoll, NY: Orbis Books

Zaehner, R.C. (1957), *Mysticism Sacred and Profane*, London: Oxford University Press

I

AUTOBIOGRAPHICAL

CHAPTER 1

Methods in My Life

The invention of Religious Studies was a personal thing to me. When I say 'Religious Studies' I mean the study of religion as an aspect of human existence in a cross-cultural way and from a polymethodic or multidisciplinary perspective. Though there had been the comparative study of religion in my youth, it was not yet really combined with the social or human sciences. It was only with the combination of the study of the histories of religions with the social sciences that you get what I call the modern 'Religious Studies'. Any tradition has its roots and its formation: these are two differing periods. For example, the roots of Hinduism lie in many places – in the Vedic hymns, in early Brahmanism, in sramanic movements, in folk mythology, in temples, images, pilgrimages, caste. So though Hinduism has ancient roots it does not really gel together till the first to third centuries CE. Similarly though Religious Studies has its roots in the nineteenth century it scarcely is formed until the 1960s.

This was surely so in Britain. There, between the two world wars, even the comparative study of religions barely existed. It was kept alive by two farseeing Anglican clergymen named A. C. Bouquet and E. O. James. In the late 1930s and the postwar period, when the Swiss theologian Karl Barth dominated – noble, creative, benighted Barth – James's Chair in Leeds was converted to the narrowest form of Christian theology. The study of religions lived at the periphery of Anglican and other divinity schools and University Departments of Theology in State schools, all of which were dominated by Anglican thought, as they still greatly are today.

This point is worthy of further amplification. Religious Studies as a university enterprise did not exist in Australia, New Zealand, South Africa or other English-speaking countries. As a discipline or sub-discipline or even as a focus of study separate from Theology, it scarcely existed in European countries other than Britain. In the United States, while something like it occurred in Princeton and in a form devised by Joachim Wach in Chicago, it was really with the advent of the subject in public institutions that Religious Studies came into full being in North America. Since I was involved in the setting up of Lancaster's Department of Religious Studies, which pioneered the subject in its full form in Britain and was to be influential in other Commonwealth countries, I was much involved in the creation of its modern form. I was fortunate to be able to work in a new expanding university which was committed to a Religious Studies Department and to be helped by various younger scholars, among them Adrian Cunningham, Robert Morgan, Michael Pye and Stuart Mews. This is what I mean by saying that the invention of Religious Studies was a personal thing for me.

The roots of my concern with the study of religion I shall come to anon. But the formation of Religious Studies as a discipline began when I was H. G. Wood Professor of Theology at Birmingham University, a Chair I occupied when I was but 34 years old. Though I entered into the world of philosophical theology with verve, I had a wider vision. One day in the middle 1960s a colleague who lived nearby, the noted Egyptologist Rundle Clark, came to see me. He came before dinner time and I brought him into my study for a glass of sherry. He wanted to discuss some university politics. Inadvertently he left behind a copy of the *Universities Quarterly*. In it was an article called 'Theology as a Discipline', dealing with the possibility of establishing Theology in the then coming New Universities. It was a new age in British higher education, with great optimism about what these new-style universities were going to do. One or two had already been started, notably Sussex. I sat down that evening and wrote a reply to this article. Because there was a post box down the street with a pickup time of ten p.m., I went out and mailed it to the journal that very evening. For me, it was a seminal article. When Lancaster University, attracted by my article, invited me to advise them about a new Department a year later, they only had one thing in mind: they did not want the old Theology. In the process of the consultation, I was cajoled into transferring from being adviser to being candidate. Many of my friends thought me insane. I was in the swim as it happened, being invited to seven posts in the USA, including the chairs of the Columbia and Pennsylvania departments, and was invited to apply for the philosophy of religion job at Oxford. Lancaster was a wonderful opportunity, however, a *tabula rasa*, a new field. The ideas I formulated were expressed in my inaugural lecture there, delivered on St Valentine's Day in 1968, and reprinted in *Concept and Empathy* (1986). In it I declared that Religious Studies, as an enterprise, is necessarily

> **aspectual**, that is it deals with an aspect of human existence, experience, institutions, ideas and so on;
>
> **plural**, both because there are many religions, and because cross-cultural work is often equivalent to experimentation in the sciences and for other reasons necessary in the field: she who knows but one religion knows none (to exaggerate a cliché);
>
> **non-finite**, because traditions and the like often classified as not being religions (such as communism, rationalisms and so forth) have some great resemblance to traditional religions and cannot be excluded from our study – the family may include some 'illegitimate children' outside, and family resemblance is the correct mode of definition of religion; polymethodic or multi-disciplinary, for obvious reasons: history, philology, archaeology, sociology, anthropology, philosophy and so on are obviously relevant to the study of religion and religions.

The department in Lancaster also started a graduate program straight away. Because of our innovative curriculum and Common-wealth connections, about 60 of our graduates presently teach worldwide in institutions of higher education. Several of these are in North America, including Ivan Strenski and Donald Wiebe, both noted for their critical acumen.

Perhaps I can outline a few of the roots of that formative period in which I came both to formulate and practice what I preached. Part of it was that after a fine education at the Glasgow Academy, I went into the military in early 1945. After sundry forms of infantry training, I was set to learn Chinese for the Intelligence Corps, mainly at the School of Oriental and African Studies, part of London University. After a year and a half of immersion in the language, my colleagues and I dreamt in Chinese. Then as officers we went East, to Singapore, then Sri Lanka (at that time Ceylon). I was roused from my Western slumber with the call of diverse and noble cultures. I had had a fine education in the Classics among other things. I had a scholarship to Oxford. When I came back from the Army to Oxford, I pursued my original avocation (Chinese and Oriental Studies had pathetic curricula) of Classics, Ancient

History and Philosophy, but at graduate level I did philosophy of religion, then a highly unfashionable thing, especially when combined with comparative religion. My main mentor was J. L. Austin of performative fame; but I also consorted with Robert Zaehner. I wrote the first dissertation in Oxford on philosophy of religion after World War II. It was also the first comparative study and likewise the first to give a performative analysis of religious language. I was too early for the times. My book *Reasons and Faiths* (1958) flowed from this work. Though original, it was not yet 'Religious Studies' in orientation. Rather, it showed what I had learned from my military 'orientalization', a work in the philosophy of religion approaching cross-cultural study but not yet arriving. In those days, when you had to go to Asia from Europe by ship, the East was still a vague notion in the European and American imaginations. My early work reflected this Western vagueness.

The philosophy which I had been involved with in Oxford was so-called 'linguistic philosophy'. This had certain merits and certain defects. Because it tried to look at philosophical questions through the lens of language, it began to encounter many of the issues which have since become fashionable, such as problems of essentialism (hence Wittgenstein's theory of family resemblance alluded to above), interpretation, contextualism and so on. On the other hand, it tended to be too much bound up with 'our' language, which therefore uncritically built in various assumptions of our own culture, that is, largely of Western culture. I found that my experience with learning Chinese, my service in the East and various other factors made me critical of restrictions in regard to common sense language philosophy as then understood. It also seemed to me important that just as the philosophy of science was beginning to take the history of science seriously, so the philosophy of religion should take the history of religions seriously as well. It is still obvious that the philosophy of religion is only very partially interested in these wider cross-cultural issues, even in the 1990s. My *Reasons and Faiths* was an early venture in this cross-cultural and linguistic philosophy of religion.

In this book I incorporated also a theory of religious experience, distinguishing roughly between numinous and mystical strands of religion and language (that is, taking Rudolf Otto in one direction and William Stace and others in another). I was much influenced however by reading in the Pali canon, and by the apparent fact that

Buddhism was a kind of 'mysticism without God'. I was thus critical of Otto's assumption that there was one central core of religious experience. I consider that the notion of two or more main types does much more to explain the variety of religions, a point I will return to below. But before that, I would like to outline some of the main themes in my own thinking as a scholar and crusader of Religious Studies from a comparative perspective.

One of the themes of my thinking is that Religious Studies scholars need to be phenomenological in the descriptive, historical task. I came to this partly from my admiration for Popper, but partly out of my reflection upon how to study religion. On the Popper side, we need clean and yet dense descriptions of the meaning of religion in people's lives. The reason is simple: if we build theories into our descriptive stance (say Marxian theory) we already cannot test the theory, for it has already infected the data. It is a simple but vital point. Second, to bring out meaning we need informed empathy. I mean empathy: a critical perspective that is sliding tragically towards meaning 'sympathy'. But neither sympathy nor antipathy is needed. Empathy is. And this subtle but powerful difference implies 'epoché', a bracketing out of one's feelings and assumptions about the phenomenon at hand. For me personally, this perspective came as a result of the influence of one of the few British values which I retain – no doubt caught from long years of playing beloved cricket, namely, the sense of fair play: the sense that our description of Buddhist or Hindu or other non-Western values has to be 'fair'. All this I characterized as 'warm neutralism'. Some of my critics say you cannot do it, that empathy without sympathy is a fraud. I, however, hold that while this is difficult to achieve in a pure sense, you can at least aim at it, aim at an approach to religions which is much better than aiming at unfairness, lack of empathy, and ignorance.

Thus, to return to my own intellectual biography, in the late 1960s I was thinking of Religious Studies as plural, polymethodic, non-finite and aspectual, and involving the phenomenological or warm neutralist method. But there was another important theme emerging in my thinking, a way of studying religions in their totality by analyzing their various common dimensions, dimensions often disregarded by practitioners.

The way this insight emerged as an important aspect of my work was somewhat unintentional on my part. I was asked by Scribners to write a book to be called *The Religious Experience of Mankind* (later in its fourth edition called *The Religious Experience*) and luckily for me the copy editor turned out to be a wise person named Dorothy Duffy. I had written an introductory chapter for this projected text which she did not much like. In 1967 I read a paper outlining a theory of the dimensions of religion at Columbia and she came along. After hearing the lecture, she urged me to make this paper the introduction to the book. The idea fit perfectly. The thesis of the paper pointed out that religion has various dimensions, of which I identified six: experiential, ethical, doctrinal, mythological, institutional and ritual. My aim in this paper was a simple one, namely, to try to ensure that scholarly descriptions of religion be balanced. At that time, and even today, there were so many treatments of religion that were not balanced, from those such as Mircea Eliade's which ignore the sociological and institutional side, to those such as Wendy Doniger's which overplay the mythological (beguilingly I do not deny), to those such as Paul Johnson's work on Christianity which overemphasize the doctrinal, and so on. By this I am not saying that each dimension is equally important in each religion. But the schema of six dimensions (later seven, the material, in a later book *The World's Religions*) created the possibility of a balance, a balance which is vital and reflects the multidisciplinary view of our subject. To deal with myth without looking at society, or with ethics without dealing with ritual, or with doctrine without contemplating experience, is to present an incomplete and unintegrated picture of religious phenomena.

So then, my view of the study of religions was that it should be conducted on a base of informed empathy, but with dimensional outreach, and with a recognition of its plural, aspectual, multidisciplinary, and nonfinite character. In the early 1970s I wrote two books to that effect. One of those, *The Science of Religion and the Sociology of Knowledge*, which included a critique of Peter Berger (of his methodological atheism, assuming the non-existence of God, rather than the more appropriate methodological agnosticism), was in line with my neutralist program. That is, I did not suppose that 'reflections' about religion had to be neutral, but simply open and pluralist. My critique of Berger is important, for it deals with the whole problem of reductionism, the tendency to speak of a religious phenomenon as if it were the result of something other than religion itself, and hence not genuine. From this perspective of empirical analysis, it is not important to us to opt for affirming either that God exists or that She does not. The question is what effects does a religious stance or institution have. If its development is more heavily affected by outside factors, then that is perhaps what people mean by reductionism. But if the other way round, then religion as a causative factor is important, at least for the period and place in question. Thus, in critiquing Berger, I worked out a theory of the focus of a religion which leaves its status as existing or not undecided. What is vital is whether it is 'real' in the minds and lives of those who participate in the religion in question. Much discussion about reductionism is confused if it does not take methodological agnosticism as the framework for empirical research.

With the creation of Religious Studies as more or less a new discipline in the 1960s and early 1970s, life for me was heaven on earth. It was made even more delightful by 1977 when I began dividing my time between Lancaster and the University of California, Santa Barbara – the two liveliest outfits in the field. Although I had taught in Harvard in the days of John Carman at the Center, in Princeton much earlier, and in Cape Town – all with fine programs – some of the places I had taught, and others elsewhere, were somewhat deficient in the breadth that I believe Religious Studies requires. For instance, comparative religion or history of religions was the norm in graduate studies in Harvard and Chicago, with hardly any emphasis on reflective, philosophical or social-scientific work. Eliade, who was highly influential, used his history of religions materials as the clothing for a religious worldview which he wished to promote. There is in my view nothing wrong with promoting a worldview either by worldview construction or worldview promotion (rather than the more descriptive higher-order activity of worldview analysis) but it is best if scholars are both aware of what they are doing and announce it. This applies both to people like Eliade and to Marxists and so on. However, the point I really wished to make that under Eliade's influence the history of religions was a kind of theology. The practice of 'epoché' becomes important in a kind of Buddhist sense, then, in otherwise being self-aware of the status of one's utterances: as intentionally descriptive and analytic, or as being loaded with one's personal agenda, and so on. The danger to Religious Studies is when some monolithic position takes over, whether Christian theology, Marxism, deconstructive theories, or whatever. It may be worth remarking at this point that while I have come in for a lot of fire from Christians, I am in fact an Episco-palian. But both in Britain and America the fact that I assault establishmentarian tendencies in the name of education leads to erroneous conclusions about my personal (as opposed to my professional) position.

At any rate, the 1970s were the most creative years in Religious Studies. The field was getting institutionalized in Canada and the United States, especially in public universities, in South Africa, Australia, New Zealand (an early leader in the field) and elsewhere in the Anglophone world. It had weaknesses, however: its professional emplacement could be peculiar. For example, the Society for the Scientific Study of Religion in the US did not coordinate with the American Academy of Religion. Much of the sociology of religion was tribal, dealing with the West but not venturing much across cultural traditions. The philosophy of religion was overwhelmingly Westernized. Colonialism still abounded in the academy. But as we are approaching the next century, it appears that these deficiencies are only slowly being remedied.

A major motif of my thinking since early days has been the impact of Theravadin studies on religious history and theory. Because of a great deal of ignorance about the actual history of religions among otherwise sophisticated scholars and even among people who regard themselves as experts in religion, various theories which appear to be called into question by Buddhism and by Theravada Buddhism in particular can survive unmodified long after they should have been altered or abandoned. The main point about Theravada is that because it does not involve belief in an Absolute or God, various concepts do not work, such as the notion of a *unio mystica* (mystical union), the importance of sacrifice, the image of a Father figure, theophanies and kratophanies, a single ultimate focus of religions, the centrality of the concept of faith, and various Western stereotypes of religion. Other traditions than Theravada might have an equally alarming affect on received opinion. But for me my early experience in Ceylon and subsequent Pali studies opened my eyes. My teacher at Yale, a wonderful linguist called Paul Tedesco, rescued from a German death camp at the end of World War II and brought to the US by Franklin Edgerton, never discussed the content of the texts beyond their immediate meanings. This focus enabled me to come to my own conclusions without being dominated by earlier, often distorted, interpretations of Buddhism. In general, I feel that scholars are much too respectful of dead people's theories (I used to say 'Who do these dead men think they are?', though I shall later make a plea for respect for ancestors). Anyway, Theravada deeply challenges various theories, chief among them the many views of mysticism, including those of Stace and Aldous Huxley, Girard's account of sacrifice and the origins of religion, Freudian analysis, Eliade's metaphysics, John Hick's Copernican revolution, Wilfred C. Smith's general account of faith, and various definitions of religion. Also though many anthropological ideas have seemed fruitful to scholarship, they seem singularly thinly grounded in major traditions, including Theravada. I am thinking of the ideas of Victor Turner particularly, but the framework of relatively enclosed societies makes some ideas plausible which would need severe modification in a wider context. In this instance, I am thinking of Durkheim and Lévi-Strauss.

Theravada also deeply challenges the assumptions of Rudolf Otto. His delineation of the numinous experience is masterly, but it does not apply to contemplative or mystical experience. I made the dialectic between these two main forms of religious experience central to my first book, *Reasons and Faiths*. In it, I evolved a theory of the ramification of language in order to deal with the problem of built-in interpretations. I published this first in an article 'Mystical Experience and Interpretation' which appeared in the first issue of the well-known journal *Religious Studies*, and more recently published a paper in Steven Katz's *Mysticism and Language* (1992) entitled 'What would Buddhaghosa have made of The Cloud of Unknowing?', involving a dense comparison of texts, Theravadin and Christian. If you asked me which of the many articles I have published were the most important I would point to these two. I was proud, by the way, that I wrote the first in 17 days aboard the liner *Canberra* between Colombo and Southampton. With 2000 Australians onboard ship and rum selling at ten cents a glass, this was surely no small feat!

An important thought among scholars during these years was that there is a vital distinction between two quite different senses of phenomenology. The sense in which I favor it methodologically is as the practice of empathy. Now it is sometimes used in quite a differing sense as meaning morphology, as in the magisterial work by G. Van der Leeuw, *Religion in Essence and Manifestation*, and as to some extent in the work of Eliade (though I am critical of his ideological slant which underlies his morphology). The morphological enterprise is designed to pick out differing and important themes among religions and worldviews more generally. This is of course a tricky task, since it is important also to make subtle allowance for context. Still, I believe that it is a possible and illuminating exercise (and I have just completed a large-scale enterprise to follow in the footsteps of van der Leeuw).

So far then my theorizing had to do with the complex nature of Religious Studies (plural, polymethodic, non-finite and so forth), the need for informed empathy or phenomenology in one sense of the term, and the need for good methods in examining the nature of religious experience. In addition, I was concerned with balance, as encouraged through my theory of the dimensions of religion. Another concern involved the teaching of religion in public schools. During the 1970s I was involved in two projects concerned with religious education in public schools in England and Northern Ireland. These projects aimed at working with teachers in introducing world religions into the curriculum, and our views came to be highly influential in the English schools system. I was also involved in a dynamic group known as the Shap Working Party in World Religions in Education, started in the late 1960s at the Shap Wells Hotel in Northern England, which has done a tremendous amount to create materials and facilities to assist the better teaching of religion and religions in schools at all levels. I believe that Religious Studies ideals are best for all ages. Even if a (say Catholic) school believes in a special regimen for inculcating values, this does not exempt it from sensitively informing all children of the history and nature of the world's religions. I was also involved in the early 1970s as editorial consultant for the BBC series *The Long Search*, widely used still in education. I learned that documentary television has already much the same values as those of Religious Studies phenomenology or informed empathy. Making the films was amazingly interesting. It added an extra dimension to my understanding of how to understand religions and how to communicate that understanding to students and the public at large.

The next main methodological lesson I would like to introduce relates to what I in 1968 had called the 'non-finite' character of the field in which I held that there is no serious distinction between secular and religious worldviews. This is a most vital point, from a number of angles. It is important from a theoretical point of view. It happens that modern life tries to make a big distinction between

Methods in My Life

religious and secular worldviews. Tax and other laws give certain privileges (wrongly in my view) to religious organizations, often on some assumption that religions are good, and somehow worthy of tax concessions and the like. Religions are both good and bad, and it is scarcely the business of the State to adjudicate. But beyond that point lies the perception that often religions and secular worldviews blend. Take, for instance, religion and nationalism. There is in some countries, notably the United States, a separation between Church and State. In my view there should be a separation between worldview-affirming organizations and the State. This would also alter educational guidelines. But whether this angle of vision commends itself, there are many areas where secular ideologies need to be brought into the discussion of religions. So, I have been increasingly preoccupied with the analysis of nationalism in particular through my schema of dimensions. My University of California colleague Peter Merkl, a noted analyst of modern German history and institutions, and I ran a conference at the end of the 1970s on religion and politics. But because the political world at that time was not quite ready for a set of essays on politics and religion, we had great difficulty in selling the book that followed from our conference thereafter. Yet thanks to the Ayatollah Khomeini, the topic soon became fashionable and the book did rather well.

What all this means is that in general Religious Studies would cover the whole aspect of human life summed up in the holding, expression and institutionalization of ultimate or higher values. While we may begin from the base of more traditional systems to which we in the West and elsewhere tend to assign the name 'religions', our field should include the study of ideologies and philosophies. There was always something unfortunate about the segregation and, indeed, protection therefore of the category of religion. Thus, the philosophy of religion became an alleged specialism rather than the philosophy of worldviews (which would be a better title, stretching beyond God-talk and the like). But perhaps the time has not come to make this move boldly. But it seems obvious to me that a person can analyze nationalism, for instance, through the application of the theory of dimensions of religion. In the old days Paul Tillich called on scholars and others to see religions in terms of ultimate concern. But he hesitated before Nazism and Communism, which he called 'quasi-religions' rather than religions. But men and women died for these causes. Nazism was a kind of hyper-nationalism, which has reaped a wondrous crop of the heroic dead. Every village war memorial in Europe testifies to this. What could be more ultimate than the willingness to die? Presbyterianism is by contrast genteel, even pusillanimous. How many die or would die for it today? Thus, when I compare nationalism and traditional religions I make use of my dimensional analysis. A nation has its myth or myths (history as taught in high school and the like, loaded history, of course, underlining heroes and national values); its rituals of various kinds, from inaugurations to memorials to the dead, even its sports and its language; its emotions of patriotism and pride, and so on; its institutions; its ethics (how to be a good citizen); its material and artistic dimension (from its land, to its monuments and music, and so on); and its doctrines (democratic ideals, ideology, religious tradition, and so on).

In the 1980s I also got interested in the analysis of modern religions – not so much the new religious movements as the trans-formation of old traditions. Here I saw the key as being colon-ialism. Again there is a strong methodological content to my interest because the new movements among major faiths have to do with something which is beyond, but of the same order, as nationalism (in fact, some cases cannot strictly be distinguished from it). The key to all this is colonialism or imperialism, which was a kind of nationalist hubris. The religions, helping to shape civilizations, needed to remake themselves in the face of the challenge of the West, which came not just imperially, but came as nations superior in science, military power, organization, to some degree culturally, and brimming with democratic modernity, not to mention a condescending breed of religion. I wrote up a lot of my conclusions in what in the USA was treated as a textbook, though by Cambridge University Press in Britain as a work of reference, my *The World's Religions* (1989). The first half of the book deals with ancient and medieval history of religions. The second half deals with the colonial period and its aftermath. This second half provides a kind of general theory of religious responses to the challenge of the West. The two main forces to emerge were types of modernism (Islamic, Hindu, Buddhist, Japanese, and so on) and forms of 'fundamentalism', returning to supposed traditional values but also in their own way modernizing. These trends were also manifest in the colonizing religions, mainly Christianity, which also experienced the pressures of the new post-Enlightenment, industrial, democratic, socially transformed modern world.

How I came to write the book was amusing. A company called John Calmann and King, very skilled and enterprising, was commissioned by Cambridge and Prentice-Hall to produce the book. Their offices are over the way from the British Museum. They called me and asked me to drop in one day. I went to see them. Larry King and an assistant talked to me, he being the boss. They wanted me to do the book but, because I already had my *Religious Experience* on the market, I said, 'Look, this new book would only be a rival to my old book.' In reply, King said: 'But you wouldn't want some other bastard to do it, would you?' I succumbed. I wrote the book with fervor and on a wholly different plan from my old one. I treated regions rather than traditions and sliced history at the colonial period. It was much more sociological (or should I say macrosociological) than the old book which was more oriented to my theory of types of religious experience. I started on July 1st of that year at my wife's place in Italy and, with only a week off for a trip down the Po valley, finished 240 000 words later on September 30th. I was near dead, but happy. I was happy because I had made an important statement. But because it was classified in America as a textbook, it has been slow in receiving recognition, though I find that texts creep into professors' theoretical consciousness slowly but surely. I do not mind if eggheads read Foucault but teach Smart! Anyway, all of my efforts in the 1980s were more oriented to the whole idea of worldview analysis as a larger category than simply the history and phenomenology of religions.

Though it will no doubt be obvious that in a broad sense I believe in comparative methods and ambitions, it is not quite true that she who knows only one tradition knows none. Consider bhakti religion. It occurs in Christianity, pretty obviously. Does the fact that it is rife in Indian theism not make a difference to our account of it in the West? Because of the high importance I assign to it (but equally recognizing the vitality of contextual analysis too), I am disturbed by two tendencies in the past 20 years or so. One is the trend to the particularization of cultures – even to the suggestion that cultures are incommensurable. This is eminent nonsense which I need not remark on except to say that it is like saying that because we are all individuals we do not have noses. It is a kind of racism, dividing humanity into subspecies. The specialists often despise comparativists, but comparative methods are common sense responses to obvious challenges posed by both similarities between traditions and differences. The second worry about Religious Studies is a product of its very successes in the past 30 years. We hire someone in Taoism, let us say, and take a powerful candidate from Sinology. But she may not really be interested in Religious Studies or the logic of our enterprise. Such already exists in both Judaism and Christian studies. In Christian studies, worse, you often get scholars who refuse to teach across the board. In my view, the pseudo-specialization of traditional Christian scholars is frequently a disgrace, but I shall refrain from going on. The net result of 'specialist' tendencies could be the fragmentation and disintegration of Religious Studies. I am deeply worried by this trend, since there are so many pressures in academic life in this direction. I know that often earlier comparativists and Religious Studies scholars could be shallow. Nowadays, monographs are deeper, and it is a great pleasure to see how many good scholars there are in the academy.

This brings me to a vital methodological point, which is increasingly influential in my thought now that we are in the mid-1990s. I was myself fortunate in having been immersed in philosophy in my early days, and having taught it in the Universities of Wales, Yale, Wisconsin-Madison, Hong Kong and elsewhere from time to time. I chose to move into Religious Studies, it is true, but philosophy gave me a sense for conceptual clarity. I have carried that over into the study of religion. I often think that some of my colleagues in the field lack it. They do not always make much effort to bring new conceptual order into their thinking. Often, they think it is enough for a person to know Sanskrit or Hebrew or Chinese. Far be it from me to decry language skills! I have spent a lot of my life learning Latin, Greek, French, Chinese, Sanskrit, Pali and so forth. But linguistic skill is often rated above conceptual insight, and wrongly so. I know a senior Indologist who is a conceptual idiot, and conversely one of the best books written on Confucius was by a relatively non-linguistic philosophy colleague, Herbert Fingarette. Often the assumptions of scholars channel their activities in unfortunate ways. I consider the critical and fresh look at categories always to be vital. Sometimes newly fashionable writers, such as Foucault in the 1980s, can loosen up and change perspectives, but not if they are turned into dogmas. It is difficult to know quite what the right word is for such conceptual freshness and clarity. I have regarded it as an important part of my contribution to Religious Studies. It is no doubt true that sometimes I stick too much to clear ideas (and perhaps they can be shallow), but I do regard it as important in a new field that people should know what they are doing, beset as they are by the Scylla of faith and commitment on the one shore and the Charybdis of unempirical and fashionable theories on the other.

Since the notion of conceptual analysis has already been pre-empted by philosophers and the application of concepts in religion needs to apply to comparative data, I shall use the phrase conceptual synthesis to stand for the intellectual tasks which I have in mind. Let me give two examples for the kind of thing I mean. First, I think it is important to distinguish between the roots and the formation of a tradition. Thus the period of the formation of classical Christianity, with its doctrines, narratives, liturgical life, and organization, could be said to be the fourth century CE, even though it has its roots in the life of Christ and the memory of ancient Israel, and so on. It is fallacious to see roots as somehow the whole of origins. This has afflicted modern attempts to see Hinduism already there *in nuce* in the Vedic hymns and the Upanishadic corpus. Again, sorting out the notion of syncretism is important: why do we count a blend between a tradition and a secular worldview as not being syncretism? Maybe, moreover, a less loaded term, such as blend, is needed. Another variety of conceptual synthesis lies in the introduction of a genuinely cross-cultural vocabulary into our field, using notions such as bhakti, li (correct performative behavior), dhyana, and so on just as in the past we have coopted totem, tabu, and so on. I carried out a bit of this program of globalization in my Gifford lectures, *Beyond Ideology* (1981).

Much earlier I adverted to my theory of dimensions of religion. This can give us entrée to a number of comparative and theoretical questions. After the monographs are written, after the texts and archaeology are published, it is surely necessary to try to make sense of human worldviews and religiosity, to piece together a general theory of worldviews. For instance, we may contemplate the relations between the doctrinal and experiential dimensions. If it be the case that mystical consciousness frequently culminates in a sense of non-dual experience, then this helps to make sense of certain doctrinal or philosophical trends: the expression in theistic religions of a close communion or union with the Divine; the notion of the non-dual experience in Hindu Advaita and related doctrines; the advaya consciousness in Mahayana absolutism; the realization of nirvana (there being no Other to be united with) in the Theravada, and so on. There appear in short to be correlations between the dimensions. Certain organizations, such as monasticism, obviously favor the contemplative life and, with it, experience. Rituals of worship and devotional prostration favor and are favored by personal theism and a sense of divine Otherness. The concept of substance in philosophy is often correlated with the use of sacramental and magical rituals. I found myself returning to this broader vision of our field's speculative power in the book I referred to earlier when speaking of van der Leeuw, entitled *The Dimensions of the Sacred: an Anatomy of the World's Beliefs* (1996).

I consider it is part of our task as intellectuals not only to theorize about the configurations of religions and worldviews, but to reflect more philosophically about the relations between religions. I addressed the idea of dialogue in a number of works, including *A Dialogue of Religions* (1960), written very early in my career, and again in *The Yogi and the Devotee* (1968). I returned somewhat to these themes in *Buddhism and Christianity: Rivals and Allies* (1993). I do not think Religious Studies should remain so purist that it eschews all philosophical and critical questions about religion. It will also be seen from my account that I prefer a road vision of what we might do. We do not want to be trapped in simply descriptive and historical researches, admirable as these are for much of what else we engage it. There is a reflective side to our field, and we should be suitably speculative, and taken notice of more by our colleagues in adjacent fields. Philosophical reflection can do much to enhance students' excitement about our field. While empirical, social-scientific, and historical studies necessarily aim at impartiality and 'objectivity', after we have surveyed the religious scene there remain some vital questions. In the long run, these questions affect educational practice. While I remain very critical of those who secretly sell a metaphysics while claiming to be empirical, there is no reason why we cannot distinguish between our various activities in the field.

But comparisons are still vital if we are to move towards theory in Religious Studies. Moreover, morphology should be dynamic, that is we should compare types of changes as well as types of more static phenomena. I consider this of some importance in my concern with the modern and colonial period. We can see differing kinds of reactive changes to the challenges of the West. Different cultures have tried to absorb differing lessons from the rampant West, and attempt to stave off domination in diverse ways. This is adapting some general approaches of Max Weber to dealing with our better knowledge of the history of modern religions. There is an analogy with recent similar work on the genesis of so-called fundamentalism.

The years since I entered the field – a little over 40 – have been a great success story, though littered too with threats and confusions. The coexistence of Christian and other theological enterprises with Religious Studies confuses outsiders. The drive to specialization may fragment the field. New theories, such as deconstructionism, do not herald well for research; too many of our fellow practitioners may have ideological or spiritual axes to grind. It is difficult to combine one's commitments and professionalism. But all in all, the story of Religious Studies, especially in English-speaking countries, has been spectacular. Moreover, the whole former Soviet empire is opening up to the field. Though the days of older scholars seem far away – men like E. O. James, A. C. Bouquet, and Sydney Brandon in Britain, and George Foot Moore, Erwin Goodenough, and Joachim Wach in America – we must be grateful to these our ancestors. Some of them kept the ideal of cross-cultural studies of religion alive in hard days. In some ways they were naive when compared with more fashionable trends today. But our intellectual forebears should be entitled to their cult of ancestors. They are the living dead. Perhaps the chief difference between those days and now is the great advance of social science and more generally cultural studies in our field. Another good change – especially in Britain – is that increasing attention is paid to Religious Studies in high schools. Our field has always held high the banner of cross-cultural studies and the repudiation of older colonial attitudes in education.

To sum up, then: from the perspective of my fairly lengthy career of scholarship and from my long-time personal and professional interest and involvement in the idea of 'Religious Studies', I see our field as aspectual, plural, non-finite and multidisciplinary. I consider the dimensional analysis of religions and worldviews is necessary to balanced accounts of religions. I advocate strongly the extension of our field to non-traditionally religious worldviews. I consider that, in addition to the expansion of monographic knowledge, we need new theories of religion and worldviews. I do not wish us in a fit of purist empiricism to cut out reflective work in our field: it is just that we need to know when we are doing what. I believe moreover that we should strive to achieve a more cross-cultural and global vocabulary for dealing with traditions both ancient and modern. The net result of such precepts is to bring religion, politics, and human life in general closer together. I think Religious Studies, provided it does not choke on specialisms or commit methodological suicide, has a marvelous future.

II

Religious Experience and the Logic of Religious Discourse

CHAPTER 2

The Comparative Logical Analysis
of Religious Doctrines

I wish to argue that the philosophy of religion is a factual enquiry closely bound up with the study of comparative religion.

The philosopher is a logician, whose job is to explore the logic of different types of proposition, including religious ones, and n o t to establish or overthrow particular beliefs (e. g., that God exists). The essence of a proposition's logic lies in the mode whereby the truth or falsity (correctness, propriety, etc.) of that type of proposition is attested, and the canons appealed to ; and thus is intimately coupled with the function, which is seen in the setting, of that type of proposition (e. g., the logic of mystical utterance can only be luminous in the setting of spiritual training and behaviour).

A rider to all this : the field of religious discourse should be regarded as autonomous, and the investigator's assumption is that religious utterances have a meaning (their own). His enquiry, then, is in its own strange fashion a factual one, and not normative, for he avoids legislating about logic.

Now we find that religious propositions occur within, or are connected with, doctrinal systems or *schemes* (a better term : they are not tautly systematic like, say, Euclidean geometry), from which they cannot be severed. For the sense of such a proposition is in part determined by what other propositions are conjointly asserted. But some schemes contain propositions of differing logics (e. g., there are differing canons of propriety relevant in respect of propositions about a Creator and of those about mystical experience), and this is connected with the fact that there are divers sorts of religious activity (e. g., worship and asceticism).

When the logician wishes to separate out the varying types
of propositions, he meets a grave obstacle, for the propositions, being woven into a scheme, are mutilated if cut apart.
He must honestly recognise that he is bound to distort,
and justify the dissection by appeal to comparative religion.
A doctrinal scheme containing one strand serves as a model
of the strand where it appears in another scheme in conjunction with, and influenced by, a second strand.

Thus, for instance, Brahmanism seems to contain two
strands : propositions about Brahman as source and sustainer
of the world, and mystical propositions about the Ātman
(to be sought within). Sānkhya, on the other hand, does
without the first strand, as does early Buddhism (the *anattā*
doctrine is largely directed against the concept Ātman as
influenced by Brahman).

Thus historical comparisons will help to give logical
distinctions content ; and so another name for the philosophy
of religion is : « the comparative logical analysis of religious
doctrines ». This should count as a specialised, and I think
important, factual enquiry within comparative religion. By
rejecting metaphysical controversy and the desire to indoc-
trinate, the philosopher can gain enlightenment from the
historian, and may even offer something in return.

CHAPTER 3

Empiricism and Religions

THERE is much scepticism today, in the English-speaking world, about the possibility of metaphysics. The notion that we can, by some form of reasoning or other, discover the truth about Ultimate Reality, is suspect. The root of this condition lies in the impact of scientific method upon philosophy: this found its formal expression in the Verification Principle. In this paper[1] I want to consider the effect of empiricism upon the philosophy of religion, with special reference to two main points. First, scepticism about metaphysics is sometimes used paradoxically as a preliminary to an irrationalist defence of revelation. I want to argue that in the present condition of the world, where the great religions are at last reasonably aware of one another, this defence, on the whole, fails. Second, it may be backed up by the thesis that there is a fundamental unity in all religions, revealed somehow in intuition or mystical experience. I want to argue (unfashionably) that this charitable view is misleading. But before going on to these major topics of the paper, I wish briefly to say something about the challenge of empiricism and its relevance to Indian philosophy.

I

Empiricism and Indian Philosophy

Some Indian philosophers with whom I have conversed have hinted that there is no need to worry much about contemporary empiricism and linguistic philosophy. This attitude perhaps stems from two considerations. First, India has from early times had its own acquaintance with empiricism, naturalism, materialism and the like; and so there is a tendency to think of modern empiricism as no new thing, as already docketed among possible views, as the kind of thing which appeals to people of a certain temperament, and therefore as something that can safely be ignored by philosophers of other schools. Second, modern empiricism appears to have a Western origin, and religious people in India may feel that it is a by-product of Western 'materialism' (in the unphilosophical sense) and of its comparative indifference to spiritual ideals. Both these considerations, though having a grain of truth, are misleading. For though the naturalistic tradition in Indian philosophy has been of considerable importance, just as it was also among the Greeks, neither ancient Indian nor ancient Greek naturalism can be compared in importance to contemporary empiricism, for a simple reason : *scientific method had not been evolved*. The theory of knowledge has to do with ways of knowing, and modern science is a way of knowing distinct from all others and tremendously fruitful. Thus ancient naturalism is a mere intuitive foreshadowing of a scientific empiricism. Again, as to the second consideration, it must be remembered that science is neither Eastern nor Western, and it would be absurd (save in a merely historical and unimportant sense) to talk of French physics or Thai chemistry or Indian zoology. (This is why the Marxists sometimes make fools of themselves by speaking of bourgeois science.) It is true that much of Western philosophers' neglect of religion is due to the indifference to spiritual values mentioned above, but this does not mean that contemporary empiricism can be neglected by the pious. Far from it, for some of the indifference arises from intellectual reasons, chief among which is the feeling that the application of scientific method leaves no room for religious truth. For this and other reasons, it is unfortunate that we still tend to speak about Indian, Chinese, British and German philosophy. What philosophy ultimately means is that the only sort of philosophy is a world philosophy. Sadly, however, national pride, West and East, and ignorance, mainly in the West, provide obstacles to the realisation of this goal. But when I say 'world philosophy' I emphatically do *not* mean that there should be some metaphysical doctrine accepted by all philosophers in the world; but only that philosophers should argue with one another openly and courteously, treating all ideas as public property, and forgetting the historical origins of these ideas. The philosopher must be a citizen of the world.

Thus contemporary empiricism is bound to have an effect on the philosophy of religion, whether religion be conceived as Christian or Hindu or Buddhist. It is true that some attacks upon religion by philosophers[2] show a total unawareness of the fact that some of the points they adduce only apply to Christianity, so that the arguments are parochial. Nevertheless, the notion that there is a transcendent Reality or state apprehended through revelation or religious experience needs to be defended in the face of modern empiricism and anti-metaphysics if it is to be acceptable to intelligent persons.

II

Anti-metaphysics and religious irrationalism

The Madhyamika is of special interest in this connection, for it illustrates very nicely the main problem arising from metaphysical irrationalism, i.e., from the view that philosophical arguments cannot succeed in establishing anything about Ultimate Reality. The characteristics of the Madhyamika relevant to our present inquiry can be summarised briefly as follows[3] : (i) the rejection of dogmatism or *dṛṣṭivāda*; (ii) the denial of the possibility of discursive knowledge about Ultimate Reality, and connectedly the attempt to show the contradictory nature of all possible views; (iii) nevertheless, the claim that there is in some sense an Absolute (*tathatā, dharmakāya*); and (iv) the thesis that the Absolute phenomenalizes itself in a revelatory way (as the *Tathāgata*).

Thus, very curiously, the breakdown in metaphysics can

still turn out to be a triumph of religion, and the abandonment of discursive thought leaves room for the acceptance of a revelation. It is curious too that a very similar position was held by Mansel, in the last century, who, in his Bampton Lectures,[4] erected a new defence of Christianity upon the basis of philosophical agnosticism and who in one way or another would subscribe to the four features of the Madhyamika described above, save that Christ, not the *Tathāgata*, becomes the phenomenalized Absolute.

Nor is this all. Kierkegaard, who has deeply influenced Christian theology, likewise subscribes to metaphysical irrationalism and uses it brilliantly and suggestively to introduce an appeal to faith and revelation. Even Wittgenstein (he loved to read Kierkegaard) hints at a similar position. Certainly, some of those who have been influenced by him have fashioned a similar 'defence' of religious truth[5]. Thus we discover, in different places, philosophers who have been driven, for varying reasons, into holding that metaphysical argument cannot yield the ultimate truth and who have used this situation as a paradoxical support for revelation and faith. It is a kind of intellectual *satyāgraha*.

The general form of metaphysical irrationalism can be expressed roughly as follows. "One feels that perhaps there is an Ultimate Reality; and yet upon scrutiny of the metaphysical attempts to establish its existence and to show its nature, one sees that they have inescapable defects. All we can do is to point dumbly towards the unknown and inexpressible X, and to acknowledge the incapacity of all thought and language. But yet there is revelation : if we seek insight into Ultimate Reality, this can be our only source. But it is a source which in the nature of the case cannot be defended by reasonings. The inexpressible shows itself to us, but mysteriously."

Now there is ample warrant in religion for the view that God or Brahman is ineffable. There is warrant too for the view that it is by revelation that we know the truth. And there is warrant again for the view that it is by faith and spiritual experience, rather than by ratiocination, that the truth is to be apprehended. So metaphysical irrationalism as a preparation for revelation seems a plausible line of approach.

Nevertheless, as it stands, it is untenable.

First, for the following and obvious reason : that if a simple appeal to revelation is made, in the context of the world as we find it, where there are differing revelations or supposed revelations, it is legitimate to ask why one formulation rather than any other should be chosen. Mansel had no warrant to identify Christ rather than the Buddha with the unknown X.

It may be replied that we do not choose revelations, but rather they choose us. But (i) revelations claim to enshrine the truth, and the fact that most people are born into, rather than choose, a religion does not entail that there is no means of deciding the truth. Likewise, people differ in traditional beliefs about morality, but this does not imply the subjectivity of morals. (ii) If the objection is an echo of the thought "God chooses us, not we Him", then we must remember that this thought itself expresses an element of revelation (theistic, moreover), and it would be circular to argue upon this basis.

But it may be further objected that revelations do not compete. They all, perhaps, witness to a single truth in all religions.[6]

This brings me to the second major topic of the paper.

III

The Fundamental Unity of Religions

Revelations employ words[7], and words seem to conflict as between one formulation of religious truth and another. For instance, it is necessary, according to the Christians, to have faith in a personal Creator, but this is unnecessary, according to the Theravada. So the following dilemma obtains : either words here mean something, in which case there is competition; or they mean nothing, in which case nothing is said. But if nothing is said, anti-religion is an equally good expression of religion as is religion, and this is absurd.

But, it may be replied, theological words are not literal and are not precisely definable. One must look beyond their overt meanings. God is not literally a Father, nor Durga literally a Mother. But this is no argument. God is not literally a Father, but in Christian theology He is not even non-literally an onion. Some expressions are more appropriate than others. This is all that is needed for the contention that here words mean something.

But if words can be, so to speak, stretched, it may still turn out that all revelations witness to a single truth. But what truth ? The rub lies in this; for the fundamental truth has to be expressed. But how ? Maybe the great religions could agree upon a highly abstract formula, but not one which would cover the following points (i) whether there is rebirth and *karma*; (ii) whether there is a personal Creator; (iii) whether there are any incarnations of such a Creator; (iv) whether if so there are one or many; (v) whether Ultimate Reality exists as the ground of the visible cosmos; and (vi) whether salvation involves identity with Ultimate Reality or not. More abstractly, one could put the argument as follows : in order to speak of the fundamental unity it must be specified, i.e., put into words. These words I shall call the 'propositional nucleus'. An empirical revelation then will consist in (a) the propositional nucleus and (b) the remainder. Even given agreement over a propositional nucleus, there will be disagreement about the remainder.

But, it may be said, the remainder is inessential. But what are the criteria of inessentiality ? It will be impossible to get the best minds (*mahājana*) of all the great religions to describe *all* the remainder as inessential. But if so, what is the point of the talk about 'fundamental unity' ?

In any case, the central truths propounded by early Islam and by the Theravada respectively share nothing significant in common.[8] It is true that there are resemblances between Sufism and certain aspects of the Mahayana. But this is not to the point, for if the best minds of the main stream of Muslim orthodoxy and of the Theravada cannot agree upon a substantial propositional nucleus, what are the defenders of fundamental unity to say ? Are they to say that Buddhaghosa misunderstood the inner truth of Buddhism ? Such an appeal to an 'esoteric' truth secretly going back to the founders of the great religions, who have allegedly been grossly misunderstood by a great mass of their followers, scarcely recommends itself to the serious historical investigator.[9]

Further, from the point of view of bringing actual unity of purpose among the great religions, such an attempt to sponsor an esoteric doctrine will fail. Does it help to tell Christians that the 'real meaning of their faith has eluded the great figures of the Christian tradition, or to tell the Theravadin that, despite the spiritual traditions and practices of the Sangha in Ceylon, Burma and elsewhere, the Buddha *really* taught belief in an eternal Self ? Even if this latter could be established, we are still left with the problem of the religious experience of countless Buddhists in the Lesser Vehicle.

Yet the upholders of fundamental unity may still be dissatisfied : for, they will say, the ultimate truth is inexpressible. But the difficulty about this belief is that if it be taken in its obvious sense, then the inexpressible truth cannot be connected with any one expression of revelation rather than any other, nor with all of them taken together (supposing that they are compatible) rather than with atheism or anti-religion. The reason why the illusion exists that there can be such a connection between the inexpressible and doctrines is that historically metaphysical irrationalism has often taken the form of the transcending of religious positions. For instance, *śūnyatā* has the flavour of Buddhist *dhyāna* about it ; Kierkegaard's metaphysical despair has the tang of a man who cannot worship enough. This is not surprising, for it is precisely this kind of *dialectical* ineffability which characterizes religious discourse—we go beyond the words of 'worship, for instance, but our silence only has significance in that context, in the context of *the words which we have previously uttered*. Thus if the appeal to ineffability is taken in its proper religious context, it is itself only intelligible given that certain propositions are already thought to be true. But the supposition that the highest truth is completely ineffable spells disaster for the very notion of truth. Silence itself can neither be true nor false. And silence is compatible with all propositions whatsoever. Thus the fundamental unity of religions cannot be defended by saying that the ultimate truth is completely ineffable.

A subtler way of synthesizing religious revelations is by saying that there are different levels of truth. At one level, say, the truth is that there is a personal Creator ; but at another level, the truth is that there is an impersonal Absolute. But though this way has been used, it does not solve our problems. For Radhakrishnan[10], one level is higher; for Zaehner[11] another. For Shankara one, for Ramanuja another. We thus have on our hands a priority decision[12] between different types of doctrine, which themselves reflect different patterns of religious or spiritual experience.

It is therefore of the utmost importance to distinguish between an interpretation of other religions or doctrinal systems from the point of view of one's own (which is comparatively easy to do) and looking at them from a 'neutral' and sympathetic point of view. The thesis of fund amental unity nearly always turns out to be a version of the former process, but buys unity at the expense of misinterpreting other faiths when these are considered *from their own point of view.*

The richness and variety of patterns of religious experience and practice must be kept in view. The idea of fundamental unity is an attempt to conceal this richness and to impose upon it a spurious uniformity.

It remains to ask why the idea is so appealing. Why should there be thought to be a single thread running through all faiths ? Part of the reason is that people are used to an outmoded form of definition. Because both Buddhism and Islam are commonly called religions[13] it is thought that they must have some doctrine in common. But, as Wittgenstein has already shown[14], the use of the same word for various things is often based upon family resemblance. A may be like B, B like C, C like D, but there may be no direct and substantial resemblance between A and D. But a more important reason for the thesis of fundamental unity is this. Since experience plays such a central role in religion, and since also it is often (and in a way rightly) defended as being intuitive, it is thought that it enhances the claim of religious experience to be veridical if it everywhere testifies to the same truth.

Thus to some degree the idea is based upon a fear : a fear that otherwise the truth-telling qualities of prophetic and mystical experience may crumble away. And yet for all that Muhammad and the Buddha can scarcely be directly compared ; and there is a wide divergence in many ways between Isaiah and Meister Eckhart. It is both clear-headed and courageous to recognize different patterns of religious experience, and it is to the credit of some of the greatest Indian theologians and philosophers that they have done so. But, as I say, there still remains the problem of the 'priority' of these different patterns, and this problem cannot simply be solved by dogmatic assertion that one or other represents the higher truth.

Our conclusion, then, is that metaphysical irrationalism as a defence of religion cannot be bolstered by the appeal to fundamental unity. In effect irrationalism involves an appeal to revelation : this appeal must fail if there are more than one revelation, for we still need reasons for deciding between revelations. Nor can we get round this by holding that somehow or other all revelations implicitly say exactly the same thing.

IV

Metaphysical Irrationalism and Natural Theology

There is a further objection to metaphysical irrationalism which we have not so far noticed. Although it has the virtue of stripping away over-intellectualism in religion, it nevertheless leaves us in the dark about religious experience, for the following reason. If someone claims to have an experience of God, he is necessarily interpreting that experience in some degree. In a theistic context he is not merely saying that he has had an experience of a certain sort, but he is further claiming that this experience is directly linked with the Creator of the cosmos. Now an unknown X is by no means necessarily the Creator of the cosmos, nor even a Being (it might, like *nirvāṇa*, be more like a state than a substance). Metaphysical irrationalism cannot help us in linking the experience of the individual to anything beyond the experience. Admittedly the experience itself may in some sense carry with it the intuition that here something transcendent is being met with. Nevertheless, men wish to know whether this transcendent entity or state has anything to do with the Ground of the cosmos, or whether the experience of the transcendent brings a cessation of rebirth. Both these questions involve metaphysical, and even empirical, argument if they are to be answered. It follows that in the widest sense of 'natural theology' (where this is evacuated of its theistic overtones), natural theology is necessary, if the traditional kind of religious belief is to be vindicated.

Of course, we may settle for something less, namely the view which I have elsewhere[15] called 'psychological pragmatism'. This is a view favoured by some Westerners who have fallen in love with Zen : what we want from religion or a way of life is experience of a certain kind, and never mind (once you have gained *satori* or whatever kind of 'illumination' is being sought) whether it reveals the truth or not. The point of religious practice reduces to the function of engineering such ineffable states of mind. Indeed, there is a close connexion between ineffabilism and psychological pragmatism. Once you adopt this position, then any conflict between empiricism and religion vanishes, anti-metaphysics is to be welcomed, and natural theology is of no interest whatsoever.

Nevertheless, psychological pragmatism is not so much a version of traditional religion (it is not even an adequate interpretation of Zen : for Western Zen and Zen are not, I suspect, the same things at all), as a new faith. No philosopher can object in principle to such a new faith. But it is his duty to point out that it is not a traditional position in new dress. Indeed, if it pretends to be, it is masquerading. All I am concerned with in the present article is the relation between certain modern ideas and religion as it has traditionally been understood, namely as a way of life presupposing certain truths about the nature of the cosmos. Since psychological pragmatism does not presuppose anything about the nature of the cosmos, it is not, in this sense, a religion. Some form, then, of natural theology is necessary if religion is to be defended. At the same time, of course, we can learn from metaphysical irrationalism the danger of thinking of religion exclusively in intellectual terms. Metaphysics of some sort is needed to vindicate the truth-claims of religious experience; but it is parasitical upon the latter in so far as without living experience religion is pointless and empty.

Both in regard to metaphysics and religious experience itself contemporary empiricism presents an important challenge.

V

Empiricism and Religious Experience

The challenge of empiricism in this context can be summed up as follows. Truths about matters of fact must be established upon the basis of experience. They must be testable by experience, and the most fruitful way of thinking about such testing is by using the concept of *falsification*. A statement is factually significant if and only if it can in principle be falsified. This provides a good criterion for evaluating scientific theories, or rather for deciding which of them genuinely are scientific theories. Now it so happens that religious truths, even if they may be claimed to be based in some sense upon experience, are such that there is no way of falsifying them in principle: we cannot conceive any empirical test which would do this, or even a mystical experience which would do this. Consequently, religious statements are not factually significant.

The matter can be put in a more informal way by saying : whereas scientific method does yield agreement, since scientists agree on how to agree, the same cannot be said about religious teachings. Look at the world (our empiricist can say) and see how the Buddha says one thing, Christ another, Ramanuja another. Look how the adherents of different faiths claim to have a view of the ultimate truth, and yet see how the views differ ! How can there be truth, when there is no methodology ? How can there be conclusions when there are no rules of inference ?

The answer to this challenge is perhaps hard to come by. But one thing is clear : the answer must necessarily involve saying 'Different realms of discourse have different methodologies'. It is not sufficient for the pious man to say : I know the truth of religion in my bones, I know it by direct illumination (or what you will). It must be shown that it is reasonable to think that religious truth is not the same sort of thing as scientific truth; and it must be further shown what the rules of religious argument are. (I know this sounds sophisticated and not at all what we expect of missionaries and the like : this is partly the fault of the missionaries, and partly the result of the fact that nature has endowed different men with different capacities—but intellectuals are necessarily sophisticated, and they also necessarily have a place in the religious community). It follows from the nature of the challenge and from the nature of the kind of answer which I have foreshadowed that a necessary element in contemporary religious philosophy must be analysis—or, as it is sometimes called, linguistic analysis.

On the other issue, namely the anti-metaphysical streak of modern empiricism, similar remarks apply, in that arguments as to whether there is a Ground of the cosmos are partly criticized on like grounds (namely, that there is no way of testing conclusions empirically). Here again we are landed with methodological problems.

Regarding the analysis of doctrines and the rules of inference in religion, it is perhaps superfluous to add that this necessarily involves the comparative study of religions. It is a very considerable weakness of contemporary philosophy of religion in the West that the arguments so commonly centre upon the Christian religion alone. Perhaps there is something typically British about this, for there is a like neglect of French, German and other Continental philosophy, and this reflects the common British feeling that once you cross the Channel you are among very strange and ignorant people, whose chief peculiarity is that they are liable not to know English! However, one must add a *caveat* about the comparative study of religions. It is a study which once fell into bad odour, for the comparisons tend to be odious, and so people searched for a new name, such as the 'history of religions'. But of course the philosopher, when he contemplates religious facts, is not merely interested in history, but in central likenesses and differences, so that the old name still has a virtue, in bringing this important aspect of religious studies out into the open.

VI

Conclusion

I have argued that the challenge of anti-metaphysical empiricism is an important one, and that the irrationalistic defence of religion fails. I have further argued that the answer to the challenge would necessarily involve us in the analysis of religious concepts and rules of inference, and that this in turn means that the philosopher must engage in the comparative study of religion. These conclusions have, as a by-product, the pleasant implication that Eastern and Western philosophers will, in regard to an important theme, be brought closer together.

NOTES

[1] Part of the paper was read to the philosophers at Banaras Hindu University in August 1960 and at Bombay University in the following month. I am most grateful for the criticisms and friendliness of these two audiences.

[2] Consider, for instance, the influential volume *New Essays in Philosophical Theology*, ed. A. Flew & A. MacIntyre (1955).

[3] I am, of course, much indebted to Professor Murti's classic *The Central Philosophy of Buddhism* (1953).

[4] *The Limits of Religious Thought* (1858).

[5] See, for instance, Thomas McPherson's "Religion as the Inexpressible" in the Flew & MacIntyre volume (see n.2).

[6] I have in mind the work of Guénon, and those influenced by him. See his *Introduction to Study of the Hindu Doctrines* (1945).

[7] This is true even in spite of analyses such as are given by some modern Christian theologians, in which it is claimed that revelation is not a set of propositions but God's self-disclosure. For already in using the term 'God's self-disclosure' we are describing and interpreting the event. See John Baillie, *The Idea of Revelation in Recent Thought* (1956).

[8] See my "Numen, Nirvana and the Definition of Religion", Church Quarterly Review, January 1959.

[9] Partly because it would mean that the techniques of historical investigation would have so drastically to be revised that the historian would be involved in a kind of contradiction.

[10] See, for instance, his *The Hindu View of Life* (1949).

[11] See his *At Sundry Times* (1958).

[12] See ch. V of my *Reasons and Faiths* (1958).

[13] For the question of the definition of religion, see the article referred to in n. 8 above.

[14] In *Philosophical Investigations* (1953).

[15] In "Yoga in the Suburbs", *Listener*, 12 January 1961.

CHAPTER 4

Understanding Religious Experience

The three terms in the phrase 'understanding religious experience' contain ambiguities. Let us look first at the concept of understanding.

In this context, it sometimes seems as if understanding is 'all-or-nothing'. This is perhaps because sometimes philosophers concentrate upon possible unintelligibility, and see intelligibility as the straight alternative. But in fact understanding is a matter of degree. Unintelligibility is the limiting case. (If you like, it is a special form of intelligibility as rest is of motion.) So when we explore how it is that we may understand someone else's religious experience, it will be a matter of what degree of understanding can be obtained and in what circumstances. This simple observation may already suggest that the thesis that you need to belong to religious tradition T in order to understand it has an air of unreality. It is rare that a binary theory applies properly to a continuum.

There is a set of distinctions which is also important for understanding understanding. There are two different forms of intelligibility we need to contemplate here. Thus first there is what may be called existential understanding, namely understanding what a given experience is like. Thus a person who has been tortured with electric shocks can be said to know what that experience is like. I have never undergone this experience, so my understanding of what it is like is not very good, though of course I can imagine. Second, there is understanding the explanation of something. Thus we might be uncertain as to how we should understand Paul's conversion. Was it due to an inner psychological crisis of some kind? Was it really Jesus speaking to him? This kind of understanding may be called *theoretical* understanding. Since there are different sorts of theories which may or may not be overlapping or compatible, there are in effect different species of theoretical understanding. As for compatibility and overlap, it could be that the psychological and theological accounts of Paul's conversion can be held together. One of the vital questions concerning religious experience is whether it is possible to have any adequate theoretical understanding without existential understanding. To such matters I shall return.

Understanding Religious Experience   11

Next we may briefly contemplate the question of what counts as a religious experience. It is, I think, useful to distinguish between religion and religions, or to put it another way between religion and a religion. This is similar to the distinction between sport and sports. A religion is a given tradition of a religious kind, and so religious experience is often picked out by considering crucial experiences in the lives of those who belong to such traditions. But it ought to be noted that there is quite a lot of evidence about experiences which hit people out of the blue, even though they do not belong to a given tradition. In the case of conversions, often the experiences occur at the frontier between non-belonging and belonging to a given tradition. So the first conclusion we can draw is that, though we should start with traditions in pinning down religious experience, we should not confine religious experience to this area. Another observation to be made is that, though we can pick out certain traditions as being religious, there are other traditions or movements which may not normally be called religious but which nevertheless have formal characteristics making them analogous at least to religions, and which represent similar human feelings, impulses, and thoughts. Thus I have argued in my book *Mao*[1] that Maoism has an analogy to the traditional religions of China, however much it may also differ in content.

Briefly, the argument is as follows. If a religion typically contains various aspects or dimensions as I have elsewhere named them,[2] viz. doctrine, myth, ethical teaching, ritual, experience, and social institutionalization, then Maoism is analogous to a religion. It has doctrines, namely Marxism as mediated by Mao; myth, such as the story of the Long March and the dialectic of history; ethics, namely its Red puritanism and evaluation of different elements in human society; the rituals of rallies and little red book-waving; experiences of conversion and exaltation; and the institutions of party and cadres. Further, the anarchist elements in Mao's thought echo Taoist themes, and Mao's anti-Confucianism replaced the Confucian ethic with a new mode of education. Marxist eschatology draws on sentiments earlier expressed in Buddhist devotionalism. Hence it is unwise to draw a sharp boundary between religion and ideological system, and consequently religion should not be narrowly defined.

Third, it may be noted that there are dramatic events in human life which have religious significance. Thus facing death is sometimes a profound and awe-inspiring experience, which naturally raises questions about human destiny and the meaning of life, and which therefore marches upon religious concerns. We may

12   *Mysticism and Philosophical Analysis*

call these dramatic experiences. Religious experiences of the tradition-oriented kind may also indeed be dramatic, but conventionally let us simply refer to these as religious experiences.

Fourth, there are experiences which may have religious significance, but which are not *necessarily* religious in character. Thus if I am a pious Christian I may think of my daily work as done to the glory of God, but that work does not need to be seen in this way. I have elsewhere referred to this phenomenon as a matter of superimposition. Thus I have elsewhere[3] sketched the following picture of the relationship between morality and religion. While injunctions such as 'It is wrong to steal' can exist and be justified independently of religious belief, they are frequently interpreted as both ethical and religious. Thus Brother Lawrence in *The Practice of the Presence of God* depicts everyday duties as modes of worshipping God. (Naturally there are some specifically religious duties which would not occur in a 'secular' morality, such as the injunction to keep the Sabbath holy.) To use different language, daily activities seen in the light of religious commitment involve *interpreted* experiences. This is, of course, a pregnant sense of 'interpreted'. To sum up so far: there can be existential and/or theoretical understanding (of different degrees) of religious, dramatic, and/or interpreted experiences, which crop up inside or outside religious and analogous traditions.

To some issues arising from these distinctions I shall come back, but meanwhile let us contemplate 'experience'. It seems to be rather specially used in the context of religion. We can see this by indulging in a little experiment. Consider some typical uses of the term 'experience' and then see what happens if we slip in 'religious' before it. Contemplate the following locutions:

1. 'He is a person of wide experience.' Compare: 'He is a person of wide religious experience.' Still, we probably are not interested in this sense of the term anyway, viz. the sense in which it has to do with having lived with a problem, various circumstances, etc.

2. 'Parachute-jumping is an interesting experience': what sort of event would need to be the subject of the sentence if we were to slip in 'religious'? In fact, the term 'experience' here often seems just to be a way of bringing out the existential aspect of an outer event or circumstance.

3. 'My experience of Henry is that he is unpredictable.' This at first might seem to be like 'my experience of God'. But slipping in 'religious' is somewhat incongruous, even if we substituted God for Henry.

It seems that when writers speak of religious experience they use it in a special sense, meaning something like a vision or an intuition. Mystical unions, prophetic visions, psychic ascents to heaven, ecstasies, auditions, intoxications – it is such things that typically get bracketed as religious experiences, and a subclass of these is mystical. And here we come to another tricky term.

I consider that it is clearest if we use the term 'mysticism' and its relatives to refer to those inner visions and practices which are contemplative. Briefly, yoga is a typical kind of mysticism, for it is a certain method or group of methods concerned with contemplation, yielding what is taken to be a fundamental insight into the nature of reality. Again, such persons as Teresa of Avila, Eckhart, Buddhaghosa, Shankara, and Rumi are mystics, for the centre of their religious life was inner contemplation. This does not exclude outer visions, for a mystic may have more than mystical experiences, and he may interpret his own quest in terms of non-contemplative religion also. For example, he may interpret his quest as part of worship which would then constitute another layer of superimposition. For though there are forms of contemplation, for instance those found in Theravāda Buddhism, which are not seen in relation to the worship of God, it is possible to interpret the yogic quest this way, just as we can also see washing dishes as a form of service to God. Also, I think it is a fair observation to make that the numinous experience so brilliantly described in Otto's *The Idea of the Holy* has an outer and thunderous quality not characteristic of the cloud of unknowing within. For this reason, it is best to draw a rough distinction between numinous and mystical experience.

But it has sometimes been fashionable among writers to count the 'panenhenic' Wordsworthian experiences of a mysterious harmony with nature as being mystical. I would rather place them near the numinous type. In any case, we are still in the early stages of any kind of refined classification of the varieties of religious experience, and unfortunately some writers, notably Zaehner, have mixed up classification problems with theological judgements. My own strictures[4] on this muddle, which are now admirably reinforced by the critique of Zaehner and others found in Fritz Staal's recent *Exploring Mysticism*,[5] can be summed up briefly as follows.

Zaehner is keen to show that there is a vital distinction between theistic and monistic mysticism (such a distinction has, of course, certain possible apologetic uses). But under the latter head he includes Sānkhya-Yoga, Advaita Vedānta, Buddhist mysticism – in short systems respectively involving many souls but no union with God; one Soul or Self identical with the Divine; and no souls at all. Mind you, Zaehner strives to get souls back into Buddhism, and this in my view involves a distortion of the relevant texts as well as contradicting the overwhelming bulk of Buddhist testimony. But if so many varieties of doctrinal milieu and interpretation of the mystical fall under the monistic bracket is it not artificial? What if I put first what I have bought into two baskets: in the one I put grapes, and in the other persimmons, pineapples, and peas, on the ground that the second group are not used to make wine. I have one basis for sorting, but not a basis which points to serious resemblances in other respects. The distinction between Advaita and theism may be less than the distinction between Advaita and Theravāda Buddhism (roughly, I believe it *is* less). So Zaehner should not have two but many baskets – or alternatively one, ascribing differences of description to doctrinal interpretation.

It may perchance be replied that such criticism relies upon this distinction between actual experience and doctrinal interpretation – and such a clear distinction cannot be drawn, for experiences are always in some degree interpreted: they as it were contain inter- pretation within them. No perception can be quite neutral. To this I would reply that there are differing degrees of interpretation, and the distinction being made is heuristically useful in providing a directive to be as phenomenological as possible about the exper- iences being reported. A way of illustrating the point is as follows. If I see a man in a white cassock driving past in a black chauffeur- assisted car, I should not jump to the conclusion that it is the Pope. It may well be the Pope (and to understand this description I have to know quite a bit about Christian institutions): but what I can report is first of all the 'lesser' description. Similarly, one needs to be on one's guard in evaluating mystics' reports, since the existen- tial impact and sacred context of the inner visions can naturally lead to wider claims for them than the phenomenology might war- rant. Now it still might be argued that such a deflationary method may prove misleading. For if I describe a goal being scored at football simply as a round piece of leather whizzing into a net slung from wooden posts, I am both literally correct and misleading. However, what is reasonably well established is that there are similarities in differing cultures between mystical reports, while at the same time there are rather divergent doctrinal claims made in the relevant traditions. It is on this basis, partly empirical, that one has reason to keep the heuristic model. If Siberians think of wolves as grey spirits of the dead and if Italians think of them as dangerous animals, reports from both quarters would reasonably raise the question of whether it is the same sort of being that is being spoken of. It is when this is established that we can go on to consider how far further attitudes to wolves are to be justified.

There is of course an important corollary of these remarks, and I mention it only because, though obvious, it is frequently ignored in philosophical practice. It is this: that philosophizing must rest here upon a reasonable knowledge of the empirical facts concerning religion and religions. The number of varieties of religious experience is largely an empirical question, though as in other inquiries there are conceptual issues too. There are thus severe limitations upon the philosophical discussion of mysticism in the abstract. The comparative study of religion thus becomes an indispensable basis of the philosophy of religion. (Naturally there are some problems where this is less directly true: as with the classical discussion of the problem of evil.)

I now turn, in view of the distinctions I have rather simply made, to certain problems which appear to arise in the exploration of mystical and more broadly religious experience. First, let us consider what limitations may exist in regard to existential understanding. Is it necessary to have a given type of religious experience in order to understand what it is like? Well, such a question has to be re-framed in view of our first point, about the degree-character of understanding. The question perhaps can be reshaped: Could one have an adequate understanding of a type of religious experience if one had never had it? Otto seemed to go far in his negative answer to this question. But it obviously spawns another: adequate for what? In the context of philosophy, the answer to this question relates to theoretical understanding. We want to know enough about religious experience to discuss intelligently theories of their genesis and validity – theories which are necessarily entangled with each other.

One criterion of adequacy here is: Do we have enough understanding of what the experiences are like to be reasonably persuaded that experiences E, F, G, and so on from different contexts are pretty similar? For if they are, then some conclusions may follow about genesis and validity. Thus if one culture has quite different family arrangements from another, but similar numinosities, then psychoanalytic accounts of genesis which relate to early childhood experience may need to be revised. And again if E

16   *Mysticism and Philosophical Analysis*

ahd F are rather similar and E occurs in the context of a possibly true religion, then thc religion in which F occurs is possibly not wholly false.

Given these reflections, we may now ask whether the diagnosis of such similarities relies in part upon existential understanding. It is perhaps theoretically possible that one might get by without an inkling of what the experiences are like, for I suppose the reports of different Martians, if available to us, concerning some type of experience which we simply do not have because we are built so very differently, might constitute some evidence of similarity. But it would surely be easy in such circumstances to be thoroughly misled – as an ignorant man might think that a person shouting 'Love' at tennis had amorous thoughts. In any case, mystics, prophets, and shamans are not Martians, and it would be surprising if we had no inkling of their sensations. For it often happens that there are analogies in experience.

This is perhaps brought out, ironically, by Otto's *The Idea of the Holy*. For Otto, thc numinous experience is *sui generis*: but in fact by skilful use of analogies he brings out the flavour of the *mysterium tremendum et fascinans*. Nor was Oppenheim wrong to call his book on the nuclear bomb *The Light of a Thousand Suns*, for the theophany of Krishna/Vishnu in the Gita is like a spiritual atomic explosion.

In so far as we use our imagination negatively also to understand certain experiences, there is a method, as it were, of visualizing contemplative experiences. Thus the emptying of the mind of mental images and discursive thoughts can be imagined, and I use this technique in trying to explicate the stages of *jhāna* in Theravāda Buddhism, in my *Reasons and Faiths* (1958). The meditative exercises are, fortunately, described in quite a lot of detail, and this makes the process of visualization easier. Thus the various levels of consciousness can be imagined much as one might be able to imagine what it is like to be weightless even though one has not experienced the state. I use the term 'imagined' here, despite its paradoxical air – the imagination produces, so to speak, a blank picture.

Still, there is no reason in principle why it should not be possible for the philosophical evaluator of mystical experience to go in for spiritual practices himself. This point is made with some force by Fritz Staal, in his afore-mentioned *Exploring Mysticism*. It might be objected that the foretaste of the beatific vision or whatever is a gift from God and not to be induced by human effort. But we climb mountains which we do not make ourselves. And the fact that something is a divine gift should not lead to human paralysis. The account in terms of grace may simply be superimposed upon an account in terms of human effort (the effort itself is a gift of God!).

A somewhat different objection might be this – that it is impossible to imagine what most mystical experiences are like since so frequently, perhaps universally, mystics refer to their experiences as ineffable, or at any rate to the 'object' of their experiences as ineffable. There is indeed a whole battery of expressions liable to occur in this context – such as 'indescribable', 'inexpressible', 'unspeakable', 'indefinable', 'unutterable', 'incomprehensible', and so on. Relatedly it is not surprising that the author of a famous account should refer to a cloud of *unknowing*. However, one should not assume that such expressions are to be taken as quite excluding describability. This is so for several reasons.

First, there is about them in any event an ambiguity. To say that God is incomprehensible may be to say not that he is utterly incomprehensible but that he is not *totally* comprehensible. There would seem to be a contradiction in saying he is utterly incomprehensible – thus nothing could be known about him including anything that might form a basis for referring to him as God.[6] Perhaps the Mādhyamika account of the Void (and so of nirvāṇa) is that nothing can be said about it whatsòever, but there have been severe difficulties about sticking to the corollary of this 'account', namely that the Mādhyamika does not have a position but only dialectically knocks down all theories, thus eliminating all apparent alternatives to a golden silence. I have argued against the consistency of this in *The Yogi and the Devotee*,[7] with the further point that a similar western view, that of Dean Mansel, also suffers from self-contradiction. T. R. Miles's 'silence qualified by parables' also may fall into the same sort of trouble.[8] The argument regarding Nāgārjuna, Mansel, and Miles is basically as follows: If we say that the religious ultimate, whether this be *śūnya* (Void) or God, is indescribable (and/or incomprehensible, etc.) and mean this literally and rigorously, then how can either the Buddha or Christ be specially connected with it? For if it is just an X then everything and nothing bears its imprint equally. Thus as a position it is empty, and cannot hope to explicate the tradition which it is used to illuminate. And if it could it could exclude no other tradition, and all religions would become equally valid including those whose positions are attacked, e.g. in the Mādhyamika, dialectically. In brief it is one thing to say X is incomprehensible, indescribable, etc., in that there is something about it which transcends description, comprehension, etc., and another thing to say that it totally eludes any sort of human grasp.

Second, we should notice the performative aspect of the string of expressions in question. Consider the following locutions: 'This news is indescribably wonderful'; 'These are the unspeakable gifts of God'; 'I simply cannot tell you how grateful I am'. In the last of these, I am actually expressing my gratitude by saying how I cannot do it! The point is: I cannot sufficiently express it by mere words, but I can show through words how my gratitude transcends the usual courtesies and formulations. There is nothing mysterious here (beyond the whole mystery of feelings and their outer manifestations); and if it is frequent to advert in religion to the unutterable this is at least partly because powerful and existential feelings come into play, and joys thought greater than the more usual earthly ones. Hence the string of expressions in question are used in a context of what may be dubbed 'performative transcendence', namely performatively using words to sketch expression beyond their conventional limits. Performative transcendence is, as I have indicated, by no means at all confined to religious contexts.

All this may be reinforced by reflecting that religion (like swearing, humour, and courtesy) fights a running battle against debasement of the currency. Repetition of words in sacred contexts may enhance their numinosity, as with the formulae of solemn liturgies; but repetition in sermons and hymns and radio broadcasts can make words lose their existential edge, their force. We need slang as a means of re-supplying vividness to our expressive language; and the indescribability of God is a reminder that likewise creativity is required in maintaining and reinforcing the means of expressing the wonder and depth of God and Brahman.

There are two further ways at least in which religious experience can be indescribable (and so on). One has to do with problems of adequacy, as above discussed; and is perhaps simply an extension of the idea of performative transcendence. It could be that for certain purposes no description is *adequate*. To this I return in a moment. The second way is just that in which *every* experience in some sense eludes description: as it were, the ocean of nuances in actual life is infinite or at least indefinitely explorable, and we can always find new things to say and subtleties to add. Even if a pre-Raphaelite can get all the details in, his 'King Cophetua and the Beggar Maid' would suffer a sea-change if Gauguin were to get at them, or Braque. But let us return to the extension of performative transcendence.

Regarding *adequacy* of descriptive utterance having a strong performative aspect, one may consider the various functions the relevant utterances may be expected to fulfil. Leaving aside attempts, for the moment, to further the scientific understanding of religion, consider the following functions – to praise God, to convert others, to arouse in others similar feelings and/or insights, to express joy. Such functions can, quite clearly, overlap. As for worship and praise – no words will do it adequately in that the meaning of God's infinity is that he is infinitely to be praised. As for conveying feelings and/or insights – the problem is that words alone cannot quite do it: something beyond them has to be there (the correct disposition of the hearer, the activity of the Holy Spirit, or whatever).

To sum up this part of the discussion: the notion of the inexpressibility of religious experience has various roots, and these centre upon forms of performative transcendence and criteria of adequacy. It is incorrect to conclude either that ineffability is a unique characteristic of religious experience or that it is absolute (for herein lies contradiction).

A further problem may be thought to arise in relation to what I have called performative transcendence. It may be said that the 'object' of religious experience is itself transcendent and so a discussion which assimilates it to 'worldly' objects of experience is misleading. Performative transcendence, or rather the need for it, really arises because of ontological transcendence. Now it would be tedious here to analyse the concept of transcendence, e.g. the transcendence of God, and in any case I have done this elsewhere in an article on 'Myth and Transcendence'.[9] Briefly I considered there divine transcendence to mean that God is non-spatial, that God and the cosmos are non-identical, and that the cosmos is pictured as a screen concealing and secretly also containing the holy God – a picture connected with religious practice and the sense of the numinous. First, not all objects of religious experience are transcendent in the sense of which a sole God is – the monotheos, so to say. For the sun-worshipper will perchance feel awe at the glorious deity, who is admittedly for him more than a red ball, a star. The monotheos's outer manifestation is the cosmos, by contrast. Second, one aspect of the idea of God's transcendence is in any case performative transcendence. Third, it does not follow that because God is conceived as distinct from the cosmos he cannot be as-

20   *Mysticism and Philosophical Analysis*

similated in some degree to it and conversely; however we may regard the source of knowledge about God there will exist an *analogia*, whether *entis* or *gratiae* or *experientiae*, or all three, etc. If not, we relapse into speechlessness, and in the absolutely unutterable there is nothing worth discussing. Consequently, God lies, as it were, along the spectrum of our experiences, and his transcendence cannot absolutely hide him away. Since anything human can be investigated and scientifically explored, so to the extent that God and nirvāṇa may appear in human experience they too can be explored, and the goal of a greater understanding of religious experience need not elude us.

There is one final issue I would like to explore concerning this search for understanding religious experience. It might be that ultimately the only *real* understanding must depend upon a theory which would incorporate within it some judgement or otherwise on the *validity* of religious experience. Genesis may be vital for true understanding. Since supposedly scientific theories, e.g. projectionist ones such as those of Freud and Marx, are liable to be in conflict with theologies, and since the evaluation of theologies is partly a matter of faith, it could therefore be held that in some manner understanding religious experience depends upon commitment. We are not in an area of 'neutral' investigation. There may be truth in this; but I would be disinclined to proclaim such a truth too loudly. For what is often forgotten is that we have a long and delicate path to pick before we are really in a position to make an evaluation; and that path is phenomenological. It means that we must be able to disentangle varieties of religious experience, have a nose for degrees of interpretation in their descriptions, see what they mean existentially, place them in their living contexts and so on. We are still in a very early stage of scientific and human inquiry along these lines, and that inquiry is ill-served if we speed too hastily into questions of theology and evaluation.

NOTES

1 Ninian Smart, *Mao*. London, 1974.
2 Ninian Smart, *The Religious Experience of Mankind* (London, 1969), ch. 1.
3 Ninian Smart, 'Gods, Bliss and Morality' in I. T. Ramsey, ed., *Christian Ethics and Contemporary Philosophy*. London, 1966.

Understanding Religious Experience 21

4 Ninian Smart, 'Interpretation and Mystical Experience' in *Religious Studies*, vol. I, No. 1 (1965).

5 Fritz Staal, *Exploring Mysticism*. London, 1975.

6 See further on this Steven Katz 'Logic and Language of Mystery' in S. Sykes and J. Clayton, eds., *Christ, Faith and History*. Cambridge, 1972.

7 Ninian Smart, *The Yogi and the Devotee*. London, 1968.

8 See T. R. Miles, *Religion and the Scientific Outlook*. London, 1959.

9 See Ninian Smart, 'Myth and Transcendence' in *The Monist*, vol. 50, No. 4 (October 1966).

NINIAN SMART, M.A., B.Phil. (Oxon), D.H.L. (Loyola). Professor Smart is the author of numerous publications, among which the most important are: *Reasons and Faiths* (1958); *Philosophers and Religious Truth* (1964); *Doctrine and Argument in Indian Philosophy* (1964); *The Religious Experience of Mankind* (1976²); *The Concept of Worship* (1972); *The Phenomenon of Religion* (1973). He has also published several dozen articles and reviews in such leading philosophical and religious journals as *Mind, Philosophical Quarterly, Religion, Religious Studies*, and *Philosophy*. He was Professor of Theology at the University of Birmingham from 1961 to 1967 and then became the first Professor and Chairman of the Department of Religious Studies at the University of Lancaster, England, a post he held from 1967 to 1975. He has also been a visiting Professor at Princeton, University of Wisconsin, and Benares Hindu University. At present he holds two chairs, one at the University of Lancaster and the other at the University of California at Santa Barbara, spending half a year at each.

III

MYSTICAL EXPERIENCE

CHAPTER 5

Interpretation and Mystical Experience

Summary. Professor R. C. Zaehner's distinction between panenhenic, monistic and theistic mysticism will be examined. It will be argued that there is no necessary reason to suppose that the latter two types involve different sorts of experience: the difference lies rather in the way the experience is interpreted. Likewise it will be argued that the Theravādin experience of nirvana, which is interpreted neither in a monistic nor in a theistic sense, may well be identical substantially with the foregoing two types. All this raises important methodological problems, in relation to the contrast between experience and interpretation. The fact that mysticism is substantially the same in different cultures and religions does not, however, entail that there is a 'perennial philosophy' common to mystics. Their doctrines are determined partly by factors other than mystical experience itself.

I. THE MEANING OF 'MYSTICISM'

Unfortunately the term 'mysticism' and its relations ('mystical', etc.) are used by different people in different senses. For the purposes of this article I shall treat mysticism as primarily consisting in an interior or introvertive quest, culminating in certain interior experiences which are not described in terms of sense-experience or of mental images, etc. But such an account needs supplementation in two directions: first, examples of people who typify the mystical life should be given, and second, mysticism should be distinguished from that which is *not* (on this usage) mysticism.

First, then, I would propose that the following folk typify the mystical life: St John of the Cross, Tauler, Eckhart, al-Hallāj, Shankara, the Buddha, Lao-Tzu (if he existed!), and many yogis.

Secondly, mysticism is *not* prophetism, and can be distinguished from devotionalism or *bhakti* religion (though mysticism often intermingles with these forms of religious life and experience). I would propose that the following are *not* mystics in the relevant sense in which the Buddha and the others *are* mystics: Isaiah, Jeremiah, Muhammad, Rāmānuja, Nichiren and Calvin.

Needless, perhaps, to say, such expressions as the 'mystical body of Christ' have no necessary connection with mysticism in the proposed sense. It is unfortunate that a word which etymologically means sacramentalism has come to be used in a different sense. Since, however, 'mysticism' now is most often used to refer to the mode of life and experience typified by men like St John of the Cross and Shankara, I shall use the term, though 'contemplation' and 'contemplative' can be less misleading.

Thus 'mysticism' will here be used to refer to the contemplative life and experience, as distinguished from prophetism, devotionalism and sacramentalism (though we must keep in mind the fact mentioned above—that prophetic and sacramental religion are often interwoven with that of mysticism).

II. PROFESSOR ZAEHNER'S ANALYSIS AND THEORY

In a number of works, Professor Zaehner has distinguished between three categories of mystical experience:

(1) Panenhenic or nature mysticism (as exemplified by Rimbaud, Jefferies and others).

(2) Monistic mysticism (as found in Advaita, Sāinkhya-Yoga, etc.).

(3) Theistic mysticism (as in the Christian tradition, the *Gītā*, etc.).

His distinction between (1) and the other two is correct and valuable. The sense of rapport with nature often comes to people in a striking and intimate way; but it is to be contrasted with the interior experience in which, as it were, a man plumbs the depths of his own soul. It is probable that Zen *satori* is to be equated with panenhenic experience, though Zen also makes use of the general pattern of Buddhist yoga which elsewhere culminates in an interior rather than a panenhenic type of experience.

But is Zaehner's distinction between (2) and (3) a valid one? He criticises those who believe that mysticism is everywhere the same—a belief sometimes held in conjunction with the neo-Vedantin thesis that behind the various forms of religion there is a higher truth realisable in contemplative experience and best expressed through the doctrine of a universal Self (or Ātman). On Zaehner's view, monistic mysticism is 'realising the eternal oneness of one's own soul' as contrasted with the 'mysticism of the love of God'.[1] The latter attainment is typical of Christian, Muslim and other theistic contemplation.

Zaehner believes in an eternal soul, as well as in God, and is thus able to claim that there is a real entity which the monistic mystic experiences, even if it is not the highest entity (which is God). In addition, he holds, or has held, that monistic mysticism can be explained through the doctrine of the Fall. Thus he is not merely concerned to analyse mysticism, but also to explain it through a (theological) theory. He writes as follows:

Assuming, as we are still encouraged to do, that man developed physically from the higher apes, we must interpret the creation of Adam as an original infusion of

_____
[1] *At Sundry Times*, p. 132.

the divine essence into what had previously been an anthropoid ape. Adam, then, would represent the union of the orders of nature and grace, the order of coming to be and passing away which is created from nothing by God, and the infused spirit of God. Adam, after he sinned, brought bodily death into the world, but did not and could not destroy his soul, because the soul was infused into him from God and therefore was itself divine. Though Adam may have repented, he was no longer able to take the supreme step of offering himself back completely and entirely to God, because he had lost contact with his source and could no longer find it again. Thus, tradition has it, at death his soul departed to Limbo, where, like all disinterested Yogins who have sought to separate their immortal souls from all that is transient and ungodlike, yet who cannot acknowledge God, it enjoyed the highest natural bliss, the soul's contemplation of itself as it issued from the hand of God and of all created things as they are in the sight of God . . . The proof, it seems to me, that I am not talking pure nonsense is in the complete difference of approach which separates the theistic from the monistic mystic. The latter achieves liberation entirely by his own efforts since there is no God apart from himself to help him or with whom he can be united.   In the case of the theistic mystic, on the other hand, it is always God who takes the first step, and it is God who works in the soul and makes it fit for union.[1]

Thus Zaehner not only distinguishes types of mysticism: he links his distinction to a theology of the Fall. Though it is not the main concern of this article to consider this theological theory, it may be useful to go into certain criticisms which can be levelled at it, since some of them are relevant to Zaehner's doctrine of types of mysticism.

III. THE THEORY EXAMINED

In linking his analysis of mysticism to a theory about the special creation of Adam and his Fall, Zaehner weakens his position, since his interpretation of the Adam story may be radically questioned. The doubts and objections which arise are, briefly, as follows:

(a) The Biblical narrative, which is the principal basis for people's belief in the existence of Adam, says nothing about anthropoid apes and nothing about an eternal soul as such. Still less does it make Adam out to be like a Yogin.

(b) Adam cannot have brought bodily death into the world, since the apes were not immortal. But let us assume that Adam was different, and was initially immortal, because of the divine essence infused into him. How does this imply that there was no bodily death for him? Does it mean that God did something to the bodily side of Adam, making the flesh and bones which Adam inherited from the apes into something mysteriously imperishable? It is not a likely story.

(c) Not all Christians would accept the theory of a substantial eternal soul. But in any case, it does not follow that this is what the monistic mystic realises in his inner contemplative experience. The Advaitin would believe that

---

[1] *Mysticism Sacred and Profane*, pp. 191–2.

he has realised the oneness of the Ātman with the divine being; while the adherent of Yoga would not. This is a big difference of interpretation, and if we were to take it at its face value we might be inclined to say that the Advaitin and the Yogin have attained different states. But do we have to take their claims at their face value? This raises important methodological issues.

Does the Advaitin make his claim simply on the basis of an inner contemplative experience? It is not so. The concept of Brahman as a divine Reality ultimately derives from an extension of the idea of the sacred Power implicit in pre-Upanishadic sacrificial ritual. The famous identification of Ātman with Brahman involves bringing together different strands of religious thought and life. It is not something yielded by contemplative experience alone, even though the latter is highly relevant to it.

Likewise, the theistic mystic, in thinking that he has attained a kind of union with God must already have the concept of God—as a personal Being, creator of the world, author of revelation, etc. His description of his experience, where this includes mention of God, is thus not derived *simply* from the nature of that experience. The mystic does not know that God is creator from a mere inspection of an interior state; rather he relates that inner state to beliefs which he already has.

Zaehner's theory, too, obviously includes data derived from sources other than those contained in mystical literature. In interpreting what happens to the Yogin he draws on certain elements in the Christian tradition. It therefore seems that the truth of his theory depends partly on the truth of Christianity (at least, negatively: if Christianity were false, Zaehner's theory would be false, though the falsity of his theory is compatible with the truth of Christianity, since the latter is not necessarily committed to beliefs about anthropoid apes and the like).

These points indicate that we must examine in more detail the methodology of the evaluation and interpretation of mystical experience.

IV. EXPERIENCE AND INTERPRETATION (AUTO- AND HETERO-)

That some distinction must be made between experience and interpretation is clear. For it is generally recognised, and certainly by Zaehner, that there are types of mystical experience cutting across different religions and theologies. That is to say, it is recognised that a mystic of one religion and some mystic of another faith can have what is substantially a similar experience. Thus as we have noted, both Christian and Muslim mystics come under Zaehner's category of theistic mysticism; while, for him, Advaitin and Yogin mysticism belong to the monistic category. But the interpretations within a type differ. We have seen a large doctrinal distinction between Avaita and Yoga. The latter believes in a plurality of eternal *purushas*, not in a single Ātman.

Consequently its account of liberation, and therefore of contemplative experience, differs from that of Advaita. Thus on Zaehner's own thesis it becomes very necessary to distinguish between experience and interpretation, when two experiences belong to the same class but have rather different modes of interpretation.

Nevertheless, the distinction between experience and interpretation is not clear-cut. The reason for this is that the concepts used in describing and explaining an experience vary in their degree of ramification. That is to say, where a concept occurs as part of a doctrinal scheme it gains its meaning in part from a range of doctrinal statements taken to be true. For example, the term 'God' in the Christian context gains part at least of its characteristic meaning from such doctrinal statements as: 'God created the universe', 'Jesus Christ is God', 'God has acted in history', etc.

Thus when Suso writes 'In this merging of itself in God the spirit passes away', he is describing a contemplative experience by means of the highly ramified concept *God*, the less ramified concept *spirit* and the still less ramified concept *pass away*. In order to understand the statement it is necessary to bear in mind the doctrinal ramifications contained in it. Thus it follows, for Suso as a Christian, that in this merging of itself in the Creator of the universe, the spirit passes away; and so on.

By contrast, some descriptions of mystical experience do not involve such wide ramifications. For instance 'When the spirit by the loss of its self-consciousness has in very truth established its abode in this glorious and dazzling obscurity'—here something of the nature of the experience is conveyed without any doctrine's being presupposed as true (except in so far as the concept *spirit* may involve some belief in an eternal element within man). This, then, is a relatively unramified description. Thus descriptions of mystical experience range from the highly ramified to those which have a very low degree of ramification.[1]

It is to be noted that ramifications may enter into the descriptions either because of the intentional nature of the experience or through reflection upon it. Thus a person brought up in a Christian environment and strenuously practising the Christian life may have a contemplative experience which he sees *as* a union with God. The whole spirit of his interior quest will affect the way he sees his experience; or, to put it another way, the whole spirit of his quest will enter into the experience. On the other hand, a person might only come to see the experience in this way after the event, as it were: upon reflection he interprets his experience in theological categories.

In all descriptions of mystical experience, then, we ought to be on the lookout for ramifications. Their degree can be crudely estimated by asking:

---

[1] See my 'Mystical Experience', in *Sophia*, vol. I, no. I (April, 1962), pp. 19 ff., discussing the distinction between experience and interpretation as propounded by W. T. Stace in *Mysticism and Philosophy*, p. 37.

How many propositions are presupposed as true by the description in question?

It would also seem to follow, if we bear in mind the notion of degrees of ramification, that the higher the degree of ramification, the less is the description guaranteed by the experience itself. For where there is a high degree of ramification, some statements will be presupposed which have to be verified in other ways than by immediate mystical experience. Thus a mystic who claims to become united with Christ presupposes that the historical Jesus is the Christ; and the historicity of Jesus is guaranteed by the written records, not by an interior experience. Again, where contemplation is regarded as a means of liberation from rebirth, the description of the mystical experience may involve reference to this doctrine (thus the concept *nirvana* presupposes the truth of the rebirth doctrine). To say that someone has in this life attained the peace and insight of nirvana is also to claim that he will not be reborn. But the truth of rebirth is not discovered through mystical experience as such. It is true that the Buddhist yogin may claim supernormal knowledge of previous lives: but this is in the nature of memory, if anything, and is to be distinguished from the formless, imageless inner experience which accrues upon the practice of *jhāna*. Also, Buddhists appeal to other empirical and philosophical evidence in support of the claim that the rebirth doctrine is true.[1]

The idea of degrees of ramification may help to clarify the distinction between experience and interpretation. But a further methodological point is also important. Descriptions, etc., of religious experience may be made from various points of view. There is the description given by the man himself, in terms of his own tradition. There is the description which others of his own tradition may give. Also, men of another tradition may describe his experience in terms of *their* tradition or standpoint. Thus if a Christian says that the Buddha's Enlightenment-experience involved some kind of interior vision of God, he is describing the experience from his own point of view and not from that of the Buddha. We crucially, then, should distinguish between a mystic's interpretation of his own experience and the interpretation which may be placed upon it from a different point of view. In other words, we must distinguish between what may be called *auto*-interpretation and *hetero*-interpretation.[2]

The difference between the auto-interpretation of an experience and the hetero-interpretation of it will depend on, first, the degree of ramification involved and, secondly, the difference between the presupposed truths incorporated in the ramification. For example, the Christian evaluation of the Buddha's Enlightenment-experience posited above uses the concept *God* in the Christian sense. The Buddhist description on the other hand does not. Thus the Christian hetero-interpretation presupposes such propositions as

[1] See my *Doctrine and Argument in Indian Philosophy*, ch. XII.   [2] *Op. cit.* p. 37.

INTERPRETATION AND MYSTICAL EXPERIENCE 81

that God created the world, God was in Christ, etc., and these propositions are not accepted in the Buddhist auto-interpretation. By contrast the Jewish and Christian interpretations of Isaiah's experience in the Temple overlap in great measure. This is because the beliefs presupposed coincide over a reasonably wide range.

These methodological observations, though rather obvious, need stating because they are too commonly neglected.

We may conclude so far, then, that a description of a mystical experience can fall under one of the following heads:

(a) Auto-interpretation with a low degree of ramification.
(b) Hetero-interpretation with a low degree of ramification.
(c) Auto-interpretation with a high degree of ramification.
(d) Hetero-interpretation with a high degree of ramification.

These can conveniently be called for short:

(a) Low auto-interpretation.
(b) Low hetero-interpretation.
(c) High auto-interpretation.
(d) High hetero-interpretation.

We may note that a high hetero-interpretation of experience (e) will usually imply the falsity or inadequacy of a high auto-interpretation of (e), and conversely. It would therefore seem to be a sound principle to try to seek a low hetero-interpretation coinciding well with a low auto-interpretation. In this way an agreed phenomenological account of (e) will be arrived at, and this will facilitate the attempt to distinguish experience from interpretation. But since (e) will often be affected by its high auto-interpretation, it is also important to understand this high auto-interpretation, without obscuring it by means of a high hetero-interpretation.

I shall argue that Zaehner's distinction between monistic and theistic mysticism partly depends on his own high hetero-interpretation, and partly on his not distinguishing between high and low auto-interpretation.

V. ZAEHNER'S DISTINCTION BETWEEN MONISTIC AND THEISTIC MYSTICISM CRITICISED

A difficulty about Zaehner's classification arises once we examine Buddhism. It is undoubtedly the case that Buddhism—and very clearly in Theravāda Buddhism—centres on mystical experience. The Eightfold Path incorporates and culminates in a form of yoga which may bring the peace and insight of nirvana to the saint. Crucial in this yoga is the practice of the *jhānas* or stages of meditation. It is thus necessary for any account of mysticism to take Buddhist experience and tradition seriously. But regrettably (from Zaehner's point of view) Buddhism denies the soul or eternal self. Zaehner, in order to fit Buddhism into the monistic pigeon-hole, denies this denial, and ascribes an *ātman* doctrine to the Buddha.

This will not do, for a number of reasons.[1]

First, even if (incredibly) the Buddha did teach an *ātman* doctrine, we still have to reckon with the Buddhists. The phenomenon of Buddhist mysticism, not involving an *ātman*-type auto-interpretation, remains; and it is both widespread and important in the fabric of man's religious experience.

Secondly, it is asking too much to make us believe that a doctrine which has been eschewed by nearly all Buddhists (with the possible exception of the *pudgalavādins*, who significantly did not dare to use the term *ātman*, even though their Buddhist opponents castigated them for wanting to introduce the idea) was explicitly taught by the Buddha. The *anattā* teaching is about the strongest bit of the earliest tradition which we possess.

Thirdly, it is easy enough to play around with the texts by translating *attā* with a capital, as 'Self'. Thus Zaehner translates *attagarahī*[2] as 'that the Self would blame', and so on. He refers us to *Dhammapada* 165 to show that evil is done by the empirical ego; so that in vs. 157, when we are enjoined to treat the self as dear, it must be the eternal Self which is being referred to. But consider the former passage. It reads: 'By oneself is evil done; one is defiled by oneself . . . by oneself one is made pure; the pure and the impure stand and fall by themselves; no one can purify another.' Does one really want to translate: 'By oneself is evil done; . . . by one's Self is one made pure'? The point could have been expressed more clearly if the author had wanted to say *this*. The whole purport of such passages is that one should be self-reliant and responsible (and I do not mean Self-reliant!). The fact is that the word *attā* is very common, and has an ordinary usage. It is a gross strain on the texts to read in the meaning ascribed to them by Zaehner.

Fourth, Zaehner thinks his case is confirmed by the passages 'illustrating what the Self is not'[3]—it is not the body, feelings, dispositions, etc. But these passages in no way help Zaehner. Their import is clearly explained in the famous passage of the *Milindapañha* (40–45), where a Humean analysis of the individual is given. The Buddha himself, furthermore, is reported as having asserted that though it is wrong to identify the self with the body, it is better for the uninstructed man to make this mistake than to commit the opposite error of believing in an eternal soul.[4]

For these and other reasons, Zaehner's interpretation cannot seriously be defended. But embarrassing consequences flow from this conclusion. It means that a main form of mysticism does not involve a monistic auto-interpretation.

---

[1] A fuller criticism is to be found in my *Doctrine and Argument in Indian Philosophy*, pp. 211 ff. Zaehner's account of Buddhism is discoverable in his *At Sundry Times* (see, e.g., his argument on p. 98).

[2] Sutta-nipata 788: see *At Sundry Times*, pp. 98–101.

[3] *At Sundry Times*, p. 101.

[4] *Samyutta-nikāya*, ii, 95.

Nevertheless, Zaehner could still argue as follows. Admittedly a monistic auto-interpretation is not present among Buddhist contemplatives: but it is still reasonable to hetero-interpret their attainment in a monistic fashion. We can still say (can we not?) that what the Buddhist *really* achieves in and through contemplation is the isolation of his eternal soul.

Such a defence, however, implies that there can be a misunderstanding on the part of a mystic as to what it is he is attaining. It implies that auto-interpretations can be widely mistaken, in so far as they are ramified.

Likewise, since Zaehner classifies both Yoga and Advaita together as monistic, and since their doctrinal auto-interpretations differ very widely, within the Hindu context it has to be admitted that wrong auto-interpretation can occur.

Let us bring this out more explicitly. According to Zaehner, Buddhist, Yoga and Advaitin mystics belong together, and fit in the same monistic category, and yet the following three doctrines of liberation are propounded by them:

(1) That there are no eternal selves, but only impermanent individuals who are, however, capable of liberation, through attaining nirvana in this life, in which case they will no more be reborn.

(2) That there is an infinite number of eternal selves, who through Yoga can attain isolation or liberation, a state in which the soul exists by itself, no longer implicated in nature and in the round of rebirth.

(3) That there is but one Self, which individuals can realise, and which is identical with Brahman as the ground of being (which at a lower level of truth manifests itself as a personal Lord and Creator)—such a realisation bringing about a cessation of the otherwise continuously reborn individual.

Now these are obviously very different doctrines. Why should the crucial difference lie between them and theism? Is not the difference between (2) and (3) equally striking? If the monistic category includes heterogeneous high auto-interpretations, there is no guarantee that we should not place *all* mystics, including theists, in the same category; and explain their difference not in terms of radically different experiences, but in terms of varied auto-interpretation. The gaps within the monistic category are big enough for it not to seem implausible to count the gap between monism and theism as no wider.

Admit that high auto-interpretations can be mistaken, and there is no great reason to isolate theistic mysticism as belonging to a separate category.

If I am right in proposing this on methodological grounds, we can go on to explain the difference between Yoga (say) and theism by reference to what goes on outside the context of the mystical life. The devotional and prophetic experiences of a personal God—prophetism and *bhakti* religion—these help to explain why the theist sees his contemplative experience in a special way. He already considers that there is evidence of a personal Lord and Creator: in the silent brightness of inner contemplative ecstasy it is natural (or supernatural) to identify what is found within with the Lord who is worshipped without.[1] *A priori*, then, there is no special call to assign theistic mysticism to a special pigeon-hole. Of course, there are theological motives for trying to do this. It avoids some ticklish questions, and it suggests that there is something very special about theistic mysticism. It is a covert means of preaching theism. Now doubtless theism should be preached; but *fairly*. Methodologically, the assignment of theism to a special pigeon-hole is suspect. The arguments are more complex and difficult than we think.

But it may be replied to all this that the discussion has been largely *a priori*. Do we not have to look at the actual words of theistic mystics? Of course. I shall, however, content myself with examining some passages which Zaehner quotes in favour of his own position.

VI. SOME PASSAGES FROM THEISTIC MYSTICS EXAMINED

An important part of Zaehner's argument rests on a couple of passages from Ruysbroeck. I quote from these.

Now observe that whenever man is empty and undistracted in his senses by images, and free and unoccupied in his highest powers, he attains rest by purely natural means. And all men can find and possess this rest in themselves by their mere nature, without the grace of God, if they are able to empty themselves of sensual images and of all action.[2]

Zaehner comments that Ruysbroeck here has in effect described (Advaita) Vedāntin mysticism. Talking of men who have attained this 'natural rest', Ruysbroeck goes on:

Through the natural rest, which they feel and have in themselves in emptiness, they maintain that they are free, and united with God without mean, and that they are advanced beyond all the exercises of the Holy Church, and beyond the commandments of God, and beyond the law, and beyond all the virtuous works which one can in any way practise.[3]

Now it will be noted that Ruysbroeck's criticism chiefly rests on moral grounds. He condemns quietists for arrogance, complacency and ethical sterility. They do not properly connect their inner experience with the God taught by the Church, who makes demands upon men, and who wishes that they may love him. But the ordinances and teachings of the Church do not spring from mystical experience: they have other sources. And moral insights are not simply derived from contemplation. In other words, the criteria for judging mystical experience are partly exterior to the contemplative life.

---

[1] See *Doctrine and Argument in Indian Philosophy*, ch. x, where an analysis along these lines is worked out in some detail.

[2] *Mysticism Sacred and Profane*, p. 170.   [3] *Ibid.* p. 171.

INTERPRETATION AND MYSTICAL EXPERIENCE   85

Thus, even given that Ruysbroeck is a good guide in these matters (and this need not be so), we might still say: the trouble with 'monistic' quietists is a failure in their auto-interpretation of their experience. They do not really see the God of the Bible and of the Church there. But this does not at all entail that, given a low interpretation (i.e. a relatively unramified account) of their experiences, these experiences differ radically in character from those of theistic mystics. In short, these Ruysbroeck passages are quite compatible with my thesis, and thus do not strongly support the Zaehner analysis.

Quietists, for Ruysbroeck, are not sufficiently aware of the working of God's grace. But the doctrine of grace (and by contrast, nature) is a theological account of God's activity. A person could have a genuine mystical experience, but be wrong in not ascribing it to God's grace. Ruysbroeck's high hetero-interpretation of monistic quietism conflicts with the latter's high auto-interpretation. But the experiences for all that could belong to the same type.

Zaehner also makes use of a very interesting passage from al-Ghazālī, part of which reads as follows:

The mystics, after their ascent to the heavens of Reality, agree that they saw nothing in existence except God the One. Some of them attained this state through discursive reasoning, others reached it by savouring and experiencing it. From these all plurality entirely fell away.   They were drowned in pure solitude: their reason was lost in it, and they became as if dazed in it.   They no longer had the capacity to recollect aught but God, nor could they in any wise remember themselves. Nothing was left to them but God. They became drunk with a drunkenness in which their reason collapsed.   One of them said, 'I am God (the Truth)'. Another said, 'Glory be to me. How great is my glory', while another said, 'Within my robe is naught but God'. But the words of lovers when in a state of drunkenness must be hidden away and not broadcast.   However, when their drunkenness abates and the sovereignty of their reason is restored,—and reason is God's scale upon earth,—they know that this was not actual identity. . . . For it is not impossible that a man should be confronted by a mirror and should look into it, and not see the mirror at all, and that he should think that the form he saw in the mirror was the form of the mirror itself and identical with it. . . .[1]

What Ghazālī is saying here—to translate into my own jargon—is that the mystic's auto-interpretation of his experience as involving actual identity with God is mistaken, and that the correct interpretation must say that there is some distinction between the soul and God. In the passage quoted he goes on to explain how the mystic, in his self-naughting, is not conscious of himself (or even of his own unconsciousness of himself), and this is a main reason for the language of identity.

This seems to me a clear indication that the monistic and theistic experiences are essentially similar; and that it is the correct *interpretation* of them which is at issue. The theist must maintain, in order to make sense of worship and devotion, that there is a distinction between the human individual and God.

---

[1] *Mysticism Sacred and Profane.* pp. 157–8.

The non-theist, not being so much concerned with devotion (though he may allow a place for it at the popular level), can more happily speak of identity with ultimate Reality, or can even dispense (as in Yoga and Theravada Buddhism) with such a concept of the Absolute. Thus the question of what is the best hetero- and auto-interpretation of mystical experience turns on whether devotion and worship are important. Or more generally: the question of interpretation is the same as the question of God. One cannot answer this by reference to auto-interpretations of mystical experience alone; for these auto-interpretations conflict, and they have ramifications extending far beyond the sphere of such experience itself.

This is why my thesis, that maybe there is no essential distinction between what Zaehner has called monistic and theistic mysticism, does not at all entail that proponents of neo-Vedāntin views of a 'perennial philosophy', involving a doctrine of the Absolute Self,[1] are right. The thesis 'All introvertive mysticism is, as experience, essentially the same' does not entail any doctrine. Truth of doctrine depends on evidence other than mysticism, and this is true even of the doctrine of the Absolute Self.

I have tried to argue that the interpretation of mystical experience depends at least in part on evidence, etc., not given in the experience itself; and that therefore there is always a question about the degree to which non-experimental data are incorporated into ramified descriptions of mystical experience. I can best illustrate this, finally, with a passage written by Zaehner himself:

We have already said that when the mystic claims attributes that are necessarily divine and demonstrably not human,—such as omnipotence and omniscience,— it is fairly clear that he is not enjoying union with God, but rather some sort of natural mystical experience. Apart from this important consideration it would seem that the mystic who is genuinely inspired by the divine love, will show this to the world by the holiness of his life and by an abiding humility in face of the immense favours bestowed which he always will see to be God's doing, not his own. Only such criteria can enable us to distinguish between the genuine state of union with God and the 'natural' or rather 'praeternatural' phenomena we have been discussing.[2]

The two criteria here mentioned can be called respectively the theological and the moral. The theological criterion shows, or is claimed to show, that the mystic cannot have enjoyed real union with God because he makes false theological claims (omniscience, etc.) on his own behalf. The moral criterion can show that a mystic has not enjoyed real union with God because his life is not holy, or not humble. Some comments are in order.

First, *both criteria are indirect*. If they are, as Zaehner here says, the *only* criteria that distinguish genuine union with God from something else, then *one cannot establish this latter discrimination on the basis of a phenomenological account*

---

[1] See, e.g., W. T. Stace, *Mysticism and Philosophy*, who comes to this conclusion.
[2] *Ibid.* p. 193.

of the experience itself, but rather on the basis of the verbal and other behaviour of the contemplative. This supports my thesis that phenomenologically there is no need to distinguish between monistic and theistic mystical experience (auto-interpretations apart).

Secondly, the first criterion depends on the truth of theism. This is why the interpretation and evaluation of mystical experience from a doctrinal point of view cannot be separated from the general question of the truth of theism. The theological criterion could not work for a Vedāntin.

Thirdly, to some extent the same is true of the moral criterion. For humility is a virtue for the theist, who sees the wonder and holiness of the divine Being; but need not be a virtue for the non-theist. In so far as moral ideas depend on theology (and they do in part), one cannot really separate the moral from the theological criterion.

VII. CONCLUSION

The above arguments by themselves do not establish the truth of my thesis that monistic and theistic contemplative experiences are (except in so far as they are affected by auto-interpretations) essentially the same: but I hope that they are sufficient to cast doubt on the Zaehner analysis.

Mysticism is not the same as prophetism and *bhakti* religion; but it may gain its auto-interpretations from these latter types of religion. But there is no need to take all interpretations as phenomenological descriptions; and this is the main point of this paper. To put the possibility which I am canvassing in a simple form, it can be reduced to the following theses.

(1) Phenomenologically, mysticism is everywhere the same.

(2) Different flavours, however, accrue to the experiences of mystics because of their ways of life and modes of auto-interpretation.

(3) The truth of interpretation depends in large measure on factors extrinsic to the mystical experience itself.

Thus, the question of whether mysticism is a valid means of knowledge concerning the Transcendent is only part of a much wider set of theological questions.

Finally, let me express my debt to Zaehner's learning and fertility of ideas. If I have criticised a main thesis of his, it is because it is itself an important contribution to the discussion of mysticism. In my view, his analysis is wrong; but interestingly false propositions are worth far more than a whole lot of boringly true ones.

CHAPTER 6

The Purification of Consciousness and the Negative Path

I

The use of negatives, or words which have a negative feel, is common in mystical literature. We hear of the unconditioned, the empty, the cloud of unknowing; we are reminded of the limits of language by such locutions as the inexpressible, the ineffable, the incomprehensible; and we tread that highway to the Beyond known as the *via negativa.*[1] Why should such blankness figure, so to speak, at the heart of mysticism? It may be useful to say something by way of analysis of the void, for even the empty can be analysed, since its context and meaning are not themselves opaque or simple.

Briefly, the reason for much of this language has to do with the purification of consciousness – the attainment of a kind of consciousness-purity. Why should such purity be thought valuable? And what questions can be raised about its viability as a source of knowledge? I shall add some remarks about these issues too. In concentrating here on that aspect of the mystical which is found in consciousness-purity I neglect external visions, interior images, numinous experiences, shamanism[2] – though I do not wish to undervalue such phenomena. But I voyage here more in the cloud of unknowing.

II

One aspect of consciousness-purification is the use of a kind of yoga or system of contemplation which allows a person to wash images, whether external or internal, from his mind. This is well delineated in Buddhist texts concerning the *jhanas*; but can be found elsewhere in manuals of the contemplative life. Thus a state of mind is arrived at which cannot in one ordinary sense of 'describe' be described, even though as we shall see the negative terminology does itself constitute a kind of description. It is common that when we close our eyes we still see things, as the metaphor has it, in the mind's eye. It is indeed quite difficult *not* to 'see' something or other, whether an after-image, or a scene from our lives or some figment. There is a strangely compelling way in which our mind wanders through slices of actual and possible perceptual experience, mimicked internally – pictures and yet they are not pictures. Such mental simulacra of outer experience are also woven into the threads of thought which tend to run like a silent dialogue through our darkened heads. No time is all this more apparent to a person than when he/she is trying to fall asleep. Thus if we define one aspect of purity of consciousness by saying that it contains no such images, no such flow of meandering thoughts, no such pictures strung on experimental threads – then we can understand one use of the whim of blankness: the purity of consciousness is empty, void; and we cannot describe it in usual ways.

For in so far as we describe our inner flow it is in such ways as the following: that 'I can see the beach at Santa Barbara where we often go' or 'I was thinking just now about the time when the children were small' or 'I was day-dreaming about Italy'. Such musings also can be summoned up somewhat at will. 'Imagine a white plate with a tomato resting on it'; and sometimes they remain consciously plastic 'I remember roughly what she looks like but I really can't visualize her features clearly'. Colours, shapes, sounds, smells, feels – all these can be called up. And we thus use their words to describe an inner simulacrum and the foci of thought, memory, fantasy, hope, fear and so on. So these are descriptions of inner experience which act by analogy with descriptions of the outer world. But if the normal flow of inner experience is replaced by a blank state, then that state is not ordinarily describable; that is, not describable in the ordinary way. But nevertheless to say 'Awake, and conscious, but not having an ordinarily-describable flow of experience' is to offer a description. Blankness is itself a property, and not nothing. Thus we may formulate a first paradox (a paradox, I say, but not a contradiction): to say that a mental state is blank and thus not to be described is to describe it.

The reason why this is not a contradiction is simply that in the ordinary sense of description – where details can up to a point be given – a blank is indescribable. But to be consistent rather than conventional a blank is, as I have said, something not nothing, and to use words about it (like 'a blank') is to describe it.

But of course it is not clear that, even though the contemplative experience may be blank, a kind of cloud of unknowing, it is *only* blank. For one thing it is a blank in context – the context of feelings and a kind of exalted serenity: and the context too of the whole search, e.g. the search for God, the return to God, the path to *nirvāṇa* and so on. It has, that is, an emotional context and in the broadest sense a conceptual context.

Still, the purity of consciousness is remarkable in itself. It is unusual and difficult – a certain heroism of yoga seems to be required. But there are many difficult and unusual events and achievements in this world. What makes consciousness-purity especially remarkable is that it acquires by blankness a number of (so to speak) metaphysical qualities. For one thing it, by its transcendence of distractions and appetites beyond ordinary feelings whether positive or negative, and by being so serene, has its own kind of bliss, as mystics so frequently testify. Not the bliss of supreme conjugal love; nor the bliss of heady worldly achievement; but the rapture of great music or great painting. All these may serve sometimes as images of the mystical. But rather it is the bliss of a kind of unshakeable consciousness, because there is no 'because'. For normally when I count myself overjoyed it is in nature of some outer good fortune or achievement, some good thing. The contemplative void is so to speak blissful (and yet not in a worldly sense blissful) in itself.

Note, incidentally, that the line between the transcendental and the worldly (the this-worldly) is not drawn between experience and what lies beyond, or between the empirical and the non- or trans-empirical. It is a line drawn between sublime and ordinary experience. That is it is a line drawn *within* the realm of experience.

Another remarkable 'metaphysical' quality of the void is that because it does not involve mental images it does not involve even make-believe time. When I daydream of Gileta Beach and what we did there in sunny days gone past, the luminescent shadows in my mind which picture the scenes contain time in hours or minutes, vague sketches of time – these are there implicitly, and slip by in a kind of make-believe and a kaleidoscopic memory. But a blank is timeless. 'I saw Eternity the other night'!, but how long did that take? Thus *nirvāṇa* is seen as a deathless place.

One can dimly picture the bright light within the mystic's skull and as he comes out from his rapture the way the world seems suddenly soaked in time and therefore in a kind of impermanence. The doctrine of impermanence in Buddhism is a sort of mirror image of the experience of the timeless.

So the blank consciousness implies a timeless serenity. The context of feeling – that somehow serenity lies beyond joy and so is paradoxically a kind of bliss, but one not to be measured by ordinary reasons – introduces a different way in which the mystical void lies beyond word.

For expressive ineffability is involved – that which operates performatively. In saying that no words of mine can adequately express my profound gratitude I am, after all, expressing (albeit inadequately) gratitude. The very use of 'ineffable' or 'I cannot say how grateful . . .' is itself a method of alleviating inadequacy. Tone of voice matters too. But leaving that on one side, the use of 'ineffable' makes the performative expression of gratitude less inadequate than it would otherwise be.

There is then a *performative* as well as a *descriptive* or constative ineffability about the supremely serene blank of consciousness-purity. This, by the way, does not distinguish mysticism from other aspects of religious experience and practice. After all, the overwhelming theophany of Vishnu in the *Gītā* left Arjuna partially speechless. But being thus struck dumb is very different from adumbrating the bliss of a bright inner void.[3]

There is, however, a set of considerations as to why an expression of feeling or of value should be inadequate. One consideration just has to do with intensity, and another relatedly with the erosion of force. Thus expressive language has its gradations, corresponding to the intensity of feeling. We might think of it as a range of superlatives: 'happy', 'very happy', 'supremely happy' . . . But 'I can't convey how supremely happy I feel' is not so much an account of failure as a way of going beyond 'supremely happy', and on the same scale. So from one point of view 'indescribably . . .' is an intensifier on a performative continuum in which feelings, etc., are ranged in a fervidity scale. Secondly and connectedly a perceptual proneness to erosion affects the force of expressive terms – for instance expletives. A previous

The Purification of Consciousness   121

generation's bad words become small change the next: 'bloody', 'damn', 'hell of a', for instance, have almost entered the polite tea party and the drawing room. Thus restlessly society keeps creating new superlatives to try to keep up with the processes of erosion. And so, in so far as the language of expression is faded, there is pressure to signal its inadequacy as part of the very task of expressing feelings. So there is here a reinforcement of the disclaimer of expressibility as itself a means of expression.

In short if we combine consciousness-purity with a sense of the sublime intensity of feeling we produce a double ineffability – the one the indescribability of what is abnormally blank, the other the inexpressibility of what is performatively beyond ordinary scales of feeling.

This analysis may be open to the objection that it fails sufficiently to take account of a paradoxical aspect of the cloud of unknowing namely that it is in so much literature pointed to as the locus of a kind of knowing, *prajña*, *vidya*, gnosis, knowledge.[4] It is paradoxical perhaps not only because it is 'knowledge but not knowledge'. Maybe it is also paradoxical because it is somehow in defiance of logic, beyond reason, etc.[5] I have said above that the noetic quality represents an objection to my analysis so far, i.e. it is an omission. This has to be taken in if the account is to be complete. But first a point about paradox and the transcendence of logic.

First, paradoxes are often rhetorical – constructive Irishisms as it were. Thus 'The only difference between children and adults is that adults never grow up', 'Sometimes the only way to get a cork out is to push it in', 'He who loses his life will save it' . . . They are intelligible challenges to assumptions: the assumption that adults are not deeply childish and vice versa; the assumption that opening a bottle implies extraction, the assumption that living can be quantitatively measured . . . and so on. Sometimes too paradoxes are not so much rhetorical as almost forced breaches of rules, though not con-tradictory ones. Thus some descriptions of strange perceptual states seem to break the rules, as when a migraine is described as including a blank in the field of vision, but not a grey or colourless patch – a real blank without any measurable width, etc. Again radio waves – waves with nothing for them to be waves of – were once thought somewhat of an effrontery to our usual talk and thought. Such paradoxes are not so much *rhetorical* as *categorical* or *analogical*. By these labels I merely mean that because a migraine blank is in a different category from the blankness of a blank wall it only has an *analogy* not a strict resemblance to the ordinary blankness. Likewise the concept *wave* in the radio case differs from the ordinary (ocean) concept and so is a wave by analogy, embedded in a different conceptual scheme from that of water and seas. It sometimes takes time to discover this: the ether hypothesis stands as witness.

Now it would not be at all surprising if mystical states were described by paradoxes either rhetorical or analogical; for the inner life is liable – especially this heroic, transcendent-gleaming sort of inner life – to issue in states which are only by *analogy* describable in quasi-visual terms. Thus the inner light. (Though I do not deny that mystics may also see lights, that is mental images of light, etc.)

Such paradoxes are not contradictions: just peculiarities, or rather, ways of stating peculiarities. Mystical states are relatively rare: if they were commonplace – and religious experiences of various life-enhancing and prayer-oriented sorts are much more frequent than the hopeful rationalist and 'ordinary man' might expect – then we would lose the sense of paradox, as has now happened with radio waves.

But what about dialectical paradoxes, the breaking down of thought, the avoidance of categorization in relation to the mystical or to the transcendent? Not either this or not-this, or both this and not-this, or even neither this nor not-this – the tetralemma seems to close off all avenues of affirmation, a *via negativa* with a vengeance. It would be hard, even with sensible brevity, to deal properly with this problem here, but let me make a few points.

First, dialectical negation has a certain direction – this being indicated in Dionysius (for example) by his use of 'super-', to suggest a negation *beyond* ordinary essences, or in other words a trans-cendental direction towards which the *via negativa* tends; and likewise it is indicated by the differing-level of truth theory in Nāgārjuna, etc. There is in brief something being pointed to. As it were: dialectics here has a denotation but no connotation (its meanings self-destruct).

Second, naturally the dialectical negations do not work unless the principle of non-contradiction holds. Whatever is done, *logic* is not what is destroyed. But it does not have any purchase on the Beyond or the Void, a different thing.

The Purification of Consciousness   123

Third, we should see the dialectical process, and indeed the whole process of philosophizing as existential, and so itself, in the context of mysticism, as a form of askesis.

But let us now return to the question of the noetic aspect of the cloud of unknowing.

The fact that it is not propositional knowledge, i.e. it is not directly knowing that something or other is the case,[6] is less transparent than one would expect; because the mystic, out of trance and out of heaven (so to speak), when she has climbed down the *jhānas* and re-emerged into the cheering light of day, no longer sees that cheer, that light, that day in the same way. The higher illumination itself becomes applied to the discursive circumstances of the world and by consequence forms the basis for what might be considered to be propositional knowledge, for instance the Four Aryan Truths. Even here we should note that the supposed propositional knowledge has an existential aspect. You do not realize the truth of impermanence simply from a textbook or a scripture. It is something to which experience and impact have to be added. Or rather, they are already ingredients of the truth to be conveyed, and so the statement is abortive unless it has such impact.

That the Brahman or the Void or God is experienced in some direct way in the state of consciousness-purity is a claim which already imparts tremendous noetic power to the experience or experiences involved. Mysticism thus involves a kind of knowledge by acquiantance which is ultimate. But this 'ultimacy' again must have an existential force. Is it not because the consciousness-purity seems itself to contain something of sublime importance, even of salvific power, that it is so staggering as an intuition? And yet how could something ineffable be so rich in suggestion?

An answer seems to emerge from a number of observations, and since these deal with questions of value and validity I shall present this part of my discussion in a separate section. But first let me sum up.

The indescribability of the pure state of consciousness which I postulate to be at the core of mysticism is not *strict* indescribability. For to call consciousness-purity 'blank', 'empty', 'indescribable' is to say that it cannot be described by any of the usual terms to signify items in or phrases in the *usual* flow of consciousness, which teems with thoughts and feelings and inner and outer pictures. Second, such terms as 'indescribable', 'ineffable' and so on are themselves per-formatives also, and help to *express* an off-scale sublimity beyond the usual rungs of the ladder of value and joy. There is nothing specially mysterious in all this; limitations on description and expression are widespread: how do you describe the sublime taste of artichokes?

III

We may approach the question of the noetic power of consciousness-purity by considering whether so much weight can be attached to interpretation that the character of the experience essentially ceases to matter. We must not, however, suppose that the experience of consciousness-purity is characterless. Moreover, it generates certain *suggestions*. As we have noted, a kind of transcendental bliss (which yet is not bliss) and a kind of timelessness adhere to the blankness of it. Thus though in no way does such experience verify or prove.that there is a timeless Ultimate, a *nirvāṇa* or God beyond God, these qualities may be said to harmonize with that thought and are therefore *suggestive* of the claim that in the experience there is an 'apprehension' of the Ultimate as described in a given scheme of things, namely the doctrinal scheme of the person involved. Eternity is ascribed to God; timelessness characterizes *samādhi*; it is not too *outré* to think of *samādhi* as thus a kind of realization of the divine.

This is not saying that anyone who had the experience would recognize God there – he would have to have the concept *God* for a start.[7] Of course this is not to say that the experience might not *change* his conception of God. Indeed, the very impact of the unknowing knowing would make it probable that his beliefs about God would be changed, emphases altered, everything seen in a new (inner) light.

Also, consciousness-purity implies the apparent elimination of the typical subject–object polarity, and so would tend to favour an interpretation involving unification of the inner self and God (but not in Buddhism which, because not postulating a Being out there nor indeed one 'in here', can economically disperse with the talk of unity, union, and so forth which is often taken to be typical of the mystical experience). There is plenty of evidence of the tension between the dualism which God-as-focus-of-worship implies and the unity which the washing away of subject and object in consciousness-purity

The Purification of Consciousness 125

suggests. Thus it is a hypothesis of some interest that, (*a*) where the mystical is combined with theism, union becomes an organizing concept; (*b*) where it is combined with a notion of a Ground of Being not so strongly perceived as Other, identity is a natural notion; and (*c*) when there is neither God nor Ground, you have neither union nor identity nor their negations (as in Buddhism and in a differing way in Jainism): isolation is the motif where souls are neither, so to speak, rising to a God nor descending to a Ground. Also, of course, where there is no Ground or God but many souls, then plurality in liberation is natural. But where there is a Ground and identity becomes central, the many souls (of course) disappear. There can only be one – the Self. In brief, one does not need much to be able to infer patterns of interpretation of the subject–object disappearance. Thus consciousness-purity itself can in differing contexts lend credence to such varying doctrinal interpretations.

It is of the essence of these remarks that the relationship of relatively unramified descriptions of mystical states to doctrines is one of *suggestion*. The fit is loose but credence-generating. We are of course used to such a loose fit in a whole range of human experience. But because of the aura of sanctity surrounding the topic, and the perhaps necessary reliance on gurus and other spiritual directors, who are typically (perhaps by definition) authoritarian, it is easy to suppose that what the mystic claims on the basis of his own experience must be the right interpretation – and this tends to introduce plurality into categories or types of experience. Though it is quite obvious that there are different varieties of religious experience; and though it is quite obvious that interpretation gets so to speak built into experiences – thus making experiences of the same type different in particular ways – it does not follow that there does not exist a type to be identified cross-culturally as 'consciousness-purity' or as 'mystical'. Such a view has the merit of making sense both of the facts the perennialists point to and of the undoubted differences of exposition, flavour, and significance as between the various traditions.

Before we go further into this question of the 'contextual value' of mysticism in a given tradition, there remains a difficulty, perhaps, in my doctrine of the *suggestion*, i.e. the view that though an experience of consciousness-purity does not entail or overwhelmingly imply a doctrinal interpretation it can be suggestive of it. Such 'looseness of fit' may not itself fit with the fact that a noetic quality is so often assigned to the higher experience, as we have seen. Is it then not knowledge after all? By acquaintance of a sort, it is, yes: but this is not to say that the doctrines and the scheme in which the ultimate presents itself in experience are necessarily as they are claimed to be.

If one takes the world view context as defining truth and falsity for those who hold it – if, that is, one holds that the claim to knowledge is internal to the system and makes no real sense outside it – then maybe the knowledge-claim can be preserved. But such a fideistic stance rests on a half-truth and the other half is that faith-systems come to confront one another in the world. In any event, even in a culture in which a system is dominant there are other strata of experience, belief and knowledge to which religion stands in some kind of cognitive relationship. When the Pope says 'I know p', we think of the Ayatollah's 'I know otherwise'.

Such mystical noesis is actually rather more like 'I knew what my duty was', even if we also know that such matters are debatable. Existential certitude can live still within the wider context of epistemological uncertainty.

But certitude is partly related to context, and to sureness about the way the world is to be diagnosed. Consequently bare consciousness-purity is not enough: it is its tie to, for example, worship of Christ or to Buddhist intellectual analysis which gives it meaning and, so to speak, direction. This is where we arrive at the question of why consciousness-purity, or any other remarkable experience, should have more than passing value. Briefly, we may see the wider importance under three heads. First, there is the impact of the experience itself, its intrinsic impressiveness, so to speak. It has a wider effect, for any really biting or solemn or deep or traumatic experience changes a person. Other experiences, other interests, look different after a glorious trip, after torture, after a sublime dive into serenity, etc. This change may itself be reinforced, in the case of mysticism, by the fact that there is an askesis used to train mind and body towards consciousness-purification. The fact that such askesis has a theory round it, normally, must be taken into account also. It may be remarked too that, if a stunning experience occurs but is not integrated into the rest of life, it is just isolated, changing tone for other experiences, but remaining a surd. It is usual for people to try to weave it into an intelligible framework. A doctrinal or other

The Purification of Consciousness　　　127

framework is to give meaning to the impact of such an experience.

Second, the characteristics of consciousness-purity have a special existential relevance. The sense of timelessness to which we have referred may give a sense of invulnerability – having tasted the eternal I may feel that life's vicissitudes cannot touch me now, for I have known a kind of completeness. The fact that we have a purity of consciousness makes us feel we have reached the soul-essence (a non-self essence!), which in other words is the pure form of the person: it is consciousness which differentiates the higher animals from the rest of creation, and the capacity to know that one is conscious differentiates men from all others. So the mystical experience is somehow a descent into the essence, perhaps even the ground of all existence, for what is the world without anything to be aware of it? Also, the mystic sacrifices her (daily) self, tames her passions, rises to a kind of objectivity of feeling, a sublime peace. It is thus not inappropriate to interpret this sublime and superior indifference as a kind of transcendence of ordinary concerns, a rising therefore above what is worldly. Thus it is valuable on a kind of superscale, beyond ordinary computations of satisfaction and dissatisfaction. As a failure of words may actually be a powerful use of language, so a disappearance of emotions may be the most potent feeling. The mystical experience is rather like the monk who in withdrawing from the world transcends worldly status – a status beyond status; the serenity of consciousness-purity is as it were above the most intense of worldly feelings. The characteristics of the experience point to the transcendent and the timeless, and thereby to a higher level of existence. The meaning of the experience can thus be thought of as giving access to something beyond. It is not just that it has a noetic flavour, but also that the noesis is of the transcendent. (But the 'metaphysical' quality of the mystical experience here is not in a positivistic sense metaphysical, for the 'transcendent' here has meaning in relation to a particular sort of human experience.)

Third, the consciousness-purity has significance in so far as it is already contextualized in a way of life, a system of doctrines, and so forth. Thus the transcendent to which consciousness-purity may be thought to give one kind of access is not 'bare' but typically embedded in a world view and milieu of practice, which means that the experience is widely connected to a web of meanings. Thus *nirvāṇa* is embedded in a milieu in which the *Sangha* mediates the

128   *Mysticism and Religious Traditions*

message, Christian mysticism has a sacramental ambience and so forth. The characteristics of the experience affect the way the ambience is interpreted. So the noetic quality of consciousness-purity may suggest new insights or what are taken for such. Thus mystical union gives a new sense to doctrines of Christ's two natures fused into one, etc.

IV

The ineffability of mystical experience is as I have argued intelligible within the context of consciousness-purification. Perhaps it is a pity that we have to use the term 'mysticism'. For though some of the classical mystics East and West have pursued such a path to a kind of inner emptiness – also a fullness in its own way – there are many other kinds of experience which are loosely termed 'mystical'. And those who aspire to consciousness-purity may have various other visionary adventures. An inventory of religious experiences seems necessary.

NOTES

References are all to *Mysticism and Philosophical Analysis*, ed. Steven T. Katz (London and New York, 1978).

1 See p. 119: Peter Moore attacks the exclusion of visions, locutions, and similar phenomena from the philosophical study of mystical experience. He is right. But still, we can distinguish. Since one can have what I refer to as consciousness-purity without these other phenomena and vice versa, we can treat them separately. But the inmost rapture which is imageless and locutionless is in my view the heart of mysticism, and correlates with some main uses of negative language and theology. But 'the heart of' may be too much of an evaluation. Never mind. Leaving aside evaluations we can still treat consciousness-purity separately.

2 P. 114: Moore refers to Paul's Damascus road experience, which cuts across such divisions as 'mystical/numinous, natural/cultivated, individual/communal and even Jewish/Christian'. As I use the term mystical it does not cut across the numinous/mystical. It just is not mystical. It is more in the numinous category, from which I think it wise to exclude consciousness-purity. The latter may be marvellous, but it is not outside and disturbing. Hair does not stand on end – for one thing it may have been shaved off.

The Purification of Consciousness   129

3   P. 211: Renford Bambrough says that the silences beloved by Otto belong
    to the *via negativa*. Perhaps. But the *via negativa* belongs primarily to the
    neo-Platonic tradition rather than the prophetic. But the speechlessness
    of being struck dumb with astonishment can meet with the speechlessness
    of the *yogin* expressing his inner insight and peace. The blend of the two
    forms of religion is not necessary, but can be fruitful.

4   Excellently discussed in Robert M. Gimello's 'Mysticism and
    Meditation', especially pp. 180ff.

5   See Steven Katz's discussion, pp. 50ff. and Peter Moore's, pp. 106–7.
    However, often the paradoxicality of mysticism may arise through a
    doctrinal and living intertwining of differing motifs of belief rather than
    in the experience itself.

6   But see Nelson Pike's example, p. 215.

7   See the excellent exposition by Moore of distinctions among retrospec-
    tive, reflexive, incorporated, reflected, and assimilated interpretation.
    Here, we deal with incorporated interpretation primarily. See also
    Steven Katz's important remarks, pp. 22–46 and 62–66, on the
    epistemological character of mystical experience and especially on how
    the pre-experiential context of the mystic influences the mystical
    experience itself. See also S. Katz's paper in the present volume for
    further details of this phenomenon.

NINIAN SMART, M.A., B. Phil. (Oxon), D.H.L. (Loyola). Professor Smart is the
author of numerous publications, among which the most important are: *Reasons and
Faiths* (1958); *Philosophers and Religious Truth* (1964); *Doctrine and Argument in
Indian Philosophy* (1964); *The Religious Experience of Mankind* (1976²); *The Concept
of Worship* (1972); *The Phenomenon of Religion* (1973). He has also published several
dozen articles and reviews in such leading philosophical and religious journals as *Mind,
Philosophical Quarterly, Religion, Religious Studies*, and *Philosophy*. He was Professor of
Theology at the University of Birmingham from 1961 to 1967 and then became the first
Professor and Chairman of the Department of Religious Studies at the University of
Lancaster, England, a post he held from 1967 to 1975. He has also been a visiting
Professor at Princeton, University of Wisconsin, and Benares Hindu University. At
present he holds two chairs, one at the University of Lancaster and the other at the
University of California at Santa Barbara, spending half a year at each.

CHAPTER 7

What Would Buddhaghosa Have Made of *The Cloud of Unknowing*?

This essay is in a self-evident way concerned with the relation between mysticism and language. It makes use of ideas first expressed
in my essay "Interpretation and Mystical Experience" (1965). It
takes two texts from different cultures, reflecting highly diverse
religious assumptions — one could hardly get a greater contrast than
Theravada Buddhism and medieval Christianity, save that both
traditions took contemplation seriously. It tries to get at the phenomenology behind the language. It uses methods sketched in my
1965 article. It argues that there are phenomenological similarities
between the differing practices despite the contrast in language
and style between Buddhaghosa and the author of *The Cloud of
Unknowing*. It appears to me that the best mode of dealing with the
issues of mysticism and language is to be found in the comparative
treatment of texts. While I have long argued for the importance of
context in analyzing doctrinal systems and mythic schemes and,
indeed, have devoted a good deal of attention to this in my book
Reasons and Faiths (1958), written in the analytic or linguistic philosophical tradition and under the influence of J. L. Austin, my

Oxford supervisor, I hold that there are genuine phenomenological comparisons to be made cross-culturally, especially in relation to mystical experience. This I hope is something that emerges from this essay.

One of the major obstacles to the thesis of a commonality between mystical or contemplative states in differing religions lies in the very diversity of contexts in which some of the most important treatises are written. Thus the whole atmosphere of the *Visuddhimagga* (*Path of Purification*) differs greatly from that of the English *Cloud of Unknowing*. Among other divergences is the way in which the *Path* is full of rather detailed instructions on the nitty-gritty of contemplative practices, while the *Cloud* is more poetic and allusive. Then there are the assumptions of the two religions. The *Path* urges recollection, for instance, of the Buddha (VII.2ff.) and the various epithets applied to him, such as "accomplished," "fully enlightened," "blessed," and so on. The contemplative therefore explicitly places himself or herself in the context of follower of the Buddha. The whole soteriology lying behind the contemplative's activities is therefore flavored with Buddhist concepts. But by contrast, the *Cloud*—though it has sometimes been accused by Christians of not being sufficiently Christocentric—is firmly planted in the tradition of Christ. Thus in chapter 4 the author says, "For in the love of Jesus shall be thine help. Love is such a power that it maketh all things to be shared. Therefore love Jesus, and all things that he hath it is thine." Consider, apart from matters of doctrine, the very different mythic ambience of the two figures: the one of royal birth, and trailing behind a whole chain of *Jātaka* stories, working out his own salvation, living to an old age, analytic in teaching, dying peacefully; and the other of artisan background, divine however, brief in public career, fiery in parables, ending his life violently with criminal execution, rising from the dead, a king, but poor. It is obvious that the meaning of contemplation must have been very different for Buddhaghosa and the author of the *Cloud*.

But there are limits on particularism. If we so emphasize the difference of context that we have room only for diversity, then no activity can be properly compared as to likenesses across culture or between traditions. But this is obviously wrong, for several reasons.

1. There are no absolute divides between traditions (e.g., between Judaism and Christianity), still less between subtraditions.
2. The thesis would destroy the possibility of using a common language to write about two traditions.
3. Good comparative studies—for example, of sacrifice in diverse traditions—have been written.

All this does not mean that we should facilely overemphasize similarities. In some ways the situation is like the one that exists between individuals. Every person has a nose, but the shapes differ and their organic placement differs. The good artist captures the generality of noses, but, more important, also captures the individual particularity of the portraitee's nose. The methodological rub is how to find a way of discerning similarities beneath the great diversities of context and conceptual cultures. In "Interpretation and Mystical Experience," I suggested using the notion of ramification in trying to resolve the problem. Less ramified language is likely to be closer to immediate experience because more ramified language—like the above references to the Buddha and to Jesus—suggests a wider epistemological context.

If one were to imagine Buddhaghosa reading the *Cloud*, the most accessible part would, from this perspective, be related to the moral qualities required of the contemplative. Although the author of the *Cloud* is conventional in listing the seven deadly sins (chap. 10), the relatively straightforward application of the ideas, uncomplicated by doctrinal presuppositions—even if doctrinal selectively lies behind their being spotlighted—would make the relevant passages intelligible. There would indeed be some matching between anger, envy, sloth, pride, covetousness, gluttony, and lust and the relevant bad attitudes found in the *Path*, themselves arising from an old Buddhist tradition. Thus Buddhaghosa treats greed, ill will, grief at privation, cruelty, joy at success, aversion, and resentment as the enemies of the four great "abidings," or *brahmavihāras*. These attitudes surely cover much of the first five deadly sins, and there are plenty of references to gluttony (e.g., I.47) and lust (I.144). So though the way virtues and vices are described varies somewhat, there appear to be fairly broad agreements about the behavior required of a person undertaking the Christian or the Buddhist life. The fact that the *Cloud* arose in a culture where great importance was attached to the monastic life helps to close the gap between Sri Lanka and medieval England.

There is, of course, a usage that might have caused problems for Buddhaghosa: the identification of the highest virtues with love. The usual story is that for Buddhism the central virtue is compassion, or *karuṇā*. This has a different flavor from that of *agape*, or reverential love of other beings. But the proper comparison would be with the four *brahmavihāras*, which could cover both love and justice in the Christian tradition. For *metta, karuṇā*, and *mudita*—that is, loving kindness, compassion, and gladness of others' successes—cover love, while *upekkhā* (equity) covers the idea of the impartial treatment of others. Of course, there are doctrinal underpinnings of love, as there are of the *brahmavihāras*: on the one hand, the Trinity as an exemplar of loving solidarity, and, on the other, the impermanence and suffering that characterize the lot of living beings.

In principle, then, there is not a huge gap between the ethical requirements of the two paths, though the Buddhist account is more detailed and analytical, and is not negatively concerned with the concept of sin, which figures prominently in the language of the *Cloud* (e.g., the heading of chap. 10: "How a man shall know when his thought is no sin; and if it be sin, when it is deadly and when it is venial"). There is, however, quite a different analysis of our troubles, more to do with original ignorance than with original sin in the Buddhist tradition.

Since in the *Path* the practice of the *jhānas* is very important, both with and without the use of devices, or *kasinas*, Buddhaghosa would have had no trouble in understanding what was sometimes strange and even shocking to English commentators—the idea of the "cloud of forgetting." Consider some things that the *Cloud* says on this matter:

> Thou art full further from him [God] when thou has no *cloud of forgetting* betwixt thee and all the creatures that ever be made. (chap. 7)

> Surely this travail is all in treading down of the thought of all the creatures that ever God made, and in holding of them under the cloud of forgetting named before. (chap. 27)

> And try to smite down all knowing and feeling of aught under God, and tread all down full far under the *cloud of forgetting,* And thou shalt understand that in this work thou shall forget not only all other creatures than thyself, or their deeds or thine, but also thou shalt in this work forget both thyself and thy deeds for God, as well as all other creatures and their deeds. (chap. 43)

> Thou shalt find, when thou hast forgotten all other creatures and their works—yea, and also thine own works—that there shall remain yet after, betwixt thee and thy God, a naked knowing and feeling must always be destroyed, ere the time be that thou mayest feel verily the perfection of this work. (chap. 43)

It is quite clear from these passages that the author urges readers to do something active about the various objects of their attention. They are to suppress thought and feeling about all entities. Moreover, they must suppress even the bare consciousness of self. This doubtless would remind Buddhaghosa of the higher *jhānas,* in which the adept passes beyond the contemplation of boundless consciousness and ascends to the realms of nothingness and neither-perception-nor-nonperception (*Path,* X.36ff.). It is obvious that putting away the thoughts and images of things does not imply that they have to be seen as creatures of God. So from the angle of unramified description, there seems to be a congruence between the procedures of the *Cloud* and the *Path.* Buddhaghosa is much more formal and detailed, as we have noted, but there is no reason to think that the two traditions point to differing systems of contemplation as such.

I stress the fact that the *Cloud* endorses activity. Despite the doctrine of grace, which the author mentions and makes use of, the follower has to make a strong effort because of the resistance of his normal self to the annihilation of self-consciousness, and because the giving up of everything and blotting it out runs contrary to his ordinary desires (chap. 29). This is analogous to the emphasis that Buddhism places on the wiping out of grasping or desire.

The *Cloud* suggests that the disappearance of the naked knowing and feeling of one's own being comes through grace, but it also depends on "ableness to receive this grace," which is "thought else but a strong and a deep ghostly sorrow." The author comments that readers have to be careful about this sorrow, so that they do not strain their body or spirit too rudely. They should "sit full still, as in a sleeping device." This perfect sorrow arises from the recognition that the person *is*. And yet "in all this sorrow he desireth not to un-be: for that were the devil's madness and despite to God" (chap. 44). Buddhaghosa would not worry too much about the devil, or Māra, but he doubtless would recognize here a parallel with the middle path. The adept desires neither to be nor to un-be. He hopes to lose consciousness of the self, but he does not wish for annihilation.

Incidentally, in the next chapter the *Cloud* makes reference to ways in which disciples can be deceived or deceive themselves, and among the delusory phenomena is an inclination "to have their breasts inflamed by an unnatural heat . . . or else they conceive a false heat wrought by the fiend, their ghostly enemy, caused by their pride and their fleshliness and curiosity of wit" (chap. 45). Here is some form of *tapas* (austerity, literally, "heat")!

The concept of the cloud of forgetting is not spelled out in detail, but there is little doubt that it refers to the systematic effort to blot out sense perception, memories, and imaginings of the world of our sensory environment and of corresponding inner states. For Buddhaghosa, this exercise would have been achieved through the *jhānas*. Thus in the *Path* there is the following interesting passage: "And when the kasina is being removed, it does not roll up or roll away. It is simply that it is called 'removed' on account of his [the contemplative's] non-attention to it, his attention being given to 'space, space.' This is conceptualized as the mere space left by the removal of the kasina" (X.8).

To explain a little: the first four stages of meditation, or *jhānas*, are the so-called *jhānas* of the realm of form because they make use of material forms as objects of concentration—for instance, a blue flower or a gray circle of clay. These so-called devices, or *kasinas*, are treated as sense data. The contemplative concentrates on the patch of blue or the patch of gray to the exclusion of everything else. Eventually, it is possible to see only the sense datum; the rest of the visual field is blank. In the next range of *jhānas*— which make use of increasingly refined formulas, such as "space, space," then "consciousness, consciousness," then "there is nothing," then "neither perception nor nonperception,"—the contemplative puts away even the sense datum, wiping out in his mind the perception of the patch of blue or gray. These formulas help to make the mind blank and, in effect, to purify consciousness. The aim is to achieve a state of consciousness that, looked at negatively, has none of its ordinary contents and even transcends the subject–object intentionality that is characteristic of ordinary human states.

It seems to me that this is how Buddhaghosa would have understood the idea of the cloud of forgetting, though he might have been a touch confused because of a different valuation on remembering, or *sati*, as he would have understood it. The notion of forgetting seems to run counter to that wide-awakeness that is typical of Buddhist spiritual manuals, in which the contemplative is super-clearly aware of his every state and is able to analyze the causes of his various feelings. This self-awareness is an important and impressive part of Buddhist techniques of self-control and self-direction. Is there a place for such *sati* in the *Cloud*? There is something parallel to it at least — the sense of the presence in them of stirring of love of the highest: "And if they think that there is no manner of thing that they do, bodily or ghostly, that is sufficiently done with witness of their conscience, unless this secret little love set upon the *cloud of unknowing* be in a ghostly manner the chief of all their work; and if they thus feel — then it is a token that they be called by God . . ." (chap. 75).

There is in the *Cloud* a kind of self-awareness in which particular qualities of the self are dismissed, and one is supposedly consciousness of one's own naked being. Although as we have seen there is not the desire to "un-be," there is an intent to paralyze the ordinary properties of the self. Perhaps the author is putting in a more positive form what in the Buddhist case is frequently seen in negative terms. That is, he may be alluding to something similar to the *anattā* doctrine. For Buddhaghosa, as for others, the purpose of recollection is to accomplish an alienation from the particular short-lived psychophysical properties pertaining to individual existence. At the same time, the Buddha wished to destroy the sense of a permanent something underlying these states, since one could also get attached to such a self. The *Cloud* does not share this way of looking at matters; but it does suggest that the individual contemplative should detach herself or himself from the usual events and concerns of inner and outer life — hence the language of "naked being." Psychologically or phenomenologically, it could be that the purification of consciousness (Buddhist) is equivalent to the attainment of nakedness of being (the *Cloud*).

It must be remembered that the *Cloud* was written within a medieval cultural context in which scholastic philosophy was the norm, and with it came the whole substance-metaphysics of Aristotle as modified somewhat by the negative theology of Dionysius the Areopagite. Pseudo-Dionysius had a great influence on the *Cloud*. But Pseudo-Dionysius nevertheless exercised his negative notions on a structure of substance. His paradoxes occur within the framework of a philosophy of being. (Thus God is said to be both being and nonbeing. To say this, however, is to deny on the surface the applicability of the term "being," but at a deeper level it is to accept that way of talking: Dionysius does not move to some radically alternative mode, such as the idea of events as point-instants, in the mode of Scherbatsky and the Theravadin tradition.) In brief, the *Cloud* was written, naturally enough, from within Western orthodoxies, even if its message was stated somewhat problematically and paradoxically. Given its substance-metaphysic, its concept of "naked being" was a radical one.

It would seem that the author envisaged, with his twin ideas of naked being and the cloud of forgetting, a contemplative attainment in which all particularities in consciousness, even self-consciousness, were put aside. Although this would have been in line with Buddhist meditative procedure, the author of the *Cloud* goes further, as can be seen in the "Epistle of Privy Counsel" (chap. 4).

> For know thou right well, that in this work thou shalt have no more beholding to the qualities of the being of God than to the qualities of the being of thyself. For there is no name, nor feeling, nor beholding more, nor so much, according unto everlastingness (which is God), as is that which may be had, seen and felt in the blind and the lovely beholding of this word *is*. For if thou say: "Good" or "Fair Lord" or "Sweet," "Merciful" or "Righteous," "Wise" or "All-witting," "Mighty" or "Almighty," "Wit" or "Wisdom," "Might" or "Strength," "Love" or "Charity" or what other such thing that thou say of God: all it is hid and enstored in this little word *is*.

In short, the various characteristics of God are ignored. I think this is an indication of what may be called the contextual nature of

God in the *Cloud*. By this I mean that of course God serves as a powerful focus of the whole life and practice of the mystic, and in this way God is a looming part of the mystic's context. But God as such is not—at least not in detail, that is, with his relevant properties—part of the higher inner experience of the mystic. We shall return to this point in discussing the so-called cloud of unknowing. But it seems quite possible that the author of the *Cloud* emphasized the absolutely nondiscursive character of the state of consciousness; he was aiming at its being free even from the more "elevated" thoughts such as of the nature, goodness, and power of God. Put linguistically, the language of theism is imposed on the experience.

There is in the *Cloud* a thesis related to this "nakedness" of experience, and of the intent that impels the person on his quest, which might have interested Buddhaghosa as indicating a parallel with Buddhist ethics. In the Buddhist case, we note a mysterious solidarity between insight and compassion (which in the Mahayana was embodied in the figure of the compassionate Bodhisattva). In an important sense, the *Cloud* is about the love of God. But whereas many writers think of love as related specifically to a person, so that loving God is loving a Person, the *Cloud* has an interesting and paradoxical twist. For true love is identified with "naked intent." This links up, as William Johnston has pointed out, with Thomas Aquinas's doctrine of perfect love, which is not inspired by any "mean,"; that is, it is not inspired by the remembrance of the goodness of God, but simply arises from the loveliness of God in Himself (p. 108). From this perspective, the love of God is the love of X, because all the particularities of the Christian myth and doctrine fall away in the cloud of forgetting. So paradoxically, it is God considered without those attributes that constitute personhood for us, which is the "object" of perfect love. The ineffable character of the focus of the mystical quest thus helps to explain the nature of perfect love. Buddhaghosa would, of course, have used very different language, but he might easily have failed to see any stateable distinction between *nirvāṇa* and God as considered nakedly, so to speak. Is there a distinction phenomenologically? I do not think it can be denied that at least the possibility of the congruence of the two experiences exists. If they are congruent, we still of course have the problem of why, outside of ineffability, such very different "trailers" were left dangling by the two concepts. That issue would take us far afield, but we may note that the numinous dread of God is something that courses down salvation history in the Jewish and Christian traditions but has no strong place in the Theravada. Naturally, too, one can point to the divergence of philosophical theory or worldview and hence of language between the two cultures. All this can be summed up by saying that while Buddhaghosa would have rejected the contextual language of the *Cloud*, he would have made sense of the notions of naked intent and pure or perfect love.

The notion that the mystic must blot out the attributes of God leads him to some passages that seem antidogmatic, as if he were heretical. Thus he writes: "Yea, — and if it be courteous and seemly to say — in this work it profiteth little or nought to think of the kindness or the worthiness of God, nor of our Lady . . ." (chap. 5). The author of the *Cloud* is a devout and orthodox Christian, but even from within the tradition there are forces that make a mystic go beyond doctrines. Buddhaghosa might consider this a kind of confirmation of the Buddha's reluctance to define or describe, except in metaphors, the nature of *nirvāṇa*.

One might add an aside here that helps to reinforce the point made about the contextuality of belief in God and the Trinity in the life of a contemplative such as our author. Given the nature of his upbringing in medieval times, how else could he conceive of his highest quest than as drawing close to or becoming united with God? But if it is the case that the essential character of the higher mystical experience is to be devoid of perceptions of images, even of God, and to rise beyond conceptualization, then there is bound to be a split between the conventional doctrines concerning God (and biblical language), on the one hand, and the mode in which the mystical experience is expressed, on the other. The teaching of the church and the Bible were based substantially on a prophetic and sacramental religion, stressing the dread character of the Almighty, the coming to earth of His Son, and the infusion of the Holy Spirit in the work and sacraments of the church. All these items — the numinous, the incarnation, the ritual dimension of the faith — can exist without the element of mysticism — that is, without the contemplative life. Indeed, there have been periods and phases in the church's history when the contemplative life has been substantially ignored (e.g., in much of Presbyterianism, in periods of

Anglicanism, and so on). The mystical tradition of Christianity has certainly been very important, and the fusion of Neoplatonic thought and practice with Christian doctrine and life has been very fertile. But the main structure of Christian thinking and experience has not derived entirely from contemplation. Hence the question must be asked: How have these noncontemplative elements affected the contemplative, and vice versa? By contrast, it is hard to think of Buddhism appearing in the varieties of Pure-Land Buddhism — and it is impossible to think of Buddhism without contemplation in the context of the Theravada of Buddhaghosa. The *Path* itself expresses the heart of Theravadin spirituality; notably absent is a sacramental kind of ritual and the very idea of a numinous supreme creator. There is no "Thus spake the Lord" prophetism in this tradition. Buddhaghosa would, then, have continually wondered how it was that the author of the *Cloud* had to import such alien ideas as God and Christ into his description of the path that led into the cloud.

So far we have concentrated on the ideas of forgetting and nakedness. But we have to deal with the cloud of unknowing itself. For Buddhaghosa it would have seemed a paradox for a special reason: Buddhism always saw the root of our problem to be, in the last analysis, ignorance — that is, lack of (existential, living) knowledge. It would have seemed strange to have valued a cloud of unknowing so highly. But of course for the *Cloud*, unknowing is, after all, a kind of knowing. The author quotes Dionysius, to whom he is much indebted (though his understanding of him was perhaps imperfect): "And therefore it was that Saint Denis said: The most godly knowing of God is that which is known by unknowing." His reasoning is: "For have a man never so much ghostly understanding in knowing of all made ghostly things, yet he may never by the work of his understanding come to the knowing of an unmade ghostly thing: the which is nought but God. But by the failing it may. Because that thing that it faileth in is nothing else but only God" (chap. 70).

Buddhaghosa acknowledges that higher wisdom, or *paññā*, differs from ordinary knowledge (*Path*, XIV.1–3). It is a penetrative understanding that differs, however, from the kind of understanding or knowing alluded to by the *Cloud* in that it involves reflection, after the highest *jhānic* experience on the nature of events in the world, revealed by contrast with the unmade, the permanent, and so forth, that characterize *nirvāṇa*. We may say that Buddhist knowledge is cyclical in character: the analysis of the world and the possibility of liberation set the scene for treading the path of purification. The worldview is used in describing and categorizing the various states and attitudes of the individual searcher. But the search ends at a higher level that, reflecting back on the world as previously analyzed, penetrates to a deeper level in discerning the nature of things. This process of beginning with a worldview and then returning to it more deeply in the light of mystical experience is less evident in the *Cloud*.

Let us now pass to the cloud of knowing, itself. How does this look from a Buddhist perspective? I think there are three points that we need to consider, which I shall take in reverse order: the nature of the cloud considered in itself; the reference in the *Cloud* to the ray of light said to pierce the cloud; and the notion of a kind of union with God. A major text here, in regard to this last, is found in chapter 67:

> Above thyself thou art: because thou attainest to come thither by grace, whither thou mayest not come by nature. That is to say, to be oned to God, in spirit and in love and in accordance of will Beneath thy God thou art: for although it may be said in a manner that in this time God and thou be not two but one in spirit—insomuch that thou or another that feeleth the perfection of this work may, by reason of that onehead, truly be called a god, as Scripture witnesseth—nevertheless thou art beneath him. For he is God by nature without beginning; and thou sometimes wert nought in substance; and afterwards, when thou wert by his might and his love made aught, thou willfully with sin madest thyself worse than nought. And only by his mercy without thy desert art thou made a god in grace, oned with him in spirit without separation, both here and in the bliss of heaven without any end. So that, although thou be all one with him in grace, yet thou art full far beneath him in nature.

This is indeed a striking passage. We may note how the author is sensitive to possible criticisms. To say that you are God would be *tout court* unacceptable in the Christian tradition. The great gap between God and humanity, bridged by Christ, must be maintained. And yet the author can figure that he is like Christ, who offers himself to God — and so, in the mystic's self-consciousness, his naked being turns out to be the being of God, and so it is God offering himself up to himself (or worshiping himself). The suffering implicit in giving up one's natural desires and impulses can be likened to Christ's suffering. The language of martyrdom, incarnation, and self-giving can thus be melded.

Yet it is fairly clear that when the *Cloud* avers that "thou art less than God" this is not based on the experience itself. There is nothing phenomenological here in the contrast between nature and grace. The exposition of the distinction owes itself to the author's general theological background and linguistic schemata, and if there is anything that is phenomenologically like grace, it arises in the idea of the ray of light, to which I shall come shortly. The distinction that the author makes comes from a prior belief in the everlastingness of God, compared with the finite character of the individual. It should be noted by the way that the assumption that the individual previously was nought in substance is not one that Buddhaghosa would make, since he believes in the preexistence of the individual (*Path*, XVII.253ff.). Given that the author of the *Cloud* believes in a divine creator, then it is easy for him to make the nature–grace distinction, and this softens the alarming character of his claim that we are "oned with God."

It is also fairly clear that in order to be oned, there have to be at least two conceived of as different. It is because the *Cloud* holds to a God over against us that it can naturally enough talk of union. In the case of Buddhaghosa there is nothing out there, though there is the unmade, unconditioned State — *nirvāṇa*. For him it does not make sense to say that the individual is united with some thing — but there is the vision of *nirvāṇa*, the realization of the unborn condition. This notion was put into the language of emptiness in the Mahayana tradition. There is considerable testimony in the mystical literature that the highest state is without distinction of subject and object, or is nondual (*advaya*). The description that the *Cloud* gives of the cloud itself and the highest experience is consistent with there occurring a nondual experience, which is naturally enough seen ex post facto as being oned with God. But Buddhaghosa might reflect that if we confine our attention to the naked realization of being, in a nondual way, and if we substitute a different ontology for that of being and substance, then there is no incompatibility between the *Cloud* and the *Path* as to the highest state and realization of *nirvāṇa*. Rather than talking of mystical union—common for obvious reasons among theistic mystics and hedged about with qualifications to effect a compromise with the language of numinous Otherness—we might talk of mystical nonduality (I hesitate to use the term "nondualism" because of its association with a kind of monism, which is not the purport either of Theravada Buddhism or of Christian mystical theology).

But there seems to be more than the cloud in the cloud; there is the striking reference to the ray of light. Thus in chapter 26, the author writes:

> Then will he sometimes peradventure send out a beam of ghostly light, piercing this *cloud of unknowing* that is betwixt thee and him, and show thee some of his secrets, the which man may not and cannot speak. Then shalt thou feel thine affection inflamed with the fire of his love, far more than I can tell thee, or may or will at this time. For of that work that pertaineth only to God dare I not take upon me to speak with my blabbering fleshly tongue: and, shortly to say, although I durst I would not.

This experience of light is recorded by a number of mystics. Richard of St. Victor writes of it as *in modum fulguris coruscantis* (*Benjamin minor*, chap. 82). Various instances are recorded by modern Buddhists in Winston L. King's *Theravada Meditation* (pp. 126, 136–37, 159–60). The language of illumination has spread widely in English and other languages. The analogy to a sudden flash may be related to another interesting part of the *Cloud*, where the author writes:

> This work asketh no long time ere it be once truly done, as some men ween; for it is the shortest work of all that man may imagine. It is neither longer nor shorter than is an atom; the which atom, by the definition of true philosophers in the science of astronomy, is the least part of an hour. And it is so little that, for the littleness of it, it is indivisible and nearly incomprehensible. (chap. 4)

According to contemporary medieval calculations, there are over 20,000 atoms in an hour, making this unit equal to about one-sixth of a second. By the unrefined methods of medieval time, this was a tiny unit, perhaps less than the normal perceptions of time would be able to cope with. Perhaps the *Cloud* here signifies, as William Johnston suggests, that the experience is somehow outside time. There are remarks elsewhere indicating that time, place, and body should be forgotten or blotted out in the spiritual life. Somehow the experience of light then suggests something from "outside space and time." Buddhaghosa might note that *nirvāṇa* likewise is referred to as the "immortal place," no doubt hinting at an "event" that is outside of time (as distinguished from ordinary events, which are in time). In brief, the account of a timeless light is within the bounds of metaphors used in the Buddhist tradition.

The passage about the beam of ghostly light implies that somehow the ultimate illuminating experience is spontaneous. For the author, this is reinforcement of the feeling that here we see the operation of grace. The final consummation of the spiritual quest is something that seems given to us. This, of course, is a theme stressed in Zen, though it is less prominent in the Theravada tradition. But an event can be spontaneous without being caused by God and as such categorized as grace. The language of grace has far-reaching ramifications, here no doubt superimposed on the mystical experience.

In saying this I am not implying that the *Cloud* is wrong. In all our experience, we superimpose knowledge gained from elsewhere. I see a patch of red outside my window, out there where the lawn finishes; it is bougainvillea. How do I know that? Not simply by looking, but out of my complex learning in the past. It may be that the author of the *Cloud* is right to diagnose his experience in the cloud of unknowing as being a kind of contact and ultimately oneness with God. Whether he is right or wrong depends on a much wider set of conditions than can be drawn from the mystical experience itself, but it is a wider set that could be put on one side by Buddhaghosa.

We may draw certain conclusions about the cloud of unknowing itself. First, from Buddhaghosa's viewpoint, it can be the same "place" as *nirvāṇa*, provided that the mystic, having reached it, were then to cast his divine eye on the rest of the world in order to contemplate it *sub specie eternitatis* and thus gain insight, or *paññā*. Second, it takes the mystic "outside time" to perceive what is transcendent. Third, the experience involves the perception of a spiritual light, so that it contains the images of both light and obscuring (a point mentioned by some other mystics, notably Willem van Ruysbroeck). In my view, it is quite possible to conceive of the experience without applying to it the whole language of nature and grace, God and creatures, and so forth, that the author of the *Cloud* naturally uses.

But it is worth noting that though Buddhaghosa might wish to put aside all that language, he would be faced with the question of how it is that the whole Buddhist analysis is to be applied to the highest stages of meditation. Since, of course, Buddhism centers on the mystical quest, which is only one main element in the fabric of Christian experience and practice, it would be easier to justify the Buddhist than the Christian analysis of mysticism. Perhaps this is already brought out by the detailed and confident analytic style of the *Path* and other works. The question of whether the *Cloud* is right turns our attention to the whole language of God, built as it is on the numinous experience and the practice of worship that have only minor places in the Theravadin outlook. Yet we should not neglect the fact that mysticism such as that of the *Cloud* has had notable effects on the language of Christian theology. There is no doubt that the whole enterprise of negative theology (such as in Pseudo-Dionysius) is erected on the practice of mysticism, and the negative language arises from the transsensory nature of mystical experience. Where the mystical strand of Christianity has been absent, other motifs become stronger, as in *bhakti* varieties of the faith and nineteenth-century Methodism. This perhaps reinforces the claim that mysticism and *bhakti*, and mysticism and sacramental religion, are independent of one another. But that is a wider question.

I think Buddhaghosa would have found the *Cloud*'s invitation to the mystical path both intelligible and attractive, but the language of God highly indigestible. The reason, of course, is that built into the language of the *Cloud* are highly ramified conceptions of the divine. That is, the author assumes the truth of classical Western theism as mediated through the Jewish and Christian scriptures and subsequent Christian theologizing and philosophizing. It is a tradition that effectively blends Neoplatonism and Christian faith. By saying that it is highly ramified, I allude to a distinction that I drew in "Interpretation and Mystical Experience." A highly ramified description is one in which a number of propositions are presupposed as true, lying well outside what could be revealed by the experience itself. Admittedly, this is a rather informal distinction. It can be intuitively recognized through the contrast between "He saw a yellow patch" (low ramification) and "He saw a black cassock" (more highly ramified). In the latter case, we have to know what a cassock is, and its function as an ecclesiastical garment. In other words, highly ramified language postulates a fairly extensive context of belief and/or action. Although the existence of ramified language is a fact, it is something that is so because of a nonlinguistic state of affairs, in the sense at least that it is a state of affairs that includes much more than the linguistic. Thus the author of the *Cloud* was plugging into a context of monastic life lying within the historic Christian tradition. The strangeness of the language to Buddhaghosa lies not in the question of translation per se, for many of the problems lie in the divergence of assumptions. Perhaps, being formerly a Brahmin, Buddhaghosa might have recognized in the *Cloud* some pre-Śankaran form of Vedanta, a kind of system of the *Brahmasūtra*.

But the *Cloud*'s language has two levels to it because the author is keen on the negative theology of the Dionysian tradition. The quoted passage from the "Epistle of Privy Counsel" makes interesting reading in this connection. Bare being differs not a whit from bare nonbeing, save that it signals the commitment to a certain style of ontology. The effect of the author's appeal to the little word "is" in effect negates the more particular concepts that he alleges are contained in it. Now Buddhaghosa could have appreciated the negativeness, for that also characterizes emptiness (*sūnyatā*) and *nirvāna*. But could he have agreed that the other terms that the author of the *Cloud* draws forth from the ultimate do so derive? Such terms as "Strength," "Almighty," and "All-witting" (i.e., "Omniscient") simply cannot sensibly be predicated of *nirvāna*. The fact is that these various predicates are not contained in "is," which is a blank term in having no definitive descriptive function. This is one reason why Buddhaghosa might not find it too uncongenial, since in the higher echelons of the process of *jhāna* he looks for emptier and emptier characterizations of the ineffable state that the adept reaches. This is why for him the *via negativa* could prove to be congenial. Of course, Theravadin ontology is event-based, not thing-based. Yet the *via negativa* still leaves unexplained the connection between the negative descriptions (or non-descriptions) and the more positive language that is secretly there through the commitment and milieu of the believer who wants the negations to apply to her or his ultimate. This is a wider problem than one that is encountered in the *Cloud* or the *Path*. Let me digress a moment before expanding on this point.

Generally the negative way has its function from three sources. One is reflective on the intellectual reasons why the ultimate eludes our grasp. The second and third are existential. The notion of ineffability has a descriptive and a performative aspect. The descriptive aspect arises from the descriptive nullity of higher mystical states. To describe something as indescribable is in this way a minimal form of description, since most ordinary descriptions arise from determinate and discriminable contents of perception. The highest mystical experience passes beyond the ordinary sphere of description; but since it is an actual state, it has some minimum describability, and mystics use various methods to delineate its higher blankness. Third, ineffability is a performative, since the sublime character of the experience is "higher"—that is, of greater value—than other experiences. As in saying "I cannot express my deep gratitude," I express my gratitude, so in saying "My experience could not be put into words," I put it into words. Ineffability, indescribability, unutterability, indefinability—such terms and their relations have a performative aspect. And pregnant silence itself becomes a kind of utterance.

But, of course, the author of the *Cloud* approaches the ultimate from a certain angle. He comes from the direction of Christian theism. He projects into the formless "is" the concepts of Lordship and Omniscience and what have you, and then miraculously finds these terms encapsulated in the "is" and so easily to be drawn forth. This is not a criticism; it is the way the ultimate has to be seen—through the linguistic path by which it (or she, or he) is attained conceptually.

But Buddhaghosa does stand for something: he stands for the observation that the languages of unity, or of communion and love, of monism or theism, are not ineluctable, for the Theravada is not ontological absolutism or a kind of theism; there is not in it a great Being out there. It differs from all Vedantas and all Western theologies—indeed, from all theologies. This poses an important question about the mystical path.

To return to the negative way: it is obvious that a totally ineffable X is, so to speak, compatible with anything. Why should we, having trod the negative way, speak of the ultimate in one way rather than another? Why should we think that Śankara's ultimate is hitched to Brahmanical practices and the Vedas rather than to Christian theism and the sacraments? Insofar as the negative way often coincides at the intellectual level with the mystical path at the existential level, we can develop the question: How can we know that the goal of mysticism is one state (such as communion with God) rather than another? It may be that some forms of mysticism have a personal quality that suggests the language of God rather than that of *nirvāṇa*. But there seem to be some forms of mysticism that end in dazzling darkness, and these seem to be compatible with both Christian theism and Buddhist nirvanism. Any decision between the two interpretations must rest on other grounds. Or do we have to decide?

It will be seen from my discussion that we cannot divorce questions of language from doctrinal suppositions, living contexts, and phenomenology. In brief, very elaborate languages, but highly diverse, were evolved around the contemplative lives of the Theravada and of medieval Christianity respectively.

References

I have used the edition of the *Cloud* edited by Justin McCann, *The Cloud of Unknowing and Other Treatises* (Westminster, Md., 1952). I have cited Buddhaghosa's *Visuddhimagga*, trans. Bhikkhu Nyanamoli, 2 vols. (Berkeley, 1976).

Other works referred to:

John of Ruysbroeck. *The Adornment of Spiritual Marriage*, trans. C. A. Wynschenk. London, 1916.
Johnston, William. *The Mysticism of the Cloud of Unknowing*. St. Meinrad, Ind., 1975.

122   *Mysticism and Language*

King, Winston L. *Theravada Meditation, the Buddhist Transformation of Yoga*. Philadelphia, 1980.

Knowles, David. *The English Mystical Tradition*. New York, 1961.

Richard of St. Victor. *Selected Writings on Contemplation*, ed. Clare Kirchberger. New York, 1957.

Smart, Ninian. *Reasons and Faiths*. London, 1958.

————. "Interpretation and Mystical Experience," in Smart, *Concept and Empathy*, ed. Donald Wiebe. New York, 1986.

IV

COMPARATIVE STUDIES

CHAPTER 8

Numen, Nirvana, and the Definition of Religion

DESPITE Rudolf Otto's remarkable contributions to the philosophy and comparative study of religion, there is a defect in his treatment of spiritual experience—namely, his relative neglect of, and partial misinterpretation of, Buddhist nirvana.[1] This hinders a fully satisfactory analysis of mysticism and militates against a correct description of the nature of religion. What I wish to show here is, briefly, as follows. Given Otto's analysis of his own illuminating expression "numinous", nirvana is not, strictly speaking, numinous; but nirvana is the key concept of (at least Lesser Vehicle) Buddhist doctrine and practice; hence it is unsatisfactory to define religion by reference to the numinous or analogous notions. Further, however, by appeal to the idea of "family resemblance", we can avoid the embarrassment we might feel at not discovering some essence of all religion. Finally I attempt to indicate how a sharp differentiation between agnostic mysticism and theism (together with pantheism and other forms of characteristically numinous religion) can lead to new insights into the structure of religious doctrine and experience.

I

Let us first examine one of Otto's rare and scattered remarks about nirvana:

> It exercises a "fascination" by which its votaries are as much carried away as are the Hindu or the Christian by the corresponding objects of their worship.[2]

It is surely clear that the use of the expression "votaries" and the implication contained in the phrase "corresponding objects of worship" accord nirvana a status it never possessed in Theravāda Buddhism and almost certainly did not explicitly possess in the earliest form of the religion.[3] Gods and god-like entities can have votaries and be objects of worship: but the serenity of nirvana is no god, nor is it even the peace of God. It is interesting to note that Otto writes, in his foreword to *Mysticism East and West*, that we must combat the

> erroneous assumption that mysticism is "one and ever the same". Only thus is it possible to comprehend such great spiritual phenomena

Numen, Nirvana, and the Definition of Religion   217

as, for instance, the German Meister Eckhart, the Indian Śankara, the Greek Plotinus, the mystics of the Buddhist Mahāyāna school, in all their characteristic individuality, instead of allowing them to disappear into the shadowy night of "general mysticism". The nature of mysticism only becomes clear in the fullness of its possible manifestations.[4]

The Hīnayāna is left out, even though it has produced such a striking handbook of mystical meditation as the *Visuddhimagga* and despite the accounts of the Buddha's Enlightenment. Further, Hīnayāna mysticism exhibits a greater divagation from theistic mysticism than does even the soul-mysticism of Yoga and Jainism.

Before listing rather briefly a few reasons for denying that nirvana, is, in the strict sense, numinous, it is perhaps as well to counter the criticism of unfairness: "Surely we owe the term 'numinous' to Otto, and if he uses it of nirvana, are we not to say that he knows best?" But once a term is introduced it becomes public property: I am not arguing against the use of "numinous", for Otto's coining has been of great service—it is only that on certain occasions he is loose or inconsistent in his employment of it.

(i) The elements in the numinous discrimination by Otto are, it will be recalled, those of awefulness, overpoweringness, energy, and "fascination". Now these certainly depict admirably objects of worship, such as gods and God. To some extent also they define many ghostly and "spooky" phenomena which Otto uses as examples. But a state such as nirvana hardly possesses all these characteristics: only, perhaps, "fascination". Now it may be replied that each of the elements should be regarded rather as a *mark*; i.e., each by itself tends to or would establish the numinousness of whatever possesses it. But apart from the undesirable looseness that this interpretation would confer upon the term, Otto analysed the numinous in the way that he did because all the elements are usually or always found in genuine objects of worship.

(ii) Experiences cannot easily be understood in isolation, but are best seen in their whole setting—in the attitude and behaviour which surround them; in particular, religious experience must be viewed in the context of the spiritual practices associated with it or expressing it. Thus characteristically experiences of awe, of an overpowering and energetic presence, are associated with and expressed by such activities as worship and sacrifice. Now altogether it is true that the mystical Path towards some inner realization as we find it in

218 *Numen, Nirvana, and the Definition of Religion*

the Christian setting is integrated with activities such as the worship
of and prayer to a personal God, in the Lesser Vehicle there is not
merely formal agnosticism, but the religion of sacrifice and worship
associated with a divine Being or beings is ignored as being irrelevant
to salvation. Moreover, such attention as is paid to numinous entities
such as *nats* and *devas* is merely peripheral, springing from non-
Buddhist sources; while the veneration of relics such as the Sacred
Tooth is moderated severely by the denial of Gotama's divinity.[5]

(iii) Otto, in criticizing the subjectivism of Schleiermacher's
account of creature-feeling, remarked: "The numinous . . . is felt as
objective and outside the self."[6] This indeed is a correct description
of how a *numen praesens* strikes the religious man; note that not
merely is the *numen* in some way "objective", but there is even a
dualism continually being expressed in religious language between
the worshipper and the object of awe. But nirvana could hardly be
counted a *numen praesens*; and it is only in a rather peculiar sense
"outside the self". Admittedly we here run into complications, on
account both of the fact that in certain spiritual contexts there is
the notion of a Self set over against the "empirical self" and of the
peculiarly Buddhist *anattā* (non-self) doctrine. But first, the *numen
praesens* is usually thought of as nearby in some spatial or quasi-
spatial way. And second, even those who would interpret nirvana as
a kind of beatified persistence beyond death[7] not unlike Christian
immortality (though without God there) give an account inconsistent with nirvana's being conceived as an object of worship. Also,
whatever may be said—and quite a lot can be—in defence of the
notion of mystical experience as "other" than ordinary experience
(thus generating the concept of an "other" Self, etc., realizable
through mystical endeavour, as in some of the *Upaniṣads*), quite
clearly there is a difference between the sense in which the Ātman
is "beyond" the empirical self and that in which God is "beyond"
the visible world and so is that mysterious Other. The difference is
indicated by that tension which we find in theistic mysticism and
which was well expressed by Rabindranath Tagore when he said:
"What we want is to worship God. But if the worshipper and the
Object of Worship are on, how can there be any worship?" Nevertheless, despite the difference, it is the genius of certain religions to
fuse together different insights into a single doctrinal scheme—so
that, e.g., realizing the Ātman is becoming Brahman and that the
cloud of unknowing is the dwelling-place of that God who appeared

Numen, Nirvana, and the Definition of Religion 219

in a very different sort of cloud to Job : this commingling of strands of religious language, experience, and practice (for the three go together) will be further considered below.

(iv) Nirvana, however, is given certain epithets which might lead one to think of it as something like Ultimate Reality — and this in turn is sometimes an impersonal way of describing God.[8] And hence we get such statements as this :

> Nirvana . . . is not stated in such a way that it can be identified with God, but it may be said to be feeling after an expression of the same truth.[9]

Thus nirvana is called "deathless" (*amata*), "unconditioned" (*asankhata*), "permanent" (*nicca, dhuva*), etc. Now even if these epithets may be held to assimilate nirvana in some degree, though certainly in a loose manner, to God, they reveal themselves upon inspection to be typically applicable to a mystical state in this life just as much as to a genuinely transcendent Being. Thus nirvana is *amatā* because it is (to quote another epithet) *akutobhaya*, "with nothing to fear from anywhere", for in attaining it in this life one loses the fear of death — and not merely because of the doctrine that there will then be no rebirth hereafter,[10] but through the great peacefulness and serenity of it. And also it is *amata* because the mystical experience at its highest level is, in being without perceptions, likewise without time.[11] Again, it is permanent partly at least by contrast with the world of compound things, which are transitory and fleeting : for though early Buddhism denied the soul of *ātman*, the distinction between the spiritual state and the world of ordinary experience is, naturally enough, retained. Similarly with "unconditioned".[12] And nirvana transcends the impermanent world by being, so to speak, other-worldly — an otherworldliness defined by the training laid down in the Noble Eightfold Path, and because it is *yogakkhema anuttara*, "unsurpassed peace", of transcendent value. That is to say, then, the epithets are understandably applicable even to nirvana in this existence,[13] without our bringing in that final nirvana accruing upon death and negatively expressed by saying that there is no rebirth.

(v) Otto elsewhere says :

> The salvation sought in Nirvana, like that sought in Yoga, is magical and numinous. It is the utterly suprarational, of which only silence

220 Numen, Nirvana, and the Definition of Religion

can speak. It is a blessedness which fascinates. It is only to be achieved by way of negation — the inexpressible wonder.[14]

Here, to put it briefly, Otto's main ground for declaring nirvana to be numinous is that it is utterly non-rational. But that a thing is non-rational does not entail that it is numinous, though the converse may perhaps hold. Otto elsewhere gives an account of what he means by "non-rational": while on the one hand we may experience deep joy, which on introspection can be "identified in precise conceptual terms", it is otherwise with religious "bliss": not even the most concentrated attention can elucidate the object to which it refers — it is purely a felt experience, only to be indicated symbolically.[15] But it is perhaps odd to say that in all non-religious contexts we can if pressed express our feelings "in precise conceptual terms". Nevertheless, there are certainly occasions upon which we can say *why* we are overjoyed, etc., and this clearly has something to do with "the object to which the state of mind refers". This understanding, however, is impossible with regard to a genuine mystical state for a different reason from that which makes it impossible with regard to a feeling of "bliss" at the fascination of the numinous. For a feeling of supreme exaltation in the context of worship or worshipping meditation is connected with God: for God is that at which, so to speak, attention is directed; and God is mysterious and overwhelming and so not to be described adequately. On the other hand, in agnostic mysticism (and we find analogies in all mysticism) the state of mind is quite empty and rapt and there is in the nature of the case nothing "to which the state of mind refers". A different sort of "non-rationality" is connected with reaction to the holy from that association with mystical liberation, though the two become fused in religions such as Brahmanism and Christianity. A second and most important point here that there is some danger in overemphazising the "non-rational" character of such spiritual experiences. This can be illustrated from the fact that Otto, in discussing the difference between agnostic soul-mysticism (such as agnostic Yoga) and the Brahman-mysticism exemplified in Śankara, remarks that the difference between their contents is itself non-rational and only to be comprehended in mystical experience itself.[16] This despairing statement hardly does justice to Otto's own achievement in discriminating the two types; but it is connected with his belief that religious concepts are merely symbolical. The danger in regarding doctrines and religious terminology as "only

Numen, Nirvana, and the Definition of Religion   221

symbols" is that they can easily this way become distorted, by being viewed as somehow pointing to the same Reality. And to say this last thing is to utter at best a half-truth. For we must distinguish between (a) describing one religious view in terms of another, (b) describing it in its own terms, and (c) exhibiting analogies. Now as for (a), a Christian or a Hindu might wish to say that the two religions are, in certain of their doctrines, pointing to the same truth; but because each would prefer or insist on using one set of symbols rather than another to depict this truth, they would in effect be interpreting the other religion in terms of their own. Similarly we may, as apologists, interpret nirvana in theistic terms, but this is emphatically not what the Buddha said, and to treat nirvana in Hīnayāna terms we have to retain the agnosticism. As to (c), it is certainly illuminating to trace the respects in which attaining nirvana may be like attaining the unitive life of Western mysticism : it is doubtless on such analogies that an interpretation of nirvana in a loosely theistic sense would have to be based. The differences too are important : but Otto in his extreme emphasis on non-rationality is in difficulty over characterizing them.

(vi) Finally, with regard to the interpretation of final nirvana as a transcendent state "beyond space and time", this indeed is a vexed and complicated subject. But even if we grant that the Buddha's negations leave room for the belief that there is some kind of entity persisting in a non-empirical state after death, the nearest model we have for picturing such a condition is the sheer tranquility of the yogic mystic in his highest self-realization; and the points that have been made above about the pure mystical state as not *necessarily* having anything to do with the numinous will hold again in this context.

Briefly, then : although Otto's analysis of the numinous fits very well gods and god-like entities and well describes men's reactions to these in experience—although, that is, it is successful in regard to those beings who are typically addressed in worship and negotiated with in sacrifice—it hardly holds in regard to those states and entities that are encountered along the yogic path. But this point is sometimes obscured because, in the circle of theistic religion (and this is what we are most accustomed to in the West), it is common to associate the beatific nirvana-like state with God; nevertheless, though it may in fact be true that the mystical vision is vision of the numinous Deity, it is not *self-evident*, it is not analyt-

222   *Numen, Nirvana, and the Definition of Religion*

ically true. We must recognize the possibility of mysticism without worship, just as all along we have recognized the phrases of religious history where there is worship, prayer, and sacrifice without any yogic or mystical path; but there is no genuine concept of god or God without worship, and conversely. The importance of nirvana is that it is a purer example of the mystical goal even than the soul-mysticism of Yoga that Otto studied, for in Buddhism there is not even the *ātman*, and it is perhaps a sign of the Buddha's rigid determination to evolve a "pure" mysticism without any theistic or pantheistic complications that he excluded the concept of an eternal soul, which in being capable of separate existence and in being described substantivally is already too much adaptable to numinous concepts — as both the Vedānta and theistic Yoga demon-strate.

2

The question arises here as to how we are to define "religion" in such a way that the term will cover not only polytheism and theism (i.e. religions which are suffused with numinousness), together with not too dissimiliar pantheistic faiths, but also agnostic and transtheistic Buddhism and Jainism. Of course the problem has exercised many before now, and for this or similar reasons Buddhism has often been regarded as a "crux" in the comparative study of religion. One way of trying to produce an old-fashioned definition is to point to some "essence" of religious phenomena; but a result of this is to distort the agnostic faiths by interpreting their negations as a type of theological agnosticism, so as to have an essential content in all religions. Another way is to place heavy emphasis on some essential spirit in all religions, such as their numinosity. In this way religions will have a common form; but again this is to distort, since for instance, the numinous aspects of popular Buddhism in the Hīnayāna are merely peripheral — it is not *nats* and spirits that makes it a living faith, but the call to nirvana. Again, one may try to avoid these pit-falls by escape into empty generality, as with Tillich's definition in terms of "man's ultimate concern"[17] — to give *this* content it is necessary to define these terms themselves, which leads back to a definition of the first type; and here we are in even subtler danger of interpreting another faith in terms, albeit vague, of one's own. But all this is unnecessary, once we abandon the old-fashioned notion of definition and throw

Numen, Nirvana, and the Definition of Religion   223

off the fascination of essences. It is a commonplace in contemporary analytic philosophy that many general words apply to a wide variety of things in virtue, not of some common property, but of "family resemblance", and so are not capable of an essentialist definition.[18] To give a crude scheme of family resemblance : suppose A has properties a, b, and c; while B has b, c, and d; and C has c, d, and e; while D has d, e, and f. Although A has nothing in common with D, it is sufficiently like B for them both to have the same name — and likewise with B and C and with C and D. Of course in actual examples the situation is a much richer one, with subtle and over-lapping similarities, as with the word "game" — though patience and hockey have no common item of content, or at least none which would help to define "game", they are both called games. To call something a game is to place it in a family rather than to ascribe it some complex essence. Similarly, perhaps, with "religion" — we can place both early Buddhism and early Islam in the same family, even though they have nothing obvious or important in common. Thus appeal to the notion of "family resemblance" has at least the following two advantages. First, and negatively, it discourages attempts to define "religion" in an essentialist manner, which leads to misinterpretations accruing upon trying to formulate some common insight in all faiths — there may be different sorts of spiritual insight. Second, and positively, it allows of a sort of disjunctive account of religion : thus, for instance (and crudely), the activities and doctrines associated with worship, sacrifice, *bhakti*, etc., on the one hand, and those associated with the yogic endeavour towards inner enlightenment and with other similar endeavours on the other hand, are two centrally important items in a number of major religions; but we need not insist on the central presence of both or of any particular one of these items for something to count as a religion.

Finally, by reserving the term "numinous" for describing entities and experiences which inspire worship, awe, dread, etc., as well as those objects, places, etc., intimately associated with these, we can take a new look at mysticism. First, *à propos* of Otto, we avoid a mistaken mode of classification : for because of his conviction that the "soul" is a numinous entity and that numinousness is central to religion, he was led to say that every higher faith includes in some way a belief in the soul.[19] This means that Buddhism, despite its *anattā* (non-soul) doctrine, has to be subsumed under the heading of

224   *Numen, Nirvana, and the Definition of Religion*

"soul-mysticism". Second, more importantly, by taking agnostic mysticism as the "typical" or "pure" variety, in the sense explained before, one is faced by a number of interesting and fruitful questions. Why should it seem natural to take this kind of experience as intimately connected with the numinous object of worship? And on the doctrinal level, why should concepts seemingly arrived at in different ways (such as *Brahman* and *Ātman*) be said in some way to coalesce? It is not sufficient to yield to the ever-present temptation in discussing these matters of saying that concepts are not important in themselves, but point to something beyond. For it is at least a *prima facie* difficulty that a concept pointing towards a Power beyond, and sustaining, the visible world should be so closely related to one which points towards a mystical "inner" experience. Nevertheless, we have already observed that there is a loose resemblance—though not so loose that the plasticity of religious language cannot absorb it—between some of the epithets of nirvana and some of those ascribed to God. Thus a theistic interpretation of mysticism is possible, though it is not absolutely forced on one. We may put the point another way, by reference to a classic example, by saying that though it may be a deep insight that Brahman and Ātman are one, this is not an analytic or necessary truth, since the concepts are arrived at along different paths and are connected with different sorts of spiritual activity: it is a welding together of initially different insights. The varying weights put upon the activities and insights by different sects and faiths, moreover, goes a long way towards explaining doctrinal differences—once the types of doctrine associated with each are discriminated. Otto has done much here in his *Mysticism East and West* and elsewhere; but his somewhat wavering treatment of "soul-mysticism" and his comparative neglect of nirvana militated against a successful chemistry of mystical, theistic, and mixed doctrines, for one element was not first isolated in its pure form.

---

[1] Hereafter I use "nirvana" by itself to stand for Buddhist *nirvāṇa*.

[2] *The Idea of the Holy*, trans. J. W. Harvey, 2nd Edition, London (1950), p. 39.

[3] Nirvana does, however, undergo some transformation in the Mahāyāna schools. For instance, on the Mādhyamika view, the Absolute (*tattva, śūnya*) is the same as *prajñā* (wisdom, i.e. non-dualistic insight, *jñānam advayam*) (Mādh. Kārikā, xxv, 19-20). This in turn is identified with the *dharmakāya* or Truth-Body of the Buddhas. Now the knowledge of the Absolute is nirvana

Numen, Nirvana, and the Definition of Religion   225

(ibid., xviii, 5); and thus there is, *via* the Three Body doctrine, a fairly close relation between nirvana as the attainment of non-dualistic insight and the numinous as displayed in the *sambhogakāya* and *nirmāṇakāya* of the Buddhas —in these forms the Buddhas come to be objects of worship.

4 Trans. B. L. Bruce and R. C. Payne, London (1932), p. v.

5 On contemporary feeling about this, see R. L. Slater, *Paradox and Nirvana*, Chicago (1951), p. 31.

6 *The Idea of the Holy*, p. 11.

7 E.g. U Agga in Shwe Zan Aung's "Dialogue on Nibbana", *Journal of the Burmese Research Society*, VIII, Pt. iii (1918), quoted in Slater, op. cit., pp. 54 ff, where survival is of "one's own mind purged from corruption".

8 Such concepts as "Ultimate Reality", "Being", etc., often have a specifically religious, not just philosophical, function, and are frequently found in close connection, though also a state of tension, with notions of a personal divinity : e.g. *nirguṇam* and *saguṇam* Brahman and the chain of identities in the Mahāyānist Three-Body doctrine. See Otto, *Mysticism East and West*, pp. 5 ff, and my article "Being and the Bible", *Review of Metaphysics*, Vol. IX, no. 4 (June 1956).

9 E. J. Thomas, *The Life of Buddha as Legend and History*, London, (1927), p. 2of.

10 More precisely the Buddha used the more comprehensive four-fold (*cātuṣkoṭika*) negation : the *arahat* is not reborn, nor is he not reborn, nor is he both reborn and not reborn, nor is he neither reborn nor not reborn (*Majjhima Nikāya*, i. 426ff and elsewhere). As to survival, however, it would be better for the ordinary uninstructed man to mistake the body for the self (*Saṁyutta Nikāya*, ii. 95).

11 E.g. the last stage of meditation (*jhāna*) is where one is "beyond the sphere of neither perception nor non-perception" in which there is a cessation of both perception and sensation.

12 I.e., it is not caused in any ordinary sense, though the way to it has been pointed out by the Buddha (*Milinda-Pañha*, IV. 7. 14).

13 The usual Pali term is *sa-upādisesa* as opposed to *anupādisesa nibbāna* (nirvana with and without substrate : see Buddhaghosa in *Dhammapada Commentary*, ii. 163—*sa-upādisesa n.* is equivalent to *kilesa-vaṭṭassa khepitatta*, "destruction of the cycle of impurity").

14 *Mysticism East and West*, p. 143.

15 *The Idea of the Holy*, pp. 58-9.

16 *Mysticism East and West*, p. 143.

17 *Systematic Theology*, Vol. I, London (1951), p. 15.

18 See L. Wittgenstein's *Philosophical Investigations*, trans. G. E. M. Anscombe, Oxford (1953), p. 32e.

19 *Mysticism East and West*, p. 143.

CHAPTER 9

What is Religion?

Often it does not matter whether we can define a term. Meaning lies in use rather than a formal translation.

But in the case of religion the definitional problems have intellectual, pedagogical and social (not to say legal) consequences. Thus in the field of religious education, we need to come to an intellectual understanding of what religion is and what the main dimensions of belief, feeling and practice are — so that in the light of this understanding a cogent educational plan can be evolved. Then, at the pedagogical level, we need to understand what elements in human (and in particular young people's) experience are relevant to the religious quest. At the social and legal level: what are the bounds of religious education? How does it engage with other areas, such as moral education?

For these reasons the definition of religion has import.

Of course we should at the outset be clear as to whether we are talking about religion or religions. Perhaps there is no such thing as religion in general — all that we meet are particular religions. However, there are religious sentiments and there are experiences, such as dying, which broadly have a religious significance, so we should not too easily dismiss the concept of religion in general. To this we shall return, but in the meantime it would be best to try to come to a clear view of what *a* religion is, in the traditional and conventional sense. Then we can move on to think about quasi-religions or movements (like Maoism) of a somewhat religious sort even if they purport to reject religion. After that we can, as I have indicated, explore the meaning of religion in general. It will be seen that this procedure is relevant to the distinction sometimes made between explicit and implicit religion (Schools Council 1971).

As for a religion — let us look first at Christianity and then at Buddhism, a good contrast of styles and content. One cannot expect a single core of content in the religions, as has been demonstrated many times in attempts at unity. The demonstration partly springs from the facts of variety, of faith and practice; but it also springs from the fate of unificatory ideologies, such as those of neo-Vedanta. That fate is stated simply. If I claim that all religions really do point to the same truth and I actually specify that truth, as in neo-Vedanta, then surely many traditionalists will reject my description of their faith. Thus many Christians will not recognise the core of their faith as being mystical and non-dualist. On the contrary they may stress the Calvinist distance between heaven and earth. So the unifying doctrine will not command agreement and it will itself become an element in a different religion. The late Aldous Huxley and the Archbishop of Canterbury belonged essentially to different faiths even if the former had in his own mind an ecumenical understanding of Christianity. So then the search for a common core is not fruitful. This does not mean that there are not considerable affinities and overlaps between elements in different religions. Of course there are. But overlaps do not help enough to form the basis of a content-related definition.

So what is to be done? Some throw up their hands and say religion is indefinable. But there is another path — and that is to seek certain common *formal* characteristics of religion. I shall illustrate it by reference to the two religions mentioned above.

I have used this approach in one or two places by invoking a six-dimensional account of religions (Smart 1968). Briefly, this is as follows. First, typically a religion has a system of *doctrines*. Thus in Christianity the Trinity doctrine tries to formalise the implications of revelation. In Buddhism the non-soul doctrine exhibits beliefs concerning the structure of human (and indeed animal and other) existence. Naturally doctrines are not simply metaphysical in aim, but relate in a complex way to practice. Interestingly on one important doctrinal matter, the existence of a creator, Buddhism and Christianity are at odds: another illustration of the difficulties of the common core. Second, religions have *myths*. This is the mythic dimension. I hope it scarcely needs reaffirmation that the word 'myth' is not used in a crude sense (as a story or idea which is false) but more technically as a story of significance somehow depicting, whether in historical event or in imaginative projection, the relation between the transcendent and the human and worldly realm. In Christianity the story of the passion and resurrection of Christ is a central myth. In Buddhism, the story of the Enlightenment of the Buddha and his temptation by Mara, etcetera, is a core myth; of course in the case of the Buddha the transcendent element is not divine, it is rather that extra-mundane state represented by nirvana as the goal and expressed by Dharma (the Buddhist way or teaching) as the message and meaning of what lies in the transactions between here and there. Thirdly, as far as belief is concerned, every religion has a set of social and ethical norms, what I call the *ethical* dimension. In Christianity the central value is love; another is humility (in line with the imitation of Christ and awe before God). In Buddhism, compassion to all living beings is vital, as also a peaceful detached attitude to the normal values of this world. The differing models of Christ, who was crucified, and the Buddha, who died of a digestive complaint at the age of eighty, dictate these norms to a great extent — always remembering the Jewish heritage of Christianity and the early Indian yogic heritage of Buddhism. Doctrines, myths, values — these are the three dimensions relating directly to belief.

On the more practical and existential side: first, a religion involves *ritual*, such as worship. In Christianity, the sacraments are at the heart of the ritual, though other activities such as the singing of hymns can be important also. In Buddhism (save in the Tantra and certain aspects of Mahayana) sacraments are not of the essence. Nevertheless the Sangha (the monastic order) depends upon rituals of initiation, preaching of the Dharma and so forth. First then in the realm of practice and fourth in the total list, there is the ritual dimension of religion. Next, we have to recognize that ritual and other external forms of religion are there at least in part to express and to evoke feelings and *experiences*. Also, experience can spring indirectly and spontaneously upon the religious man — consider Paul on the Damascus Road, the Buddha under the Bo Tree. The love of God in Christianity is inculcated through arousing sentiments via hymns and sacraments; other means are used to induce serenity and detachment among Buddhists. In addition to the ritual and experiential dimensions of religion, every religion is institutionalised, often through a separate organisation or set of organisations such as the churches in Christianity and the Sangha in Buddhism. A religion thus has a *social* dimension.

With regard to religions which are coterminous with some group such as a tribe, there is no strict differentiation out of religious from non-religious institutions. But similarly even in 'world' religions we may detect what may be called the superimposition of the religious upon what otherwise would be the secular. Thus, for example, though marriage can exist as a 'secular' social institution, in Christian societies and in Christian thinking it is seen as a sacrament. The concept of sacrament is superimposed upon the 'secular' situation.

The six-dimensional analysis can be used to see how far some ideologies may have a religious meaning.

If we consider Maoism, we note that it has a set of doctrines: it has a mythic dimension (the Russian Revolution, the Long March, The triumph of Mao and so forth); it has a strong ethical dimension — a new anti-Confucian puritanism; it has a ritual dimension — rather, the use of the Little Red Book, etcetera; some experiential aspects — conversion-experience being important; and of course the Communist Party and cadres as the institutional transmitter of the teachings and correct practice. Though Marxism does not, like orthodox religions, have an other-worldly transcendent reference, and perhaps has some of the dimensions more weakly than traditional religions, it has a sufficient resemblance to make it profitable to make comparisons. Further, since an ideology such as Maoism rivals traditional religions, the study of religions needs to take it into account.

I conclude from this that the concept of a religion is non-finite in the sense that, surrounding religions proper, are certain secular systems of belief which somewhat resemble them. Thus the study of religion needs to take account of these ideologies.

There is another lesson to be learned from the six-dimensional approach, namely that we need to give a rich account of a religion if we are to bring out its nature. It is not enough to recount doctrines as though they were meaningful in themselves outside the context of ritual (worship), experience and so on. This does not mean that religious education involves direct worship, for the ritual presupposes particular belief and this cannot be counted on or demanded in a plural society. But it does mean that religious education has to explore ways in which the reality of worship and religious sentiments can be conveyed effectively.

The study of religions then in principle is plural and dimensional; and it is non-finite in going beyond the traditional religions to the ideologies and systems which resemble and challenge the religions.

What, now, of the notion of *religion* as distinguished from that of *a religion*?

Here we can perhaps begin by asking what a religious question is. Here we do not mean a question concerning a religion, such as 'Why do Muslims go on pilgrimages to Mecca?' or 'Why do Sinhalese Buddhists lay flowers before the Buddha image in the temple?' Rather we mean a question of human existence to which the religions supply answers. Thus 'Why do men suffer?' 'Why does anything exist at all?' 'What lies beyond death?' — these questions would seem to be religious questions rather than simply questions concerning religion. Indeed in an important sense they do not immediately concern the religions. They spring from problems of human existence and meaning.

Here a word about the meaning of 'meaning' may be useful. When we use the expression in some such phrase as 'the meaning of life' we are not thinking of 'meaning' in the ordinary sense, as applied to words. Rather, we are looking to matters of *value* or *purpose*. If I say that my job is meaningless to me, I mean it has lost its savour, its importance — it no longer seems worthwhile. In other words, the questions of human meaning are essentially to do with value — with its conservation and enhancement. This is why sometimes men are hostile to certain philosophies which in a sense devalue values — such as emotivism, namely the theory that all 'statements' of value, such as 'Stealing is wrong', are all essentially expressions of emotion, amounting to 'Boo to stealing!' So, then, the idea that values are objective — guaranteed somehow either by God or by the structure of the universe or in Buddhist terms by the Dharma — this notion is one which reaffirms the meaningfulness of existence, just as also the historical dialectic in Marxism has a similar effect.

To put the matter crudely, the questions about ultimate meaning that can be regarded as religious are to do with *values*.

'Ultimate': what does this term, which I have so easily and obscurely slipped into the discussion, signify? After all, we may recall Tillich's talk of ultimate concern and the like. For him religion is what concerns man ultimately. Incidentally the formula shows that he is only secondarily concerned with religions and ideologies. Man is an abstraction, likewise ultimate concern. One can understand the drive of his thinking, but he did tend to underestimate the diversity of men and their actual concerns. How then can we understand the inner core of Tillich's idea? I suspect that the word 'ultimate' is not quite right. What he was after was the thought that some of our concerns — our questions about meaning and therefore about value — are deeper and more towards the limits of life than many everyday value-questions.

Let me illustrate. I happen to be concerned about the way universities operate. But this is, though fairly important to me, of less 'ultimate' (that is, deep) concern than the problem presented to me existentially by the death of our youngest child. 'Problem' is of course too weak a word. Death, then, especially when particularised, is a deep concern, or presents religious questions, even if not in a traditional way. After all, I could Stoically hold that death must be accepted just as it is — in modern terms this Stoicism turns out to be J.P. Sartre's existentialism. Incidentally, there is a reason why there is an amplification of the existential impact of death. Apart from the particular sorrow, there is the more general reflection that death threatens values. That is, since much of life seems to get its value from ongoing projects and institutions, death represents a question mark over that value. Hence the grim horror and hopelessness of *On the Beach*. If death claims us, then does it not thereby claim the long-term purposes in which we cooperate with our fellow men?

So then we can reckon some questions about value to be sufficiently 'deep' and serious to warrant their being called religious, even if they are not posed in explicitly religious terms. But since the degree of value is not absolute, but a matter (to be obvious) of degree, it follows that all value-questions have some degree of religious significance. It is only that the more highly charged ones have such an amount of 'ultimacy' that their religious significance becomes obvious.

In brief, Tillich and others have been wrong in supposing that ultimacy is absolute — rather it is a matter of degree of depth.

However, it would be very foolish to think that all value-questions are *ipso facto* religious. Even if such questions are a matter of degree, it does not at all follow that the degree of degree is unimportant. Whether I should have cheese or fruit for the final course of lunch is a value-question, but not deep. It is true that one might consider the choice important (after all, austerity in food is significant in a number of varieties of religious practice). Even so, considered in itself from the 'secular' point of view, the choice is not all that vital. Hence it is a choice which would not normally be included within the ambit of religious 'ultimacy'. In brief then, the *implicit* questions regarding religion and the implicit outreaches of experience arise from those value-questions (therefore related to human life) which are the most important — not just at the limit of ultimacy, whatever that is, but near there, for the truly important questions of value also can raise religious problems and therefore gain religious answers.

Let us expand a little on this point. It is fairly fashionable in these later days to look on life as a series of *questions* or *problems*. That is indeed right from more than one point of view. We live in a plural society where folk, even very young folk, have to make up their own minds, in a context where people generally think, whether in Parliament or in school and whether teaching or learning, that religion is a 'private' matter — a matter for individual choice. Given the previous analysis, all this means that though all value-questions have in principle a religious aspect, in fact it is more practical to see the deeper value-questions as religious. Individual choice is now, in our society and in our world, implicit in the very idea of religious education, so the study of some of these deeper questions will be part of RE.

New Movements in Religious Education

We can sum up the argument hitherto as follows. Firstly it is important to recognise that a large part of our concern with religion is to do with religions. In other words, religions represent facts and feelings and for this reason represent also the elements of answers to living questions implicit in life. Since ideologies also have a similar role, and have a dimensional analogy to religions, the exploration of religions passes over into the exploration of ideologies. When it comes to considering *religion* (as distinct, at least in conception, from the religions) we are here dealing with 'ultimate' value-questions related to the meaning of human life. And to understand a religion we need to have some grasp of its relationship to these values and meanings.

Since I have on the 'implicit' side stressed the connection between religion, meaning and values, it might be useful to spell out something of the logical relationship between religion and morality — and also in view of what I have said about ideologies, between religion and politics.

First then, morals.

The connection is hard to grasp because morality is both inside and outside religion. It is inside because the ethical is one of the dimensions of religion. After all 'Love thy neighbour as thyself' is one of the two great commandments. But it is outside religion in as much as moral beliefs can be articulated and justified without a necessary appeal to a religious belief-system. It might be argued that *some* ideology or other would be presupposed, but even this is doubtful, for one can have a 'common-sense' morality — perhaps utilitarianism counts as this — which accounts at least for a wide range of moral rules.

We must then move to the question as to what difference it makes if morality is within religion. How does a religious (or indeed ideological) morality differ from a secular or common-sense one? Mainly, I suggest, in the way a religious morality perceives morality itself as being not *just* morality, but also as something religious. This may seem obvious, but it needs further explanation.

That explanation is to do with what may be called *superimposition*. For example, if I wash up, I may regard this service to my family as a way of praising God. It is not that washing up can only be justified in terms of God's commandment to me: the reason for doing it has its own common-sense' justification, for it rests upon respect for persons and in particular those persons who are bound closely to me by family ties. But as a Christian, though I recognise this obligation, I may see my actions as being in continuity with my Sunday worship. I am (to use the phrase of Brother Lawrence) involved in the practice of the presence of God. This, then, is what I mean by superimposition. Loving action is seen as worship too (though other men might not see it so). This is the 'superimposition' of religion on morality — though this is not to say that there is some kind of historical sequence here. So there is a kind of congruence between moral questions and those which we have called 'implicit'. In both cases the questions do not demand religious answers — in the conventional sense of 'religion' — but they can do so. Just as the approach to death can evoke thoughts of Christian or Buddhist survival (different indeed as they are), so too the approach to moral values — whether to do with killing, abortion, streaking or whatever — can raise the issue of whether a religious backing to morality is necessary. But that presupposition of superimposition is only one (though a major) part of the story of the relationship between religion and morality (see Chapter 4).

Similar remarks apply to politics. There again some of the deeper 'implicit' problems of value and meaning arise. It is of course absurd here in such a brief compass to say anything about the various ways in which political institutions in different countries may operate. But it follows from what has been said about morals that likewise the political aspect of human life should in principle attract a superimposed interpretation. But more particularly we need to consider the role of political ideologies — as analogous to traditional religions. If a secular society is also pluralist, partly because in a secular society there is no immediate cohesion between people and ideology or religion — if then a secular society is pluralist, then by contrast totalitarian societies, such as China and Russia, are not really secular. They may claim to be anti-religious but they are committed societies analogous to the Scotland of John Knox or the medieval situation of the Papacy. In brief the ideological bosses are in their own way Popes — and they are certainly not attuned to the plural

world of certain Western societies. The democratic theory of
such open countries, by the way, is that pluralism is in line
with the long search for spiritual truth. So it may turn out in
a curious sort of way that my theory of plural politics is in
conflict with the ideological stance. But this is only to say
that the sort of exploration of religion which logic and
pluralism dictate cannot occur in China or Russia. This is a
penalty that these countries pay in their search for cohesion.

In brief, then, I have tried to outline what religious and
religion mean. The consequences for religious education are
fairly clear: it must concern itself both with religions and
with values — and both in a plural, not a dogmatic, way.

References

Schools Council (1971) Working Paper 36 *Religious Education in
  Secondary Schools* Evans/Methuen.
N. Smart (1968) *Secular Education and the logic of Religion* Faber.

CHAPTER 10

Theravāda Buddhism and the Definition of Religion

It is an obvious, but yet not always recognised fact that the Theravāda tradition of Buddhism does not fit substantial theistic and absolutistic types of definition of religion. There is no underlying Ground of Being. As a non-theistic religion, it, like Jainism, evades many of the Western characterisations of religion, in so far as these are tied to describing a certain core ultimate.[1] If there is an ultimate in Theravāda it is not a God and not a Being. It is true that the Buddha has some analogies to a God, but according to the Theravāda's own doctrine, he is not strictly speaking "there." Nirvāṇa is like Gertrude Stein's Oakland: there is no "there" there. The Buddha is not a persisting individual who could re-enter communication with the world: and the strict Theravadin would not regard the homage paid as being worship properly so-called. Even if pragmatically the peasant's homage looks like worship, yet the doctrines of the Theravāda do not permit us to say that the Buddha is God. It is *anissara*: without the doctrine of a Lord, that is it is non-theistic. The gods end up as forces, but merely somewhat unusual denizens of our world. This is why there is always difficulty in trying to say that all religions worship the same God or the same Reality. It could of course be said that unknowingly Theravadins believe in the impersonal side of God, and that they perceive in Nirvāṇa that indescribable aspect of God which lies, like the other side of the moon, behind her personal face. But that is a claim to be made from the standpoint of some theology or philosophy: some version of the Perennial Philosophy.

All this does not greatly help in the framing of a scientific definition of religion. But such a definition can be method-ologically very important, both in terms of the scope of our field, and in pointing us towards a balanced approach. Also, pragmatically the definition of religion will affect politics and the law. For instance, if we cast our net widely we may end up, under the head of the separation of Church and State, or religion and the State, with a separation of all worldview-affirming bodies and the State (a position I favour).[2]

Theravāda Buddhism affects the scope of definition for it represents a possible boundary in the circumscribing of reli-gions; beyond it lie the so-called non-religious worldviews. Such worldviews often want to reject, root and branch, what are conventionally held to be religions - but critiques of reli-gion, such as their otherworldliness, alleged projectedness and falseness (all of which a Marxist might wish to affirm) are dubitable distinguishers. What is true and false is a soft matter. Marxism can as easily be a projection as theism. A secular ideology is often just as otherworldly, because the future of this world is as far removed from the present "this-world" as the transcendent. The distance from utopia to heaven is short.

Let us look at the question from the end of scope, firstly, and then from the angle of balance, secondly. Do we want religion to cover secular symbolic systems or not? I consider it highly desirable, from various points of view. First, there is the tendency to have an aspectual study[3] which does not cover all of its human life - rituals, ultimate beliefs, myths and so on - then it is bad if a whole chunk is left out, and it leads to con-fusion including scientific confusion. We have had studies in the past which begin from a particular worldview and inter-pret others from the categories and values of that worldview, notably in sociology. (E.g. Berger's *The Sacred Canopy*.[4]) They can be illuminating, such studies, but they do not deal with the problem of distinguishing themselves from what reg-ularly goes on in theology. There is a decent worldview-neu-tralism we should strive for, hard as it may be: because at least then our hypotheses are open to testing. But it does seem odd that we should analyse the ritual of the Theravadin temple and not that of the Sri Lankan State.

There are fruits from dealing with not just religions but with more broadly worldviews (suitably deepened to include their performative structures). One is a new view of syncretism or blending. If Catholicism absorbs Mexican saints who are old gods, we say "syncretism", or we might think of the Unification Church as blending Confucian and Christian motifs. But it is just as much syncretism when Lutheranism takes on board the values of liberalism, or Catholicism blends with Marxism in the shape of liberation theology. So one fruit might be new theories of blending.

Another fruit is to see continuities of function. The true heirs of the old Church-and-State solidarity of Lutheran, Anglican and Presbyterian countries and principalities in Europe are - or were - the Marxist States, not the rather wishy-washy establishmentarianism of England and Sweden. It was in these Marxist States that you had, to get on in life, to affirm (so to speak) the Thirty-Nine Articles of the Church of Lenin.

Again, the washing away of a fundamental distinction between religion and secular worldviews enables us to ask more sensible questions about the function of systems of believe, and perhaps to use religious studies insights in the analysis of modern societies: what are the important rituals? What are the myths? and so on. Regarding myth, for instance, it is obvious in the modern nation-State that the basic myth is given in history and literature - the history of the people helps give it identity, and its military heroes are complemented by the poets. And musicians, too.

We can ask too about privatisation. As authority in religion is affected by modernity (and post-modernity, which is after all just a new phase of modernity), so we are finding increasing numbers of citizens who, not irreligious in the traditional sense, are not affiliated, and who make up their own religious beliefs in various blends of motifs.[5]

I would argue that there are gains in stretching the scope of religious studies and so in effect the definition of religion. It is of course awkward in ordinary conversation. So I use the term "worldview" and the phrase "worldview analysis" for what we do. It is not the best of words, but the English and other languages are very poor in vocabulary for discussing beliefs, ideologies and the like. Often the vocabulary of a people simply reflects its own religious history and that is typically not good for describing other systems. It is a problem with which we have to struggle as best we can. Eventually eclectically we may be able to borrow from other tongues, and absorb such terms as *mārga, karma* and *dharma.*

I referred to the study of religion and religions as aspectual: in this it is like politics and economics. Everything has at least some slight religious or symbolic meaning. Some things are intensely economic or symbolic - the Stock Exchange and the Mass. It is, as I said, unfortunate if the aspect of human existence that concerns us is artificially divided by human language, and one corner put out of bounds to students of religion thereby.

Because of the absence of a single focus of religions, and even more of worldviews, it is not much use defining them in terms of Focus. The best we can get to is something Tillichian. It is better perhaps to have a kind of functional account, or as I like to say dimensional account. The aim of this is so that we can have a balanced picture of a religion when we come to delineate it. In the recent *Encyclopedia of Religion* there are quite a number of articles which could have done with balance. Some give you the history of a movement with some depiction of organisation and ethos, but almost nothing of doctrines. Others tell you about doctrines but not about ritual or religious experience and so on. This reflects general practices in the field. I offer my dimensions not because they are the best (if there are better ways of doing these things then critics can surely supply alternative balances). In looking to the ritual-practical, legal-ethical, emotional-experiential, doctrinal-philosophical, narrative-mythic, social-organisational and material-artistic dimensions I proffer a schema which offers balance.[6] I am not pretending that all these dimensions are equally important in all religions or ideologies. So it is that ritual is less important among Unificationists than tantric Hindus; the artistic is less vital among Jehovah's Witnesses than Eastern Orthodox; ethics is more important for Humanists than Shintoists; experience is more central to Southern Baptists than to Confucianists; organisation is more focal for Buddhists than for New Agers. And so on. But at least the attempt to use this checklist to characterise a movement will be useful in supplying a balanced picture. So it is worth noting that certain functionalist ways of dealing with the definition of a worldview or religion can remedy one-sided approaches in the field of analysis.

The Theravāda is an important catalyst of questions because of the difference in its assumptions compared either with the Hindu tradition or the Western theisms - or for that matter the Western secular ideologies. The differences can be bridged in one sort of way by the stepping stones of family resemblance definition, if we are looking at their ultimate and fitting it into the same picture as the Western ultimate. There are stepping stone that is from Nirvāna to God, via such systems as Yoga and Advaita to theistic Vaisnavism to faith in Allah. If we wish to, using family resemblance, we can draw our boundary of religion at the Theravāda. But why? Well, we may argue that by dimensional analysis it is surely a religion. It has doctrines aplenty; it has the myth of the Buddha, including his previous lives, and the myth of Sr Lanka; it has meditation and various rituals; it purifies consciousness and has thus an important experiential side, revived in recent times; it has the Saṅgha as primary organisation; it has ethical teachings; its temples and beauties abound in material form. But using the dimensions to draw the line there is shaky. Does not the Chinese form of Marxism have its doctrines? Does it not have its myths, from the dialectic of history through the Long March, etc? Does it not have its rituals, faded perhaps lately? And so on. By dimensional criteria we push our definition outwards from the Theravāda.

If we do all this we merge the study of religion into others, such as anthropology. Why not? No scholarly quest is an island, and our divisions themselves are imperfectly thought-out accidents of Western intellectual and organisational history. In any event, it is obvious that religious studies has to be multidisciplinary.

And so the Buddha, remembered for his footprint in Sri Lanka, already bids us turn our gaze away from Rome and Banaras; but strangely our eyesight yields another vision, beyond Adam's Peak we see shadowy suggestions of John Stuart Mill and Karl Marx, and of a cloud of national heroes, from Herzl to Mazzini, and from Gandhi to Nelson Mandela.[7]

One major consequence of my argument is that philosophy of religion will become philosophy of worldviews. It may also become more self-conscious about how often Western philosophy is heavily determined by a particular worldview - scientific humanism. And it, like all other worldviews, is capable of defence, but uncertain. A soft non-relativism reigns.

ENDNOTES

1   I first noted this in *Reasons and Faiths* (London, 1958).
2   See Paul Badham, ed., *Religion, State and Society in Modern Britain* (Lampeter, 1989), article "Church, Party and State".
3   See Don Wiebe, ed., *Concept and Empathy* (London, 1986), article "The Principles and Meaning of the Study of Religion".
4   Peter Berger, *The Sacred Canopy* (New York, 1967).
5   Wade Clark Roof, *A Generation of Seekers* (New York, 1993).
6   Ninian Smart, *The World's Religions* (Cambridge, 1989).
7   Ninian Smart, *Religion and Nationalism The Urgency of Transnational Spirituality and Toleration* (Centre for Indian and Inter-religious Studies [CIIS], Rome, 1994)

CHAPTER 11

The Work of the Buddha and the Work of Christ

I

THE aim of this paper is to set out the likenesses and differences between Christian and Buddhist conceptions of the way in which the Buddha and Christ bring about salvation or liberation. Since systems of religious belief and practice are organic,[1] similarities between features of two systems have to be seen in the perspective of crucial divergences elsewhere. The present investigation, then, aims to throw light not only on the particular similarities and dissimilarities between beliefs about the work of the Buddha and the work of Christ, but also upon the underlying dynamics of the two systems.

In a way, though, it is an over-simplification to speak of only two systems, since the changes and developments within Buddhism especially must make our comparisons multiple. This in turn means that a treatment confined to a single essay must be impressionistic and selective: nevertheless, this may turn out to be an advantage rather than the reverse, in letting us go to the heart of the matter.

II

At first sight, Theravāda Buddhism has no concept of a saving god. Not only is it agnostic about a Creator, so that there is no

Supreme Being for an earthly figure such as Gotama to embody or manifest in his person, but also the Buddha himself is not, strictly, an object of worship. It is true that the expression *devātideva* ('god above gods') is used of him in the Pali writings;[2] and he is also said not to fit into human categories.[3] But the former epithet is a way of signifying that the Buddha transcends in value the gods, who are not spiritually important. For this reason, H. Zimmer coined the term 'transtheistic' to describe Buddhism and Jainism[4] (though it would be more natural to refer to them as 'transpolytheistic': the gods, in the plural, are not denied, but the highest truth and salvation cannot be obtained from them—'transtheism' would be a term more appropriate to Advaita Vedānta, where it is theism which is transcended[5]). And the Buddha's not fitting into human categories is at least partly a means of expressing the transcendental nature of the attainment of *bodhi* and *nirvāṇa*. It would thus be a considerable misrepresentation of the Theravāda to think of the Buddha as a kind of incarnate deity. Since salvation in the Christian tradition essentially involves a relationship with God, there can be no question of a strict parallel between the Christian and Theravādin conceptions of the work respectively of Christ and the Buddha.

Nevertheless, the Buddha did do something which looks like a 'saving work': he provided a prescription for liberation from the world's ills. As the spiritual doctor, he provided a diagnosis and a therapy.[6] Still, this is essentially saving men through *teaching*, not, as most Christian theories of the Atonement claim, through the performance of an act which has a cosmic effect, the benefits of which are available to the faithful. This is in line with an important strand of Indian thought, namely that men and other beings owe their sufferings and dissatisfactions ultimately to ignorance, rather than to sin or moral evil—so that the cure essentially involves knowledge, rather than repentance. For this reason, when the Buddha said that after his passing the faithful would still have the *dhamma*,[7] he was not, according to the Theravādin tradition, affirming the identity between himself and a transcendent principle, as the Mahāyāna *trikāya* doctrine asserts, but pointing only to the continued importance and saving power of his teachings.

Ninian Smart

These are efficacious in themselves, and are in a sense only contingently related to the historical Buddha: for the charismatic authority of the Buddha is qualified by the injunction to his followers to test the teachings in their own experience (in this way, Buddhism is much more 'experimental' in its flavour than Christianity—the truth is *ehipassiko*, not just authoritatively revealed). The emphasis upon the saving work of the Buddha's *teachings* contrasts with the main Christian theories of Christ's saving work: it is not so much Christ's words which help us, but Christ as the Word. If Jesus' teachings were detached from their historical context and significance, and regarded as a sufficient prescription for salvation, then the result would be the kind of ethical theism found in Unitarianism; but it would be notably different from Christianity as traditionally understood.

It should be noted that the concept of the liberating power of knowledge in Buddhism, and to be found in other strands of Indian religion, is mainly a result of two factors. First, the absence of belief in a divine Being, and the relative insignificance of the gods, mean that there can be no special place for the notion of sin as separation from, and as the converse of, the Holy. Notions of ritual and moral 'uncleanness' and the sense of unholy inadequacy before the *mysterium tremendum et fascinans* are not evident in the central tradition of the Theravāda.[8] Second, the essential concentration, in the Theravāda, upon contemplative or mystical experience gives the concept of *knowledge* an obvious importance. For mystical experience is like a direct acquaintance with something (*Brahman*, God or the state of *nirvāṇa*, etc.) and this has analogies with one sense of 'knowing' (e.g. 'He knows Macmillan, Loch Lomond, etc.'). Again, it brings a kind of certitude, and knowledge as contrasted with belief is like this. Finally, one sees the 'point' of the doctrines associated with the path through which one attains the experience: one knows *that* such-and-such is the case on the basis at least in part of direct experience.[9] But of course, all this must not be conceived merely as intellectual, like seeing the truth of the Binomial Theorem, partly because the emptiness of mystical states precludes discursive knowledge;[10] and partly because the path typically involves some degree of asceticism,[11] since the right total view of the world itself requires the taming of desires which lead to attachment to, and implication in, empirical reality. By contrast with Buddhist yoga, theism stresses belief and a personal relationship to God through faith. Not unnaturally wrong belief tends therefore to be traced to sin, or wrong relationship to God. But wrong belief in the Theravāda is conceived ultimately as the product of a failure in spiritual perception.

Nevertheless, it might be thought that there was some analogy between the Buddha's defeat of Māra and the 'classical' theory of the Atonement.[12] Just as the Buddha, at the time of his Enlightenment, defeated Māra, so Christ, through his life, death and resurrection, overcame Satan. In an excellent recent work, Dr T. O. Ling has surveyed the Pāli material on Māra; and his conclusion is plainly correct: 'the figure of Māra represents an *approach* to the Dhamma (from animism), but is no part of the Dhamma itself . . .; he is a doctrinal device, not an item of doctrine.' [13] Māra shows that the ills of life are not to be dealt with piecemeal, in an animistic manner. But the symbol is transcended, as indeed is animism and polytheism, in the realization of the peace and insight of *nirvāṇa* and in the formulation of doctrine which expresses that insight. Indeed, the essential Theravādin view could be said to rest on the text of *Dhammapada* 276:

> *tumhe hi kiccam ātappam, akkhātāro tathāgatā,*
> *paṭipannā pamokkhanti jhāyino mārabandhanā.*

Thus the virtual absence of Māra from the Abhidhamma is no accident.[14] Now it is true that Satan has come in for symbolic treatment, and is now liable to be demythologized.[15] But of course he has been regarded much more as a metaphysical reality, partly because his existence has a doctrinal function to play in connection with the problem of evil—whereas agnostic Buddhism does not have to concern itself with reconciling God's goodness to the ills of the world.

Still, though at the doctrinal level Māra is not ultimately significant, the symbol of the Buddha's overpowering is not without similarity to the defeat of Satan. Māra, both etymologically and mythologically, is associated with death, and his defeat, like that of Satan, means the overcoming of death, in so far as death is looked upon as the finishing of a life still stained with evil.[16] Again, both Satan and Māra represent the forces hostile to men's endeavour to lead a truly religious life, and therefore try to deflect the respective Teachers from their path, only to find that the attempt is unsuccessful. But in the New Testament, the ultimate victory over Satan is through the performance of an act, namely the sacrifice on the Cross;[17] but it is the knowledge of Māra, i.e. of the real nature of evil, which is the key to the Buddha's victory.[18] Thus the concept of Māra illustrates clearly the centrality of contemplative insight in the Theravādin tradition.

So far, then, there is no strong analogy between the work of Christ and the work of the Buddha, But it is worth noting that there is an exemplarist strand in Buddhist soteriology. There was evidently too some feeling that the docetic ideas associated with the Lokottaravāda undermined this exemplarist position, for then 'we are mere men and unable to reach the state of a god'.[19] This no doubt is the main reason for the Sarvāstivādin insistence on the humanity of the Buddha. However, the like orthodox Christian insistence on Christ's humanity has largely a different cause, namely that Christ's reconciling sacrifice, in so far as it is expiatory or propitiatory, requires his solidarity with mankind, so that a phantom Christ would be sacrificially irrelevant.

III

The absence of a concept of God as a supreme object of worship precludes the Theravāda from having any doctrine of reconciliation and from any idea of salvation as some kind of intimate union with God. Mahāyāna developments partly altered the situation. First, the cult of Bodhisattvas and celestial Buddhas made these beings, phenomenologically considered, divine. Not only from the side of the devotee is *bhakti* important, so that the inner aspect of worship complements the externals—the cult of images, etc.; but also these beings acquire mythologically the attributes characteristically ascribed to numinous powers elsewhere. The sword of Mañjuśrī and the thunderbolt of Vajrapāṇi express the *tremendum* on its fiercer side; the supernatural marvels of the *Saddharmapuṇḍarīka* express its dumb-founding and fascinating side. And though the total cosmos remains uncreated, in accordance with the Buddha's ban on undetermined questions and agnosticism, Buddhas are now conceived as partially creative, through the idea of the *buddhakṣetra* or 'Buddha-field'.[20] Not only this, but their celestial habitations are psychologically distant enough to function as virtually transcendent places, not so different from the ordinary Christian's conception of heaven as where God is and as the goal of salvation.

Unification of this complex pattern of belief and practice was brought about from two directions. the religious and the metaphysical. This indeed was no accident. E. J. Thomas has written:

Two aspects of Mahāyāna doctrine, which seem to show no relation to each other, stand out in great contrast. There is the religious side of the worship of saintly beings with the ideal of a succession of lives of heroic virtues, and the philosophical side developing the boldest speculations in logic and epistemology. The cause of this contrast was inherent in Buddhism from the beginning—the division into the monastic order and the laity.[21]

But this judgement is most misleading: for the Mādhyamika and Yogācāra systems, for instance, are not purely intellectual. As nearly everywhere else in the field of Indian philosophy, the determinative ideas in these systems are born of religious experience. Buddhist metaphysics is ultimately concerned with defending a spiritual view of the world. Thus the unification of Mahāyāna belief and practice was achieved both at the religious and metaphysical level in a harmonious way. First, this was done through what was later systematized as the *trikāya* doctrine. Thus the multiplicity of celestial and earthly Buddhas has a transcendent unity in the *dharmakāya*. Whereas *dhamma* in the Pāli canon refers to a body of propositions, the Mahāyāna evolved a doctrine analogous to what happens elsewhere, which can be called 'identification with the reference': i.e. the propositions no longer constitute the *dharma*, but the *dharma* essentially *is* the being or state which the propositions centrally allude to.[22] Likewise, *śruti* in the Hindu tradition is sometimes thought of as what propositional *śruti* refers to; and rather recently, for partly different reasons, revelation has been treated by some Christian theologians in a similar manner.[23] But the *dharma* referred to by scriptures is somehow specially manifested by, and taught by, the celestial and earthly Buddhas; and so it cannot simply be viewed as a state to be achieved, like *nirvāṇa* in the Theravādin sense. In a more substantial sense it underlies the numinous Buddha-figures. Thus, from the point of view of popular religion, the doctrine of the *dharmakāya* achieves something like the unification of polytheism expressed in the famous lines of the Dīrghatamas hymn, *Rgveda*, I, 164, 46: the one reality has different names.

It is against this background that the Mādhyamika and Yogācāra should be viewed. The *śūnyavāda*, for instance, is not a restatement of the virtual pluralism of the Theravādin ideal (with its affinities to pluralistic Jainism); yet neither on the other hand does it try to express something quite foreign to the Theravāda. For both these Mahāyāna schools and the Theravāda have as their central concern the mystical or contemplative experience which is the starting-point of Buddhist doctrine. It seems superfluous to postulate radically different kinds of mystical experience to account for the variation in Indian doctrines, whether Hindu, Buddhist or Jain, and in particular within Buddhism, in view of the methodological distinction between experience and interpretation,[24] and in view of the phenomenological principle that the goal is in some degree affected by the path leading to it.[25] Thus the Mahāyāna stress upon *karuṇā* may well give a special flavour to what is found in contemplation, without however affecting its essential nature. In general, in the Indian context at least, there seems reason to suppose that the interpretation of mystical experience is only partially determined by the nature of the experience itself, but is normally also affected by the weight given to other forms of religious experience. For instance, the experience of a personal Being, expressed in the reaction of loving adoration or *bhakti*, affects theological attitudes to mystical experience and to its doctrinal interpretation.

This last point could be expressed in a very crude way by the following equations, where the numbers roughly estimate the weight given to the different kinds of experience. The left-hand side gives the kind of experience or associated activity considered relevant to the perception of the highest truth about reality, and the right-hand side gives the correlated doctrines.

0 *bhakti* + 2 *dhyāna* = agnostic/atheistic pluralism (Jainism, and the virtual pluralism of the Theravāda)

1 *bhakti* + 2 *dhyāna* = transtheistic monism (e.g., Advaita)[26]

2 *bhakti* + 1 *dhyāna* = transmonistic theism (e.g. Rāmānuja)[27]

One can indeed generalize such equations, by contrasting the numinous and the mystical in their many modes of combination (and failure to combine), and by observing the correlation between the intensity and importance attached to these two kinds of experience and the doctrines associated with the relevant religious movements.[28] It is often because of its association with *bhakti* or with a prophetic tradition that mystical experience is not given that minimal doctrinal interpretation which the Theravāda represents (putting it crudely: you have to have the concept of God already if mystical experience is to be interpreted as a kind of union with the divine).

These general remarks show how the monism of the Mādhyamika and of the Yogācāra can be explained. The substitution of the *śūnya*, *tathatā*, etc. as a kind of substance—albeit a pretty shadowy one—for the Theravādin *nirvāṇa* conceived as a *state*, i.e. the introduction by the Mahāyāna of an Absolute,[29] is in line with the need to accommodate the religious concept of the numinous as somehow concealed behind phenomena and yet as being a personal object of devotion.[30] Thus, the Theravāda stands to the Mādhyamika roughly as Sāṃkhya-Yoga stands to Advaita. It is not fortuitous, even apart from historical connections, that both in Advaita and in the main stream of Mahāyāna thought which we are now considering at least a secondary place is given to *bhakti* in the religious quest and to the experience of numinous beings. The many Buddhas, then, have a concealed, mysterious unity in the *dharmakāya*, even if this unity is ultimately viewed as a kind of non-dual (*advaya*) Emptiness, in accordance with the deliverances of the contemplative consciousness. But, as in the Theravāda, the latter remains supremely important: in this, both Lesser and Greater Vehicles are, largely, at one, and where they differ is as to whether anything else is important, i.e. whether *bhakti* has any basis or significance. The Mahāyāna doctrines are a means of synthesizing two forms of religion, with the religion of worship in second place. This balance is altered in some phases of the later development of the Mahāyāna, notably in the Far East, so that eventually there can arise sects which stress faith only, and where the underlying Buddha-principle is conceived as essentially personal: thus bhakti and paradise are substituted for *praj ñā* and identification with the Absolute as the soteriological means and ends.

This excursus into the dynamics of Mahāyāna doctrines, and of the Mādhyamika and Yogācāra schools in particular, as centrally representing 'main-stream' Mahāyāna, is necessary for the understanding of the comparison between Christian and Mahāyāna soteriology. With the evolution of the idea of the Buddha as a divine being, it could be expected that salvation would be seen as a kind of communion with the Buddha, and the overcoming of the gulf fixed between the worshipper and the object of worship. Now it is true that the colourful picture of Amitābha's paradise reflects the hope of something analogous to the beatific vision of God, even if in theory the Pure Land is merely a place specially favourable for the attainment of *nirvāṇa*. Nevertheless, the different dynamics of Mahāyāna doctrine mean that in the last resort the communion is differently conceived: for ultimately the devotee attains the highest goal, the contemplative goal with its non-duality. And because of this non-duality, there can be no distinction between the devotee and the Absolute: which in religious terms means that the devotee is indeed the Buddha. There being no overriding concept of a personal Lord to check the mystical tendency towards non-dualism,[31] the devotee in highest truth is, in worshipping, only worshipping his future self.[32] It happens too that there were other forces impelling the Mahāyāna towards the same conclusion—principally the emphasis on morality and compassion, for the attachment of these ideals to the figure of the

Bodhisattva meant that the universal requirements of goodness and self-sacrifice could be seen as presupposing the future Buddhahood of all men.

But though the provisional nature of the distinction between men and the divine Reality (as contrasted with the radical distinction presupposed in most of the Judaeo-Christian tradition, which sharpens the Christological paradox) means that the work of the Buddha still centres on his teaching and that it is contemplative knowledge that ultimately saves, nevertheless the provisional truth incorporated soteriological elements which have some analogies to Atonement doctrine. The most famous of these is, of course, the concept of *puṇyapariṇāmanā* or the transference of merit. The self-sacrificing Bodhisattva can out of the treasury of his merit, the *guṇa sambhāra*, convey some of it to the otherwise unworthy devotee. This gives to Buddhist mythology a strong flavour of the Christian idea of Christ's sacrifice as bringing about an immense or infinite abundance of merit available to the faithful. Thus St Thomas Aquinas writes: *Christo data est gratia non solum sicut singulari personae, sed in quantum est caput Ecclesiae, ut scilicet et ipso redundaret ad membra; . . . manifestum est autem quod quicunque in gratia constitutus propter iustitiam patitur, ex hoc ipso meretur sibi salutem . . .*[33] But there remain differences between the two doctrines. First, the Buddhist concept has as its background the doctrine of *karma,* so that the acquisition of merit has a kind of causal effect; but by contrast the Christian counterpart, in theory at any rate, is the direct activity of God. Second, the acquisition of merit by Christ was conceived as a consequence of his self-sacrifice upon the Cross,[34] and 'sacrifice' here had a ritual sense. Although Old Testament concepts of ritual sacrifice were transcended in the New, their transcendence presupposed their initial acceptance. But the self-sacrifice of the Bodhisattvas is essentially moral, and has little of a ritual background to be transcended and given new significance. It perhaps may be that one or two instances of a moralizing of ritual sacrifice occur in the *Jātakas* and elsewhere, e.g. the hare's famous self-immolation;[35] but this does not involve an explicit acceptance of the quasi-causal effects of ritual sacrifice. And although a ritual significance is given to self-offering through the *pūjā* involved in following the path of Bodhisattvahood,[36] the ultimate emphasis remains on treating this as a means rather than an end—whereas worship by contrast in the Judaeo-Christian tradition is the intrinsically appropriate response of men to the Holy One.

Furthermore, in both the Mādhyamika and the Yogācāra, the empirical world is in a sense illusory—for where there is in essence only one reality the multiplicity of the cosmos as viewed from the ordinary common-sense standpoint must ultimately be an illusion. This means that the docetic tendencies of the Lokottaravāda are reinforced in the fully-fledged Mahāyāna. The plurality of earthly Buddhas likewise puts pressure in the same direction: for where the divine Being 'appears' in many forms, it is a natural inference that these are *mere* appearances; while the Christian insistence on the uniqueness of Christ preserves two features which Atonement doctrine requires, namely Christ's simultaneous humanity and divinity. It is as though, in having only one Incarnation, God fully commits himself to the earthly life, and is not just arranging a theophany in human form.

The docetism of the Mahāyāna and its relative unattachment to historicity is signalized by the concept of *upāya-kauśalya* or 'skill in expedients' (Edgerton also suggests a nice translation, 'diplomacy'[37]). The Buddha is essentially a pragmatist, engineering human relations so that men will be brought to the truth. At one stroke the Mahāyāna has a piece of apologetic *contra Hinayanistas* and an explanation of the secondary importance of *bhakti* and the whole elaborate scheme of popular Buddhist cults. These are only means, both from the side of the individual and from the side of the Buddha-principle itself, for bringing about a certain spiritual result.

In turn this reminds us that Christian soteriology has always been conceived as closely tied to history. God's saving work is thought of as manifested in history (i.e. in the flow of human events) and as grounded in history (i.e. in historical evidences). On both counts, and in both senses of 'history', Buddhism has a different attitude. The general backcloth of the cyclical immensity of time makes the brevities of human life seem unimportant, and in so far as Buddhism speaks of a direction of events in our epoch it is one of decline rather than progress. And historical evidences are not vital where the truth is seen in inner experience.

IV

In brief, the picture of the crucified Christ and that of the suffering Bodhisattva may appeal to the same stirrings in the human heart; but the moral hero and the mediator diverge precisely because in the one system the ultimate reality is the contemplative intuition of Emptiness, while in the other it is a personal God. Both the Theravāda and 'main-stream' Mahāyāna are at one in stressing the centrality of *prajñā*, even if they differ about whether or not the religion of worship and devotion should be given doctrinal recognition. The Buddha's liberating work is bringing men to a type of *gnosis*; Christ's is the reconciliation of men with a numinous Object of worship. The Buddha bridges the gap between men and *nirvāṇa*; Christ bridges the gap between men and the Father.[38]

NOTES

[1] That is, in a sense analogous to that in which a work of art is organic: see my *Reasons and Faiths* (1958), p. 12; H. Kraemer makes a similar point in speaking of a 'totalitarian' approach (*The Christian Message in a Non-Christian World* (1938), p. 145), but the term 'organic' seems for various reasons more suitable.

[2] *Niddesa*, ii, 307, etc.

[3] *Anguttara Nikāya*, ii, 38, etc.

[4] See *Philosophies of India* (1951), pp. 181–2.

[5] The concept of transcendence in *this* sense is of considerable importance, and implies that where the concept of A is transcended by the concept of B, the former concept is not denied to have spiritual value, but is subordinated to, and ultimately interpreted in terms of, the latter concept. Here 'transcendence' is not meant to express, but only to describe, a value-judgement, which the comparative religionist need neither endorse nor fail to endorse. For the senses of 'transcendence', see my 'The Transcendence of Doctrines' in *Sri Aurobindo Circle*, No. 16 (1960), pp. 93–8.

[6] 'The so-called Four Noble Truths of Buddhism correspond exactly to the four successive problems which the Hindu doctor is taught to face in treating a patient.' H. Zimmer, *Hindu Medicine* (1948), pp. 33 ff.

[7] *Dīgha Nikāya*, ii, 154, etc.

172   *Ninian Smart*

[8] For which reason, Rudolf Otto's analysis of religion is not entirely success-ful: see my 'Numen, Nirvana and the Definition of Religion', *Church Quarterly Review*, March, 1959, pp. 216-25. Of course, it is true that numinous elements enter into popular belief, but they have little or no significance at the level of the *Abhidhamma*. Moreover, rituals are of little importance (cp. *Saṃyutta Nikāya*, ii, 99), though, as Keith points out, there are references to ritual bathing, etc. (*Buddhist Philosophy in India and Ceylon* (1923), p. 114, n. 2.

[9] *Reasons and Faiths*, pp. 176-7.

[10] Thus the contrast between *jñāna* and *yoga* in the Indian tradition is more a matter of emphasis than a radical distinction: as Eliade points out, 'the two methods, that of the "experimentalists" (the *jhains*) and that of the "specula-tives" (the *dhammayogas*), are equally indispensable for obtaining arhatship' (*Yoga: Immortality and Freedom* (1958), p. 176). The teachings are tested in con-templative experience and in turn are used to interpret it.

[11] For this reason, there is not a firm division between *tapas* as a soteriological technique and *yoga*: it is true that the Jains, because of a materialistic view of *karma*, stressed *tapas* very strongly, but the interior quest of the Jain ascetic is clearly analogous to that of *yogins* in other traditions. Thus *dhyāna* is used in Jainism, and the Buddha's condemnation of *tapas* extends only to extreme self-mortification. *Tapas* is praised as meaning *brahmacariyā* and *saṃvara* (see *Pali Text Society's Pali-English Dictionary* (1922), p. 131a).

[12] To use Gustav Aulen's term (see *Christus Victor* (Eng. trans., 1953)).

[13] *Buddhism and the Mythology of Evil* (1962), p. 94.

[14] Ibid., p. 163.

[15] See, e.g., a rather Buddhist approach in Don Cupitt's 'Four Arguments against the Devil', *Theology*, vol. LXIV, No. 496 (Oct. 1961).

[16] Ling, op. cit., pp. 56 f.

[17] As in, e.g., Colossians 2:15.

[18] Ling, op. cit., p. 63.

[19] *Lalitavistara*, 100, preserving Sarvāstivādin doctrine according to E. J. Thomas in *History of Buddhist Thought* (1933), p. 174.

[20] Indeed, Buddhas take on the attributes of Hindu creators, so that it be-comes hard to draw a firm line between the ontological status assigned to the great gods and Buddhas in the Hindu and Mahāyāna traditions respectively.

[21] Thomas, op. cit., p. 198.

[22] Thus in the *Lankavatāra Sūtra*, the distinction is made between word (*ruta*) and reference (*artha*). Words are subject to intellectual understanding, but their essential reference (i.e. the reference of the scriptures in particular) is an ex-perience; the relation between *ruta* and *artha*, and that between *akṣara* and *tattva*, are like that between the finger and the moon (D. T. Suzuki, *Studies in the Lankavatara Sutra* (1920), p. 109). Thus the *dharma* is no longer propositional, no longer *akṣarapatita*, but is the 'object' of contemplative experience.

[23] For a Hindu example of 'identification with the reference', see P. N. Srinivasachari, *The Philosophy of Bhedābheda* (2nd edn., 1950), pp. 11-12; for the history of the new Christian concept of revelation, see J. Baillie, *The Idea of Revelation in Recent Thought* (1955). But whereas in the Indian context it is typically experience, or the Absolute or divine Being as experienced, which is what the scriptural words point to, the Christian case is complicated by the fact

Buddha and Christ 173

that God's self-revelation occurs in a concrete historical process, so that Christ rather than the New Testament, is what is essentially meant by 'revelation'.

[24] The distinction is clearly stated by W. T. Stace in *Mysticism and Philosophy* (1960), pp. 31 ff. See also my 'Mystical Experience', in *Sophia*, vol. i, no. 1 (1960), pp. 19–26.

[25] This in two ways: both through the current doctrinal interpretation put upon the mystical experience, which will affect the manner in which the believing contemplative will see his own experience; and through the kind of training involved in the path, which may reflect the doctrinal milieu—e.g. Buddhist compassion influences Buddhist meditative techniques.

[26] I use 'transtheistic' in the unZimmerian sense suggested above: Advaita does not deny theism, but considers it only a provisional and secondary truth.

[27] That is, Rāmānuja is close to the doctrine of the *Bhagavadgītā*: 'Though the Brahmam is again and again referred to as the highest abode . . . , yet God in his super-personality transcends even Brahman' (S. N. Dasgupta, *History of Indian Philosophy*, vol. ii (1932), p. 476).

[28] *Reasons and Faiths*, chap. v.

[29] I use 'Absolute' not in the sense in which Dr Conze uses it in *Buddhist Thought in India* (1962) (by the term he means that which is unconditioned or out of relation with anything else); but as that which underlies, embraces or is the essential nature of reality. This brings out the similarity between Śankara and Nāgārjuna, and makes the equation *nirvāṇa = saṃsāra* meaningful.

[30] *Reasons and Faiths*, p. 35.

[31] That is to say, because of the fact that the mystic is—in the interior vision— withdrawn from ordinary perceptions, the normal sense of a duality between perceiver and what is perceived is absent; hence the mystic, if he conceives himself as having an experience of Something tends to think that he is identical with that Something. Thus the division between subject and object is likely, in this context, to be abrogated; but where on other grounds the mystic regards the distinction between men and God as fundamental, he is more inclined to use such images as that of spiritual marriage, which combines a sense of distinctness with a feeling of the greatest possible intimacy. See my *Theology, Philosophy and the Natural Sciences*, University of Birmingham (1962), p. 12.

[32] See T. R. V. Murti, *The Central Philosophy of Buddhism* (1954), p. 202.

[33] *Summa Theologica*, iii, Q. xlviii, art. 1.

[34] *Cur Deus Homo?*, ii, 11 and 14.

[35] *Jataka*, iii. 51. But note that the term used, *pariccajati*, has no ritual significance (as in the English 'self-sacrifice').

[36] See Bhikshu Sangharakshita, *A Survey of Buddhism* (2nd edn., 1959), pp. 446–8, following Sāntideva.

[37] *Buddhist Hybrid Sanskrit Grammar and Dictionary*, vol. ii (1953), p. 146b.

[38] I am grateful to Dr Conze for sending me a copy of his essay for the present volume, while I was in process of writing my own. Thereby I have avoided some errors and (I trust) too much overlapping in our treatments of a very similar theme.

CHAPTER 12

The Logos Doctrine and Eastern Beliefs

CAN we detect a Logos doctrine in the traditions of India and China ? The answer, perhaps predictably, is both yes and no. I say ' predictably ', because on the one hand every faith is both organic and unique, so that similarities are never precise, and on the other hand the study of religions notoriously has revealed parallelisms between different cultures. I shall not in this article attempt any theological appraisal of the situation (though it is clearly important in the dialogue of religions for Christianity to give theological recognition to possible signs of God's revealing activity outside Christendom). Rather I shall attempt the important preliminary to such theology —an analysis of the possible parallels to the Logos doctrine in Eastern religions. For want of space and for other reasons, I shall confine attention to Hinduism, Buddhism, and Taoism.

There are at least three dimensions of the Logos concept in St. John's Gospel. One relates to the idea of God's revealing Word; another to the Philonic-Stoic notion of a creative pattern; another to the incarnate manifestation of the foregoing. It is the second of these dimensions which promises the best parallels in Eastern religions, though some comments on the other dimensions will, as we shall see, be in order. C. H. Dodd (*The Interpretation of the Fourth Gospel*, p. 285) concludes a detailed discussion of the Logos by offering the following rendering of the opening words of the Gospel : ' The ground of all real existence is that divine meaning or principle which is manifested in Jesus Christ. It was this principle, separable in thought from God, but not in reality separate from Him, that existed before the world was, and is the pattern by which, and the power through which, it was created.' This interpretation allows us to give a more detailed analysis of the concept of the creative pattern. The following elements can be separated out.

First, the Logos is both identical with and yet different from the Divine Being. Perhaps a better way of putting this would be to say that the Divine Being comprehends within Himself the Godhead and the Logos. But from the point of view of the present analysis, we can simply say that the Logos doctrine includes the notion of two entities within the Divine Being in a relation of identity-in-difference. As we shall see, this is a feature of some non-Christian doctrines. This element can be called, for short, ' divine identity-in-difference '.

Second, the Logos is the power through which the world was created. In a sense, therefore, we can simply refer to the Logos (or Christ) as Creator. But in view of the element of divine identity-in-difference, this is oversimplified ; for if a doctrine of Creator is held in conjunction with divine identity-in-difference, the creative act is a double act, even though ' primarily ' associated with the Logos. Hence Dodd's phrase ' the power through which ', which implies that the Logos is not, as it were, alone in its creative action. The second element, then, in the Logos concept is what may be called ' the creative element '.

Third, and less easy to state clearly, the Logos functions as a pattern or principle reflected in the created world. For St. John's Gospel, this aspect, of course, connects up closely with the Incarnation —for the whole point of the Prologue is to say that the true pattern is manifested in the life of Christ. In principle, this concept of a pattern is separable from the idea of creative power (it is perhaps this aspect of the Logos which the ' New Theology ' concentrates upon, leaving aside rather the doctrine of Creation). Perhaps we can describe this element of the Logos concept thus : that there is an underlying principle in the universe which is manifested in Christ. But since this element is connected with the creative element, the underlying principle is not something inert. As other faiths, *ex hypothesi*, do not focus revelation upon Christ, it is convenient for the present analysis to treat this element as consisting in the notion that there is an underlying principle which has some particular manifestation or manifestations in the world. For short it can be called the ' underlying element '.

Do we find these elements in other faiths ? Let us look first to HINDUISM. It is important here, of course, to recall that Hindu theologies are many and diverse, so that the following remarks apply only to part of this complex religious field. But it would be readily conceded that the various systems of Vedānta hold a central place in the Hindu tradition, and here there are to be found some analogies to the Logos doctrine.

In Advaita Vedānta (Non-Dualistic Vedānta) as propounded by Śaṁkara we discover the element of divine identity-in-difference, though in a rather special way. Strictly speaking there is only one Reality, namely Brahman or the ' Holy Power ', a concept drawn ultimately from Brahmanical sacrificial religion as interpreted in the classical *Upaniṣads*. The inner nature of the Holy Power is summed up as consisting of being, consciousness, and bliss, characteristics (if they can properly be called such) which point to the connexion between Śaṁkara's theology and the interior, contemplative life so prominent in the Indian tradition. Now although there is, strictly speaking, only the Holy Power, also identified with the Self lying behind individual psychological states, the world of common experience has to be accounted for. This is described as *māyā* or 'illusion'. Judgments about experience are valid within this world of illusion, though they are ultimately transcended when one realizes one's identity with Brahman. Thus Śaṁkara operates with, so to say, a double-decker theory of truth. At the lower level there is the world, and at this level the Holy Power is seen not merely as an underlying reality, but as Creator. Thus from the ordinary point of view we can distinguish a higher and lower aspect of the Holy Power: the indescribable Brahman and the Lord (*Īśvara*) who creates the world. Thus in some sense we may discover the elements here of divine identity-in-difference and creativity. In so far as the underlying principle is manifested in the life of the liberated man, the third element is present too, though in a very different context.

However, there are diversities. First, the doctrine of *māyā* undermines the value and significance of the Lord: ultimately the Creator too is transcended in non-dual experience. However, some modern interpreters of Śaṁkara, notably President Radhakrishnan, have played down the doctrine of *māyā*, for a number of reasons. Śaṁkara's criterion of illusoriness was impermanence—*i.e.* the 'defectiveness' of worldly existence—is that it lies in the sphere of impermanent things and satisfactions. But, as Rāmānuja and other critics of Śaṁkara pointed out long ago, impermanence and unreality are not to be equated. Further, it is doubtful whether the *Brahma-Sūtras*, upon which Śaṁkara based his primary writing, held the doctrine of *māyā* of the sort that he propounded. If, then, we regard Śaṁkara's emphasis on the illusoriness of the world as a departure from the intention of the *Brahma-Sūtras*, it is possible to see in the Vedāntin tradition a doctrine of identity-in-difference not dissimilar from that of the Logos. Indeed, Fr. Raymond Panikkar's recent *The Unknown Christ of Hinduism* exploits such an interpretation of Vedānta in presenting Christ as the 'unknown' term between Brahman and the world.

However, it may be noted that the flavour of Advaita is to treat the Holy Power as rather impersonal and the Lord as personal; this is something of an inversion of the Logos language, where God is assumed to be personal, but the Logos is slightly abstract (an impersonality counterbalanced from the start in St. John's Gospel by the presentation of the Logos as manifested in the flesh, in the personal form of Christ). It may also be noted that in many respects Rāmānuja's Qualified Non-Dualism is much closer to Christian theism in its general theology, without, however, including anything strongly analogous to the Logos doctrine. Nevertheless, modern Hinduism is moving in the direction of a synthesis between Rāmānuja's theism and the Non-Dualism of Śaṁkara (one can point, for instance, to the teachings of the Ramakrishna Mission). This being so, it is worth stressing the general likeness between a realistic (and not idealistic or illusionistic) version of Advaita and the Logos doctrine.

Yet there may be coincidental aspects of the similarity. Advaita itself is a synthesis between contemplative and devotional religion, with the latter in a secondary position of esteem. The worship of the Creator-Lord is transcended by the inner realization of oneness with Brahman. Contemplative mysticism no doubt played some part in the formation of Philo's Logos doctrine and so contributed a little to the Prologue of St. John. But contemplative mysticism was not in general a strong feature of the Old Testament, nor of the New.

BUDDHISM might at first sight seem an unpromising field for finding a Logos analogy, in view of the creative element's forming part of the network of ideas lying behind St. John's Gospel's use of the concept. It might seem unpromising because it repudiates the notion of a Creator of the universe. Further, the Buddhism of the Pali canon does not involve any belief in a personal Object of Worship, nor of an underlying Reality. It confines its attention to the state of nirvana as the goal of endeavour, and this is neither something which in principle could (literally) be adored nor a source of being—nor indeed is it an underlying Something quietly informing the whole of existence. Nevertheless, Buddhism developed in one direction which is suggestive of a parallelism with Christianity. It happens too that this direction was one which influenced Advaita. It was not for nothing that Śaṁkara was accused by his opponents of being a crypto-Buddhist: for he borrowed much from the *Śūnyavāda* of Nāgārjuna. This in turn was one contributor to the religious development of the Mahāyāna. This development can be briefly recapitulated as follows.

Though (probably) original Buddhism did not treat the Buddha as in any sense divine, there slowly evolved the cult of Buddhas and Bodhisattvas (Buddhas-to-be) as divine or quasi-divine beings. Naturally the historical Buddha, Gautama, was included in such devotionalism (*bhakti*), though a great part of the latter was directed at celestial and mythological figures, such as Amitābha—later to follow a powerful career, as Amida, in the Pure Land Buddhism of Japan, itself mediated by devotionalism in China. The cult of Bodhisattvas was ethically significant, since it was a means of expressing what the Great Vehicle felt to be a contradiction in the Lesser. The latter stressed compassion, for this was a central feature of the Buddha's moral attitudes ; but at the same time it held out sainthood, through the attainment of nirvana, as the supreme goal and this could be interpreted in a selfish and uncompassionate way. For inevitably there was a feeling that the prospective *arhat* was seeking his own salvation : how was this compatible with striving compassionately for the good of all living beings ? The ideal of the Bodhisattva, however, was that of the Great Being who sacrifices himself, even to the extent of putting off his own deserved nirvana, on behalf of others through countless lives. This ideal was connected up with the worship of Bodhisattvas, and was possible for ordinary men, in so far as they took themselves the vow of following the path of Bodhisattvahood.

Concurrently with these religious and ethical developments there was an evolution of Buddhist philosophy, issuing in the concept of an underlying Absolute informing and embracing phenomena. This was expressed in a negative and dialectical way by Nāgārjuna in his *Śūnyavāda* or Doctrine of the Void. Reality is indescribable and insubstantial : hence the term ' Void '. Although some interpreters have seen Nāgārjuna's aim as being purely negative and nihilistic, in fact the philosophy of the Void School was used in a positive and clearly religious way. At one level, ultimate reality was described as the Void or as Suchness (a term well adapted to bringing out its ineffability) ; at another level—the ' empirical '—the Absolute manifests itself as phenomena and religiously as the celestial Buddhas and as the historical Buddha. This two-level theory of truth or reality is one of the contributions Buddhism made to Advaita. All this was synthesized in the *Trikāya* or ' Three-Body ' Doctrine. The Buddha is conceived as having three aspects : his Truth-Body (*dharma-kāya*), identical with the Absolute ; the Bliss-Body (*sambhogakāya*) where the Absolute manifests itself as the personal Lord, the celestial Buddha or Buddhas ; and the Transformation-Body (*nirmāṇa-kāya*) whereby Buddhahood is manifested on earth, in the shape of Gautama, the historical Buddha.

It is not hard to see that certain elements of the Logos concept are present here. First, the divine identity-in-difference is apparent in the way in which the Absolute manifests itself as personal Lord. Second, there is the notion of an underlying principle manifested *par excellence* in the figure of the Buddha, corresponding *mutatis mutandis* to third element which we distinguished in the Logos doctrine.

It is interesting to note that both Nāgārjuna (or at least his followers) and Dean Mansel used similar aguments in support of differing religious loyalties. For Nāgārjuna ultimate reality is void and indescribable, but fortunately phenomenalizes itself as the Buddha ; for Mansel, the Absolute is an unknown X, which, however, manifests itself in revelation, *i.e.* in Christ.

Absent, however, from the Buddhist conception is the belief in the creative dependence of the world on God, even if celestial Buddhas are sometimes described as having limited creative powers. Though there is a kind of analogy to incarnation, through the Three-Body doctrine, there is far less emphasis on historicity in the Mahāyāna than in Christianity. This is brought out by one of the beliefs regarding salvation prominent in the Great Vehicle. According to this, the Buddha, as a celestial Lord, can save living beings by transferring to them merit from the illimitable treasury of merit which he has gained through his countless self-sacrifices. The otherwise unworthy faithful are translated thereby on death to a paradise, the Pure Land, where the conditions for attaining nirvana are peculiarly propitious. Though this whole nexus of ideas is analogous to medieval views of the operation of the Atonement and of grace, the basis is essentially mythological. The sacrifices of a Buddha occur overwhelmingly in stories of previous lives and have no empirical basis. This is not necessarily to be regarded as a defect in the belief (so Great Vehicle Buddhists would argue), for imaginative knowledge of reality can be gained by the spiritually perceptive in ways which do not require the kind of spelling out involved in historical acts, like those of Christ.

There is some contrast with Advaita. Whereas the latter emphasizes more the first and second elements of the Logos idea, the Mahāyāna stresses the first and third (always remembering the *mutatis mutandis* clause).

The connexion between contemplative mysticism and Advaita doctrines referred to earlier can be paralleled in Buddhism. Though Theravāda Buddhism is essentially contemplative, and does not incorporate *bhakti* devotionalism, the Mahāyāna represents a synthesis. Though contemplation may remain the predominant motif, by and large, in the Great Vehicle, piety is importantly focussed, but at a secondary level, on ultimate reality as manifested by celestial Buddhahood. This synthesis is in part achieved by the identity-in-difference implicit in the Three-Body doctrine.

The emphasis on contemplative union with ultimate reality in both systems accounts in part for their view of revealed truth. In both cases the higher truth is to be directly experienced : consequently revelation is only indirectly expressed in words. The words point to something beyond them. This ' non-propositional ' view of revelation can be compared to modern interpretations of the Biblical concept of revelation. But an important difference remains. For Advaita and the Mahā-yāna Void doctrine the reference is to what can be met in contemplation : for Christianity the reference is to the divine acts in history and above all to Christ. Though the Buddha may manifest the Absolute, he does so obliquely, for one has to see beyond the fleshly manifestation to the Truth-Body. The fleshly manifestation remains at the lower or empirical level of reality.

Thirdly we may turn briefly to TAOISM. It is well known that many different interpretations of the *Tao Te Ching* have been offered ; and the virtually certain non-existence of Lao Tzu precludes any serious attempt to penetrate to a single ' original gospel ' of Taoism. But commonly in the Taoist tradition the *Tao Te Ching* has been understood as a religious document, propounding a poetical metaphysics as well as an original social attitude. The presence of ascetic and contemplative techniques in early Taoism is, in this context, significant.

The *Tao Te Ching* does not present anything like a formal doctrine of identity-in-difference (indeed it does not present a formal doctrine of anything). But the book does incorporate a kind of synthesis between the earlier concept of Heaven (*T'ien*) as creator of the world and the concept of Tao as the underlying principle in the universe, to be followed by the sage. In fact the latter conception already merges two strands of thinking : on the one hand the Tao is an entity underlying and pervading the world, and on the other hand *Tao* retains something of its meaning of ' way ', *i.e.* the right path of behaviour. Thus the Tao is both a reality and a method, and by following the method one gains union with the reality. Since that reality is imperishable, here there is the secret of eternal life. This Tao, both reality and method, replaced Heaven, as we have said, as creator. Thus the Tao is at once the underlying reality of things, the creative source of them and the method of gaining eternal life. But whereas the Hindu concept of Brahman has strong overtones of power, the action of the Tao is paradoxically passive. Hence the famous pacifism and quietism of early Taoism.

The replacement of Heaven by the Tao in early Taoist thought involved a certain ' depersonalization ' of ultimate reality. This is where the analogies between the Tao and the Logos can be deceptive, since, as has been remarked earlier, the latter concept, though impersonal or abstract in flavour, is placed firmly in the context of a personal Christ (and for that matter of a personal divine Father). Thus although the Tao displays the creative and underlying principle elements, any close similarity with the Logos is eroded by the lack of appropriate organic connexions with the necessary context. The analogy here is much weaker than that discoverable in the case of Hindu theology. It should, however, be noted that the Tao and the Absolute of Mahāyāna were easily identifiable—a synthesis finding its best-known expression in Zen.

It is hoped that this brief account of some parallels to the Logos in Eastern religions may help to clarify ideas in preparation for the further, theological, task of interpreting God's revelatory activity amid Hindu, Buddhist, and Taoist traditions.

CHAPTER 13

The Comparative View of the Person: East and West

In this presentation I want to concentrate on India and the West, though I shall also include a few remarks about the Far East. In fact the differences in the ideas of the person between the cultures of the Hindu and Buddhist traditions on the one hand and of Christianity and Judaism on the other are rather marked. This contrast or set of contrasts (for Hindus and Buddhists tend to have rather divergent analyses) is obscured by the fact that we loosely use the word 'soul' to stand for rather differing conceptions. Let me begin however by some remarks about the Buddhist analysis of the individual, where in any case the notion of a soul, whether of East or West, is inapplicable.

As we well know the Buddhists deconstructed the individual human being by dissolving her into a series of *khandhas* or *skandhas*, that is of bunches of events of diverse types. An individual is composed of bodily events, feeling events, perceptual events, impulses and conscious events. Stick all these bunches together and you have a functioning human being. Moreover, that individual is somewhat controlled by kamma or karma, and so is in causal continuity with previous lives and future lives, unless she has attained sainthood or nibbana. Moreover, because of Buddhist emphasis upon causality the swarm of events making up an individual radiates out and is radiated into by events. So perception is a dynamic process of interchange with the environment. And so individuals are in interplay with other individuals both at the conscious and subconscious levels. While a Buddhist view is not absolutely necessary for a sense of the outer radiations of causality it does facilitate it. I think if our perceptual apparatus were more sensitive, we would see a cloud or aura (so to speak) accompanying each individual and indeed everything. What happens however is that our perceptions necessarily simplify what we encounter. It is useful simplification which we project upon the world. It is nice for

4   *East-West Encounters in Philosophy and Religion*

us : a beautiful sunset is better than an incredible jumble of radiating particles.

At the core however there is no permanent entity. This idea of a changeless self is both morally unfortunate and metaphysically inept. The changeless can never explain change (so much for God by the way), and egocentricity is constantly to be guarded against. This sometimes however brings puzzles about how the Buddhist virtues work. The cardinal virtues or divine abodes (*brahmaviharas*) are, as you will recall, friendliness, compassion, sympathetic joy and equanimity. How can you be friendly or compassionate towards others if there is so to speak no other there? Now in Mahayana things became a bit different because of the evolution of the notion of the Buddha-nature which in some respects became a substitute for a soul. It is that potentiality for enlightenment lying within every living being. We are all Buddhas in the making. There is a parallel here with Western conception of Christ residing within each individual, emphasized perhaps more in Eastern Orthodoxy than elsewhere.

The emphasis in the Theravada is more on the rights of the other as flowing not from themselves as from the duties of all others to help them in their dissatisfaction and suffering. But of course there remains a contrast between the Buddhists view of the emptiness of the individual and the Western emphasis upon the sacredness of the person. Note however, that there is a curious convergence at another level. The Buddhists acquired a well-developed metaphysics of emptiness, and the Christians had a narrative or mythic notion of how in following Christ we empty ourselves—finding our souls by losing them. (I explored this in a recent book called *Buddhism and Christianity : Rivals and Allies*.)

I would add a rather different observation about the *khandhas*, and by analogy also the Samkhyan somewhat differing breakdown of the individual into such entities as *buddhi, ahamkara, manas*, etc. Is it not curious how the models of differing cultures and traditions diverge so much? Every language has word for nose and ear and even (usually) for inner organs such as the liver and pancreas : but there are wildly diverse inner psychological vocabularies. This must tell us something.

This by the way points to an important function of comparative philosophy—to raise critical questions across boundaries. Think of the great investment in the West on discussions of the will. Despite Schopenhauer's affinity with Buddhism and the Upanisads, what is the Indian thinker, bereft really of any precise counterpart to the will, to think? If a Mahayana Buddhist he might prefer *The World as Process and Representation* or even *Energy and Representation*. But *Will*?

Ninian Smart 5

Also as we have noted there is the divergent aspect of kamma and rebirth. The Buddhist individual is in fact a macroindividual. The person Buddhadhatta stretches back beyond his Buddhadhatta manifestation to uncountable previous lives. Though this does not diminish the value of the present manifestation it sets it in a different perspective. Hence the individual's abilities and circumstances are put within a moral framework of past lives which differs from the Western frameworks, which ascribe a person's advent in the world to luck or bad luck, or see in her circumstances the work of God's direction.

Moreover, as in other Indian systems, the person is also placed in a spectrum of living beings. Admittedly humans are the top, from the point of view of soteriology, for you can only gain liberation if you are born a human [story of the turtle]. Gods, though more splendid in their life-style, have to take second place. But also of course the Buddhist sees the person as part of a range of other personal beings, namely living beings.Because of Christianity's rigid confinement of souls to humans, the ideas of animal rights and the like have had to be argued specially, and only rather recently. On the other hand the relevant Buddhist cardinal virtues apply towards all living beings.

Because of Buddhism's permeation of Chinese, Korean and Japanese cultures such values clearly affected these civilizations. Confucian perspectives are rather different : there is perhaps a clearer view here than in Buddhism of the social placement of the individual, whose sacrality is as it were ensured by the li or correct behavior of others. This points to something vital, namely the performative notion of the person. This is thought of in a wider than ethical context in the Confucian tradition; in the Buddhist context as we have noted it has an ethical application. That is the individual is valuable in so far as others should treat her with compassion, etc. Both systems imply that value is precipitated in the individual by society.

If we now turn to the Hindu tradition, we have here various notions of an eternal something residing within or in connection with the individual. These ideas range from the concept of the *purusa* in Samkhya-Yoga, often translated 'person', to the one Atman or Self in Advaita Vedanta. In between there are the many selves of Visistadvaita which are as it were offshoots of God. The nearest to the Buddhist doctrine is Non-Dualistic Vedanta : if there is only one Divine Self then there are not differing selves for individuals. This is one reason why the system was regarded as cryoto-Buddhist. The many *jivas* or individual life-monads are impermanent, like the persons of the Buddhist tradition. So the more

6   *East-West Encounters in Philosophy and Religion*

important examples of contrast are those systems which believe in many souls or selves. Now here there is a problem once more of terminology. The big contrast, so paradigmatic and pervasive in Indian thought, is between the permanent and the impermanent. *Cit* or consciousness, supposedly permanent, is not part of the apparatus of the psychophysical organism, but lies as it were behind it. Our mental attributes, such as the *manas* or synthesizing common sense, and the ego-maker or *ahamkara*, as well as the senses and feelings, are really all part of the *prakrti* or 'nature.' They are all material, though often material in a highly refined sense : subtle matter plays an important role in Hindu cosmology. On the whole the Western soul is more intimately involved with mental operations. The function of *cit* is so to speak to illuminate the mental apparatus, as a light illuminates the film in the projector. Consequently on the Samkhyan scene liberation, meaning in effect the disconnection of *purusa* from the transmigrating bodily manifestation, becomes thoroughly empty from the perspective of individuality and so somewhat like nirvana, though expressed within the frame of a divergent metaphysics.

In short Hindu views of the person as expressed in traditional philosophical systems draw the line in a different place than do Western systems, typically, though Visistadvaita more resembles Western soteriologies.

In general, it is worth remarking that certain traditional theological ideas in the Christian context have certain analogies. Here what is important is to concentrate on the idea of the divine as being immanent in individuals. The notion that Christ or the Spirit exists 'within' does not deny that God is essentially transcendent. The concept of the transcendent needs analysis of course, but basically it is the same (as I have argued elsewhere) as the immanent : given that both are 'beyond' the world, one inwardly and the other 'beyond.' These ideas of beyond and within, though superficially spatial, have deeper meanings. Both imply that the entity in question is non-spatial (except in some metaphorical way) and yet in interaction with spatial events. The divine 'within' lies beyond the mental and physical, beyond even the spiritual resources available to people within their psyches. And so it turns out that the divine spirit dwelling 'within' the individual has an analogous place to the *antaryāmin* or inner controller of the Indian tradition.

So far we have been talking of traditional notions of the person. In the Indian case, both Hindu and Buddhist, we are involved in very different cosmologies from those of the modern West. Modern secular cosmologies see profound value in the individual, especially the human. If there is something which tends to unite the very diverse systems it may lie in the perceived potentiality for liberation and some divine status contained in traditional views of where we stand. Things may be different if we are thinking of modern liberal humanism. This outlook sees something of profound worth in each individual. But there is some illusion in seeing personal worth as depending upon some interior changeless entity. For, to repeat a point made earlier, the changeless cannot help the changeable.

The connection between the person and cosmology is also worth noting. In *śramanic* and in particular Buddhist and, later, Hindu thinking the universe pulsates, virtually beginningless—and the same applies to the individual. But in the Jewish, Christian and Muslim cosmologies the world starts with a sudden fiat. Many secular cosmologists see it all starting with a big bang. Likewise the individual is not seen as pre-existent. I caricatured this conceptual lack of adventure with some verses about Peter Strawson. In his book *Individuals* he has a chapter exploring the idea of disembodied consciousness after death. At that time Strawson identified himself as a descriptive metaphysician.

Peter Strawson has laid a logical curse on the thought of a never embodied person :

> Such a naked soul just wouldn't be viable,
> But worse it'd be *unidentifiable*.
> But things may be better than we had reckoned—
> For couldn't a soul for about a second
> Acquire a body and get an identity
> And so become a respectable entity?
> It's a bit of a chore is this body filling
> But the flesh is brief and the spirit is willing.
> Yet it's bad to be shamed into apparition
> By a merely descriptive metaphysician.

I would like to note one or two modern developments. Since this is Chicago year I may mention Vivekananda. He adapted Advaita Vedanta in a way which makes his doctrine of the universal self seem closer to the idea of the divine presence within a person familiar to traditional Christianity. Also significantly he responded to utilitarianism by insisting on the transcendental character of true happiness.

In the Theravada, thinkers such as K.N. Jayatilleke and Padmasiri De Silva have brought Freud into play (he too of course has his somewhat idiosyncratic inner psychic geography). Since notoriously Freud does

8 *East-West Encounters in Philosophy and Religion*

not fit the Theravadin case among others you might suppose that Freudian theorists would have qualms, though they don't seem to.

Jayatilleke and Padmasiri can use Freud to criticize Western religion, while Buddhism remains unscathed on the whole.

But I mention these developments as indicating that traditional Hindu and Buddhist views of the person are perhaps shifting.

At any rate such simple crosscultural reflections as I have spun out here should lead us to see divergences as challenging and thought provoking. If so far Western ethicists and psychologists have not paid too much attention to comparative philosophy and religion that is because of lingering tribalism, pervasively evident in our whole educational system.

CHAPTER 14

Buddhism and the Death of God

THE somewhat dramatic title which I have selected points to some problems in the relationship between Christianity and Buddhism. It happens that in recent years Christian theologians have been experimenting with radical ways of presenting the Gospel in these latter, sceptical and technological days. Such radicalism involves modifying or even scrapping belief in God as previously understood by the traditional worshipper. Largely, this process of experiment has been carried on the milieu of Western culture, without much regard to the total religious situation in the world or to the challenges implied by other great traditions, such as Buddhism. Buddhism, by contrast, has never taken the idea of a personal Creator with ultimate seriousness—and indeed Theravada Buddhism has largely eschewed the pietism which brings parts of the Mahayana closer in spirit to Christian theism. For the Theravada Buddhist, there is no question of having to modify or even scrap belief in a personal God. This belief has just not been important. This being so, does the present theological radicalism represent a kind of convergence of the two traditions? Is it a new way towards a mutual understanding?

Before I turn to answer these questions, let me amplify further what I have said about the Theravada and theism. For it is a strange thing, at first sight, that such a gap should have been fixed between it and the theistic religions which share something of a common heritage—I mean Judaism, Christianity and Islam. For those brought up in the ambit of these faiths it is perhaps puzzling that a great and successful religion should have maintained itself with ideals so different from those involved in the worship of God and of obedience to him. For the Theravadin, the Buddha is not a being to be worshipped and he saves largely through his teaching. He is not Creator; nor is there any Creator of this ceaseless, impermanent universe. Liberation, nirvana, indeed is possible, but it does not consist of relationship to a personal Deity. I stress this *via negativa*, a way of 'nots' to be trodden by the theist if he is to rid himself of preconceptions about the nature of religion and of Buddhism in particular. There is another negation, however, that I must stress: it is not correct to identify Buddhism with

4

the Theravada, and if in this lecture I draw upon Theravadin texts, it is only because this tradition represents the clearest challenge to traditional theism (and perhaps I was a Theravadin in a previous existence). I can perhaps also add here that one of the reasons why Buddhism and some other religious movements have attracted recent interest and concern in the West, and especially among the young, is precisely their non-theistic nature. I admit that the Hare-Krishna movement is not without support in California and elsewhere (as I have recently had occasion to note in the streets of Hollywood)—a movement of fervent devotionalism stemming back to that great teacher of *bhakti*, Caitanya. But the main mood is introvertive, disillusioned with a personalistic approach, among those who have experimented with the teachings and methods of the Eastern world.

I can perhaps bring out something of the spirit of the early Theravada by drawing upon some poems in the *Theragāthā*, a collection of Pali verses belonging to the Khuddaka Nikaya of the Theravadin canon. These poems are often autobiographical, and help us to understand the development of the Theravadin ethos—in particular the modes of conversion-experience and liberation-experience thought to be important. I hope to indicate not merely the attraction of the Buddha's message as understood by these early *bhikkhus* but also the essential otherness of their whole approach to the personal devotion to God of Christian and Jew. By bringing out this contrast, it will be possible to penetrate further in the quest for a synthesis which would make intelligible the very divergence of the two kinds of faith.

First let us consider one of the more austere and doctrinal of the poems. In this, as in the other translations, I have tried to convey the rhythm of the original Pali prosody.

> There is no everlasting life: no compound things
> Can be eternal, but living beings dissolve
> Again and again into their constituent parts
> And are reborn. Knowing this painful truth, I have
> No lust for life: dead is the lure of all desires
> And I've destroyed all drugging and confusing thoughts.

For the Christian and more generally for those brought up in the Western tradition, there is a strange paradox in the message here conveyed. How can it be, so to say, *good* news that there is *no* everlasting life? And at first sight too it looks as though the author of these lines is highly cerebral in his emphasis—stressing the disappearance of the wrong kinds of thoughts, as though clarity of intellect were to be prized above all as the key to liberation.

These initial impressions, like most perceptions of other men's cultures, are misleading and yet also contain a certain truth. They are misleading because they neglect the whole cultural context, the web of ideas and actions and institutions within which the lines quoted have their meaning and force. They contain a certain truth because in exhibiting what is (from a Western, Judaeo-Christian point of view) a puzzle they lead us on into an exploration to make sense of what is said—and in this exploration the organic web of ideas and actions and institutions will progressively become revealed.

Let us return to the question of everlasting life. The accent here is upon duration and the possibility of individual existence's enduring for ever. By a seeming paradox nirvana (*nibbāna*) is described often as *nicca*—'the permanent'. How can it be that there is no everlasting life and yet there is the chance of a liberation which is permanent? Note that the author of the verses I have quoted refers to the dissolution of living beings again and again into their constituent parts. This is of course a way of describing the process of rebirth—but before we turn to this most crucial of Buddhist assumptions, it is important to realize that for Buddhism individual things and beings are essential composite. They are conjunctions of factors; and it is the nature of the composite to perish. This leads to one of the intellectually most intractable features of Buddhist eschatology—the thesis that we cannot talk of individual existence after death in nirvana. It is neither correct to say that the saint survives after death nor that he does nor that he both does and doesn't nor that he neither does nor doesn't.

At one level this ultimate silence is the consequence of the general structure of Buddhist metaphysics. But the lack of concern for individual survival among those who have attained nirvana has an important existential, experiential side to it. For the serenity and insight which the Theravadin saint (*arhat*) obtains takes him into a kind of selflessness where craving for individual survival vanishes. Thus we see in another poem:

> In the woodland thickets beyond Ambataka park
> Lucky Bhaddiya lives, his craving pulled up by the root,
> In meditation. Though some like the music of drums
> Or of cymbals and mandolines, my delight as I sit
> By a tree is the sound of the Buddha's message. And if

6

> The Buddha would grant me a wish and the wish were mine,
> I would choose that the whole world might constantly
> Be alert to the transience of all physical things.
> Such men as have measured me by my bodily form,
> Who are under the spell of language, are beguiled
> By sensuousness, and they do not know me. For fools
> Entangled on every side cannot recognize
> What's within, nor can they see what's outside this.
> They are led astray by a sound ... .

As has sometimes been remarked, the problem of survival is quite different in Buddhism (and indeed elsewhere in the Indian religious tradition) from that which the Judaeo-Christian tradition confronts. If there is a question for us as to whether we persist beyond death—a question of whether indeed salvation consists in part of immortality beyond the grave—for the early Buddhist the problem was the opposite. The doctrine of rebirth posits continued existence in various forms virtually for ever unless something drastic is done, which would lift the individual into a kind of transcendent disappearance. Nirvana is of course under one aspect the attainment of serenity and insight in this world, but a crucial characteristic of its other aspect is that the process of rebirth is discontinued. To state the contrast starkly and over-crudely: in Western salvation there is another form of individual existence, in Theravadin Buddhist salvation there is no individual to speak of. In the one case immortality, in the other case the cessation of immortality. In the one case, the individual carries on; in the other, individuality as we know it is destroyed. As another poem puts it:

> Days and nights pass away: with them
> Life's consumed and the span assigned
> To mortals soon evaporates
> Like water in the mountain streams.
> Yet the fool still does evil deeds
> And fails to understand that soon
> A bitter fruit will follow on,
> The sure reward of wickedness.

In other words, it is the foolish person who prolongs his existence by failing to take account of the effects of actions. More sharply the point is put in another poem:

7

In the round of existence I arrived at hell and again
And again arrived in the world of spirits.
Long did I suffer ill in the many forms of animal life.
I was glad to become a man, but rarely did I gain
A heavenly body. In the realms of form and formlessness,
In the realms of perception and non-perception I was placed.
I knew well these conditions of life—they are without essence,
Conditioned, unstable and forever drifting. Knowing this
By understanding the origin of my self,
Self-aware I have attained true peace.

It is noticeable—and here we come across another seeming contrast
to the Judaeo-Christian frame of reference—that the author here speaks
of heavens and hells. More correctly the word for 'hell' might be
translated 'purgatory'—in the sense that such a realm of existence is
not ultimate. However long a person may suffer the torments of
punishment, he will emerge at the end to a higher form of life. Conversely, heavens and the realms of form and formlessness mentioned
in the poem are impermanent. Nirvana transcends even the highest
type of heavenly life: it transcends the life of the gods, even of the
great god Brahma, who supposes himself wrongly to be creator of the
universe. To the question of the gods I shall return shortly: but meanwhile it is worth observing that there is an oblique reference to
methods and stages of meditation (the *jhānas*) in this poem—methods
which can take you up to a purified state of consciousness in which
there is neither perception nor non-perception—an inner state corresponding to elements in mysticism elsewhere. But even these states
considered in themselves are impermanent. They are part of what is
typically involved in the attainment of nirvana, but it is only nirvana
itself, as a rooted disposition and as a transcendent state, which is
finally permanent, the true 'deathless place' (as it is sometimes called).
The correlation of higher realms of being with stages of meditation is
further evidence that Buddhist metaphysics and cosmology are not
simply theoretical and intellectual, but at the same time existential.
Thus in Mahayana Buddhism the subtle dialectic used in the Madhyamika school to break down all theories of ultimate reality itself serves
not just as a piece of philosophizing as we might understand it in these
latter Western days but also as a method of meditation. The arguments
used are meant to be both valid and salvific.

It is in the light of this existential character of early Buddhism that

8

we must set the ideas of knowledge and insight, and their opposites. We have already noticed in one or two passages the reference to those who are 'foolish'. They are not fools in the ordinary sense. What they lack is spiritual insight. They are victims of *avijjā*, that ultimate ignorance which entangles people in the round of rebirth. If salvation involves a kind of knowledge, the *gnosis* of nirvana, the unsaved, unliberated state involves a deeper kind of ignorance. Indeed one might count ignorance in this sense as being the counterpart of original sin in the Christian tradition.

This means that the Teaching, the *dhamma*, has a very central role in Theravadin eschatology. The Buddha cannot be said to exist (or not to exist) any more: he has disappeared trackless and unfathomable at his decease. But he leaves behind him the Sangha or order of monks and nuns and the *Dhamma*. This teaching is something which men can test in experience, and through its guidance they can tread the Path which will hopefully bring them to liberation. It is therefore primarily as Teacher that the Buddha saves. It is the *Dhamma* which is the light to guide men to a higher destiny. (By contrast it is Christ as actor rather than as Teacher, that classical Christianity has seen as the bringer of redemption, by his life, death and resurrection.) But the *Dhamma* is more than a set of propositions, albeit that it is clothed in propositions and injunctions. It points to something, and in a sense incorporates that something—which is why in the Mahayana the *Dharma* and *nirvana* could be equated. In the Theravada the atmosphere of the *Dhamma* can perhaps be brought out by the following poem:

> The peacocks shriek. Ah the lovely crests and tails
> And the sweet sound of the blue-throated peacocks.
> The great grassy plain now runs with water
> Beneath the thunder-clouded sky.
> Your body's fresh, you are vigorous now and fit
> To test the Teaching: reach now for that saintly rapture,
> So bright and pure, so subtle, so hard to fathom,
> The highest, the eternal place.

The Dhamma therefore points to the highest state to be achieved by man. It is itself the product of transcendental insight: for it was discovered by the Buddha in his Enlightenment and passed on by him to succeeding generations. Yet those generations can only know what it really means if they too have the insight. Thus another poem:

See how that insight of the Buddhas blazing
Like fire in the middle of the night
Gives eyes and vision to those who, approaching,
Manage to discipline their doubt.

Owing to the enormousness of the time-scale of life in Buddhism, the constantly recurring evolution and decay of the cosmos, the vast and indeed limitless procession of births and deaths for any given individual, it is not surprising if the task of breaking free from the entanglements of craving and ignorance should be thought to be a strenuous exercise. The mood of these poems is undoubtedly ascetic. It is true that the Buddha preached a middle path between self-torture and self-indulgence: but these extremes are relative. The middle path of those days might seem mortifying to us in these later days. One form of meditation practised widely by Buddhist and other ascetics was to frequent the charnel-ground—where not all corpses were reduced to ashes and bones, but others were in those days simply exposed to rot and to be eaten by wild animals and the less attractive birds. A reflection of this grim practice is found in another poem:

The woman Kali strong and crow-like
Breaks off a thigh-bone, then the other.
She breaks an arm off, then the other,
And the skull too, like a milk-bowl.
She prepares them all and is seated.
The man who has no understanding
Stupidly fashions the foundation
For future birth and keeps returning
To pain. Therefore the man of insight
Builds no rebirth, but keeps repeating
"May I never lie with a smashed skull-bone."

And yet on the other hand the recluses who composed these poems were also able to delight in nature:

When I see the pure white plumage of the crane
As she flaps in fear before the dark clouds,
Seeking a shelter and storm-free haven,
Then the river Ajakarani
Is a sweet thought for me.

10

When I see the clear white plumage of the crane
As she flaps in fear before the dark clouds
Seeking a refuge beyond the horizon,
Then the river Ajakarani
Is a sweet thought for me.
Who would not love the sight
Of the rose-apple trees
Arrayed on either bank
Behind the hermitage?
Where the frogs, safe from harm. . . .
Will indolently croak:
"It's not yet time to go
And leave the mountain-streams:
The Ajakarani
Is peaceful: it is blest
And delightful here."

We have seen that even the gods are impermanent. It must be remembered that Buddhism has never really rejected belief in gods. It is only that they do not bring salvation. Here there is a characteristic ambiguity, arising from the psychological, existential interests of Theravadin Buddhism. This can perhaps be well illustrated from the position of Mara, the Buddhist Satan (if one can make so crude a comparison). This evil, death-dealing spirit is mentioned in a number of the poems: he symbolizes the forces hostile to liberation (as is well brought out in Trevor Ling's *Buddhism and the Mythology of Evil*). Does he really exist? It seems so, and yet once he is perceived for what he is he is defeated, driven away by the Buddha's and the saints' insight. He only has power over those who do not know him as he is—just as the gods and ghosts have a certain mundane power, but become quite irrelevant to those who gain liberating insight. This ambiguity of Buddhism's attitude to the gods and supernatural beings allows it to live harmoniously in societies where gods and ghosts and the like are part of the cultural furniture. There is no need to destroy such beliefs: there *is* need to bring home to people that ultimately these forces are utterly transcended both by the Buddha and by liberation. The Buddha vanquishes Mara and is a 'god beyond gods'—and yet he is not really a god. Thus is expressed, merely, the transpolytheistic character of Buddhism. It is not, incidentally, unnatural for the Buddhist to treat the Christian God and the Jewish God after the same fashion—psychological forces, so to say, but ultimately to be transcended by peace and insight.

To sum up some of the attractions and characteristics of early Buddhist loyalty, as exhibited in the *Theragatha*, perhaps I can quote part of a long poem of aspiration:

> When shall I go to live alone,
> Migrant among the mountain caves,
> And see the impermanence of things?
> When oh when will it come to be?
>
> When shall I go in ragged robes,
> A yellow-clad recluse, with all
> Hate, passion and illusion dead,
> To the jungle joyfully?
>
> .   .   .   .
>
> When shall I draw insight's bright sword,
> The searing weapon of the saints,
> And smash the Tempter's army while
> He's still triumphant on the throne?
>
> .   .   .   .
>
> When will the pure rain of the black
> Monsoon cloud come to drench my robe
> As in the woods I take that Path
> Which wise men tread? When will it be?
>
> When in the wooded hill ravines
> Will twice-born tufted peacocks call
> And rouse my will to try to gain
> The immortal? When, when will it be?
>
> When shall I get the power to soar
> Over Ganges, Jumna, Saraswati
> And the awful yawning jaws of hell
> Without falling? When will it be?
>
> When like a vagrant pauper pressed
> By creditors, who finds a cache,
> Shall I come joyfully upon
> The Great One's saving word? Ah, when?
>
> .   .   .   .

When will abusive words no more
Cause me to be upset, and praise
Cease to induce in me a thrill
Of pleasure? Oh when will it be?

It will, I hope, be seen from the foregoing that the atmosphere of early Buddhism, as expressed at any rate in these poems, is different indeed from that of (say) 4th century Christianity. The themes of Creation, atonement, worship of God, sacramental participation in the divine life, original sin and many others are absent; and often do not have analogues.

This 'lack of fit' has sometimes induced both modern Western and some Eastern commentators to doubt whether Buddhism of this form is properly speaking a religion. Of course, if we define religion by reference to belief in gods or in God as the ultimate reality, Theravada Buddhism is not a religion. But it is more realistic to define religion in a broader way—though this is not now an issue that I have time to explore. In any case we can perhaps consider what may be described as the 'spiritual logic' of the Theravada: and this may begin to throw some light upon the questions about the death of God with which I started.

I have stressed in my exposition the importance of insight, knowledge, as opposed to the ignorance and foolishness entangling men in the round of rebirth. The emphasis upon insight in Buddhism may be said to arise both from the historical origin of the faith and from the nature of the central Buddhist experience. First, the Buddha unmistakably belonged to the groups of *samanas* or ascetic teachers who existed in dialectical interplay with the sacrificial Brahmanical religion of the time. Their emphasis was upon self-control, interior states and liberation from rebirth. The inward-looking character of Buddhist meditation belongs to this tradition, even though of course the actual shape of Buddhism was characteristic, idiosyncratic, highly original—a testimony to the creative power of the Buddha himself (about this we can have little doubt, even though the quest of the historical Buddha is so hard). Second, the meditational practice of early Buddhism, especially the practice of the *jhānas*, was oriented towards purifying and controlling inner states, so that the saint could perceive the transcendent—the deathless, the permanent. This did not entail that there is a deathless soul within—the whole Buddhist analysis opposed the concept of such a substantial self. There is no self: the individual is but a congeries of impermanent states. But at any rate it was in this inner experience above all that the saint was enabled to find assurance of liberation. The originality of the Buddha's anti-substantialist metaphysics may blind us to the fact that the true analogue of the perception of nirvana is the mysticism which runs like a thread through religions wherever the contemplative life has been prized. The Theravadins had their own interior castle, however differently described may have been their universe.

This is relevant to the question of God—for it is a fallacy to suppose that contemplative mysticism needs always to be interpreted in terms of union with a personal being. The teachings of Sankara, of classical Yoga, of some phases of Taoism, of Buddhism itself, testify in the opposite direction. The Theravada is, if you like, mysticism without God: the transcendent, yes—the personal Creator and redeemer, no. Hence the diagnosis of man's condition is not to do with sin, that is alienation from God. Rather it is to do with ignorance, that is the lack of that deeper insight which assures liberation. Hence too there is no ultimate concern with personal survival, which in a theistic context can above all mean the continuance of relationship with God. Rather, the concern is with a purely transcendent state, where the question of personal relationship does not arise. These diagnoses are of course placed within the wider context of rebirth, but even apart from this, there is a logic in the emphases. Again, the fruit of insight is a supreme serenity, which chimes in with the whole ethos of self-control, and with the perception that there is nothing to be related with in the final analysis—no self to cling to anything whether transcendent or not. Hence too the gods, not being ultimate, are themselves the victims of ignorance and illusion and so are without ultimate power. Even the power of the Evil One vanishes before insight.

If this is a satisfactory view of the Theravada (and of course I miss out here the whole subtlety of the Sangha's engagement with society), it may help us to see something of the present mood of the death of God. Of course, the new radical Christian theologies have distinct roots, very different from those of the Theravada. Yet there are analogies: and I may be permitted to explore them briefly. One main root of the modern radicalism lies in the contrast between the Gospel and religion found varyingly in the writings of Barth, Kraemer, Bonhoeffer, Harvey Cox. The contrast enables people to subject the religious and traditional elements of Christianity to a critique. Most radically, the picture of a personal God is itself consigned to the sphere

14

of religion, transcended by the Gospel concretely manifested in Christ. God becomes treated in this way as a mythic symbol which needs to be used but then transcended (this is itself incidentally a traditional motif in its way: compare the whole question of analogical predication). Here is a modern counterpart to Buddhist ambiguity towards the mythology which it incorporated into its fabric. Secondly, modern radicalism has roots in Existentialism: for instance, in the use of a form of Heidegger's account of existence, as exploited by Bultmann and his followers, the Christian message is represented in a form concerned with the inner, personal meaning of the old myths. This again has an analogy to Buddhist treatment of contemporary religion. Though Mara appears as a personal figure in the story of the Buddha's victory over ignorance and craving, the point of the story can be presented doctrinally, yet only on condition that the doctrines of rebirth, craving, ignorance, non-self and so on are seen in their true meditational and existential context.

In these ways there is a certain convergence between modern Christian radicalism and the outlook of the Theravada. Nevertheless it is a convergence from very different directions. It is fair to comment that modern radicalism is largely a Protestant phenomenon, even if now Roman Catholicism is showing signs of moving in a Protestant direction. What characterizes Protestantism, from the crude and wider perspective of the history of religions is first a strong concern for the logic of personal numinousness in God, reflected grace (for only God can save), a certain secular orientation consonant with a rediscovery of the prophetic role of the new Israel, a flexible use of rituals. But second Protestantism has been less concerned than either Catholicism or Orthodoxy with the mystical, contemplative life. I do not deny that there have been elements of this in Protestant history, such as the life of Boehme and the idea of the inner light among the Society of Friends. But even so the major emphasis has been upon the relation of the individual to a personal God in worship and in the experience of conversion. This is a main reason for the present crisis in Protestantism —for it is easier to demythologize inner experience and one's existential relationship to the world (for instance to death) than it is to demythologize a personal God.

To return to the convergence—as I have said, it is from very different directions. In Indian terms, the existential nisus in Protestantism is from the direction of *bhakti*, a fervent devotionalism, or pietism if the word is preferred; while the interior emphasis in Buddhism is from the direction of the contemplative life. It therefore appears to me that the most fruitful kind of dialogue between Theravada Buddhism and Christianity will occur on the frontiers of Catholicism, precisely because of the high investment by the Catholic tradition in the contemplative life: and it is the contemplative life, however differently described, which lies at the heart of Buddhism. But in moving in a 'reformed' direction it could be that contemporary Catholicism is making it less easy for Christianity to see the chief point of Buddhism.

Yet this is paradoxical in terms of the present situation in the world, where moon-shots and hamburgers disenchant the environment, so that men seek the truth within themselves—naïvely and technologically sometimes by taking LSD; equally naïvely perhaps by looking to a Westernized Yoga; but increasingly by following new religions of meditation and self-development. By 'men' here I chiefly mean Western men. And one thing we must escape is this wretched identification. Christianity will ultimately be tested not in the secular city, whose prototype is Chicago and New York, but in the hearts of those who have tasted the canned fruits of the post-Christian West and found them tasteless.

The quest for an interior serenity and insight into reality, such as is exhibited in the lives of those who concocted the *Theragatha*, is not at all ignoble. And precisely because these men did not wait for the so-called death of God (for they had no God to die) it may be that they can tell us something which transcends the vulgarity of the new moral radicalism afflicting secularizing Christian theologians.

It may also be important for Judaism, though it is presumptuous of me to say so, to continue the rediscovery of its mystical heritage, the Kabbalah and Hasidism.

CHAPTER 15

Types of Religious Liberation: An Implicit Critique of Modern Politics

Introduction

Much of contemporary life is taken up with the twin pursuits of freedom and happiness. The religious traditions of the world also in their own ways are concerned with these goals. But they provide a perspective from which to criticize secular aspirations for them. For what, in the ultimate analysis—or should we say "in the light of the ultimate"—is happiness? And in what consists true freedom? Thus for the Christian, Christ's freedom is something that goes beyond a merely commonsense absence of restraints; for the Buddhist true welfare or happiness (sukha) is in part consequent upon the recognition of the illfare and unhappiness that otherwise characterizes all sentient life. However, though the main religious traditions converge at certain points, there are also not inconsiderable differences. In the first part of this essay I wish to lay forth some of the chief varieties of belief in liberation or salvation; in the second part I will reflect briefly on them and consider how far they can be seen as complementary.

Types of Liberation

Since the main religions have a conception of the ultimate as somehow transcending "this world," however that may be analyzed, it is natural that liberation or freedom should be seen as becoming close to or realizing one's unity with, or attaining, the ultimate and thereby throwing off the restraints of this world. Liberation thus is seen as something transcendent itself or closely tied to what is transcendent. There is therefore, ineluctably, an otherworldly element in liberation. But as we shall see, this need not mean that we should not see salvation or liberation as having an important this-worldly component.

Religion and Society: Issues and Cases

To flesh out my point: consider the following ways of seeing the state of salvation. It is the final departure of the soul (jiva), in the Jain tradition, from the karmic round of rebirth and its lodging motionless and omniscient at the summit of the universe. It is likewise, in Sāmkhya and Yoga, a state of isolation and absence of pain beyond the round of rebirth. In Theravāda Buddhism, there is no soul, but somehow in the disappearance of individuality there is attained the state of nibbāna in which and from which there cannot be any more rebirth. In Advaita Vedānta, liberation involves realization of one's essential identity with Brahman and the cessation of the karmic round. In theistic Vedānta on the other hand, through transcendence of the round of reincarnation (a common factor in the mainstream Indian traditions), salvation is pictured as everlasting life in heaven close to God. Incidentally, heavens are, of course, present in the Buddhist and other nontheistic traditions, but are thought of as places of nonpermanent residence, and since permanence is often seen as the mark of true and ultimate value, such heavens turn out to be no more than pleasant consequences of virtue, not ultimate goals to be striven for. Theoretically, this is the way it is seen in Pure Land Buddhism, that great efflorescence of Buddhist bhakti: but since in the Pure Land so many fervent spiritual hopes are centered, the goal of final nirvana beyond even the Pure Land itself fades—so that phenomenologically this variety of Buddhism approximates the Hindu theisms as much as the nontheistic schools. So far we come across two main motifs with variations: disappearance from rebirth into a static, blissful (or at least pain-free) state; and ascent to a permanent heavenly state close to God. The Advaita variant is in a sense intermediate: one is God, the Divine Being, and as such is liberated, save that you typically do not know it. In the first case, this-worldly individuality is lost. In Samkhya and Yoga and Jainism, liberated souls are "base," "nude," unclothed in bodily and psychological modes. In Buddhism, there is no real question of personality surviving since nirvana is delineated with a whole battery of appropriate negations. In Advaita, too, the worldly individual disappears, since the true self, which is discovered existentially to be divine, is not mine or yours, but unindividually universal. Similar remarks can be made about those Mahāyāna developments where the Buddha nature, as a kind of quasi-self, is spoken of. It is ultimately empty (sūnya) and suchness, and in no way is embedded as a swarm of individual Buddha natures in different living beings.

Types of Religious Liberation

It is useful here to make a distinction. In Sāmkhya and Dvaita Vedanta, for instance, there are many individual souls. But in Sāmkhya they are "standardized" so to speak—they are individuals but without individuality. Liberation means continuing individuation, but there, as they say, "once you've seen one you've seen them all." On the other hand, there is a Dvaita, a sense of individual uniqueness, and this is also the usual interpretation of the Christian doctrine of the resurrection of the body. So it may be useful to distinguish between a pluralism of individuals or souls on the one hand and the notion of the individuality or uniqueness of each soul on the other. For short I will call the first the doctrine of *numerous* individuals or souls and the second the doctrine of *personal* individuals or souls.

In the major Western traditions of Christianity, Judaism, and Islam, reincarnation of course had not had much prominence, so the whole nexus of ideas surrounding karma, samsāra, and liberation does not apply. Rather, notions of heaven predominate (and hell, etc.) Also the concept of the resurrection of the body has entered into mainstream Western theism. This latter notion has as part of its cash value the notion that what is sacred is the whole personality, as embodied. Perhaps for most purposes this is the whole of its cash value, since both traditionally and today the resurrection of the body has often been seen as mysterious, as involving God's creating new bodies perhaps not of earthly stuff. So by consequence the difference between this idea and that of a personal soul becomes diminished. The problem of the soul idea is its abstractness and lack of clear relation to personhood; the problem of the resurrection idea is its overconcreteness and propensity to degenerate into speculations about material reconstitution, for example, of ashes.

So far we can perceive various patterns of belief concerning liberation. First, there is the doctrine of numerous individuals who have transcended the round of rebirth. Second, there is the doctrine of liberated personal souls somehow related to God. Third, there is realization of unity with the ultimate in which both the idea of numerous souls and that of personal souls disappears (Advaita and Sūnyavada in Mahāyāna Buddhism).

We should also mention the conception of ancestors. Though not primarily a notion of salvation or liberation, it does have a role in our thinking about an afterlife. Ancestors typically are important in extending the community; the latter is seen not merely as constituted by the living, but extends to those who have passed into the

Religion and Society: Issues and Cases

invisible world, but an invisible world still close to us. Thus the cult of ancestors—giving them offerings, say—is just an extension of the veneration given to the old and the wise. It reminds us that sometimes freedom or liberation or salvation can also be viewed as a collective matter. This can be so in a narrower or a wider way.

More narrowly the focus may be primarily on a given people, such as Israel. The people may look forward to "last things" in which God will, perhaps through some charismatic leader or messiah, restore the people and settle them in peace forever. Secular ideologies such as nationalism and Marxism can echo this concept. Indeed, it is worth noting that in modern times "freedom" very often is thought of in terms of a collective national or social liberation. (But freedom also has to do with individual rights, and collective and individual liberties can collide.)

The broader way in which a collectivity of liberation may be conceived is universalism—that is, the doctrine that all eventually will be saved and that since no one can be finally happy while others suffer, individual and collective bliss becomes notionally simultaneous. This idea occurs in some Christian theologies and in the bodhisattva ideal in Mahāyāna Buddhism. For the bodhisattva puts off his own liberation until all are liberated.

We may observe that only one type of liberation is strongly personalistic. Neither nontheistic systems that hold that there are numerous individuals or souls nor those that believe in a monistic unity of all souls conceive of liberation as personal. It is by contrast characteristic of Dvaita in the Hindu tradition and theisms that emphasize heavenly liberation after some kind of judgment and reconstitution of the individual that have a place for salvation of the person. Yet of course it is a paradox: for though I may thus be guaranteed my ego, yet that self now is seen as truly happy when dependent on God. As it is said, "whose service is perfect freedom."

So you can, it seems, have perfect happiness as a person in a state of dependence or perfect freedom if you are prepared to give up your individuality. Happy slavery or unconscious freedom—is this the choice?

But the contrast between the nonpersonal and personal (which are also theistic ideas) is not as strong as it at first seems. For the nonpersonal systems also hold to the concept of the person who is "living liberated" or jīvanmukta. Such a one has attained assurance of release while alive and indeed is already liberated. His body and mind of course continue to operate, but there will be no rebirth

Types of Religious Liberation

when death arrives. As the usual image has it, he is like a potter's wheel continuing to spin after the potter has taken his hand off.

This notion of living liberation or jivanmukta means that we have the idea of an individual who will indeed lose his particularity at death (becoming either unutterable as in Buddhism or a standard soul as elsewhere in nontheistic Indian traditions); but on the other hand he is objectively a person. So he is a liberated person, or saint. I stress personhood twice here to drive home the point that here we have a living model of personal liberation, which does not in principle differ ontologically from that of the saved person beyond the grave in the theistic traditions—except only there is no relationship to God. But there is relationship to others in the community here and now. Also, of course, in theistic traditions there is sometimes the idea of living salvation, as when the believer has assurance that he is saved, because of some direct experience of God's grace, for example.

So far we have looked at ideas of liberation and salvation without asking the question "from what?" Here there is, of course, a variety of beliefs to consider. It is typical, however, of the Indian tradition that the most typical answer is at one level duhkha or illfare, suffering, pain (different translations are common but the first of these is what I favor). Deeper down we find that illfare arises in the last resort from ignorance, lack of insight. But monism does not see the problem simply in these terms because the doctrine itself implies that the multiple world of appearances is an illusion. So ontologically the world we transcend is unreal. Elsewhere it is real, but unsatisfactory. In gnosticism there was often the more radical idea that the world is evil. But it is only possible really to think of the world in this way if there is an evil creator of it (demiurge); for evil is an attribute that applys to the effects of an evil actor. Otherwise the world can be painful or illusory. On the whole, modern religious traditions have moved far from the concept of an evil God or even of a Satan. On the other hand, if there is but one God then the evil in the world is his responsibility unless you ascribe it to some primeval catastrophe, and this is where the Christian doctrine of the Fall comes in, and with it the idea that it is sin we need saving from, not ignorance.

Sin has come to have two components: one is that of alienation or estrangement or, in more traditional terms, unholiness in the sense of falling short of the holiness of God; and the other is moral evil and disobedience toward God. If we are to put matters positively,

Religion and Society: Issues and Cases

then the aim of those who would wish to be liberated from sin would be gaining holiness and communion with God on the one hand, and moral goodness on the other. But the very essence of a religion of the holy is a sense of duality between God and worshiper—that is, ontological difference—even when the sense of alienation is overcome. So salvation is not seen as merging or actually becoming God, but rather as being in the closest possible relationship to God. It is this sense of relationship, even in the life beyond, that no doubt accounts for the personalism of theistic salvation. Conversely, because liberation in the nontheistic traditions means isolation or unutterability, it is in *this* world, where relationships still exist, that we have the liberated person.

The holy or numinous character of God means that liberation can, strictly speaking, only come through his agency. For as the one God he possesses ultimately all the holiness there is—nothing beside him is holy. (If in Hindu devotional religion there seem to be gods and goddesses besides the Lord, they are, in the end, parts of him, refractions so to speak—which is why we may call such a system of myth and cult refracted theism.) Holiness flows from God, thus the ·idea of grace and of the transfer of merit. Even if we do things that are not admirable and are out of accord with his will, he can forgive us and count them as nothing. In such a way, though being good is in a sense a means to salvation, it is ultimately not so—for only grace is a means thereto. The moral endeavor is swallowed up in a wider and deeper sense of meaning.

On the other hand, in nontheistic systems, where there is scarcely any call to think of grace (except where bhakti and devotional religion begins to make itself felt, as with the growth of the bodhisattva ideal), moral action becomes an important ingredient in the path to liberation. It becomes much more directly a means of salvation.

But it is morality still in a context, and this supplies three motifs that typically affect the way goodness is considered. These are karma, tapas, and dhyāna—or in English, reincarnational effects, austerity, and contemplation. Belief in rebirth means that morality often becomes a mode—*the* mode sometimes—of acquiring merit and so of gaining a better life next time. Such a life may be in a heaven, but even here the worm of impermanence and potential suffering persists, for no heaven can provide ultimate freedom. So karma theory stretches the effects of moral striving. As for asceticism, in the Indian tradition especially there are deep impulses

Types of Religious Liberation

toward self-mortification as a means of neutralizing the effects of deeds, and we have as the ultimate symbol of this the great nude Jaina statues where creepers growing up the legs of a saint show how impervious he is to the environment, how indifferent to worldly things. Self-starvation becomes the perfect death. To the ascetic outlook belongs a view of the world not so much as illusion, as painful, or as sinful, but as entangling. Freedom must mean cutting off all those impulses that get you more deeply entangled.

But it is contemplation that possesses the greatest present-day interest. For it is characteristic of the Yoga traditions of India, of which Buddhism is in many ways the greatest, that they see the acquisition of a special type of higher consciousness as being the key to liberation. This higher consciousness is empty and pure, and yet it also brings knowledge. For the world seen now *sub specie eternitatis* has a different look, and the analysis that is part of the context of self-training is perceived existentially. So the world view of the yogi thus has confirmation in higher experience, and liberation also involves some kind of jñāne or viveká or prajña—in Greek, gnosis, a kind of what I call for fun "gnowing."

Such contemplative mysticism is not, of course, absent from theistic traditions, but there it has a different context and significance. For one thing, higher consciousness is seen as union with but not identity with the ultimate; and it is itself considered a product of grace. Moreover, since mysticism is not the predominant form of life in theism, where worship and sacraments are more pervasive, it has less centrality as a means of liberation than in the nontheistic religions.

We have seen some polarities and contrasts. Thus there is the sense of personal, heavenly salvation versus nonpersonal liberation in nirvana. There is individual versus collective liberation. There is liberation from sin and from ignorance and entanglement. There is the world as real and the world as illusion. There is grace as means of salvation versus austerity, morality, and contemplation. I wish now to reflect about some of these typical patterns in the more secular context that is becoming so pervasive in today's world.

Reflections on Traditional Concepts and Their Contemporary Relevance

Contemporary Western culture is dominated by utilitarianism, namely the doctrine that social policy should be aimed at maximiz-

Religion and Society: Issues and Cases

ing happiness and minimizing suffering. We are descendants of Adam Smith and John Stuart Mill. There is much to commend in modern economics, and in social democracy there is an attempt to adjust and curtail the workings of "the market" in order to alleviate the suffering of the poor and needy. At the same time the most vital political force in modern times is nationalism, and this has sometimes run contrary to the individualism inherent in utilitarianism. Moreover, Marxism, with its collectivist thinking—especially as vulgarly understood by the ruling classes of Marxist countries—reinforces nationalism in practice, for it has proved a potent instrument of liberation from colonial and neocolonial bonds, which have largely been to the old capitalist nations of the north.

These reflections might seem far removed from the varieties of salvation I have been analyzing in this essay. But this is not so, for a number of reasons. First, the individualist ethos of liberal capitalism creates two problems, one of what may be called *external* identity, and the other of *internal* identity. As social persons we find identity in belonging to a group. For each person there may be an overlapping set of groups, but the most important is what may be called, in a somewhat Tillichian phrase, "the group of ultimate concern." In a nationalist era it is often the nation that functions thus, as that which demands if necessary your life in its service, and a large slice of your earnings and expenditure as a toll. Betrayal of the nation attracts the deepest opprobrium, as treason. But though national and ethnic identity may be built into the individual through his upbringing it need not be overriding. Its ultimacy may be questioned.

This is so in both theistic and nontheistic religion. Although one may be sympathetic to struggles for liberation (by Basques, Zimbabweans, Palestinians, etc.), the universal religions cannot see this political liberation as ultimate, for there is a higher community, of Christians or Muslims or Buddhists. Even where a faith is tied to a particular ethnic group (as appears to be the case with Judaism, except that the *ethnie* is both a matter of descent and of religious affiliation so that the religion defines the *ethnie* and not conversely), it may have a universal meaning, so that the group is a "light to the Gentiles" or an example to other nations. This means that though the group may be ultimate, its wider life is seen in a universal context.

Moreover, as well as widening our gaze horizontally to all humans as the ultimate group or even all living beings, the religions also expand it vertically, to the transcendent. And this becomes relevant to the problem of individual internal identity. It is by

Types of Religious Liberation

worship, in the case of theistic faiths, that you connect yourself to the transcendent, and by self-discipline and inner contemplation that you can aim for a "living liberation" as the ultimate ideal. This of course is relevant to the utilitarian program. For in both cases religions offer something beyond the usual this-worldly ideas of happiness or of suffering. Higher welfare need not of course be world negating, but they are what can be called world deepening and world transforming. They deepen the world, as in Buddhism, by inviting us to "see through" common sense. They can deepen it in theistic religions by creating a vision of the world as everywhere, even in its darkness, manifesting the Divine Being.

In all this, traditional religion becomes a critic of modern secular ideologies. It criticizes the flat happiness of materialist individualism; it criticizes the flat collectivism of Marxism; and it criticizes the narrowness of nationalism.

Yet the spirit of our secular age is pervasive. After all, how many people can believe, without effort or special commitment, in life after death or in rebirth? There is not much point in criticizing the ideologies of our time if it is from a radically foreign point of view. In certain important respects the old images of heaven and judgment and rebirth have to be taken now as regulative pictures. Let me briefly explain my meaning here.

One of the central problems, perhaps *the* central problem of philosophical theology, is how we conceive the junctures between the transcendent (whether God or nirvana or Brahman) and this world. I can understand the experience of realizing one's essential identity with Brahman; but how does this experience cause rebirth, a this-worldly phenomenon, to cease? I can understand how God supports and pervades the whole cosmos; but the manner of his becoming Christ eludes clear understanding. Again, how is it that there is a liberation, nirvana, and yet nirvana has no cause? In a sense, all questions of survival are such "juncture" questions: for if I survive only as a bull in the Argentine or as any kind of this-worldly being, how is that ultimate salvation? It is mere prolongation of life. So the images of redemption and the liberated state can hardly be clearly explicated. Rather, they help to point us to the ground of any hope and freedom, and that is the existence, as being or state, of that blessed transcendence to which the religions in varying directions point. In essence, then, the religions provide criticism of the secular because they have a transcendental outreach. This in turn means in human terms that a deeper experience of the

Religion and Society: Issues and Cases

world is found than in flat utilitarianism. Such depth experience helps us to see the world transformed.

This makes a difference to the significance of liberation theology, as distinguished from secular ideologies of liberation. The essential reason for seeing the material bases of human poverty and exploitation is that exploitation itself is an attack on human dignity, and that dignity is guaranteed by the divine spark or Buddha nature in each one of us. The worth of men and women relates not to class or ethnic group, but to their relation to the beyond and indeed reflection of what is transcendent.

The ideas of individual "disappearance" into the state beyond (in the style of Buddhism and other Yoga traditions) and of communion with God are complementary, for they point to two sides of religion and human life—a side that is full of images, worship, and outer cosmic vision, and a side that is empty of images, is contemplative, and seeks an inner light. We cannot know what liberation in the beyond is like, but we can here and now see its incarnated representatives. Thus the concept of liberation or redemption provides for transformed persons, who themselves are critics in their lives of the flatness and cruelty around us that follow from human nature and sometimes callous ideologies.

This is not to say Mill and Marx have not contributed to our world, but only when we see that material change and prosperity is essentially related to dignity do we see it in perspective. As I have said, the theories of salvation in the religions provide a deeper such perspective, even if we cannot say much about heaven or nirvana.

V

Religious Studies and Religious Education: Method and Theory in the Study of Religions

CHAPTER 16

Religion as a Discipline?

IN a recent article, 'Theology as a Discipline?',[1] Dr. W. A. White-house has discussed the case for theology in the university. His dissatisfaction with much of what goes on in conventional Departments of Theology ('a few harmless courses on the Bible and Christian doctrine') will be felt by many; and his proposal for small experimental Departments pointing the students towards live research work may also find support. But a much more radical view of the place of theology and religious studies is needed. The concept of a Department of Religion, rather than that of a Department of Theology, is the best answer. Perhaps some people will regard the concept as tainted because of its American associations (a red rag, it seems, to many of our John Bulls). But let us give it a good hearing.

Why is religion intellectually important? For two separate reasons: first, because it is a widespread and highly significant human phenomenon; and second, because of its claims about the nature of reality. In regard to both these sides of religion, conventional Departments of Theology display serious deficiencies. Part of the trouble is that theology lives on sufferance. True, the cunning manipulation and reinterpretation of charters have allowed it a place in universities which once would never have admitted it. But there is great sensitivity about it all round, and this has led to sad results. To be respectable, it has had to go in for tough and 'scientific' pursuits. Biblical studies are just right for this—plenty of Hebrew and Greek, textual criticism, minute historical enquiries. Church History too, being a branch of history, is undoubtedly all right. But the formulation of Christian doctrine, apologetics and the like are doubly suspect. Their methodology is obscure, and their conclusions, some may think, are prejudiced. The concentration upon the Biblical and historical side has had at least three evil consequences. First, it has restricted enquiry into religion as a human phenomenon: the non-Christian religions scarcely get a look in, and topics like the sociology and psychology of religion are regarded as largely irrelevant. Second, it has made theology rather dull for those who are interested in religious truth (and falsity). Third, theological studies are not presented in a candid way in our universities. Everybody knows very well that the Bible is selected for treatment in depth because it is fundamental to the Christian revelation. Everybody knows very well that it is no accident that the Fathers of the Church are so fully studied. But as for discussion as to whether the Bible does after all enshrine the truth and whether the formulations of the early Church are worth heeding—these are left in uncandid darkness. Yet these discussions are important; and the main issues of modern theology (largely a product, not unnaturally, of non-British theologians) are not negligible. That the universities have no quarrel with such fundamental discussion, provided that it is conducted in an open manner, is evident from the fact that it sometimes occurs in Departments of *Philosophy*.

These miseries are made worse by the fact that nearly everyone who studies theology is professionally interested and confessionally committed. Nearly all are prospective parsons and teachers of religious knowledge in schools and training colleges. The idea of going in for religious studies because they are interesting and important in themselves is largely wanting.

The cure for these evils is to rid religious studies of the grip of the Christian establishment. In the very nomenclature—Departments of Theology—it is tacitly implied that studies are devoted to Christian theology. This prevents an openness of approach, and means that interested agnostic, Jewish and other 'outsiders' are discouraged from taking up the subject. This is where the mere change of name to Religion is a blessing. Not only will it point towards a greater interest in descriptive studies, such as the sociology and psychology of religion, but also it will encourage more attention to topics such as the roots of modern atheism and agnosticism. And this in turn will generate greater concern for apologetics on the Christian side. Moreover, it should not be forgotten that the apologetic situation greatly affects the formulation of doctrine. For instance, the aftermath of the Theory of Evolution has brought an agonizing reappraisal of the doctrines of the Fall and of Original Sin. In short, a Department of Religion could well do far more than present Departments of Theology to stimulate research and debate about the two fundamental aspects of religion mentioned above—its ramifications as a human phenomenon and its validity or otherwise in claiming to give us an insight into reality.

But the project might well be suspected from two angles. The theologian may feel that disestablishment is a kind of surrender, while others may be unnerved by the prospect of the candid teaching of doctrine and apologetics. Yet these objections obviously contain a paradox. For it is precisely where, in a Department of Religion, theology is liable to be subjected to the cold winds of criticism and to the need to respond to the challenge of humanism, Marxism and the like, that serious theology gets done. It is no accident that (despite all the vagaries of American education) systematic theology flourishes more luxuriantly in the States than in England, or even than in Scotland. In brief, the theologian will in fact benefit, from his own point of view, through the change. Instead of being a hole-in-the-corner affair, on the edge of a Faculty of Arts, theology can once more resume some kind of real intellectual challenge. The truth or falsity of the Christian religion, and of other religions, is a serious matter; and discussion of it should not be the academic perquisite of a special group. Even the atheist will no doubt, moreover, wish to reject the strongest, not the feeblest, statement of the religious position.

But apart from this, the theologian should surely welcome the opportunities presented by the new approach. There are many areas of enquiry to which the history and phenomenology of religion are vitally relevant. The social sciences cannot ignore the phenomenon. Asian and African Studies, now burgeoning through Hayter, need the services of the Comparative Study of Religion—a Cinderella in the present theological world. History needs Church history. Philosophy needs doctrine to get its teeth into. In countless ways, and for obvious and long-standing reasons in the nature of human culture, the study of religion can be relevant and helpful to other disciplines. But as it is, people in other Departments are discouraged by the narrow interests of theology. Moreover, it is all too easy for agnostics to slip into thinking: 'Because religion is not true, and is not important to *me,* we need not consider it in trying to understand actual human behaviour.' This is a fallacy, but a prevalent one. A Department of Religion, then, could well be a source of service to other disciplines. Already, of course, there are some theologians who do perform such services: but not on a large enough scale.

But what of the other objection? Is not religion too explosive a subject? Will not the candid presentation of doctrine and apologetics mean that the universities are betraying their duty of impartiality? These fears are misdirected and out of date. Nobody questions

RELIGION AS A DISCIPLINE? 51

the right of political scientists and political philosophers in the universities to discuss the history and principles of Marxism. If a Marxist teacher chooses to *expound* Marxism, this is no intellectual crime. Only if Marxists take over Departments of Politics and stifle open discussion is there such a crime. But again there is a paradox. The suspicious non-Christian should reflect that it is the very refusal to have open discussion of theology that leads to the present set-up, where undoubtedly theology is an enclave of the Christian establishment. Sensitivity about the teaching of doctrine (except as mere history) is, as we saw, a main cause of the existing lack of candour in our universities about religion, and has made it all the easier for Christian scholars to keep religious studies as their special perquisite. There is nothing terribly sinister in this, and no doubt Christian theology will always be more important in our country than, say, Muslim theology. But the suspicious non-Christian, as well as the theologian, should surely be happier with a more open approach to religion.

But yet, it may be said, even admitting that this new approach is desirable, is it practical politics? To this there are a number of answers. First, it is unclear as to what is and what is not practical politics in the new universities being set up. Second, a start can be made in existing Departments of Theology by offering Religion as a subsidiary course for those reading honours in other subjects. Here co-operation with people in other disciplines may be essential, though its shape will depend on who there are and in what subjects. A course in Religion could suitably include work on the Bible and Christian doctrine; on religious and anti-religious thought in the last hundred years; and on the philosophy, psychology, sociology or comparative study of religion. Third, there is no reason why in one or two existing universities, and especially at London University, a special degree in Religion should not be established. In such ways it may be possible to attract more graduate students into the field—vital if the supply of suitable teachers of Religion is to be adequate.

Dr. Whitehouse, in the article mentioned, considered how a new adventurous Department of Theology, consisting of three persons or so, could operate. This is clearly an important kind of question. For a new university will not be likely to incorporate at the outset a fully fledged Department of Religion. What, then, could three people do effectively? In such a wide field there are many possibilities. Let us look at just one, as a sample of the range.

52   UNIVERSITIES QUARTERLY

Consider a Department consisting of a comparative religionist, a systematic theologian and a Biblical scholar. It would then be feasible to run a three-year course with two sides to it. Thus, on the European side, one could begin with a review of the present state of Biblical studies and the demythologizing movement. Quite clearly, scholars' critical questions about the historicity of the Bible are determined largely from outside—e.g. from the growth of scientific knowledge which has created problems of a philosophical and theological nature about the categories of ancient Jewish and early Christian thought. Thus the linguistic and Biblical studies could go hand in hand with an historical and critical investigation of the last hundred years of religious and anti-religious thought, including the changes in philosophical, scientific and theological views. These courses could well be supplemented by two or three others devoted to specific topics, such as creation and atonement, considered in the light of modern cosmology and psychology, and of philosophical criticisms of the Christian faith.

On the other side, and complementing these studies, a fairly extensive treatment of Eastern religions, notably Buddhism and Hinduism, would have great advantages. First, it would free the student from the European cultural tribalism which so bedevils thought about religion (and much else). Second, it would correspond to the real growth of interest in the great Eastern faiths as a possible alternative, and certainly a challenge, to Christianity. Third, out of this subject there arise in a very natural and incisive way most of the philosophical and apologetic issues which the Christian has to face. For example, the Western concept of the importance of the historical process is largely foreign to these faiths, and the notion of a personal God is altogether less prominent. This raises questions about the basis of theologies in religious experience; and so we are able to gain an insight into the sources of religion from the phenomenological point of view. In these last matters, the two sides of the course clearly come together and illuminate each other.

This is one sample. Not only would it constitute a degree course which would be lively, interesting and serious, so that the 'outsider' might well be attracted to it; but it would be quite as good a professional training as existing theological courses. Moreover, there are obvious points of contact between such a Department of Religion and other disciplines in the university. Our sample would be, for instance, just right for a university embarking upon Asian studies.

RELIGION AS A DISCIPLINE? 53

In brief: religion is too important both as a phenomenon and in its intellectual claims to be treated as it is now in our universities. As to the claims, maybe theology is bunkum, and maybe again it is not: but whatever the truth, the claims should be intelligently presented and openly discussed. As to the phenomenon, no-one can surely deny, whatever their beliefs, that it has been and is profoundly influential— and extraordinarily interesting. In a way, it is perhaps more interesting for the agnostic than for the believer. For men do strange things under the influence of religion—strange, strange things. Who has yet given us an absolutely authentic insight into the explanations for these things? There remains so much to be understood. The study of religion has its own important contribution to make.

NOTE

1 'Theology as a Discipline?', in *Universities Quarterly*. Vol. 16, no. 4, 1962.

CHAPTER 17

What is Comparative Religion?

The comparative study of religion as it is actually carried on in academic circles covers a number of different pursuits. As I shall try to show, one of these properly bears the title, while the others, though legitimate enterprises, can better be classified under such other general heads as "history" and "theology". I do not think that at the present time there is a clear consensus among comparative religionists as to how one tests conclusions, nor about the methods to be used. I shall try to illustrate some of the difficulties on these scores by reference to a thesis which I myself have propounded, mainly in relation to Indian religions, and which is open to a number of criticisms.

It is useful to look at the present place which comparative religion plays in religious studies in this country. Mostly it is an optional subject to be taken by students reading theology. It can, however, be taken as a separate discipline at Manchester University, and at least one new university is intending to set up a Department of Religious Studies rather different from the usual pattern in civic and ancient universities. In addition, much work in Oriental studies bears on religion, and sociologists of religion often do work which, but for the pigeonholing of subjects, would count as the comparative study of religion. But largely, as has been said, comparative religion is tied up with theology. This accounts in part for the diversity of pursuits comprehended under the name, though the pervasiveness of religion in human history means that almost any arts or social science subject is going to have something to do with it.

Let us clear away first those pursuits which are not, in my view, properly called comparative religion, though sheltering under the umbrella. First, there is the (in this country mainly Christian) theology of other faiths. Obviously some account has to be given, by the theologian, of other faiths—as to whether they contain truth, and if so in what ways. Professor R. C. Zeahner's *At Sundry Times* for instance contains a liberal, yet still Catholic, interpretation of some major world religions. George Appleton's *On the Eightfold Path* does something similar for Buddhism; Raymond Hammer's *Japan's Religious Ferment* for Japanese religions. Such works include a lot of factual material, but they tend to look at other faiths from a specifically Christian point of view. The converse is possible.

Thus many of President Radhakrishnan's writings interpret Christianity from a Hindu point of view. These exercises, though legitimate, depend on prior doctrinal assumptions : they are not either purely descriptive or "scientific". Second, and relatedly, there is the topic known by the barbarous neologism of missiology, comprising not just the history of missions but more importantly their aims and tactics. This incorporates conclusions of a theological nature. Again legitimate, but not in the required sense descriptive and scientific. Third, and again relatedly, there is the currently fashionable enterprise of the dialogue between religions, in which participants eirenically discuss mutual viewpoints, both for the sake of clarification and for the sake of possible agreements. This is a kind of polycentric theologising. It would have no point if each participant did not start form a prior position. These three pursuits are essentially theological. But the comparative study of religion, though in part *about* theology, is not itself theology.

Next, there is the history of religions. It is interesting to note that the world organization coordinating studies in comparative religion calls itself the International Association for the History of Religions. Properly, of course, the history of religions should be dubbed the histories of religions. In the main, for instance, Indian religious history has occurred independently of European religious history. Thus the history of Indian religions can in principle be treated quite separately. There is not a single subject "the history of religions", unless one counts its formal methods as giving unity to the discrete narratives. The separate histories do not count as comparative religion, for the obvious reason that they are not (save implicitly) comparative. Thus comparative religion has to be distinguished both from the history of religions and from theology.

What then does it aim to do? It feeds on the hope that one can make some sense of the similarities and differences between separate religious histories. This implies first that it is necessary to give a fair descriptive account of religious beliefs and practices. These are the data that may suggest accounts of why there are coincidences and variations. To give such a fair descriptive account one must suspend prior doctrinal judgements and value-prejudices (except perhaps for the higher-order principle that what is important to people is worth studying). But it is also necessary to enter sympathetically into the religious world one is considering. This involves a kind of make-believe, though it differs from the ordinary sort. The latter is such that one makes-believe that one is on the Moon, say, when one knows all the time that one is not. The former sort does not necessarily involve this conflict with what is known. Even for the committed Christian, for example, the entertaining of belief in nirvana is not *ipso facto* the entertaining of a belief which one knows to be false, for a number of reasons : for one thing, it might turn out that nirvana and the higher reaches of Christian contemplation have an affinity; for another thing, the concept of *knowledge* does not apply straightforwardly in relation to religious loyalties. In brief, then, the descriptive side of comparative religion is not just a recording of data : it is the attempt at a warmly dispassionate delineation of the outer shape and inner meaning of religious phenomena. Needless to say interpretation offered should conform to the typical interpretation given by the adherent of another faith. One is looking at the world from his point of view.

Would it not be enough, then, to collect accounts of faiths as given by their adherents? Not normally, for we have an eye to comparison. There is no guarantee that the adherent of faith A will be able to bring out the ways in which it differs from and is similar to faith B. To do that he must have entered at least imaginatively into faith B. Even if he be a convert, and so can encapsulate both faiths in his own experience, there are human troubles to consider—the zeal of the convert, his tendency to propagandize, the small chance of warm dispassion. There are some who can do it : many who cannot. There is no formal prescription for selecting in advance the good comparative religionist.

The need to straddle both sides of a comparison ought in principle to be recognized by the historian of another religion. For naturally one comes to another culture with certain prior views about the shape and nature of religion. These can be misleading, as Buddhological studies have clearly shown (the absence in Theravada Buddhism of the worship of anything like God and disbelief in an eternal soul have been too much for many Western scholars to stomach—they have tried, even quite recently, to smuggle one or other of these missing items back into the "original gospel" of Buddhism). The best way to deal with prior assumptions about religion (often deeply felt because religion remains controversial) is to bring them out in the open. But to do this is to embark on explicit comparisons. In brief it is to do a bit of comparative religion. But in so far as the chief aim is historical, one can still justly call the results the history of religions rather than the comparative study thereof.

There is then already a sense in which the acquisition of the data is comparative. But one wants to go beyond this. One wants, for instance, to see whether one can detect any correlations within the various dimensions or levels of religion. For example, does a certain kind of theology go with emphasis on a certain type of religious experience or practice? Such a question, though, is complicated by the organic nature of religious systems of belief and practice. Thus the Christian concept of a Creator is not quite the same as the Muslim or Jewish ones, closely related as these are. For the notion of the Creator God is modified by its juxtaposition with belief in the Incarnation. Any given proposition in a doctrinal scheme has its meaning affected by what other propositions are asserted in the scheme, and of course by the atmosphere of worship, etc., i.e. by the shape of religious practice which provides a milieu for the scheme of belief. This organicness of religious systems has led at least one writer (H. Kraemer) to argue that no proper comparisons between the Christian Gospel and other faiths is possible.

Now it is true that every faith is unique—i.e. it has properties not shared by other faiths. For instance, only one religion has as its chief prophet Muhammad. Only one was founded (or refounded) by the Buddha. It is true also that there are sometimes substantial differences in the content of belief and practice. Thus as we have seen no role is assigned in Theravada Buddhism for the worship of a God. Christianity alone focuses itself upon a single and exclusive Incarnation of God. But such uniquenesses by no means rule out valid comparisons, even given the organicness of religions. Sometimes there are mythological correspondences, such as the idea of a holy figure's having been born without benefit of human paternity. Sometimes more deeply there are doctrinal and experimental correspondences, such as belief in grace (as in Ramanuja and Paul) or likeness of mystical experience (as say between some Sufis and some Christian contemplatives). The organicness does not rule these out, any more than it rules out making certain comparisons between American and Rugby Football (even though these assign different meanings to terms like *goal* and have a roughly similar kind of organicness to that found in religions).

Some confusion perhaps has been caused over the question of uniqueness by the fact that it has entered into apologetic arguments. Obviously if you hold the same beliefs as everyone else, you have nothing to offer. If you think you have something to offer you are keen to stress uniqueness. Combine this with a simple appeal to revelation (not an uncommon attitude in Christianity and some other religions) and you end up thinking that in establishing uniqueness you have somehow established truth. Looking at it dispassionately, however, we must say: Yes, what you hold is in at least some respects unique. As to truth, that is another argument (and not one incidentally which lies within the province of the comparative study of religion proper, even if the latter can furnish some very suggestive and sometimes apologetically embarrassing results).

Though sensitive, then, to organicness, and hence in fact to uniquenesses, the comparative religionist hopes to draw out ways in which there is some sort of explanation of likenesses and variety in religions. I take as my main example the problem of how to account for the diversity of doctrines in the Indian tradition, bearing in mind the recurrence of certain patterns of religious practice and experience. Thus some traditional systems (Jainism, Samkhya-Yoga) are atheistic, but believe in a multiplicity of eternal souls implicated in rebirth and in the possibility of release. Buddhism likewise denies a personal Creator, but does not believe in eternal souls, though it does believe in many individuals implicated in rebirth and in the possibility of release. Medieval Dualism (Dvaita) believes in everything found in the former systems, plus a personal Creator controlling the destinies of the eternal souls. Qualified Non-Dualism (Visistadvaita) is very similar, but more firmly emphasises the intimate dependence of the world and souls on God. Non-Dualism only believes in a personal Creator at a lower level of truth, at the level of illusion (maya). In highest truth, the soul and Brahman are identical. Realizing this identity brings release. This two-decker Absolutism, as we may call it, is parallel to a main school in Mahayana Buddhism, the Madhyamika (as commonly interpreted). So we have a series of systems, ranging from atheistic soul-puralism, through theism, to Absolutism.

On the other hand, there is a simpler set of distinctions in religious practice and experience. (Naturally here I over-simplify.) There is a contrast in the religion of the Upanishadic period between sacrificial ritual (administered by the Brahmins) and tapas or austerity, usually the prerogative of holy recluses. These are both rather formalistic. But they in part provide the milieu for more "experiential" types of religion. On the one hand, there evolved the religion of bhakti or loving adoration of a personal God, exemplified in the Gita and in medieval theism. On the other hand, the practice of yoga was held to bring one to higher contemplative states which could be a sign of liberation. Confining our attention to the bhakti-yoga polarity (the polarity between devotionalism and contemplation), we may note that the two types of practice and experience can occur independently, though they can also occur together. If they occur together one may be stressed more than the other.

142

They can also of course appear as equals. But let us leave aside this possibility. So far the polarity yields four paths. First, there is yoga without bhakti. This is exemplified in the non-theistic systems—Jainism, Yoga, Theravada Buddhism. The first leans towards formalism, tapas being stressed. Second, there is yoga plus bhakti, with the latter rated as secondary. This is exemplified both in Shankara's non-dualism and in the central schools of the Mahayana. Third, there is bhakti plus yoga, with the latter in second place. This is exemplified in Ramanuja's theology. Fourth, there is bhakti without yoga, exemplified in some of the more fervid poets of Tamiland and in evangelical Christianity. It can also paradoxically be discovered in some forms of Pure Land Buddhism —paradoxically because Buddhism in origin and heart emphasizes the yogic path to liberation.

This quartet of possibilities suggests immediately a thesis : that bhakti is correlated with theism, that yoga is, when by itself, correlated with non-theistic pluralism, and that the combination of bhakti with yoga with the latter in first place yields absolutism rather than theism. Necessarily the foregoing brief account is crude. But it works as a suggestive theory in comparative religion. It works outside the Indian context. Eckhart's distinction between deitas and deus, for instance, is not far removed from Shankara's theology. Some Sufis have used absolutistic language. The theory, however, may be a bit unnerving for pious Christians, for it suggests that contemplation does not have to be interpreted as union with God, etc. It also casts doubt on a simple neo-Vedantin view, that mystical experience essentially involves the realization of the Absolute Self, though it is favourable to the notion that mystical experience is essentially the same, though contexts, intentions and interpretations differ. But the theory by itself cannot directly settle the truth claims of the various religions and doctrines.

The theory, whether it be correct or not, illustrates the point that one must go beyond comparisons and attempt some kind of explanation of likenesses and differences. If is an explanatory theory, for it tries to bring out a correlation between doctrines on the one hand and religious experiences and practices on the other; and it tries to treat the latter as dominant. But such explanations can run into a number of methodological difficulties.

First, we must be sure that definitions (e.g. of "contemplative life", "mysticism", "yoga", etc.) *realistically* differentiate forms of the religious life. It is worth noting that great sloppiness has usually characterized the use of "mysticism" and its cognates. Second, it is not so easy to know the grounds for treating one arm of a correlation as more important than the other. That is, which is explanatory of the other? Third, the attempt to generalize inevitably brings in its trail problems about description. For instance, the *lingam* in Hinduism can be assimilated to other symbols elsewhere by describing it as phallic; but this is not the description favoured by those engaged in the cult. Fourth, and connectedly, accounts of religious experience need to be sensitive to the distinction between reporting and interpretation. But it is a tricky matter drawing the line in practice. Thus there are those who distinguish between theistic mysticism and other sorts, on the ground of differences in what appears to be reporting—and yet the use of a term like "God" in such reporting (as when the contemplative describes himself as attaining an inner apprehension of God) makes us alive to the possibility that here a whole set of beliefs grounded outside the experience are being brought to bear in its description. For the very organicness of religion means that its central concepts come "not in utter nakedness . . . but trailing clouds of theory".

The complexity of many of the comparative tasks is, moreover, increased by the fact that religion, in often arousing strong feeling, renders secondary sources, whether in the form of books or of the testimony of individual (and perchance highly idiosyncratic) adherents, deserving of highly critical evaluation. Religions are not often typified by the avant garde, and one should listen keenly for the noise of grinding axes.

Needless to say, we are at a very primitive stage in the understanding of religions and of the deeper reasons underlying the attractions of one sort of belief and practice over another. Since religion is part of the whole fabric of human cultures, the comparative study of religion must branch out into cultural history and sociology. The complexity of the enterprise means that it will only be through a cooperative effort that advances will be made. This implies that a clearer notion of the aims of such study must be developed. I have suggested in the present article that a main feature of it should be the attempt at explanatory correlations between elements in the different dimensions of religion. But since religion has its wider milieu, as has just been noted, these explanatory correlations should be extended, e.g. through considering the psychological and sociological roots of certain religious phenomena, and the converse, the religious roots of some psychological and social phenomena. This in turn means that psychology and sociology need the right kind of information and sensitivity to tackle religious themes. Ignorance has in the past held up a decently scientific approach to religious problems—Freud's acccount, for instance, of the genesis of religion is culturally very idiosyncratic. In short, the comparative study of religion is a vital ancillary to other studies, just as they can be to it.

CHAPTER 18

The Structure of the Comparative Study of Religion

Since so many different activities are clustered under the title 'comparative study of religion', it is important to make some distinctions. This essay is chiefly devoted to this task. But before settling down to this, it is useful to say a word about the position of the subject in the United Kingdom. In higher education, its most likely niche is within a syllabus of theology (divinity, etc.); and the most likely rationale is that it is important for students of Christian theology to take other religions into account. It is this situation that causes the subject to be treated as shorthand for 'the study of non-Christian religions'.

This situation is largely illogical. The study of religions should not of itself make any sharp divide between Christian and non-Christian religions. The judgment that Buddhism is the most important non-Christian religion could equally be met with the judgment that Christianity is the most important non-Buddhist religion, and so on. If there is any logic at all in the treatment of comparative study of religion as having essentially to do with non-Christian religions, it must arise out of the sense that in studying Christian theology the student is *doing* theology, i.e. Christian theology; while in studying non-Christian religions he is describing them 'scientifically'—or at any rate is not *doing* Islamic theology, etc. Even so, the logic of the distinction is not very logical; since the Christian tradition itself needs descriptive, 'scientific' treatment, even apart from the theologizing.

The distinction between *doing* theology and studying religion objectively is, however, an important one. In relation to the study of religions, one can broadly divide activities into two groups: I shall dub these the A group and the B group respectively. In the B group one is concerned with expressing, criticizing, evaluating a religious tradition, or traditions, from the standpoint of a faith (or anti-faith). Christian theology, Islamic theology, Buddhology, philosophy of religion, certain sorts of dialogue—these activities have their natural home in the B group. Comparative study of religion has its natural home in the A group: but, as we shall see, once we disentangle the variety of objective studies of religion there will be a strong motive for dropping the use of the phrase 'comparative study of religion'. A revolution in nomenclature is called for.

THE A GROUP:

1. *Histories of religions.* The histories of particular religions are in principle independent, save in so far as religions historically intertwine. While on the one hand it is possible to treat the history of the Reformation without paying attention to Buddhism or even much to Islam, there are also obvious cases of intertwining. Thus early Islam and contemporary Christianity and Judaism have to be seen in historical relationship with each other; and the history of Zoroastrianism has intertwined with post-Exilic Judaism and early Christianity. But in principle the history of a faith, or of a phase of a faith, can be described independently, and for this reason there is merit in talking of *histories* in the plural.

Of course, as any historian knows, historical explanation involves more than simple narration, and thus woven into the fabric of historical enquiry are various (usually unformalized) laws or generalizations about human behaviour, institutions, etc. Even to ascribe an action of a politician to ambition is implicitly to call upon a generalization, namely, that ambition is a motive normal in the circumstances and one which tends to issue in certain sorts of behaviour. Likewise, in concentrating upon religious aspects of an historical epoch, the historian of religions may call upon cross-cultural generalizations. This itself presupposes the possibility of a typology. Thus we can classify different actions as being motivated by ambition (psychological typology); while in the more directly religious context, one can make use of types such as *prophecy, rites of passage, sacramental, prayer, sect,* etc. This brings us to the second activity falling under the A group.

2. *Typological phenomenology of religion.* The variations in breadth and depth manifested by scholars working in this field are great. As an example of an intendedly comprehensive typology, one can cite Gerardus van der Leeuw's *Religion in Essence and Manifestation.* Rudolf Otto's *The Idea of the Holy* is a case where the main emphasis is upon religious experience (in addition Otto appends to the pure phenomenology a philosophical theory about the *validity* of religious experience). On a narrower band is the same author's *Mysticism East and West,* dealing with the analogies between the doctrines and experiences of Eckhart and Sankara. Sometimes works which at first sight appear to be simply typological and descriptive in intent may have an apologetic foundation, as in R. C. Zaehner's *Mysticism Sacred and Profane*—such a work hovers uncertainly between the A and the B group. This by itself is no fatal criticism, provided an author knows what he is doing. Since there is a great deal of confusion about the aims of the comparative study of religion, this is not always a wise assumption to make.

It may be noted that the comparative descriptive task involved in typological phenomenology must be sensitively undertaken, with due regard to the principle of intentionality—namely to the principle that in human experience and activity the way the person involved sees his activity or experience is an important part of the description.

Some of the doubts liable to be expressed about the validity of the phenomenological, comparative approach are caused by the principle of intentionality. How can it be respected and at the same time generalization preserved? First, it might be objected, every religious experience, institution, etc., is historically particular, and thus particular in regard to the intentions of the participants. Second, the participant may not see his action as the phenomenologist does. For example, the latter may see the *lingam* as a fertility symbol, or some of Charles Wesley's hymns as fervent expressions of *bhakti* religion: but these are not the terms which the participants might want to use (and indeed could react against them). Despite these objections, however, sufficiently sensitive work in phenomenology has been achieved to justify it. As for the first objection, it merely draws attention to the fact that there are particularities, and phenomenology cannot hope to capture them all. Likewise, though it is true to say that the tree in my garden is an oak, it has its own special shape. As for the second objection, this merely draws our attention to the way in which the advance of the human sciences makes a difference to human consciousness itself. Once people become sensitively aware of parallels between different religions, including their own, they will inevitably come to look upon their own faith in a different way. In brief, phenomenology has its repercussions on the phenomena. Similar situations have arisen in psychology and sociology (consider the way in which the idea of the Freudian slip has affected the manner in which educated people look upon their own verbal errors).

We have already seen that sometimes phenomenology has a hidden apologetic basis (and to that extent is no longer pure phenomenology). It can also have a different sort of debatable basis. Thus the work of C. G. Jung on the *mandala*, for example, is highly charged with Jungian theory; and much of Eliade's later work is likewise affected about a general theory of human existence and historical consciousness. There is some merit in separating such work out from purely typological approaches (pure comparison and contrast, as it were). This leads us then to the third activity in the A group:

3. *Speculative phenomenology of religion.* Naturally, sometimes such a speculative approach has a relationship to apologetics, since it tends to be informed with a general *Weltanschauung*, which may be favourable or unfavourable to a particular faith-stance. The materials may tend to be arranged according to a preconceived pattern, itself incapable of being thoroughly insulated from theological (or anti-theological)

NINIAN SMART

assumptions. It might be replied that the study of religion can *never* achieve such a virgin objectivity as I have implicitly been arguing for. However, much harm has been done by theological subjectivism in the field of the study of religion, for it can too easily be used as a licence for unfairness, lack of clarity and the tendency to be guided by apologetic considerations rather than by respect for the facts viewed relatively dispassionately. (Contrarily, the phenomenology of religion can be distorted by over-rationalistic approaches, e.g. to the phenomenon of myth.)

The classification of religious experiences, institutions, doctrines, etc., is, however, only laying the groundwork for deeper explorations. That it is relevant to questions of religious truth (in the B group) goes without saying. But it is also central to the enterprise of explanatory theories of religion, as in psychology of religion, sociology and anthropology.

4. *Sociology of religion, anthropology.* From an explanatory and theoretical point of view, in the social sciences, religion is of obvious and great importance. Thus much of the central work in sociology and anthropology—the work, for instance, of Max Weber, Emile Durkheim and Claude Levi-Strauss—has concerned the role of religious institutions in society. It will, moreover, readily be agreed that at least part of the explanation of a given style of belief, as institutionalized in a religious structure, has to do with the social forces at work in the society in which the community is embedded. To this extent, sociological (and anthropological) explanations of religious phenomena are in order. Conversely, there are dynamic elements in a religious tradition which help to shape a given social milieu. In both sorts of interplay historians and sociologists are seeking explanations. Since a main feature of scientific enquiry is the search for explanations, there are good reasons to dub this sort of investigation of religion as 'scientific'. It is true that, as to some extent in other branches of science, a given theory or set of explanations may be *debatable*—so that one should avoid the vulgar equation of 'scientific' with 'well-established'; but the main rationale of calling a given pursuit 'scientific' is that it is in broad terms committed to a certain methodology. It is not that

the social sciences need to ape the physical sciences in detail; rather it is that they seek explanatory theories, tested against the data as far as possible.

But here a problem arises. One cannot put history in a test-tube; nor can one get a society inside a laboratory, to perform experiments on it. This is a severe limitation upon the experimental aspect of the social sciences (and indeed upon psychology in so far as it is intertwined with sociology and anthropology). The best that can be done is to test hypotheses against the data supplied in a variety of independent living societies and in their histories. This was a point seen with the greatest clarity by Max Weber. Hence his studies of Indian, Chinese and other religions, in conjunction with his work on the spirit of capitalism in relation to the Protestant ethic. Comparative, cross-cultural testing functions as a form of experiment and a check on theories. Thus it is of the essence of sociology, if it is to become scientifically validated, that it is comparative. In regard to religion, therefore, typological phenomenology must play a crucial role, for it supplies an ordering of the data. Consider, for instance, the function of the concept of *prophecy* in Weber—and consider also the question of whether from a phenomenological and historical point of view Weber's concept is justly delineated and applied.

Similar remarks apply, naturally enough, to work in the psychology of religion.

5. *The psychology of religion.* There is a clear overlap between this and the foregoing category. The overlap can be put in the following way. In so far as psychology has to do with the explanation of individual actions, occurrences, etc., it has to take cognizance of the norms operative for society in a given milieu. For instance, in a tribe where men and women go around naked, no special explanation is called for if a given individual is walking around on a sunny morning wearing no clothes. But the observation of a man walking down Piccadilly with no clothes on might call for some investigation. It could be that he is doing it for a bet or as a protest; but there is *prima facie* evidence from the *social* situation, as well as from his action, that some special

26   NINIAN SMART

psychological explanation of his action needs investigating. Hence it is hard to disentangle psychological and sociological approaches to human behaviour, including of course religious behaviour.

It is thus no surprise that part of the enterprise known as psychology of religion is cross-cultural, for the same reason that sociology needs to be comparative if it is to be as fully experimental as the subject-matter allows. For instance, the Freudian account of the genesis of the Father-figure in religion needs to be tested not only against the historical evidence in the Judaeo-Christian tradition, but also by reference to *prima facie* counter-examples in other cultures (e.g. Theravada Buddhism, which has no special place for a supreme personal God).

Some concluding remarks about the A *group.* The delineation of these categories of descriptive, scientific studies of religion appears at first sight to leave on one side what is likely to be in the forefront of many people's minds—the task, simply, of *understanding* a given religious tradition, whether one's own or another's. Surely, it will be said, a prime task of the comparative study of religion is to give insight into particular faiths—not just historically, not just phenomenologically, not just sociologically and not just psychologically. And insight into another faith can be an important element in promoting international, inter-community understanding, etc.

However, this objection misses the mark: for it is implicit in the notion that one can study (and come to understand) the history of a particular faith (A 1 above) that one can come to terms with a cross-section—a temporal cross-section—of that faith. For example, one can come to terms with *contemporary* Islam. But to see Islam in the round, one must not merely know something of its past, above all the past that enters into the intentions and consciousness of contemporary Muslims; but also about its social institutions and its psychology. To some degree also one is bound here to be engaged in typological phenomenology; for the understanding of, for example, Muslim prayer is already to see it under a category of religious activity. It is moreover no bad thing if comparisons and contrasts between one's own tradition and another are made explicit, for it is by bringing them to the surface that one can begin to see another faith in its own right, by transcending what might otherwise be inept, comparative presuppositions about it.

It is, however, worth stressing that a religion is organic—interwoven of a complex of doctrinal, mythical, ethical, experiential, ritual and institutional parts. It is artificial to abstract from a faith, therefore; nor one must lose sight of the principle of intentionality. If a faith is organic, so likewise is the intentionality, the consciousness, of those participating in it. It would thus be illusory to suppose that one may exhaust the meaning of a faith by typological phenomenology as applied to it. The historical aspect of the study of a faith safeguards, fortunately, against this tendency, and brings out the uniqueness of a faith (of every faith, indeed).

A final remark about group A: since the process of comparison is simply the activity of doing phenomenology (unless apologetic and other B-group interests obtrude), there is no special need to retain the clumsy title 'comparative study of religion'. Indeed, in view of the interlocking character of history, phenomenology, sociology and so on, it is probably simplest to talk about the study of religion. Since, however, that term might be most naturally used to cover both A and B activities, one might particularize somewhat and use the term 'scientific study of religion'.

This is probably the best course, provided it is remembered that much of it can be debatable and some of it speculative, so that there may be interactions with activities properly falling under the B group, such as the philosophy of religion.

THE B GROUP:

1. *Theologies.* A main task of the religious intellectual is to elaborate or develop a theology expressing his own and the community's faith. The need for a theology is itself often the product of changing social and cultural patterns, which bring out the need for a continued re-statement of the traditional faith. The theologian in systematizing or otherwise intellectually

28   NINIAN SMART

expressing the core of faith typically also is expressing value judgments, since a faith has ethical and social consequences. Thus the taking up of a theological stance is also taking up a value-stance: it is not just theory, it recommends practice.

Though it is common in this country to identify theology with Christian theology, it is transparent that there can be analogous activities such as Islamic theology, Hindu theology, etc. Historically, it is true that the term 'theology' does not always fit too snugly e.g. in Buddhism ('Buddhist theology' is a paradox when there is scarcely a Theos). But this is a merely terminological difficulty. It is quite clear that Swami Vivekananda (for instance) was theologizing from a Hindu, or from one Hindu point of view, just as Karl Barth was expressing a Christian point of view.

An important feature, in these latter days of increased mutual awareness as between the religions, of a theology is theologizing about other religions. In the West it has sometimes been that the Christian theology of other religions has been mixed up with the comparative study of religion. Obviously, descriptive and phenomenological studies are a necessary prerequisite of a sensitive theology of other religions; but the task of theologizing is different from that of describing, etc. It is worth noting in addition that as it is legitimate for the Christian theologian to try to make sense, from the standpoint of the Christian faith, of non-Christian religions, so likewise is it for the Hindu to try to make sense, from the Hindu point of view, of Christianity and other non-Hindu traditions.

For the sake of completeness, it is useful here (if again a little paradoxical) to count atheistic doctrine as a kind of theology. The atheist too is taking up a standpoint, and from it he judges the religions. It is in this connection unwise to treat the non-theological character of sociology of religion, for example, as signifying a sort of implicit atheism. It is easy to think that because a scientific study of religion does not start from faith or from appeal to authority, etc., it is against faith. The illusion is indeed fostered by the fact that sometimes atheistic doctrine creeps into supposedly scientific studies—there is an important way in which Freudian theory has incorporated a kind of atheistic critique of religion. But strictly it is not the function of the sociological or psychological study of religion to determine, off its own bat, the truth or otherwise of faith.

Now it is clear that sometimes a theology comes into conflict with a science, as happened notoriously over evolutionary theory; and so in principle a theology could come into conflict with phenomenology, sociology or psychology. All I am here wishing to point out is that there is no *a priori* necessity for such a conflict. Moreover, any phenomenology, sociology or psychology which does not take seriously the particular contents of a faith or faiths is liable to be bad science. Distortions can occur both because of uncritical theological zeal and because of uncritical rationalism.

However, the intellectual future is always somewhat unpredictable. The future relations between theologies and the social and other sciences cannot be laid down in advance. Here there are liable to be boundary disputes, to be settled largely by philosophical considerations. This is one way in which theology cannot be partitioned off absolutely from the philosophy of religion. And since the philosophy of religion moves in debated territory, it is ever liable to issue forth in appraisals of truth-claims in Christian and other theologies (including atheistic). In this way it is not a neutral enterprise, and can thus form a second category in the B group.

2. *Philosophy of religion.* Though I have said that philosophy is not neutral, in one aspect it can be, namely in the analysis of religious language, if this is undertaken without hidden apologetic aims. However, since natural theology, philosophical theology and the settling of boundary disputes are likely to remain central to philosophizing about religion, it is more realistic to place the subject in the B group rather than in the A group. Indeed, philosophy of religion in some of its manifestations falls directly under the head of apologetics, and thus is a kind of theologizing.

It is worth noting that great gains can come to the analysis of religious concepts through use of phenomenology and histories of religions. It is unfortunate that much analysis has been pursued in a non-comparative manner. Generalizations about religious language as being essentially parabolic (for instance) would not so easily stand up to the evidence if that evidence included a consideration of some of the major non-Christian faiths. But also the existence of differing world faiths brings out the need to consider the question of criteria of truth in religion in this wider context. This is a task as yet severely underdeveloped. It is not, incidentally, simply to be equated with so-called 'dialogue' between religions, as will be shown below. The question of criteria in some ways goes much deeper than dialogue.

3. *Dialogue between religions.* It happens that at the present time dialogue is a fashionable activity, and this is a good thing, for it signifies that men of different faiths are happy to enter into conversation and exchange. It is the starting-point of a wider ecumenicity, necessary if the scars of inter-religious conflict are to be healed and necessary too for the burial of European ideas of cultural-religious superiority. However, what does dialogue in essence amount to? At one level it is simply a means to mutual *understanding.* In this respect it is a personalized way of doing history of religions and phenomenology. But at another level it is part of the process of mutual theological adjustment, and the attempt to work out new faith-perspectives. At this level, it is a kind of polycentric theologizing. Thus there is reason to place this activity in the B group, even if, as we have said, part of what goes on is personalized history and phenomenology.

CONCLUSION

I have attempted in this essay to sketch out some of the more important intellectual activities falling under the study of religion. The comparative study of religion (so-called—for as we saw there may be merit in dropping this title) is most centrally concerned with histories of religions and the phenomenology of religion. It thereby provides substance for the sociology and psychology of religion, and is a necessary element if anyone wants to go on to theologize or philosophize about other religions and about the criteria of truth in religion. But the comparative study of religion at its heart is more concerned with *understanding* than with adjudicating. It is not a sort of theology and does not begin from a faith or an anti-faith stance. In this sense it is 'objective' (or at least it is not subjective).

Naturally there are ways in which the activities of the A group and those of the B group interact. It is unlikely that the study of religion can ever be fully rich without including both sorts of approaches; but in this country the B group activities especially have tended to be dominant and the world of the A group left as rather marginal. This is a great pity, not only because educationally the field of the study of religion has been unduly restricted, but also because our understanding of religion and religions at the A level is still in a relatively primitive state. Phenomenology, sociology and psychology are relatively recent growths. The latter part of the twentieth century is a time yet early in the history of these endeavours; there is much indeed to be learned in the future.

Fortunately for the study of religion, the shrunken world of jets and the mutual presence to one another of men of differing faiths and ideologies make it plain to see that the subject is well worth investing brains and effort in. And hearts—for only by finding how things feel to other men can we claim to have gone far in exploring the content of faiths.

Though it has not, save by implication, been a theme of this essay, it is worth finally reflecting that non-religious ideologies themselves in some degree play in the same league as religious faiths. Thus laterally the study of religion needs to branch out towards the study of 'non-religion'. Perhaps the world of Mao Tse-Tung can be understood by some of the approaches being developed in the study of religion.

Professor Ninian Smart is Professor of Religious Studies, University of Lancaster.

CHAPTER 19

Scientific Studies of Religion

THE HISTORY of religions and comparative study of religion, the sociology and psychology of religion—such studies are sometimes called 'scientific'; and this is a way of showing what they are *not* attempting to do. Roughly one can describe the object of Christian theology as being to explore, present and apply the Christian faith (see note 10 on p. 318) in successively changing cultural and intellectual situations. The 'scientific' study of religion is, on the other hand, not concerned with presenting or applying a particular faith, though it is relevant to such a task. Naturally, much of what comes under the head of the scientific study of religion is used in an ancillary way by those who are doing Christian theology, but I shall confine attention in this chapter to those aspects which are less closely tied up with theology as traditionally understood. I shall, however, indicate ways in which these studies and Christian theology are liable to interact.

In order to exhibit something of the logic of the study of religion, it is necessary to make some remarks about the different types of approaches and fields which it embraces. These remarks unavoidably over-simplify; but they may provide a map of the subject. It is useful to begin with the problem of what can be intended by the commonly-used phrase 'the comparative study of religion'. Very often this is used loosely to refer to the study of religions other than Christianity. This is illogical for two reasons. First, Christianity is itself a religion, and the study of religions naturally includes the study of Christianity. Second, one may study a religion or religions without having any intention to compare. We shall later see what the point of

PREFACE TO CHRISTIAN STUDIES

making comparisons is; but it is not a *necessary* feature of studying a faith, for one might simply be exploring the history of that faith.

It so happens that the title 'comparative study of religion' has been open to criticism in that sometimes those who have made comparisons have been inclined to draw unfavourable ones, sometimes because they start from a position in one faith and see others as defective in the light of that faith. Of course, it is legitimate for a person or a group to evolve a theology of other religions—expressing (say) a Christian perspective on, and interpretation of, other religions. But such an exercise falls more clearly under the head of theology (see pp. 21 and 31 above) than of the scientific study of religion.

For such reasons, it has become more common among scholars to speak of the 'history of religions'. For instance, the international organization for co-ordinating work in the field is called the International Association for the History of Religions. But even this title needs some elucidation. Consider a situation where one person is studying the history of Zoroastrianism, another the history of Buddhism, another the history of Shinto, another the history of Christianity, and so on. These could be so many separate studies (except in so far as the stream of events in one tradition flows into and out of another: for example, Zoroastrianism had some influences, via Judaism, on early Christianity). Is there any special need to group these separate studies under one head as 'history of religions'? It might turn out that phenomena in one tradition can throw light on those of an independent tradition (cf. pp. 31 and 300 f.), and that methodological tools employed in one history can be applied in another. But this would be, roughly, because each history would be dealing with the same sort of aspect of human existence, namely the religious aspect. There would be a parallel here with economic or political history. Economic history abstracts from total history an aspect of human existence, namely the economic behaviour of men. So likewise it can be argued that histories of religions abstract the religious aspect of the traditions concerned.

Necessarily there are problems here about the definition of

SCIENTIFIC STUDIES OF RELIGION

religion, which I shall leave on one side for the moment. Let us summarize briefly some conclusions that might so far be drawn from the foregoing. (1) There are various social traditions, very often largely separate histories. (2) There are various histories which can be studied, therefore; and it is possible to study them from the point of view of abstracting one aspect of human existence, namely the religious aspect. (3) There remains the question of the point of making cross-cultural comparisons of features of these histories.

Here it is possible to point to a positive sense in which the study of religions may be 'scientific', as distinguished from the negative sense mentioned earlier, namely that such a study is *not* theological in intent. At one level of scientific enquiry, not admittedly a very high one, there is the task of classification, of typology. Thus an important part has been played, in the early stages of the evolution of botany as a science, by the systematization of the data—by classifying plants according to genera and species, etc. (Similar remarks apply to zoology, ornithology, philology and so on.) It is not therefore unreasonable to expect that it is possible to construct a typology of religious experience, belief, ritual, etc. Such a typology is central to modern phenomenology of religion (see below). It is part of what was meant by the comparative study of religion, for the whole essence of a typology is to arrive at cross-cultural classifications, inevitably and truistically entailing comparisons. Of course there is a limit to such typology, for a given religious tradition is bound to have unique features. Nevertheless, there is no reason why one should not classify, say, Eckhart (*c.* 1260–1327) and Buddhaghosa (fifth century A.D.) together as mystics, or sketch out a typology of initiation rites, etc.

The phrase 'phenomenology of religion' as used in the modern context has connections with the work of Edmund Husserl (1859–1938), who advocated a descriptive method of discovering the fundamental structures of human consciousness—a programme which he saw as central to philosophical enquiry. However, the title is not now generally used to indicate any particular attachment to a philosophical school; and the main emphasis is on the *descriptive* character of religious typology. On the other hand, speculative elements sometimes enter into phenomenological enquiries, in as much as the typological material moves scholars to speculate about the origins of religion, the functions of certain myths, and so on. Thus speculative elements occur in the work of the foremost phenomenologists of this century, e.g. Rudolf Otto, Gerardus van der Leeuw, Raffaele Pettazzoni and Mircea Eliade (most notably, perhaps in the writings of the last-mentioned). This brings us to another level in which the study of religion may be 'scientific'.

A crucial property of scientific endeavour is the search for explanations. Crudely, an explanation is provided by a *theory*. So the formation of theories to explain data is crucial. Naturally a theory may turn out to be false; but this does not imply that it is not scientific. Darwin's evolutionary hypothesis might, say, turn out to be radically wrong; but this would not detract from its status as a scientific theory. It is in this way that theories, for instance, about the origin of religion can be said to be scientific, even if none of them can as yet be shown to be correct and most of them are virtually certain to be false. Thus as well as descriptive typology (phenomenology of religion in its 'pure' sense), there is the search for theories to explain types of religious behaviour, beliefs, etc. One might distinguish such theories from historical explanations in that the latter are primarily orientated towards the particular sequence, the 'narrative', through which the particular developments of a particular tradition occur. For instance, the attempt to raise money for the building of St. Peter's is an important element in the historical explanation of the events of the Reformation; on the other hand it might be possible to give a typological explanation of Luther's religious experience.

It would be natural here to ask: If a theory purports to explain the genesis of religion, or of a particular feature of religions, in terms of *what* does it so explain? Are not some explanations *reductionist*—that is, do they not explain religious phenomena in terms, say, of psychological phenomena (e.g. in the work of Freud)? Before we can look at this problem, it is necessary to essay something towards a definition of religion,

SCIENTIFIC STUDIES OF RELIGION

or at least a characterization of it as it typically manifests itself. Without entering into recent discussions of definitional issues, I would here propose some features often or always present in religious systems.

Typically, a religion has a belief-aspect and a practice-aspect. The belief-aspect often comprises doctrines (notably where a religion has developed a written literary heritage, etc.); myths (in a wide and neutral sense—neutral because the use of the term as a technical one does not imply that a myth need be false or fictional); and norms of conduct. The practice-aspect comprises rituals (again in a wide sense, and including such activities as worship, prayer, sacramental occasions, etc.); experience (dramatically, the experience of prophets and mystics; but more generally the numinous and other experiences of the faithful); social institutions (such as a church, a framework of initiatory customs, and so on). Naturally the meaning of the practice-aspect has to be found in the belief-aspect and the meaning of the belief-aspect in the practice-aspect (cf. p. 28). For example, belief in a God implies belief in a focus of worship, so that worship here gives meaning to doctrine; while the content of worship has in turn to be defined doctrinally or mythically. In terms of this characterization of religion, one can see overlaps between religion strictly so called and ideologies. Thus Maoism, as currently evolved in China, contains doctrinal, mythic, ethical, ritual and institutional elements—though these as it happens are not focused on a transcendent being or state (a feature of the more prominent religions of history). It is useful therefore to characterize some ideological systems as 'quasi-religions', in order to indicate that religions have a large penumbra in which the student of religion can legitimately take an interest.

The above profile of religion indicates ways in which varying branches of enquiry can be brought to bear on religion. In so far as religion is institutionalized socially, and in so far as this institutionalization is connected up with the other dimensions of religion, there is the possibility of doing 'the sociology of religion'. In so far as religious experience and its related beliefs is present, there is the possibility of doing 'the psychology of

PREFACE TO CHRISTIAN STUDIES

religion'. Again, the nature and functions of myth are in part illuminated by anthropology. (Matters of the *truth* of doctrine and myth are crucial to theology and philosophy—see p. 22; but the main emphasis of the present article is not on this area of enquiry.)

It is possible now to say something, admittedly crude, about kinds of theory in regard to religion. There are those which are, so to say, intra-religious (explaining one feature of religion in terms of another)—for example, trying to show systematic connections between types of religious experience and types of doctrine; and there are those which are extra-religious (explaining a feature of religion through recourse to some feature or features of human existence which is not specifically religious)— for example, Freud's theory of the genesis of the Father-figure in religion. There are also mixed theories, exhibiting the interplay between religious and non-religious factors (perhaps Max Weber's classical work in the sociology of religion comes into this category). Some proponents of the phenomenology of religion, have strongly upheld the autonomy of religious categories and therefore of the study of religion. This is a way of resisting a totally reductionist view of the scientific study of religion and has a certain justification, in my view; for whatever one might say about the genesis of, for example, the sense of the numinous, as depicted by Otto (see p. 181 below), there can be little doubt that this sense has to enter into some explanations of human conduct, etc., from the religious side. That is, religion has its own dynamic, even though it be affected, as we all know, by the dynamics of other aspects of human existence. Thus the study of religion needs to steer a course between a totally intra-religious body of explanation and a totally extra-religious one.

The foregoing discussion can be summed up as follows, by listing areas of enquiry. (1) There are histories of religions. (2) There is descriptive phenomenology of religion, aimed at cross-cultural typological classification. (3) There is speculative phenomenology of religion, concerned primarily with intra-religious explanations of religious phenomena. (4) There is sociology of religion. (5) There are anthropological data and

SCIENTIFIC STUDIES OF RELIGION

theories important for explanatory purposes in relation to religion. (6) There is psychology of religion. In the ensuing, I shall attempt to give some guide to the material under some of these heads. For the sake of convenience, I shall conflate (2) and (3). I shall conclude with some remarks on the relevance of these studies in the theological and philosophical context.

HISTORIES OF RELIGIONS

Since the beginning of the nineteenth century, a vastly creative period in the development of scientific scholarship, there has been a remarkable explosion of historical work in relation to religions, stimulated in part by the rise of comparative philology and of great investments in the editing of the texts of the great religions. A signal monument of this endeavour was the *Sacred Books of the East* series, edited by Max Mueller. By the first part of the twentieth century, it was reasonable to say that Western scholars and general readers had available, for the first time in history, the basic materials to understand the great non-Christian traditions (though the literary, philological approach to other religions may have placed undue weight on scriptures —seeing other religions as having a relationship to scripture analogous to that of the Christian Church). There has also been in the last century and a half a vast amount of work done in archaeology and ancient history, yielding an understanding of great religious traditions now dead or virtually dead—for example, ancient Near Eastern religions other than Judaism; pre-Columbian religions in America; Greek and Roman religion and the mystery cults; and so on. Prehistorical researches and the fashion for evolutionary views of culture in the late nineteenth century helped, in addition, to stimulate enquiry into the origins of religion—an enquiry often linked to growing anthropological researches, on the principle that the modern 'primitive' might yield clues to primeval myth-making, etc.

It is perhaps useful to introduce here a classification of religions, to provide an inventory of the histories of religions. Beginning with the rough distinction between living and dead religions, one can list the former as follows: (1) Three major

PREFACE TO CHRISTIAN STUDIES

traditions springing from an overlapping Semitic background: Christianity, Judaism and Islam, together with various latter-day offshoots (e.g. Christian Science, Mormonism, the Baha'i, etc.). (2) Religions originating in the Indian sub-continent: Hinduism, Jainism, Buddhism, Sikhism (the last containing, however, Muslim elements). (3) Religions originating in China and Japan: Confucianism, Taoism, Shinto, together with latter-day offshoots (the new religions of Japan). (4) Ethnic/tribal religions: in Africa, the Americas, the Pacific and elsewhere, together with modern offshoots. The last group is often treated as 'primitive' or 'primal', terms which are open to objection. That a society is 'primitive' in the technological sense in no way entails lack of sophistication; and although 'primal' avoids the pejorative overtones of 'primitive' it suggests unnecessarily a sense of tribal peoples as standing, so to say, at the dawn of history—whereas it is platitudinously true that tribal religions have long histories (but ones which are not easily available to the scholar because of the usual lack of a written literary tradition).

Of the dead religions, the most important are as follows: (1) Ancient Near Eastern—Sumerian, Babylonian, Egyptian, etc.: these have attracted much attention not only because they constituted an aspect of the living milieu of Judaeo-Christian origins but also because of the strategic place of the ancient Near East in the growth of urban culture and civilization. (2) The religions of Indo-European speakers (other than those comprised under (1) and other than those which have continued in living form, e.g. Vedic religion): e.g. Celtic religions, Greek and Roman religions—and perhaps Zoroastrianism should be included here. The continued existence of a relatively small Parsi community gives Zoroastrianism a slight 'living' status. (3) Pre-Columbian religions of America—Aztec, Inca, Maya, etc. (4) The proto-historical religions of mankind, important in relation to problems about the genesis of religion.

These lists are not quite exhaustive, but map out the major areas of historical researches. It may be noted that the religions under (4) in the living category tend to be more widely investigated by anthropologists than by religionists.

SCIENTIFIC STUDIES OF RELIGION

Generally speaking, the main focus of interest among those concerned with Christian theology is in the so-called 'world religions' (usually held to include categories (1) to (3) in the first list, since these faiths provide both a challenge to Christianity and an opportunity of dialogue). From an ancillary point of view, the ancient Near Eastern religions are often linked to the study of biblical history and religion. I shall revert to the matter of world religions in the last section of this essay.

PHENOMENOLOGY OF RELIGION

The discovery of certain apparently recurrent patterns in religion has led to a series of attempts to bring the materials together in an ordered way. Sometimes such attempts have been connected to a theory or theories of a speculative character about the nature and genesis of religion, as in Sir James Frazer's work. Some themes, e.g. as to the nature of magic (prominent in Frazer's discussions), have also figured centrally in anthropological work. Some of the more ambitious exercises in religious typology attempt to cover the whole field of religious phenomena; others compare particular elements of doctrine, experience, ritual, etc. It will bring out the range of such studies best to mention some of the better-known authors and works in this field. These works are listed in the bibliographical section at the end of this chapter.

Of what we may call 'holistic' phenomenologies—covering the whole range—probably the best-known is Gerardus van der Leeuw's *Religion in Essence and Manifestation*; earlier attempts on the same scale include W. Brede Kristensen's lectures on phenomenology. Rather less wide in scope is Nathan Söderblom's *The Living God,* investigating basic forms of personal religion.

Perhaps the seminal work in the present century has been that of Rudolf Otto, who coined the term 'numinous' to characterize the basic religious experience which, in his view, is central to religion. Though his theory does not fit mysticism so easily, he was also an important modern pioneer of cross-cultural studies of the contemplative life, in his work comparing

PREFACE TO CHRISTIAN STUDIES

Eckhart and Shankara. The topic of mysticism has generated quite a large literature, a significant and prolific recent contributor to which is R. C. Zaehner (though he does not always write from a strictly phenomenological point of view, since he works theological judgements into his descriptions). Otto also addressed himself to the problem of the relations between doctrines and experience, a case of intra-religious explanation— explaining one element of religion in terms of another.

Particular aspects of religion covered by Mircea Eliade include shamanism and yoga; but he is rather more widely known for his general theory of myth, which bears some relation to the psychology of Jung, though more oriented to the relation between time, history and responsible action. Thus Eliade holds that profane human acts are given cosmic significance through myths describing archetypal acts 'at the beginning of time' which are constantly repeated and recreated through ritual, etc. From this point of view, the idea of unrepeatable history, as expressed in the Judaeo-Christian revelation, represents a radical break with archaic, mythic thinking, so that the man who has no longer the security of the archetype is 'fallen'. (This part of Eliade's work is, naturally, speculative, but illustrates the way in which phenomenology may rise to theories bearing a theological significance.)

As well as many particular studies of such topics as the judgement of the dead in different religions, the mother goddess, the high god, prophecy, etc., the phenomenology of religion has naturally supplied material for various theories of the genesis of religion, as well as providing evidences for and against wider ranging theories in psychology, sociology and anthropology. This is very obvious when we consider that one of the seminal figures in the sociology of religion, Max Weber, made use of a typology, including such concepts as prophecy and charisma, in his works on Indian, Chinese and Western society, etc. As one of the few approximations to experimentation in regard to wide-scale sociological and psychological theories is to apply them to independent, or relatively independent, cultural histories, the phenomenology of religion must in principle play a crucial role here.

SCIENTIFIC STUDIES OF RELIGION

SOCIOLOGY OF RELIGION

Very roughly it is possible to divide approaches to the sociological investigation of religion into two kinds—the theoretical
and the inductive. On the one hand, there are theories about
the role of religion, or of particular aspects of it, in society; on
the other hand, there is the gathering of data about religious
behaviour, etc. As elsewhere, theories are fruitful in suggesting
what data to look for; while conversely religious statistics may
themselves suggest hypotheses to explain them.

On the theoretical side, the most influential figures have been
Emile Durkheim and Max Weber. The former's functionalist
theory of religion implied that religious rituals and beliefs
fulfil a cohesive function in society: they correspond to men's
needs to overcome the contingency and frustration inherent
in their being subject both to the forces of nature and to the
restraints imposed by social living. Despite the mythological
and transcendental dressing concealing it, the true focus of
religious activity is society itself. Such a functionalism is often
taken to imply that religion is a necessary feature of man's
existence. Weber's approach was subtler and more far-reaching
than Durkheim's, and his thesis that religion can be a powerful
element in social causation (notably worked out in his *Religion
and the Rise of Capitalism*) went well beyond Durkheim's rather
static functionalism. This is partly because of Durkheim's
looking for his main models in 'primitive' societies, which
possess a less fluid and plural character than more wide-scale
cultures, such as that of Europe at the Reformation or India.
Another significant contributor to sociology of religion was
Ernst Troeltsch, whose distinction between church and sect—
the former conserving, the latter protesting against, the given
social order—has stimulated much recent investigation of
sectarianism, for example in the work of Bryan Wilson.

Social changes in the twentieth century, and in particular the
apparent secularization of some major industrialized societies,
have posed questions about sociological theory—for instance,
it casts doubt on functionalism. At the same time, religious
thinkers and organizations have shown an increasing awareness

PREFACE TO CHRISTIAN STUDIES

of sociological determinants of religious behaviour. Hence the emergence of what might be called 'religious sociology', namely the investigation of the data, etc., with an ultimate view to remedying the decline in faith, etc. Conversely, secularization has stimulated a form of secular Christianity, as in Harvey Cox's *The Secular City*.

Meanwhile particular, more inductive studies multiply. Ultimately it is to be hoped that the theoretical and inductive sides can be welded closely together, for this has been the form of advance in other sciences. Necessarily, sociological theory has hitherto contained a heavily speculative element. Weber's programme of cross-cultural testing of theory remains important, and it is inevitable that the sociology of religion should be integrated with phenomenology and history of religions, and in such a way that it is not simply reductionist (see above, pp. 176, 178). This in principle is the view of the most important American theoretician, Talcott Parsons.

Needless to say, there is no strict boundary between anthropological and sociological approaches to religion (indeed a great deal of Durkheim's material was drawn from anthropology). The differentiation between anthropology and sociology is in part to do with the kind of society each tends to study (for example, the study of mortuary rites among the Wisconsin Winnebagos would tend to fall under anthropology; the mortuary rites of the citizens of Oshkosh, Wisconsin, would tend to provide material for sociological research).

ANTHROPOLOGY

The creation of modern anthropology in the nineteenth century coincided roughly with the vogue for evolutionary theories of human culture; so that not surprisingly much effort was devoted to evolving theories of early stages of religion by reference to newly discovered anthropological material. Thus E. B. Tylor, sometimes regarded as the founder of modern anthropology, saw the beginnings of religion in animism: belief in such spirits he explained somewhat rationalistically as due to primitive speculations about dreams, death, natural

SCIENTIFIC STUDIES OF RELIGION

forces, etc. By contrast R. R. Marett emphasized the centrality of the experience of *mana*, a sacred, awe-inspiring force (he drew the word from Polynesia). Such a force can be looked at as magical and religious; but it is out of it that religious development springs. It was characteristic of the late nineteenth-century and early twentieth-century anthropological discussion that much weight was laid on the relations between magic and religion. Thus Frazer saw religion as emerging out of magic, finally to be displaced by science. In an important sense, both Tylor and Frazer could be described as reductionist—explaining religious phenomena in non-religious terms; while Marett, after a fashion, resisted such a reduction. Similar disputes, but in a different key, still operate. By reason of the natural concentration upon the *social* dimension of religion among social anthropologists there has been a strong tendency not to take sufficiently seriously the dynamic function of religion as a system of meanings. Nevertheless, there are also trends—for example in the work of Evans-Pritchard and of Clifford Geertz—towards a reappraisal of religious experience and symbolism, and one which is neither simply functionalist nor reductionist.

Somewhat at a tangent to these developments is the work of the French anthropologist Claude Lévi-Strauss, evolving a sophisticated way of looking at the structure of myth in terms of its formal properties and those of the social institutions, rituals, etc., with which myths are associated in a given society. In this, Lévi-Strauss hopes to show the logic of 'primitive' thinking. What he does not deal with much is the question as to the way religious meanings continue to have force though moving from one culture to another—for example, the story of the Incarnation and Resurrection retains something of a continued pattern of meaning through all the transformations of Christianity in its transitions from one cultural milieu to another.

Though there is a natural interplay between anthropology and the sociology of religion, there remains a certain lack of mutual fertilization between these studies and the history of religions and the phenomenology of religion. As yet there is no 'all-round' study of myth, for instance—the work of theologians, philosophers, sociologists, anthropologists and so on have not been integrated. This is a point to which I shall return in the concluding section.

PSYCHOLOGY OF RELIGION

The growth of modern psychoanalysis and psychology has inevitably raised questions about the origin and shaping of religious emotions. Freud's account, in *The Future of an Illusion* and elsewhere, has been profoundly influential. Though Freud himself considered that religious symbols were psychological projections of inner needs, there have been attempts to make use of Freud's general structure within the framework of a psychologically more self-aware Christianity. If Freud's theory is conflictual, in the sense that religion arises out of childhood conflict, Jung's is collective. For Jung, religious symbolism represents the uprush of primordial archetypes from the collective unconscious. The latter is, as it were, a storehouse of the experience of the human race, inherited as a common factor by each individual. To illustrate this view, Jung and his associates were at great pains to collect mythic and symbolic data from a variety of cultures, notably Eastern ones. Both for Freud and for Jung and for other psychologists with wide-ranging accounts of religion, there are problems about testing the theories from a statistical point of view; and there are also philosophical problems about concepts such as 'the unconscious' and 'the collective unconscious'. At the same time the relatively wide acceptance, in psychotherapy, of elements from Freudian psychology, has meant that a whole new concern has developed to relate religion to mental health. This in turn has produced, particularly in the United States, but to some extent in Britain, new ways of treating pastoral theology. Traditional ideas about the cure of souls have begun to suffer a sea-change in the wake of the new psychology (cf. p. 234f.).

Some classical studies of religious experience, for instance William James' *The Varieties of Religious Experience* and James Leuba's *The Psychology of Religious Mysticism*, overlap very

SCIENTIFIC STUDIES OF RELIGION

considerably with phenomenology of religion; but they go beyond the descriptive aspect of the latter in so far as they offer explanations (whether favourable or unfavourable to traditional religion) couched in psychological theory. On the other hand, statistical attempts to check on theories of religion themselves are necessarily intertwined with work in the sociology of religion —as in Michael Argyle's *Religious Behaviour.*

Developmental psychology, and in particular the work of Jean Piaget, has recently made a strong impact on educational approaches to the teaching of religion, since there seems to be evidence that children's emotional and conceptual development is such as to preclude their understanding of certain kinds of religious teaching in the younger age-groups (intuitively obvious, perhaps, but a conclusion liable to have profound effects, when spelt out in detail, upon religious curricula, whether in the Church or the school context).

As in the case of sociological theory, it is hard to avoid the conclusion that psychological theories need cross-cultural testing. It may turn out, for instance, that Freudian psychology has a rather confined range of application—more plausible, say, for late nineteenth-century middle-class Vienna than for Nepal or Sicily. Here again the history of religions and the phenomenology of religion remain crucial.

THE RELEVANCE OF SCIENTIFIC STUDIES OF RELIGION TO THEOLOGY AND PHILOSOPHY OF RELIGION

The history of religions brings to light in a concrete and striking way the variety of religious beliefs and experience. It thus immediately confronts the Christian theologian with the problem of the appraisal of other faiths. Crudely, two types of attitudes tend to be manifested in the face of world religions (for it is they above all that supply a living question mark to the Christian faith). One is to stress the 'wholly-otherness' of the Christian Gospel. In recent times this attitude has drawn on the distinction between the Gospel (i.e. Christ) and human religion, as found in the work of Karl Barth—so that the Gospel stands in judgement upon all religions. This position was elaborated in a sophisticated way by H. Kraemer in his *The Christian Message in a Non-Christian World,* written just before World War II and of continuing influence in the mission field. (see p. 299f.). The other attitude is to recognize an overlap between Christian theology and practice on the one hand and the beliefs and practice of non-Christian religions on the other. From this point of view there is truth and illumination to be found in the world religions, even though of course for the Christian theologian the Christian faith is the highest. It is difficult to avoid the conclusion that there is overlap, from the point of view of the descriptive phenomenology of religion.

Reflection also shows that other faiths may adopt this second attitude in reverse—in effect this is the position of Sarvepalli Radhakrishnan, a chief exponent of modern Hinduism. This in turn raises the philosophical question of the problem of criteria of truth in religion. Put crudely and artificially, this question is: What grounds can there be for accepting the truth of one revelation rather than another?

A further relevance for philosophy of the history and phenomenology of religion is this: inasmuch as the philosopher of religion is concerned to delineate the nature of religious discourse (see Chapter 9), it is necessary to see the latter concretely in its varieties of manifestations. Christian discourse does not exhaust religious discourse.

We have seen that both in the phenomenology of religion and in anthropology, from rather different angles, there has been debate about the nature of mythic thinking. Here is an example of a search for understanding which is related to important tasks in modern theology. Rudolf Bultmann's project of demythologization (see p. 55), that is the re-presentation of the Gospel by penetrating to the inner, living meaning of New Testament myth and by discarding the outer shell of mythic concepts (such as the literal picture of Jesus' ascension upwards into heaven), depends upon a certain analysis of myth. This may have to be tested in a wider context. This must remain an abiding issue, in that the Christian theologian must always be re-presenting the Gospel afresh, and this must involve at one

SCIENTIFIC STUDIES OF RELIGION

end as rounded an understanding as possible of the cultural condition of the early Church.

We have noted that sociological and psychological theories of religion are sometimes reductionist, explaining away the transcendent focus of religious belief and action. In part this is a consequence of the fact that in the nineteenth century, the seminal century for scientific studies of religion, there was thought by many intellectuals to be a collision between scientific and religious thinking. The debate about Evolutionary Theory, for instance, often suggested that the Church was wedded to an anti-scientific literalism. But the question of the ultimate incompatibility between faith and science is highly complex, and essentially a philosophical question. Thus with regard to theories about religious experience, it is necessary to ask: Even though the psychologist may be able to speculate about factors predisposing a person towards a religious experience of a certain type, how does this affect the question of whether such an experience is of God? It might, for instance, be argued that God sustains the whole cosmic process and hence the factors predisposing a person to such-and-such an experience. For a proper investigation of such issues, it is necessary to have a clear understanding of the nature of a given experience (history and phenomenology of religion), a testable theory (psychology of religion), and a view about the conceptual relations between that theory and theology (philosophy of religion). The last of course presupposes a reasonably well defined theology, which itself may be affected by interaction with the scientific study of religion.

It can thus be seen that though scientific studies do not primarily have a theological intent, they supply materials which are necessarily of theological significance. The Christian theologian, if he is to be equipped to re-present the Gospel in the present (and future) situations of burgeoning knowledge and theories about religion, needs to take seriously the change in perspective brought about by seeing Christian belief in the context of world religions, in the context of sociology and in the context of modern psychology. Here are challenges which can only be met creatively—not be compartmentalizing the

PREFACE TO CHRISTIAN STUDIES

study of theology, but by opening it up to the new intellectual and cultural forces released by the nineteenth century's often fumbling but undoubtedly dynamic attempts to form a science of religion.

For further reading

1. HISTORY OF THE STUDY OF RELIGION:
Jan de Vries, *The Study of Religion*, Harcourt, Brace and World, New York, 1967.
John Macquarrie, *Twentieth Century Religious Thought*, S.C.M., London, 1963.

2. HISTORY OF RELIGIONS:
Trevor Ling, *A History of Religion East and West*, Macmillan, New York, 1968.
Ninian Smart, *The Religious Experience of Mankind*, Scribner's, New York, 1969.
Charles J. Adams, ed., *A Reader's Guide to the Great Religions*, The Free Press, New York, 1965.

3. PHENOMENOLOGY OF RELIGION:
Van der Leeuw, *Religion in Essence and Manifestation*, Harper and Row, New York, 1963.
Rudolf Otto, *The Idea of the Holy*, Oxford University Press, London, 1923, and Penguin Books, 1959.
Sidney Spencer, *Mysticism in World Religion*, Penguin Books, London, 1963.

4. SOCIOLOGY OF RELIGION:
Max Weber, *The Sociology of Religion*, Methuen, London, 1965 (with an introduction by Talcott Parsons).
Thomas F. O'Dea, *The Sociology of Religion*, Prentice-Hall, Englewood Cliffs, N.J., 1966.
Vittorio Lanternari, *The Religions of the Oppressed*, New American Library, New York, 1958.

PREFACE TO CHRISTIAN STUDIES

5. ANTHROPOLOGY:

Robert A. Manners and David Kaplan, *Theory in Anthropology,* Routledge & Kegan Paul, London, 1969.

6. PSYCHOLOGY OF RELIGION:

Paul E. Johnson, *The Psychology of Religion,* revised and enlarged edn., Abingdon Press, New York, 1949.

Michael Argyle, *Religious Behaviour,* Routledge & Kegan Paul, London, 1958.

7. OTHER TOPICS:

Hendrik Kraemer, *The Christian Message in a Non-Christian World,* International Missionary Council, London, 1947.

Paul Tillich, *Christianity and the Encounter of World Religions,* Columbia University Press, New York, 1961.

Ninian Smart, *World Religions : A Dialogue,* Penguin Books, London, 1965.

Note: for some bibliographical and other advice, the author is indebted to his colleague, Stuart Mews.

CHAPTER 20

Religious Studies and the Comparative Perspective*

Since different people mean differing things by "Religious Studies", let me start with a brief delineation of the field as I see it. Then we shall seek to explore the relevance of its plural and comparative character to reflection about our world - not to mention the next world. That human history has displayed both vast variety and a recurrence of patterns in its religious history is undeniable; and the depth of the religious roots of the major cultures gives the study of religion a special place in the understanding of the way the human world works. And if we extend religious studies realistically to include the exploration of secular ideologies too, for they too are symbolic systems with ultimate concerns, then this wider field - which I like to call "Worldview Analysis" - has a crucial function in education and practical life, as well as in the theory of the human sciences. But though I think that religious studies should have this wider worldview outreach, I shall for the purpose of this paper keep to the old term. What then, is the study of religion?

It is like politics and economics. In these fields we abstract from total human behaviour and institutions and products one major aspect: political behaviour and institutions and so forth; or economic behaviour, institutions and so forth. So we abstract from the total of human behaviour, institutions, products that aspect which is religious. It may turn out that there is nothing, or very little, which fails to have religious meaning - just as too there are few things which do not have some political or economic meaning. Briefly, then, the study of religion is aspectual.

You may think: But what about the non-human? What about God or nirvana or the Tao, the sacred stars or the holy murmuring sea? Well, for descriptive and theoretical purposes (for phenomenological or scientific purposes as some might say) we have to include the foci of human religion, but those foci need to be bracketed. We examine the experience of God or of liberation, or the worship of Visnu or Christ, or sacrifices to Pusiedon or Allah; but we do not (in that frame of warm dispassion which we sometimes know as phenomenology) preach Allah or affirm Posidon, nor deny God or nirvana, but rather we bracket these living-foci and objects of reciprocity. We practise thus methodological agnosticism. So we recognize thus the Transcendent, but as it relates the human behaviour, institutions and so forth. The fact is that Allah as bracketed focus has great power to move people and thus enters in to human history, and we can say this without committing ourselves to Him or against Him. Such commitment does not belong to the warm dispassion of the human sciences, but it belongs rather to the realm of faith, preaching, worship.

Next, the study of religion is quite obviously plural. There are many traditions, new movements, religious ideologies, living and dead, East and West, North and South. We of course are more and more aware that even those great moving entities we label Christianity, Buddhism and so forth are really federations and swarms of variegated movements.

5

Part therefore of the study of religion is the histories of these many traditions and sub-traditions. This study is of course valid in its own right, but it generates comparative questions.

It asks us how we delineate one tradition from a perspective outside it.

It suggests hypotheses about patterns of development and patterns of symbols, experiences, and so forth.

It suggests that we may up to a point to give explanations of a religious kind for human behaviour, social change and so on.

In brief, the pluralism of the study of religion proposes methods, themes, theories. The current debate about phenomenology is to do with method, the debate about mysticism deals with a theme, and the discussion of projection theories belong to the realm of explanation. In fact I believe that the boot is on the other foot, once we accept methodological agnosticism, for religious foci and experiences have an evident dynamism, as do ideologies in the modern mode, which helps to shape society and technology. Perhaps we are projections of the gods.

Above, I put the question of how we delineate one tradition from a perspective outside it rather abstractly. More humanly the question is how we enter into the minds and hearts and contexts of others. Clearly the means we use are not just the language of the learned paper and the format of the book: documentary television, literature and other means can well delineate the meanings of other people's lives in and out of religion. We sometimes forget this: phenomenology is in principle multimedia, as the study of religion is multi-disciplinary.

It is multidisciplinary, or polymethodic as I prefer to call it, because in analysing myths or explaining the emergence of doctrines or exhibiting the meaning of the sacraments or evoking the ethos of a faith or ideology, we can benefit from the insights of anthropology (say Geertz and Levi-Strauss), sociology (say Weber and Bellah), history of religions (say Otto and Eliade), Asian Studies (say Basham and Needham), Classics (say Jaeger and Kirk), philology (say Barr and Egerton), history (say Hobsbawm and Bainton), history of art (say Kuhn and Cipolla), history of ideas (say Berlin and Dasgupta), African Studies (say Vansina and Kenyatta), Church history (say Marty and Ware), theology (say Bultmann and Robinson), and so forth.

So the study of religion is aspectual, phenomenological, plural (and so comparative) and polymethodic.

It is also not bounded. The definition of a religion, of what it is for something to be religious, is not so secure or so self-evident, nor are human beings so compartmentalized, that it is reasonable or feasible to draw a line between religious and non-religious symbol-systems. As I indicated earlier, the study of religion should in principle extend itself to the study of worldviews: at the descriptive and theoretical level, to Worldview Analysis.

6

Hitherto I have been trying to delineate the study of religion, but there is more to Religious Studies than the quest for history, phenomenology, explanation. There is also the question - or rather the next of questions - of truth, that is, the truth of religion. What worldview is true? What worldview has ethical validity? What are the criteria of truth and validity? We pass here directly into the levels of theology and theologies, buddhologies, ideologies, philosophy, morals, public policy. Before we get there let us pause a moment to consider why the more descriptive and phenomenological side of religious studies is important and how Worldview Analysis is so neglected in our educational and intellectual milieu.

Religious studies and Worldview Analysis are important because they throw light upon the mental and symbolic engines which shape cultures and individual actions. Considering the amount of time we spend on economics and technology it is surprising how little time we spend on crosscultural studies. It is extraordinary that we have people educated to a great degree of sophistication about machines and a great ignorance of the world-shaping items within the most glorious machine of them all - ourselves. Because, however, religions and ideologies and values are areas of delicacy, whether because we wish to preserve the separation of Church and State, or because it is necessary not to argue about values in case we disturb one another at sensitive points, or whether it is because we are somewhat in the grip of a partial technosophic ideology (technosopic in the sense of thinking that we can get by with technological expertise to solve our problems) - whatever the cause, there is a curious lack of educational investment in the business of trying to understand one another crossculturally. It seems however to me that one of the noblest as well as one of the most immediately practical of human endeavors is that attempt to voyage into other minds, to walk in the moccasins of others, which is represented in the study of religion by the phenomenological method.

As the native American proverb says "Never judge a person till you have walked a mile in his moccasins". Not much is done to develop this art in high schools, and on college and university campuses it is broken up: some is done in anthropology, but that tends to be much about small-scale societies; sociology does some, but is pretty much culture-bound (sociology is about 'us', anthropology about 'them'); philosophy tends to be judgmental rather than descriptive and historical; religious studies is often absent from the campus, and where present tends not to do much about secular ideologies and may often be very Western in emphasis; political science looks to ideologies somewhat but tends to eschew religions; history is often us-regarding - and so it goes on.

But apart from the practical value of Worldview Analysis there are the larger reflections it gives rise to, and I shall return to these after looking to the constructive, expressive, normative aspects of Religious Studies and (of course) Theology. It seems to me that Religious Studies must engage with truth and criteria questions, and also with spiritual, ethical and in some degree political policy questions. It cannot just remain at the descriptive and theoretical level if only because philosophical issues arise in theoretical enquiries (thus Freudian projection theory depends upon a view about the truth and origin of religion).

Conversely the theologies have to take account of the study of religion. Obviously Christian and Jewish theology have been profoundly affected by the use of historical methods on the scriptural material. But they cannot either ignore the facts of pluralism in religious traditions and sub-traditions. No Theology can fail (if it is to be at all gripping in the modern world) to have a theory about other religious traditions than its own. Some of the questions thrown into relief by the material are disturbing to insulated faith, of course (which is why comparative religion is supposed to make people comparatively religious, as Ronald Knox snootily said, and wrongly, I believe: since the voyage into other religions can also deepen understanding of one's own).

Religious studies differs from Theology, obviously, because even in discussion of normative and constructive issues it must remain plural, indeed pluralistic. It is in this respect a kind of market place of the worldviews of the world. Now it may be that in many places Christian or Jewish Theology as incarnated in seminaries or divinity schools is plural in its outreach and incorporates great swathes of the modern study of religions and religion: but its essence remains rooted in a tradition and a commitment. That is something which religious studies as institutionalized cannot (and rightly cannot) do. Individuals may have commitments of course, but the enterprise is essentially many-sided.

If the word 'philosophical' may be used as shorthand for saying that religious studies is concerned with truth and criteria as well as descriptive and theoretical issues, and incorporates theologies too in its purview; if 'many-sided' is shorthand for the essential institutionalized pluralism of religious studies, then we can move to a full, but brief, delineation of the character of the field.

It is aspectual, phenomenological, plural, comparative, polymethodic; and it is philosophical and many-sided.

And if we wish to extend our field to make of it Worldview Analysis and Evaluation, then it is all those things I have listed but in an unbounded form, unbounded that is by the fact that the definition of religion is confined to those systems and phenomena traditionally regarded as religious.

We may now turn to consider the constributions of the comparative study of religion as I have delineated it to the human sciences, firstly: and then its relevance to reflections about the present state of humanity.

First of all, Worldview Analysis raises the question of the importance of the 'mental component' and religious and cultural outlooks upon the variegated development of human society.

Second, our field calls in question culture-bound theories of human nature, for instance Freudian theory (which fares ill in its application for instance to Sri Lankan Theravada Buddhism). Other culture-bound projection theories (e.g. Peter Berger's in **The Sacred Canopy**) would have to undergo severe modification and change if they are to have a chance of surviving.

Third, our field generates material for a genuine theory of varieties of religious experience, and this in turn lays the foundation for hoping for some intra-religious explanations making use of types of religious experience. This means going beyond fertile but simplistic 'one-type' theories - e.g. Rudolf Otto. It is elementary that if religious experience is to be brought in as an item which helps to explain other items (e.g. types of doctrine) in religion, then the variety of religious phenomena implies more than one main type of religious experience. I think numinous (awe-inspiring, polarized) and mystical (contemplative, percep-tually empty) experiences are the two main types, but there is need for a general theory of religious experience.

Fourth, the phenomena of new religious movements, in America, Africa, Oceania and elsewhere not only can throw light on the genesis of past 'new movements', but also may illuminate the relationship between belief and identity.

The symbolic themes drawn out of the material of the religions by Eliade, Turner and others have an important role to play in analysing contemporary motifs, and can have the effect of reinvigorating our self-analysis, i.e. in showing some of the deeper meanings of what at the surface seem to be rational arrangements and ideas. There is here a whole field of Symbolic Analysis as a derivative from and adjunct to Worldview Analysis.

Sixth, the comparative study of religion is important in helping us to get the feel of a world which is a kind of global city - one, and yet with many cultures living cheek by jowl. We have of course entered a period when the many different streams of history, Chinese, African, European and so on, have merged into one great waterway of world history. This implies the emergence of a world culture, and that needs to have knowledge of its multitudinous ancestors. So for us now the ancestors include Lincoln and Confucius, Christ and Mao, Aquinas and Sankara, Asoka and Muhammed, Leonardo and Hokusai . . .

Seventh, the study of religions can supply materials towards a general theory of li, ritual or performative acts (we are only at the beginning of a grammar of the performance).

Eighth, we are at the beginning of a productive period of intra-religious explana-tions in which the differing dimensions of religion are related. Thus the relation between doctrine and experience involves on the one hand considering the way interpretation is built in (so to speak) the raw types of religious experience (consider the discussions in Steven Katz's **Mysticism and Philosophical Analysis**); and on the other hand considering how experience shapes doctrines (e.g. grace in Paul and Ramanuja). Comparatively based theories on these matters are the most effective, since theories of their nature have general application (but we must also note particularities, by the same token: uniqueness can only be dis-. covered in a comparative context).

9

As another example of inter-dimensional explanations, we can look to the way differing types of religious experience and practise shape differing kinds of ethics: thus the yogic techniques of pacification of the passions tend towards a prudential and gentle ethic of self-control and harmlessness, while the numinous dynamism of prophetic religion is more activist and authoritarian. So there is here one side to the whole enterprise of comparative religious ethics. Another side to it is the way the imitation of holy persons shapes morality. Still another is the way ritual can be 'superimposed' on ethical action - so that doing good is seen as a form of worship or humility is seen as a form of reverence towards God or as a sacrifice - and so on. All these and other approaches to understanding variations and similarity between cultures as to ethical ideals and rules is burgeoning now under the general rubric of "comparative religious ethics".

These then are a few of the ways in which the comparative method opens up fruitful explorations of the phenomenon of Religion.

Although it is not my primary aim here to consider the direct relationship of these avenues of exploration to Christian (or any other) Theology, it is obvious that there are ways in which such Theology is challenged and enriched by the comparative method. Thus briefly: it suggests that any particular tradition is a 'tradition among traditions', and that it may share features with other religions - bhakti in Paul, analogies of mystical experience in Ruysbroeck and the Sufis and others, similar symbolisms (Jungian at altars and in hymnody), and so on. It suggest that the question of criteira of truth as between religions must be faced in a complex way: by their fruits ye may know them, but how do oranges and persimmons compare? It suggests that differences are often essentially difference of interpretation, and how then are these decided? And the raw material of religions suggests all sorts of fascinating and tremendously mysterious echoes and insights.

Also the history of religions can often make life uncomfortable for those who try to produce simple unities: Guénon and Radhakrishnan and the perennial philosophy does not seem to me to match up to the facts, for instance of Theravada Buddhism, but indeed also the complexities of Western theism. Hick's Copernican revolution suggests one sun: maybe we orbit religiously round a binary star, or a quasar. So even if in the end we came to accept such unity doctrines, it would only be after a debate with the material. Incidentally, because of its otherness in many respects both from Hinduism and Western theism, Theravada Buddhism seems to me the most important example which any theory of religion has to take account of. This seems to me a profound weakness in the writings of some more theologically orientated comparativists, from Otto and Van de Leeuw to Zaehner and Wilfred Cantwell Smith, however profound their contributions in other respects.

Moreover old-fashioned natural theology has to be reshaped if it is to survive at all, partly to take in the discussions of other cultures such as Indian arguments for and against Ísvara, and partly because the human concern for the ultimate turns out after all to be a striving for several sorts of ultimates.

Finally, on Theology and related matters, much is to be learned by the Christian (or other) Theologian from others: thus we can cite new insights on the via negativa in the Buddhist tradition, new ethical values in the Confucian doctrine of li, new ways of looking at the relation of God and the world in Ramanuja, and so on. We are at a most fruitful juncture in the quest of a divine eclecticism.

However, now I wish to turn to something less directly Theological, but rather some reflections, born of the comparative perspective and Worldview Analysis, about our present age. I offer these reflections not as something 'established' by the study of religion, but suggested by it, in the mind of one practitioner. The important thing is not the particular conclusions, but the debate. It is important for Religious Studies to enter the intellectual, political and ethical debate of our times. Too often it is left to narrowly based exponents of particular worldviews (often authoritarian religious worldviews and varieties of secularism).

First, the very attempt to look at secular ideologies as symbolic worldviews is important, because it begins to erase the ideologically loaded distinction between the religious world and the secular. Thus we are often confused in thinking about Church and State. The most important modern practitioners of the old principle **cuius regio eius religio** are the Marxists and totalitarians. Now one reason why it is important to separate a worldview-imposing-community from the State is so that there shall be the possibility of genuine pluralism. Now since in fact the criteria of truth in religion and in worldviews in general are so unclear, and since proofs are wanting, from the very nature of the case, then logically and epistemologically pluralism is indicated. To put it more humanly, each religion or worldview finds itself in the modern global city, living side by side with other faiths and customs, and it is hard to resist the conclusion that we have to shape societies to a multi-faith context. So though there is much evil and external exploitation infecting the social democracies of the North, they stand for pluralism and for the mutual respect of traditions. But because they are also heirs to a broadly racist outlook on other cultural traditions (nearly everyone given the chance alas is liable to be racist), and also because capitalism (which seems to be a necessary ingredient, though not the sole ingredient, in a plural society) is often externally exploitative in a quite shameless way, for instance in Central America, northern pluralism needs to enter into dialogue with southern and eastern cultures, which also are concerned with a kind of pluralism as the condition of the survival of their indigenous values.

A second main reflection of Religious Studies is this: that the fallacies of technosophy must be resisted. By technosophy I mean the notion, also pervasive in northern countries, that the problems of humanity can be resolved technically, by machinery and economic expertise above all, without regard to the mental and spiritual components of action, or as if what is rational is transparent to us. The segregation of religion itself reduces the degree to which a flat, technological secularism can undergo criticism. Worldview Analysis becomes itself a means of criticism, in that it attempts to delineate various alternative belief and value system, and so makes us conscious of many of the unspoken assumptions of our own society. This is a region where Religious Studies can supply materials for a more conscious and critical view of our world.

Though it is by no means entailed of course by the study of religion as part of the human sciences, yet there is some pressure from the material (in my view) towards also a kind of federalist approach to religions and worldviews. Because there are great varieties of religious and other outlooks and because there are no easy proofs of truth, we cannot achieve epistemological certainty by at best a kind of open certitude. By this I mean that on the one hand appeals to experience or revelation or argument can engender counter-appeals, alternative revelations and counter-arguments, so that at best our criteria of truth in religion are soft; while on the other hand we live but one life apiece and need therefore a worldview or commitment, which we can hold to hopefully with assurance while recognizing the alternatives. Those who claim a kind of certainty 'out there' seem thus to be wrong, and in the modern world there is also the pervasive presence of plural living. So certainty cannot legitimately be attained, though certitude of a kind has to be grasped. Or if you like, we can have faith but not proof, and cannot then reimpose faith itself as proof. Consequently, we are bound to be faced, both in logic and reality with a continuing symbiosis and pluralism of worldviews. The persistence of this living together of systems points to a kind of federalism of the spirit. I believe in any case that since claims to unity of all religions or of the Focus of all religions are debatable (to say the least) a federal outlook is the nearest to unity we can foreseeably attain.

In this connection I have recently (**Beyond Ideology**, being Gifford Lectures for 1979-80) explored the notion that Buddhism and Christianity for instance have a **complementary** relationship. They serve as complements to one another and can function as mutual critics. This way each is both challenged and strengthened by the other. Perhaps this critical path is one which can be more generally used, for it does not try to wash away genuine differences and contradictions between systems.

Moreover, criticism is part of the essence of the process of discovery and theory-building and theory-testing. It is part of artistic and other forms of creativity. This critical mode, stressed among others by Popper in his delineation of the logic of scientific and other research, can be echoed in religion: for though religious worldviews are not simply scientific they have to pay attention both to the method and content of science in depicting our place in the cosmos. So the congruence between religious federal openness and the scientific outlook is important for our world.

Another reflection out of Religious Studies concerns the nature of our modern condition. The last two hundred years have seen the emergence of a new religious mode: religion **aware of itself**. Religious Studies has as a major component of its endeavors the task of holding up a mirror to religion - more generally, holding up a mirror to worldviews. Unfortunately our educational systems across the world are only dimly coming to understand this. There is still concern to instil the values of the nation or the tradition, as if we did not now belong to a world society.

Finally, let me here come to a paradox. I - as is apparent from the preceding argument - hold structured empathy and the process of fair and evocative delineation of the beliefs of others in the highest esteem: I think Religious Studies and more generally Worldview Analysis are crucial to humanistic and realistic education. I think they are noble endeavors too, and desperately underdeveloped and under-rated. But part of the enterprise is a kind of higher-order neutrality, a kind of warm dispassion. But this attitude itself finds itself in conflict with some of the worldviews under consideration. It would have had short shrift from Hitler, or from Stalin, and is unwelcome to some of the Moral Majority, strongly motivated Muslim politicians, many Marxists and so forth. My dispassion goes better in a pluralist society and in federalist contexts. Thus Religious Studies as we know it is not taken seriously in Poland or Romania or many traditionalist Catholic countries nor in Islamic countries: and so on. The paradox then is that the effort to be neutral comes down on one side, for it favors separation of Church/Party and State, it favors pluralism and openness of enquiry.

But this is fine. The human sciences as well as the physical and biological sciences point towards openness. The values of human dignity and human knowledge walk hand in hand.

But yet here is another paradox. Those suspicious of Religious Studies and Worldview Analysis will point a finger and say "So your vaunted neutrality is not neutrality after all! Your attempt to find an ahistorical, 'higher' standpoint from which to describe others' worldviews after all turns out to be vain." Who said **ahistorical?** Who denied the relative relativity of our enquiries and descriptions? But the reason why we come down (as you may put it) on the side of freedom and pluralism is that the attempt genuinely to get at the inner facts of people's lives and at the structures of their beliefs itself requires openness. But - and here is the paradox - only if I am committed to fairness, evocation, openness, objectivity so far as one can, warm dispassion, in a word a kind of 'neutrality' - only on this basis can I become committed to a politically pluralistic worldview. Only by espousing lack of bias can I have the licence to become biased in favor of lack of bias.

In this paper I have explored some of the possible fruits both of the comparative study of religion and of reflection stemming from it. We are only in the early days of our field. We are only, also, in the early days of the new global city.

*Paper for the Pacific Coast Theological Society, Berkeley, California
April 2 - 3, 1982

University of Lancaster

Ninian Smart

13

The Study of Religion as a Multidisciplinary and Cross-Cultural Presence among the Human Sciences

[This item has been re-keyed. Page numbers in square brackets have been inserted to indicate the format of the original.]

The modern study of religion is one of the great intellectual developments of the recent past. But many academics do not yet understand that we have moved far beyond what used to be called theology, that is, Christian theology, and the kind of enterprise typical of seminaries and divinity schools. Our aim in the comparative or cross-cultural study of religion is to explore religion and religions as a force in human affairs, at varying times and places, weak and strong. It is the power of religion, rather than its truth, that primarily concerns us. The Ayatollah was what he was independently of the value which we in the West might place upon his theology and actions. Now this attempt to appraise the dimensions of religion in terms of their power to influence other aspects of human existence and in terms of the ways they are affected by those other aspects is, of course, highly relevant to both the humanities and social sciences – what I here shall for short dub the human sciences. I shall spell out some of the connections later.

I take a somewhat functional approach to religion and like to deal with it in relation to seven dimensions through which religions manifest themselves, namely the ritual, ethical, doctrinal, narrative, experiential, social, and material dimensions. Religions typically have practices or rituals, ethical and legal precepts, doctrines or philosophies, narratives or myths, experiences and emotions, seminal and social or organizational arrangements, and material or artistic products. It is not that this scheme of mine is sacrosanct: there are others that would work. But it is an attempt to ensure that by treating all these dimensions we will give a rounded and realistic view of how a religion functions. If we were thinking of Scottish Presbyterianism we would note the style of worship, preaching, Sabbath-keeping and family involvement; we would depict the ethics of inner-worldly asceticism; we would note the teachings on Calvin and how they have been adapted to the Scottish scene; we would see the narratives of the Bible and the Reformation as normative; we would depict and evoke some of the sober feelings and the sense of election typical of Presbyterian life in Scotland; we would observe the religious establishment and the social embedding of the Kirk in Scottish life; we would look at the generally plain churches and generally aniconic mode of Calvinist representations. The exploration of the role of the Kirk would obviously be vital to an understanding of Scottish life.

But it is fairly obvious that this functional approach could also apply to quite a few manifestations of secular ideology. For instance, East German Marxism had its rituals – parades, flags, the use of revolutionary language; it had its doctrines – Marxism-Leninism of a particular kind; it had narratives – the history of the revolution, the pre-revolutionary struggle against the Nazis etc.; it had its ethics – an adherence to revolutionary ideals and proletarian values, etc.; it had its emotional side, enhanced by songs and music; it had its social organization – the East German Com[5]munist Party; it had its material embodiment – the architecture of the Stalinallee, socialist-realism in painting, etc. For these reasons I prefer to extend our studies to the study of worldviews in general and not just to religions. For practical purposes the comparative study of religions is the comparative study of worldviews. There are some interesting consequences: for instance we would consider the relations between the party and the state in Marxist countries as a special case of church-state relations. The heirs of Lutheran establishmentarianism were the Marxist regimes of Eastern Europe and such regimes as the Chinese.

I have laid some emphasis on social organizations. Of course in today's world there are lots of floating individuals – practical humanists or eclectic searchers with a more spiritual emphasis. These, too, are a vital phenomenon of the modern world, and though unorganized, they have an important social presence. Many such searchers and humanists are found among our students.

Obviously our exploration of religions and worldviews must be cross-cultural. There is no excuse for Western tribalism, though it is prevalent. In any case, the West's chief religion, Christianity, has moved south. Its center of gravity is no longer in the North. Its most populous regions are Africa and Latin America. I do not wish to decry the emphasis on European and American culture which prevails in our schools, but it must surely be heavily supplemented by Chinese, African, Islamic, and many other strands. Buddhism, Hinduism, Confucianism – these and many other great traditions need to be part of our explorations, and this is why we in religious studies put a heavy emphasis upon world studies. We can thereby supplement much that goes on in the academy: not just Western studies of various kinds, but Asian and Asian-American studies, Chicano studies, African and African-American studies, Native American studies, Middle Eastern studies, and so forth. I would like for us, perhaps through the Interdisciplinary Humanities Center here, to promote a study and inventory of worldviews prevalent among the Pacific Rim nations: Japanese, Korean, and Chinese values; the particularities of Indonesian Islam and the ideology of the present political systems; the Pacific Way in Oceania; Australian and New Zealand values, including Aboriginal and Maori ideas; the Westward-facing Hispanic States and their values; the ideology of California and of western Canada and Alaska; the attitudes of the Soviet Union; and the worldviews of the Inuit and their Soviet relatives.

Because the exploration of religion is cross-cultural, we put a lot of emphasis on methods of imagination and fieldwork as well as on the more traditional dealing with texts. We have to be ancient and modern. To understand ancient times you need time travel, and for many studies you need a kind of space travel. We have to think ourselves into other thought worlds. Data are vital, of course, but imagination or empathy are also. Religious studies has its analogues in anthropology. For many purposes [6] we are the same discipline. Geertz works in religious studies, as does Mary Douglas (she is currently visiting professor in religious studies at Lancaster University); and other scholars such as Jack Hawley and Mark Juergensmeyer do a kind of anthropology. I think informed empathy is a central ingredient of the humanities. How does a boy feel what it is like to be a girl, or a White grasp the important values of Native American life, or a Vietnamese understand Europe, or an African-American imagine what African existence was like in the Gambia or Angola? In all cases we need to cultivate the imagination.

This is an area where literature can play a vital part. I like to introduce students to Eastern Orthodox Christianity through *The Brothers Karamazov*, to the Hindu tradition through *A Passage to India* and Narayan's *The Guide*, and to nineteenth-century Catholicism in Italy through *The Saint* by Fogazzaro. You can all think of many variants. Literature is a great enhancer of informed empathy. Scriptural texts also can have a like effect: the poems of the *Thera-* and *Therigatha*, the numinous theophany in the *Gita*, *Job*, the *Platform Sutra* – to name but a few. Of course, in terms of my informed empathy we need much more than literary texts. For the non-Jew *Leviticus* may seem dry stuff, but we need to enter the world of the Jewish student and observer of Torah. (Incidentally, one of the least understood religions in the West is Judaism, since people brought up as Christians think – wrongly, of course – that they know what it is. This makes a current tendency to inwardness in Jewish studies – Judaism studies by and for Jews – a bit unfortunate. Happily, here at UCSB we have a broad and outward-looking approach to Jewish studies, largely because of the pioneering work here of my colleague Richard Hecht, recently supplemented by two new colleagues, Randall Garr and Barbara Holdrege.)

In any event, informed empathy is nothing special to religious studies but is vital throughout the human sciences. And already because of it, we see affinities between the exploration of religion and the comparative study of literature. Another bond lies in the necessary concerns with hermeneutics, or theory of the interpretation of texts, where we have many fascinating examples in the religious sphere of modes in which the evolution of the varying dimensions of religion has affected the hermeneutical practice of a faith or worldview. One of the most striking puzzles comes out of India: how is it that the same Upanishadic texts were interpreted by Sankara, Ramanuja, and Madhva (to name but three) in such a diverse manner, ranging from full-blooded monism to strict dualism? One becomes suspicious: perhaps the texts, vital as they are, came to be outweighed by diverse conceptions of piety and practice.

There also arises in my mind the question of whether literature departments, if they have canons, are not branches of a worldview, with professors as mullahs, high critics as ayatollahs, and students as the faithful? You will, of course, excuse the speculation. We tend to see [7] religious structures everywhere.

It is, of course, fairly evident that the multidimensional character of worldviews means that the means to explore them will be multidisciplinary. In addition, the fact that religions are both ancient and modern underlines the need for historical perspectives, often thought to be primary. The social dimension means that we need sociology and anthropology, the narrative dimension points to literary methods, the doctrinal dimension overlaps with the history of philosophy and intellectual history, the ethical and legal dimension has relations to law, experiential aspects of religion relate to psychology, and ritual studies can be important in anthropology. Material products are part of the subject matter of art history and the history of architecture.

So we import a great deal from the various disciplines I have listed and from others. Our work is enriched by such figures as Weber, Geertz, Levi-Strauss, Victor Turner, Hirsch, Gadamer, Foucault, Rodo, Beteille, Narayan, MacIntyre, Jung, James, Mary Douglas, J.L. Austin, Gombrich, and Kramrisch.

What does the study of religions and worldviews have for export? First, it has the ineluctable cross-cultural perspective. This is vital to us here in California and is relevant in most of the rest of the world. Our citizens are Christians of various kinds, Buddhists, Hindus, Jews, Muslims, Sikhs, New Agers, and a whole variety of other movements. They come from Iowa, Vietnam, Africa, Nicaragua, Mexico, Native American enclaves, China, Korea, Japan, Laos, Texas, and a host of other milieux. It behooves us to be cross-cultural throughout the human sciences. We in the Department have experimented with seminars and other help for high school teachers to teach some material on world religions through their cultural manifestations in California, a program known as Religious Contours of California. I shall return to this question of the cross-cultural perspective in talking about philosophy.

Second, in relation to sociology, there is a great increase in interest in world-systems theory and the like. The global way of looking at human life is important, and religious studies can supply both data and theory relevant to this. For instance, the varying reactions of religious traditions conceived as cultural forces during and after the colonial period are very important for the process of modernization in countries such as India, China, and Japan. It is important, too, retroflexively in the USA. One can speculate as to what difference it makes when the modernizing forces are internal to the imperial power rather than external.

I would hold that some of the same reactions occur. Liberal Protestantism has affinities with the modern Hindu ideology of Vivekananda and Gandhi, while various neofoundationalist (or fundamentalist) responses sacrifice a slice of science in what is otherwise a modernization of Christian ritual and other dimensions.

Third, the establishment of departments of religious studies [8] redresses a balance. Many political scientists and historians have fought shy of religion as a factor, whether for ideological reasons or by the dynamics of religionless curricula. Peter Merkl and my book of a few years ago (*Religion and Politics in the Modern World*) is one of the early manifestations of a new wave of political science interest in religions. They are obviously important in a whole host of modern political contexts – the Sudan, Northern Ireland, Cyprus, Israel, South Africa, Poland, Iran, Afghanistan, Tibet, the Philippines – to name just a few countries.

Fourth, constitutional questions are affected by the new broadened scope of religious studies to worldview analysis. Church-state theory has to be re-examined in the light of queries about definition. If Shinto could be declared by the Japanese constitution not to be a religion, then that had profound effects on the freedom of worship in Meiji Japan. But the same applies, as we have seen, to Marxist countries. The debates about civil religions can be clarified further by attention to these definitional issues.

Fifth, it may be that religious studies can help to unify anthropological and other approaches to religious change. The study of new religious movements in small-scale societies is well developed, and sociological explorations of new religions in western countries are likewise richly embodied in the literature. To this we need to add a theory of changes in large-scale religions. This is attracting the attention of comparativists such as myself. All three types of exploration could well be unified. Large societies need not be all that different from smaller ones.

Sixth, worldview analysis remains a vital ingredient in area studies. You cannot fully understand Japan without the exploration of her religious and other values. Too many area studies may neglect the input of religious studies, and we can offer a piece of the action which moves towards an integrated and rounded view of cultures. In the past there has sometimes been a regrettable tendency to take ideological stances: Because I don't think religion is good or important (thinks a scholar), it is not important in reality. This is, of course, a fallacy. All of us reject Nazism, but it was a singularly dynamic ideology, alas.

Seventh, classical-style phenomenology of religion in the manner of G. van der Leeuw and M. Eliade can provide, in principle, a universal human 'grammar of symbolism'. I am aiming to embark on a new large work along these lines once I have completed a study of world philosophies. Such a 'grammar of symbolism' would have relevance to literature, anthropology, sociology, and art history.

Eighth, it is worth saying a word about philosophy. I have myself taught philosophy in various places: Wales, Oxford, London, Banares, Wisconsin, and the University of Queensland. I was a visiting professor for a quarter in the philosophy department of the University of Hong Kong in the fall of 1989. It is always a pleasure for me to pursue one of my early avocations. But philosophy departments can be highly culture-bound. This is partly because often they wish to be involved in rational thought [9] and to uphold the ideals of the Enlightenment. But there are a whole lot of other traditions in the world, and these should get some recognition in philosophy departments. There is, however, something even more important to say. That is, no worldview or part of a worldview – such as central-state materialism, which is not only fairly widespread in the USA, but is the preferred view of many Australian philosophers and pioneered there somewhat by my brother J.J.C. Smart – fails to run into some powerful objections, and no worldview can be proved. Worldviews drift in and out of fashion, and new ones emerge. The unprovability of philosophical systems can be illustrated by how we regard the giants of yesteryear: James, Russell, Peirce, Dewey, and G.E. Moore all look terribly dated and in parts highly unbelievable. This does not mean that we need to be relativists. We should, in my view, be soft non-relativists. But it does mean that there can be no rigid reason to exclude other possible philosophies and worldviews. In fact, then, the philosophy of religion, which should examine cross-culturally the criteria for truth or acceptability as between religions, might herald a new philosophy of worldviews (from Davidson to Marx to Nishida to Bhattacharya), which might probe the assumptions and relevant criteria as between worldviews. It would be a philosophy of philosophy. That is a contribution that a new cross-cultural philosophy of religion might suggest. I expect my philosopher friends will murmur in dissent. Good: that means we have an argument on our hands, and it is arguments which keep philosophers in employment.

In talking about philosophy we are speaking of questions of truth. Generally speaking, religious studies in its modern form does not want to make judgments about the truth of religion, since we explore its power, rather. But insofar as philosophy is part of the array of disciplines we incorporate, we rightly cannot escape some consideration about criteria of truth. Our practice is, however, necessarily plural. It is not for the university to lay down that Christianity or any other faith or non-faith is true or that all are wrong. But the university is interested in providing a sensitive arena in which young and old can debate the verities together. The philosophy of worldviews is simply a systematic attempt to learn lessons from such debates.

Ninth, it is worth noting that religious studies in its broader interpretation has something to offer to business and economics schools. For part of the secret of development is the right ethos, and such an ethos springs from a worldview. The Protestant ethic, it turns out, is not the only successful ethos. Post-Confucian

Buddhism, as in Japan, with its blending of religions, seems effective, combining discipline, hierarchy, individual motivation, spiritual self-containment, and a scientific faith. A pluralistic variety of Neo-Confucianism seems effective in Singapore. The idea of a Methodist and responsible individualism powers Mrs Thatcher. Various Marxisms substantially fail. The analysis of worldviews should be an ingredient in business education. [10]

Tenth, let me underline a point which I made near the beginning. We in religious studies have the honor to complement many area studies. The exploration of the worldviews of China, Korea, and Japan contributes to East Asian studies; of South Asian religions to South Asian studies; of Christianity and Judaism to classical and medieval studies; of modern Christianities and other religions to modern American studies; of pre-Columbian religion and Hispanic Catholicism to Chicano studies; of African and African-American religions to Black studies; of Eastern orthodoxy to Soviet studies; of Pacific religions to Pacific Rim studies; and so on.

Let me now, having sketched these exports of religious studies, say a few words to a number of significant people. To the chancellor I affirm this:

> *Note that modern religious studies, with its imaginative empathy and cross-cultural scope, has a key role to play in the education of the young who are entering a plural world.*

To the director of the Interdisciplinary Humanities Center I say:

> *We are enthusiastic about the interdisciplinary enterprise, for that is our substance, and remember that we can help you to be cross-cultural: beyond the glories of the West lie those of the East and the South.*

To historians and social scientists I say:

> *We can let you hear more clearly the sound of symbols.*

To the atheists I say:

> *The exploration of the power of worldviews is compatible with everything you stand for, and everything which you oppose.*

To the pious I say:

> *It is your decision to be pious: our task is analysis and synthesis. You are part of what we have the privilege of understanding.*

[11]To the world I say:

Forget your reactions to religion and heed the importance of a cross-cultural pluralism: as we shrink into a single, interconnected global society, so our devotion to delineating the riches and tragedies of religion and of various human worldviews becomes all the more relevant to the preparation of globally oriented citizens.

CHAPTER 22

Comparative Religion Clichés

[This item has been re-keyed. Page numbers in square brackets have been inserted to indicate the format of the original.]

Crushing the Clichés about Comparative Religion and then Accentuating the Positive Value of the New Religious Education

Most people have views about religion and an image of what the teaching of religion is. Sometimes the image is hateful; sometimes it is too comforting. Typically, it stands in the way of an appreciation of the role and nature of the new religious education of which comparative religion is an important component. Here I shall firstly concentrate on the clichés which need to be wiped out if a proper view of the study of world religions is to be widely shared. I therefore here look at a few of the main clichés (not always consistent with one another or held by the same people), and then go on to deal with the positive qualities of the new religious education.

'You can't understand a faith other than your own.'

A corollary is that commitment becomes a qualification for teaching a given faith. The cliché can be used both to justify a simply confessional religious education and to exclude the teaching of non-Christian religions. It is wrong for a number of reasons:

(a)   Understanding is a matter of degrees, not an all-or-nothing-at-all affair. A greater understanding is better than a lesser one.

(b)   First-century Christianity is perhaps more culturally distant from twentieth-century Britain than twentieth-century Buddhism.

(c)   The cliché would wipe out such undeniably fruitful subjects as social anthropology, history of other cultures, etc. – for all these subjects and enquiries involve explorations into religion, among other things.

(d)   The adherent can be in a worse position than the so-called outsider: does a Martin Buber or Claude Montefiore know less about Christianity than an Enoch Powell or Cliff Richard?

(e)   Besides, many children and young adults – consumers, so to say, of religious education – are either through their parents or in themselves not Christian (I am thinking here primarily of the indigenous Briton rather than of the immigrant, where the point is even stronger).

'Comparative religion makes men comparatively religious.'

A cliché derived from a vapid witticism by Monsignor Ronald Knox. Its force derives from two thoughts – first that confrontation with deeper choices from abroad will cause men's hold on Christianity to weaken; second, that the study of religion and religions attracts half-committed, rather superficial folk. It is silly for a number of reasons:

(a)   In that other profound traditions exist in the world (other that is from Christianity) this is a fact to be recognised, learned from, digested. If it leads some people away from Christian adherence or makes for scepticism (as in a way it is bound to do), the answer is for the Christian to face up to the challenge. The modern world is like the first centuries of Christianity, when it was making its way in a multi-religious and multi-philosophy Roman Empire; but now it is the wider world of the planet.

(b)   The cliché supposed that we are *only* concerned with inducing some kind of religiousness. Knowledge of religions, extending at least to the often-despised 'outer facts', should be part of the educated person's awareness, irrespective of commitment and salvation.

[5]*'The teaching of "comparative religion" is for older children, i.e. young adults, and for adults: it is unsuitable for younger children.'*

This is an educational cliché in this country, heard even from those who wield Bloom's taxonomy. The reasons given are usually: first, that the understanding of other religions is especially difficult (see our first cliché!); and second, that since the real point of religious education is to bring pupils to a position where they can make some responsible choice, it is silly to confuse very young and otherwise irresponsible children. The objections are at least as follows:

(a)   Some religious feelings overlap religions, so why should not children (sometimes supposed to be especially good on emotions if rather poor on concepts) enter into alien religious feelings?

(b)   Many young children meet children of other faiths – Jews, Muslims, Hindus, Sikhs. They need to come to terms with these other traditions which is to some extent within their own power.

(c)   Commitment is scarcely the only objective.

(d)   Religion is not divorced from life, and life is multifarious and planetary. Unless young children are to be deprived of realities (related to their own experience, hopefully) they will have a poor initiation into the ways of the world.

(e)   Traditional, biblically based religious education is no more suitable for young children than Buddhist analogues. But this shows nothing about the possible excitements of a wider perspective.

'A Christian cannot be committed to the teaching of religious values in competition with the Christian Gospel.'

This cliché derives properly from the 1944 Education Act as usually interpreted, and is not to be despised, for it contains an important existential truth about the recruitment and ethics of many teachers of religious education. One can well appreciate that the transition to the new R.E. could be distasteful and painful to many teachers of the subject. However, though this is important as a political and human factor, it should not entirely sway our thoughts about how to deal with religious education; and it should be set side by side with psychic wounds suffered by Jewish and many other young people (many ex-Christian) who have seen the insensitivity of a certain sort of 'commitment'. Anyway the cliché is silly because:

(a)   It depends partly on the *sort* of Christianity professed by the Christian.
(b)   The so-called indoctrinating policy in religious education (it does not matter whether the charge is true: it is *felt* to be by a substantial number of children and parents and others) is counter-productive and alienates many from the Christian faith. If the latter depends upon extending Sunday schools to weekdays, the grace of God is weak.
(c)   Very many people, perhaps all, are interested in religion and in making sense of the universe: this is true of children and young adults. They would be more interested in Christianity if it were not forced down their throats.
(d)   Most importantly: children and young adults are swift to perceive the difference between religious education and other subjects; they soon find out if there is an unacceptable bias in the presentation of Christianity – hence the alienation. Conversely, an open presentation of religious issues can arouse enthusiasm. In brief: even from the point of view of the Christian message the open situation is more effective – but this is not to say that preaching is the ultimate meaning of teaching religious education.
(e)   In bringing out the nature of Christianity or of any other tradition the education process in a sense presents it. In this respect there is no need for preaching! Let religions and religious figures speak for themselves.
(f)   A Christian should be committed to working fruitfully in the world. A Christian teacher should be, therefore, committed to good education and this may be incompatible with some attitudes (apparently but perhaps not truly Christian) which the cliché relies upon.

'Religious education is a matter for the churches – so it is the churches' attitude to other religions which should be taken most seriously.'

This is an institutional version of the previous cliché. It neglects any real distinction between denominational and maintained schools – in a way justifiably because the 1944 Act made 'establishment' assumptions (though stretching 'establishment' beyond the established church to other denominations). However, the general assumption that religious education is a matter for the churches is silly, because: [6]

(a)   There are religious groups outside the churches, e.g. Sikhs, Muslims and so on.
(b)   In any event it is not fully justifiable (to say the least) to suppose that a branch of education should be shaped by the interested parties who constitute the object of study and understanding; would we tolerate Politics Agreed Syllabuses determined by conferences of parties, including of course Plaid Cymru, Marxists, Conservatives and so on? If we did so it would be to protect fairness, not to propagate a particular political tradition.

'Teachers are so ill-equipped that teaching other religions could do much more harm than good.'

A good point in a way, but:

(a)   If so, the situation is a disgrace arising often from narrow and unacademic (i.e. badly biased) syllabuses in higher education, which has produced the teachers.
(b)   Where there is a will there is no need for a counsel of despair.
(c)   Anyway, teachers are not frozen by their training – and learning can be a co-operative enterprise: the teacher does not need to conceal his ignorance.

'There's no time for a decent treatment of Christianity, so …'

(a)   The small time devoted to religious education in schools is a symptom of its lack of esteem, arising from its *not* being the new R.E.
(b)   Whatever the slice of time, the times devoted to different areas within the subject should be a genuine reflection of the shape of the subject.

So much for some of the clichés. But now let us 'accentuate the positive' regarding the new religious education.

What is the new religious education?

It could be described as being a stage which goes well beyond the idea of 'open-ended' religious education. Why does 'open-ended' religious education need to be open-ended? Because it starts from a relatively closed position. It is fine in its way, but it is only fine within the context of the church. It is in a sense the church (in its teaching mission) at its best. But it is not essentially based upon the inner logic of the subject (if subject be the right word for the area of religion).

However, this way of presenting the new religious education is still negative. More positively: –

The new religious education is concerned with initiating young people into the meaning of religion and religions, and not only the Christian religion.

The new religious education recognizes that education in this area is dictated by the 'logic of the subject', namely:

(a)   The dominant religion of the cultural environment must be given the treatment which its dominance demands, but this must be seen in relation to the other principles contained in the logic of the subject.
(b)   Any religious tradition should as far as possible be seen from the point of view of those who belong to it; and more than one tradition should be presented to pupils or students.
(c)   Questions of the description of religions (important culturally and as part of the general education of people) should be treated descriptively, not distorted by external judgments of value and truth.
(d)   Questions of truth and value should be clearly seen as such.
(e)   The new religious education must elicit the religious dimension from the experience and reflective powers of the pupil or student.
(f)   The understanding of a religion should no more preserve beliefs, but bring out their living social and experiential context.
(g)   The bad side of a religion should not be ignored – within the framework of the principles cited above.
(h)   Non-religion and irreligion should find a place in the syllabus.

In brief, the new religious education tries to stare facts in the face; and to present the living world in all its rich plurality. Sympathy, criticism, plurality – these are some of the slogans the teacher needs to use in adapting his understanding to that of the pupils. The presentation of religion and religions must not be merely 'religious' however: that is, it is absurd to look on a religion without seeing how its institutions and psychology are embedded in the society or societies in which it exists. Or to put matters in another way, sociology must supplement history and the other disciplines needed for the understanding of religion. Further, [7]it is useless to discuss religion or to look deeply into it without recognising that there is a strong agnostic and atheistic secular stand in the modern world. It is absurd, for one cannot insulate pupils from the actual world.

In short, the new religious education is realistic, impartial, and sensitive. No indoctrination: only initiation into understanding, and so a resistance to the pressures one way and another of a conformist world. Questions of the truth of religion and religions need to be intertwined with questions *about* religion and religions.

It is a delightful and hopeful future that religious education has, provided that it absorbs integratingly 'the new R.E.'.

Ninian Smart is Professor in the Department of Religious
Studies of the University of Lancaster

CHAPTER 23

The Political Implications of Religious Studies

There used to be a model of the study of religion which in different parts of the world still persists somewhat, and that is the view that the primary purpose in studying a religion is to practise it, and that the main consequence of advanced study is theological expertise. This model is the traditional Christian theological one; in other forms it is to be found in Judaism, Islam and elsewhere. It assumes the truth of a given religious tradition or subtradition, and it believes that citizens' children and citizens themselves should be exposed to those ideas. It tends to think that the State is justified in using the money gained from taxpayers to pay the salaries of those who teach the tradition or subtradition in question. It is a model which has and still has immense influence upon humanity. Moreover, if we extend the study of religion to the study of secular worldviews it may stimulate us to reflect that the same situation prevails, secularly, in Marxist countries: a main job of schools and universities is to train people in scientific atheism and to drill them in the values of the Marxist tradition. Somewhat similar things may happen in rightwing countries too, where some local ideology will be *de rigueur*.

This model of theology and religious education may be generous-minded. It may allow that minorities, such as Jews, can withdraw from school lessons. Provisions may be made for Jewish higher education. It may be too that in some part of the theological faculty provision is made for the study of world religions other than the predominating one.

It is obvious that this model cannot stand up to the arguments for pluralistic study contained in my previous chapter. But the idea that we have a certain set of values which need in education to be handed on is a strong one. It is not it would seem unreasonable to set forth and transmit something of the tradition which has formed us. If we have a Christian heritage, then we should pass on the Christian faith as the norm. Such is the sentiment which lies behind the older model which underpins so much in education and theology in our schools and universities. But the model is fallacious – and indeed pernicious – and it has origins which should remind us of the ways in which it has fostered the oppression of minorities and even in many cases majorities.

The model is a hangover from the principle of *cuius regio eius religio*: citizens need to follow the religious commitment of the ruler, or in different terms citizens should obey the religious and ideological dictates of the government. The model depends upon the principle of established religion, or more generally of established worldview. In my opinion there should be no established worldview other than that implied in the doctrine that there should be no established worldview. The sooner our citizens are educated in this the better. Moreover, such a pluralistic principle is in accord not only with the spirit of the university but also with the new realities of our citizenry, which is drawn from many countries as well as the prevailing group, and which also espouses, even in the prevailing group, quite a number of different beliefs and non-beliefs, and of varying practises.

It may be replied that probably the majority approves of universal Christian religious education, and would be quite happy to have Anglican or Presbyterian divines in theological posts in Glasgow or Oxford. Even if the majority thinks that Christian religious education makes people into better citizens and better human beings, this is by itself no argument. The majority can tyrannize. One of the stupidest concepts of modern political life is that democracy consists somehow in majority rule. The only way in which majority rule where the minority is tyrannized is better than minority rule where the majority is tyrannized lies in numbers. The truly free country is one where the minorities have rights too. Moreover, the fact that the majority may believe that Christian education produces better citizens is fairly irrelevant, in that the majority can be wrong in any event in its judgments. Also, by the way, being a good citizen is not the highest state: the good citizen is taught to give up part of his wealth, and some of this goes to manufacturing arms with which to kill non-citizens. Citizens that do not follow government orders to kill non-citizens are deemed disloyal, and may themselves be killed. I am not saying that there are not just wars: but only that being a loyal citizen of a modern nation-State is not the highest ideal.

The idea of *cuius regio, eius religio* derives from an old thought, or rather from two old thoughts. One is the authority of the ruler: the other is that there has to be agreement in worldview for citizens who are joined together in a common State. The second principle is usually interpreted to mean 'a substantive worldview'. Kings debated whether to adopt Christianity or Islam, or Catholicism or Protestantism, or to stay with Yggdrasil or look instead to the Cross of Christ. They adopted Buddhism or Hindu cosmology as a means of rule; or Confucianism or State Shinto ... and so on. In Britain it turned out that the State religions rather sloppily, but excellently for the times, varied: the Welsh, with their 18th and 19th century Non-Conformism, and the Irish with their stubborn Catholicism, rebelled against official ideas. But the apparatus of a State religion in Britain, though much of it remains in place, is inappropriate, and this should have strong social, political and educational consequences, to which I shall come.

The United States of course has constitutional principles running in the opposite direction. It is true that priests and rabbis may say prayers at Inaugurations of Presidents: there is what Bellah has called America's civil religion.[1] But there is at the same time a ban on using taxpayers' money to subsidize chairs of theology or to finance the teaching of any one religion in school. It is constitutional to teach about religions, but unconstitutional to teach a particular religion, in the public school system. Of course pluralism allows private schools and private universities. If Harvard wants to have a Divinity School it can have one, and it can treat the teaching of world religions as an element in its operation. But the public system, both higher and lower, has been chary of any religious studies. Thus in the University of California, all campuses have departments or programs of philosophy, but only a minority have Religious Studies, and only one campus, Santa Barbara, has a fully fledged Department offering doctoral work. There are other State Universites which have no teaching of Religious Studies. The vast majority of schools have nothing on religion, save some historical scraps falling by the wayside of social studies. This leads to an irony in my life: in Britain I fight for pluralism against the assumption of Christianity; in the United States against the assumption of nothing.

If the United States constitution is the chief counterexample of the *cuius regio* principle, the chief exponents of the doctrine in modern times are less the rather enfeebled establishmentarianism of Scotland or Sweden, but rather the Marxist countries. Only we would now need perhaps to re-translate it, as 'Of whom the rule, of him the ideology' – *cuius regio, eius ideologia* or *cuius regio, eius philosophia*. This incidentally is where the question of the definition of religion becomes of great importance. Had Communism been treated as a religion or quasi-religion, it would have been hard for McCarthyism to maintain its impetus. Once we think in terms of worldviews, rather than something rather narrowly conceived of as religion, the applications of the rules begin to change in a very heady fashion.

This, by the way, might lead us to view the distinction betwen religion and the secular as itself an ideological distinction.[2] It draws the line a particular way which suits modern society, e.g. in regard to taxation, the definition of a charity, and so forth. It separates out religion and in some degree thereby tames it. Religion is assumed often to be a 'private' matter, and not something that can rightly enter into the main substance of politics. If the narrower definition of religion, distinguishing it from secular worldviews, is indeed an ideologically determined choice, then it needs to be treated with scepticism. But there are plenty of other grounds for not accepting a narrow way of looking at religious worldviews as if they were *toto coelo* differentiated from secular ones, as we have seen.

All this suggests that in a pluralist and democratic society, no worldview-affirming institution (no church in a very broad sense) should be officially adopted by the State. No citizen should be disadvantaged for holding to one worldview rather than another. As I have remarked, it is the Marxist countries which are now the chief exponents of the old principle, and it means that citizens are disadvantaged for not belonging to or affirming support for the official worldview-affirming institution, namely the Communist Party of the relevant country. Citizens may be disadvantaged for other reasons, e.g. being part of the left-over bourgeoisie, or for ethnic reasons, but primarily it is disloyalty to the *credo* of the rulers that brings problems, ranging from prisons and torture to lack of oportunities and advancement. Such States can claim to have religious freedom but this is not the

same as worldview-freedom, even where practise of cults is relatively open. So from the vantage-point of Marxist orthodoxy,
again, the narrower treatment of religion as in a separate categorial
basket from secular worldviews has a certain advantage. We may
note that in such States there is forbidden the teaching of religion;
State schools, which are the only ones, must teach scientific socialism; and to all intents there is official worldview-transmission.

The radical alternative to this is to have a pluralistic curriculum,
in which various worldviews are presented (in principle, all the
main worldviews of the world), and in which none is seen as the
'official' view: leaving choice openly to the students and citizens.

But it will be objected that this radical alternative is not after
all so radical: does it not itself imply a worldview? And so is it
not merely masquerading as an alternative path? It is really the
same idea, but presented in a more genteel and bourgeois and
Western fashion. I think we need to investigate to see that it
is in the way of a worldview which the pluralistic alternative
implies.

First, it implies an epistemology. It implies that there are no
absolutely clearcut ways of proving one religion over another or
one worldview over another. This soft epistemology implies that
worldviews are, from the angle of criteria and proofs, opinion.
Where opinions predominate then the educationalist points to
the alternatives; and the democrat allows for divergences of belief
in society. Only where there is proof would one be justified
in teaching anything with certainty as the truth, the 'received
opinion'.

In other words, a soft epistemology implies toleration. But there
is more than softness: there is productivity lying behind the
notion that we should have an open society. Knowledge advances
by imaginative exploration and criticism – not taking any position
as established, probing and seeking weak spots. This is the epistemology of Karl Popper. It claims that the open society, in encouraging criticism and debate, is a better engine for the production
of new knowledge than is the closed society. But we cannot
arbitrarily restrict enquiry, for instance by thinking of worldviews
as not open to debate, but of scientific hypotheses or literary
judgments as so open. So a society open in one way will need
ultimately to be open in all. And this entails pluralism.

But liberty is not simply something instrumental to greater
knowledge, important as that may be. It is something to which

individuals and groups have a right (the democrat may think), provided that in the exercise of that right they do not infringe the liberty of others. Now this principle, which I believe is that which in Western democracies we all at least pay lip service to, allows great variation of practice, but it does pull some of the teeth of the worldviews whose practice it makes room for. It is a tame Islam or Catholicism or Marxism that it may allow: it is Islam without Islamic society, Marxism without Marxist revolution, Catholicism with limited sway for the Pope. For how could a pluralistic democratic society agree to the Shari'sa as the law of the land, or to Leninist secret police, or to Papal dictates about censorship? So the Muslims, Marxists and Catholics who operate in a democratic society do seem to have their teeth pulled. But this does not mean that they do not have real freedoms in such a society.

The Muslim has the freedom not to eat pork, to arrange marriage in accord with Islamic law, to worship at his mosque, to pray daily, to go to Mecca. It is true that there are some restrictions on the full implementation of Muslim law, but he does have a large measure of traditional Islamic activity open to him. He will have more freedom than would a Bahai under Islamic law. So there is at least in principle a maximization of pluralism, to the greatest degree possible, that is, for one group in relation to the susceptibilities of other groups.

But all this is based upon a doctrine of human rights, and why should we accept *that*? This is where we return to the questions of epistemology. Only if you can be sure that something is wrong are you entitled to prevent someone else from doing it. Now some rules, against murder, stealing, lying, for instance, are necessary for the existence of any society, and so we need to obey them. But lots of other rules, about eating pork, marriage, homosexuality, etc., do not have this necessary status, and can be left as matters of 'opinion'. Moreover some issues, such as abortion, have ambiguous status for there are problems generated by conflict of rules. I would say that about a variety of religious and other practices we cannot, in the public arena, be sure. So these rules cannot be taught as certain nor imposed upon others. As a Muslim I may be against the sale of alcohol, but it is wrong to impose it upon all. But people are entitled to hold for themselves views and precepts which are deeply held. I would think, incidentally, in a pluralistic society there could be accommodation over such rules as marriage. Why should a Muslim in a pluralistic society not fully follow traditional Islamic marriage law, provided there is protection of the rights of women?

But this appeal to the softness of the epistemology is not going to be very agreeable to dedicated Muslims, Buddhists, Christians, Atheists, Marxists and so on. Will they not by definiton be sure of what their faith entails?

They are in one sense of 'sure' entitled to be sure of whatever it is that they are committed to; but this certitude is different from public certainty. If I may use the word 'certitude' for subjective sureness, and 'certainty' for public sureness; or if you prefer it 'certitude' for private commitment and 'certainty' for public provability; then, we need to distinguish between the epistemological softness as a publc matter, and private conviction. I may be sure that Geronimo is going to win the 2.30, but I have no right to erect that into a public fact before the event. As far as others are concerned it is just an opinion that he is going to win. It is ludicrous to suppose that there is a public proof of the truth of Christianity or of atheism. Those who have thought that there was such public proof have done much harm, in trying to force obedience to what should have been presented as opinion. There was no justification for the Inquisition, or for Luther's Biblical castigation of the Jews.

But does all this represent a worldview? Does pluralistic openness itself constitute a worldview? I would say not; but it does represent a theme in the spirit of the modern world, mainly since the Enlightenment. As such a theme it might be held to be a worldview-theme, if not by itself a fully fledged worldview. It is higher-order in basis, but it does have lower-order consequences.

Let me then admit that it is at least a thematic element which worldviews need to take account of. As a worldview-theme it may, despite being second-order, have that degree of softness in epistemology which we associate with other worldviews. But it is a powerful theme, and one that religious and secular traditions need to take seriously, and so try to work into the fabric of their own beliefs. In fact there are forms of liberal Christianity, Judaism, Islam, Buddhism and so forth which work pluralism into their schemes of belief and practice. In fact, liberal protestant Christianity was the main pioneer of liberal religion in modern times. It has been followed, through the aftermath of Vatican II, by the Roman Catholic Church, which now incorporates heady drafts of

Religion and the Western Mind

liberalism within its softening structure. It has been expressed
well in liberal Judaism in America and elsewhere.

But, it may be replied, if liberal worldviews are best, they
cannot be proved to be so. They fall under the rubric of epistemological softness like every other worldview. It may be so. But
let me just add a point which in this context in which we are
speaking and hearing, reading and writing is significant. There
is the context of the university. The university institution as we
understand it is one dedicated to the pursuit of truth, and it is
in its internal nature as such dedicated to the epistemology which
brings truth. It should be host to criticism and debate. It should
be open and plural. Largely, modern universities do have this
character. It is no coincidence that it was Lancaster, a new university, which advertized its Chair of Religious Studies as open
to someone 'of any faith or none'. Sir Charles Carter, the first
Vice-Chancellor, sometimes quipped that I was Professor of Any
Faith or None. It is not that universities always strictly follow the
principle of openness. Schools of thought develop and take over
Departments or whole disciplines. But it is surely impossible for
a university to deny the principle of pluralism, of open enquiry.
So even if such a worldview theme cannot in general be proved,
it has certainty within the commitments of the university.

There are of course matters of emphasis. Chinese should no
doubt do more work on Chinese history and literature, Russians
on Russian, Scotsmen on Scots, and so forth. No doubt a Christian
country will harbour more studies of Christianity than will a
Buddhist country, which in turn will have some emphasis on
Buddhism. But neither country would be right in shutting out
alternatives from its educational system.

There will be those who say or think: But learning about Buddhism will confuse the young, and might draw them away from
the Christian faith. What pitiful thinking! If the young are confused they have a right to be: it is a confusing world; and if the
presentation of Buddhism makes Christianity seem less certain,
so be it – it does, in one sense. Surely the Christian faith is strong
enough to see Buddhist virtues and learn from them: it does not
need the spurious shield of concealment in order to maintain its
vigour.

It would seem from these remarks that I am treating university
and schools on a par. I am by implication urging pluralism in the
high schools, in the primary schools even. That is right. I see no

reason why a subject should be in principle different at school level from what it is at university level. The degree of attainment will of course differ. The complexity of conceptual apparatus will be a good deal less at primary school than at high school or at college. But I see no special reason to think that we have some different *subject* at school from what we have at the university, and so the same principles ought to apply. If openness and pluralism are important at university why should they not be so in our schools?

There is a major point that needs to be put in parenthesis here. It happens that the teaching of Christianity in a non-pluralist tradition is hopeless and narrowly conceived. It has been common in Britain and some other countries to concentrate the teaching of Christianity on learning from the Bible. The reason for this is that at least differing Christians from diverse traditions can agree upon the importance of the Bible. There is also a very heavy emphasis upon Biblical enquiry in theological schools in universities and elsewhere. Now I am not one to say that the Bible is not important for Christians; but it is ludicrous as a source for learning about Christian life and Christian pratice, especially in the school context. In most Christian denominations the Bible is read in church: it is interpreted: it is woven into the very fabric of Christian living. Maybe it is the bones of Christianity, and the sacramental and spiritual life is the flesh. What is happening is that the Bible is plucked from its usual living context, and treated as a textbook.

More relevantly one would teach Christianity through a variety of living and historical examples, and no doubt the Bible would have to appear somewhat there, for it was precious to many Christians. Similarly it is best to treat of Buddhism by looking at the various dimensions: ritual, experience, institutions, stories, teachings, ethics, art. Through the lens of Theravadin Buddhism in Sri Lanka one could look back upon the texts of Buddhism. But it would be absurd to judge the whole of Buddhism by the texts.

The notion that it is best to teach the Bible because Christians agree upon the Bible also imports the wrong judges. The clergy are of course vital to the faith: but they are not as such educationalists and they are in fact nearer to being the living data than the teachers about those data. If Christians disagree about a lot of things that is something which the young need to know.

34   *Religion and the Western Mind*

It will show them that there are Christianities not a monolithic Christianity. If dispute between Christians is a bad thing (and I suspect some of it is, though some of it is not), then that is relevant to their judgment about the truth of the faith. They should look at it, warts and all. If they fall in love it will be despite some of the warts. So a better-fleshed treatment of Christianity is called for. But because chairs and syllabuses have been created in the past in the context of seminary-type training, and because ministers and priests need to be able to preach from texts, an excessive investment in Biblical Christianity is to be found in our universities, and far too little of the rich variety of forms of Christian spirituality. But all that is an aside.

The chief conclusion my argument comes to is that we ought to have education in plural worldview analysis in the schools, colleges and universities. Young people ought to learn about the mental geography of our planet, as well as the mental geography of their own country or region. But this is based upon a political principle, that there should be no established worldview-institution, whether church, mosque or party.

The natural drift of this is towards individualism: let the individual choose her worldview, her commitment. This is because the pluralism exhibits more nakedly the breakdown of authority. If there are real alternatives to the Pope, then loyalty to the Pope becomes elective. He is chosen, and he does not choose. So there is in the very process of crosscultural study an erosion of traditionally conceived authorities. But such erosion often leads to backlashes. In fact, if we conceive of the cultural complex which gives rise to emphathetic worldview analysis as a separate tradition, then when other traditions meet it, something occurs which is typical of the wider world, where traditions meet. A meets B and each affects the other, so that we get *Ab* and *Ba*. But this can generate a backlash. We get *Aa* and *Bb*. So in this sort of way you get a kind of traditionalist backlash, which at one level was represented in the writings of Karl Barth (other religions became quite irrelevant to the revelation of God in Christ); and at a cruder Biblical level in the teachings of the so-called fundamentalist Christians.[3]

The question to be posed here is whether those who at least in overt ideology are not individualists, who affirm the authority of scripture with great vehemence, who wish to create new Christian communities in a state of uncritical solidarity, can be coped with happily enough in my version of disestablishment? Can the more individualistic philosophy which I have presented deal with more collectivist and authoritarian views? I think so: for pluralism implies toleration for groups as well as individuals. If individuals give up their freedom to choose, by joining a sect, so be it. If Muslims or Buddhists wish to continue their religious and cultural customs, that in itself presents no problem. The only real condition attaching to such peaceful coexistence is that conversion be by persuasion and that the general, necessary rules of society be observed.

The individualism which tends to flow out of the pluralistic ethos is a rich individualism. It is not the restricted individualism of rationalist liberals and the classic libertarians. That is, it is an individualism which stresses the importance of groups and traditions. It wishes to walk in many moccasins: the green ones of Islam, the saffron ones of Buddhism, the royal blue ones of Eastern Orthodox Christianity. It wishes that such traditions maintain a degree of vigour, to increase human choice and insight. It does not demand that the individual have no family. It does not despise pedigrees and histories and mythic belonging. It loves what humans love, even when humans do not love individualism. It does not say that the human being need be alone. But it does say that the individual in the last resort makes a choice. If he does not like Catholicism after all, let him walk out. If she does not like purdah, let her cast off the veil. If she does not believe in humanism any longer, let her join a Church. And so on.

Does all this mean that the truth of worldviews is irrelevant? Does it mean that in the grey night of individualism all the cats of belief are equally grey? No: there is no need to assume that everyone is right, only that everyone has a right to be wrong. The varying sects and denominations and movements and churches and religions are all there with something to offer: without it they would scarcely survive. So I have no doubt that there is some truth or value in everything. But there are bad things too. It is for us to provide an education which at least helps the young to make up their minds about these things. They must become as far as possible *religiate*, worldview-sensitive. So there is no need to conclude with indifferentism or relativism. There are criteria of truth; but they are, we must recall, soft criteria. So we have to see at least darker and lighter shades of grey.

36   *Religion and the Western Mind*

The rich individualism which flows from the pluralistic viewpoint allows, then, for crosscultural empathy. In principle it
embraces the whole of human civilization as we know it today.
It provides at the same time the groundwork for a critical view
of one's own tradition and national culture. It appreciates
traditions, but it has some explosive things to say about our own
society. For one thing, it means disestablishment seriously.

In Britain the most serious educational entrenchments of
religion or worldview probably lie in the theological faculties and
departments. It is true that the number of Chairs explicitly tied
to clerical appointments is diminishing, and is not now great. But
it is no coincidence that the great majority of chairholders have
been Anglican clergymen, in England, and Presbyterian clergy in
Scotland. The position in England is more significant for many
departments of theology are in civic or what might be called
'state' universities, outside of the traditional faculties of divinity,
whereas in Scotland all posts styled 'theology' or 'divinity' are in
traditional faculties. In other words, the Anglican or more broadly
the ecumenical establishment moved out from Oxbridge after
World War II and happily ensconced itself in the new departments
of theology which were being formed or expanded up and down
England.

Now it is true that in a pragmatic way the departments of
theology began to accommodate a more plural perspective; but
keeping the name 'theology' was itself of some moment. To use
the term without a prefix (actually people studied Christian, not
Jewish or Islamic theology, except for a touch of Buber and Ibn
Rushd), was to affirm that there is such an academic study – as
if God were there, pure and undefined, waiting like the moon to
be an object of study. Without prefix the subject is fraudulent:
with a prefix it is egregiously particular, and cries out for pluralism. So although many fine things go on in theology departments
and though I myself sometimes practice Christian theology, I
would argue that the notion of theology *tout court* is inappropriate
to our times, and represents a neat way of affirming a kind of
ecumenical establishmentarianism.

Mind you, all this is a small matter. So many ways of arranging
academic divisions are irrational. But of course it is symptomatic
of a much larger question. If we cannot legitimately talk about
'theology' *tout court* it implies a recognition of alternatives that
would make an established religion also inappropriate. So let us

be clear, that the very pluralism implied in the conception of Religious Studies or of Worldview Analysis itself drives us towards a radical political view, namely that no one symbol or set of doctrines is adequate to the beliefs of the nation. For sentimental reasons, though, given the history of a country like Scotland, is it not surely all right to give the Kirk an honoured place? An honoured place, yes, but no preeminence in regard to belief or teachings. If my thesis is correct, then there should in an open society be no official belief, no worldview institution entrenched in the affairs of the State.

But what if, as in Ireland or Poland, a religious tradition is part of the distinguishing character of the nation? Well, that is something to tell in the story of the nation, the myth of identity; but it in no wise follows that the worldview in question should be given privileges of institution.

Because the individualism which flows from the field is what I have called a 'rich individualism' it does not really need much or any substance. Its body is above all procedural. It is methodological in stance: it asks us to recognize a certain epistemology, to use empathy in understanding others, to be tolerant. In this way it can make room for entertaining a rich variety of beliefs and practices; but it does not need to affirm any one worldview. So if it contains a worldview theme it is one of attitude rather than content.

The attitude of being openminded, empathetic and tolerant is not by itself enough to govern one's own life. One needs such attitudes in a liberal democracy; but as for the particular directions of one's own existence there is need for choice, and this involves choosing a substantive worldview. But the nation does not need a single worldview.

One of the reasons for this is that the nation is not after all the community of ultimate concern. Or it ought not to be. It only has provisional status. For the individualist should if possible be free to choose her nation too. It is true that we are born as Americans or Italians or British people. But one of the best things about human civilization at its best is the possibility of emigration. Now there are constraints upon it, very severe ones in certain cases. The use of that horrid instrument, the visa, is growing in some of the traditional immigrant countries, such as Australia. But it was a nice thing in the days when *cuius regio* was formulated that the dissenting citizen was free to leave, and mostly free to arrive. Despite the growth of the resources and demands of the modern State there is still some freedom to move. One of the great symbolic powers of America is that it is the land where virtually anyone could emigrate to: it was the great alternative to southern Poland or Sweden or Kampuchea. But in so far as it is a country based upon a constitution and upon the rights of the citizen, it sets a higher law above that of national feeling. It symbolizes, for all its patriotism, the transcendence of older ethnic and religious nationhoods. It symbolizes the fact that the nation is in the last resort not ultimate: it is not the very last resort.

If there is a society of ultimate concern it should be humanity as a whole. We are now arranged in nations across the earth, but our primary loyalty ought to be humanity as a whole. Nations are ways of giving people modernity and a sense of identity: but not, if I am right, ultimate identity.

This implies, by the way, that education should prepare the young of Scotland, California or Chad in the meaning of belonging to the whole of humanity. Here Religious Studies has a vital contribution to make in telling something of the story of the world's values. One of the effects of crosscultural study is the thought that there are fine things to discover in all cultural traditions.

One of the major political problems which emerges from these wideranging concerns is the tension between individualism and liberty on the one hand and economic welfare on the other. This happens as a result of the configuration of our world at the end of the colonial epoch. It is a reasonable hypothesis that some measure of capitalism is necessary for a pluralistic society. There are no cases of completely non-capitalist societies in which individual freedom exists. This of course is not to say that capitalism always *favours* freedom. Far from it: it often favours the Pinochets of this world. Repressive and corrupt dictatorship is often the choice of big companies. In its dealings with the people of the South, capitalism has often gone into alliance with varying forms of colonial exploitation. So there is often conflict between capitalism and the desires of the poor for a better life and for newly found national independence. So although capitalism in some degree may be so far as we can see a necessary ingredient in a pluralistic society, it is also often in conflict with desires for collective liberty, and may even be in conflict with ideals of political pluralism. It is not unreasonable for people in the Third

World sometimes to think that the solution to their problems may lie in socialism, a kind of anti-capitalism. Your enemy's enemy may be your friend.

Moreover, the pluralism I advocate may not be at first a primary aim of anticolonial liberators: solidarity and nation-building may be thought to be a good deal more important.

In this way, anticolonial movements shift in a variety of directions. But the world market is dominated by the North. The prices of commodities are fixed in London and New York, Chicago and Hong Kong. What can the poorer countries do?

The state of the world is reminiscent of the times when Roosevelt came to power. There are many, many poor in the world; but now we are not just dealing with the economic problems of a single, albeit large society, the United States, but with the whole world, as a single complex market-place. As Brandt and Heath recognized in their commission which produced *North–South*,[4] a kind of Neo-Keynesian solution is now needed on a world scale. More resources need to be put into the South, so that it can buy the products of the North. We need a new way to a cycle of prosperity, and that in turn involves sarifices which will yet be in the long term interests of the North. The programme envisaged is a kind of social–democratic one, on a global scale; and it may be that the function of governments is to act like unions on behalf of their citizens to exert pressures on the Northern multinational corporations. To all this a Marxian analysis is not particularly relevant. Human experience with welfare socialism, that is social–democratic, forms of economy is good; but with absolute socialism it is on the whole bad. And that is encouraging – for it augurs reasonably for relative freedom in the emerging countries, when they recognize the productivity of freedom.

But times are not propitious in other directions for individual freedom: computers create too much information and mis-information about people; we are currently in a conservative mood politically in many of the Northern democracies, and not all that active in maintaining a pluralist perspective; new technologies of brain control may emerge from neurophysiological research. So we need to be on our guard. And here the religions themselves can make a special contribution. For in so far as they speak with two voices, one earthly and the other heavenly, they may have a more potent direction from which a critique of secular values can be made.

Religion and the Western Mind

That is, given that now there has been a crumbling of authority, it does not mean that religion has become irrelevant. On the contrary that 'other shore' to which religion points and of which it speaks is the place from which to criticize this world. The task of religious doctrine is now one of criticism, not dogmatism. The visions which the faiths inspire are alternative pictures of this world, and modes of rescuing individual dignity from the toils of a technocratic civilization. So the aim of the study of religion – to understand the other – may be supplemented by drawing on those very resources which religion reveals, in order to criticize the shortcomings and oppressions of this world. This is where what I have called a rich individualism scores over the restricted individualism of an older liberalism. It is liberalism plus a variety of cultures, plus the depth supplied by the resources of the transcendentalist religions. It is Popper, empathy and heaven!

If the liberalism I have been advocating is against establishment in education, it is also of course against it in the State. In Britain religious establishment focuses finally on the Queen. I am not so radical as to say we should do away with the Royal Family; but we could surely evolve it away from its religious connections. If there is to be a way of entrenching pluralism it could be done through a Senate in which representatives of many differing viewpoints could be included, as part of some balanced way of inducing variety. But I am not sanguine about such structural changes in British society. Maybe the best that we can do is at least to begin to *think* plurally.

This will have great effects in all of education. In history it should mean that all history should be in the context of world history. It may be countered that we have enough to do already with British and European history. But with syllabus-designers we always have enough, more than enough. To cover greater areas you need to be more selective, of course. But that is not in itself difficult. Then in literature we shall have to be comparative. One of the best experiences I had when young was being introduced at Glasgow Academy to Russian literature by an eccentric but gifted teacher, who had no special business introducing me to Russian literature seeing that we were doing English literature. Since then I have had my life enriched by Turgenev and Dostoievsky. That Mr Crosbie was an educator with a feel for the wider world, and I here pay tribute to him. So: literature should be comparative, and set in world perspective. And the teaching of worldviews should be plural and empathetic, and only then critical. The teaching of science should be enlivened by the history of science so that young folk may see that most scientists in the past were wrong. Only in mathematics should we allow talk of proof! But even here Riemann and Lobachevski should haunt the geometers: let noone without these geometers enter the academy! The educated young person in Britain would be already feeling a world citizen, would be self-confidently critical in her opinions, and tolerant of varying points of view.[5]

All this might involve a weakening of traditional loyalties: if a Catholic, then a questioning Catholic; if a Presbyterian, a Presbyterian interested in yoga; if an atheist, an atheist with slivers of vision of the Beyond; if patriotic then critical of national values; if virtuous, then pluralistic in values; if committed, then freely committed. It is an ideal difficult to achieve, but it is implied by the logic of worldview analysis.

It might be argued that the ideal is not only difficult: it does not appeal to political leadership. Its erosion of obedient patriotism is not something which a government will wish to encourage. Why should taxpayers subsidize teachings which undermine the loyalty of citizens? On this several observations are apposite.

First, in so far as the world-wide, pluralistic outlook is itself a worldview,it is one that overlaps greatly with the ideals of liberal democracy. Now it may be asked whether there is not an implicit conflict between liberal democracy as a universal ideal and the particularism of nationality. There is such a tension. But a nation's citizenry needs more than just appeal to nationality if the continuing sacrifices demanded of it are still going to be willingly made. In the past, often the overriding ideological justification from intra-national altruism has been a traditional religion. In Marxist countries it has been Marxism–Leninism. In America it has been a blend of values including those of the Enlightenment, as embedded in the Constitution. So the fact that I appeal to universal values of global solidarity and critical pluralism is natural enough: there are no greater difficulties combining these ideas with British patriotism or any other variety than in combining (say) Christianity. In the one direction we have clashes between national interests and universl human concerns, in the other direction between patriotic war and the Lord's Prayer, especially in Spanish!

There is nothing noble in putting your own national or tribal group first in policy. We are often deceived into thinking that ethnic selfishness is noble because individual people, often young men, need to make the most stupendous sacrifice, of life itself, on behalf of ethnic interests. Extra-national selfishness depends upon intra-national altruism: often our citizens are sold on the latter by appeal to universal moral principles, so that teaching Christian values can be seen to coincide with teaching intra-national altruism. What is good for the tribe is found, in this way, in the Sermon on the Mount. And in a way death for the tribe would for many be unbearable if it were not that somehow it is death for humanity. Perhaps on occasion it is – as in the fight against the Nazis. But the Nazis themselves represent a disease of nationalism, not something which attacks the root of the patriotism that Churchill mobilized to defeat Nazism. Well, if we sometimes bring in universal principles to back national identity, why not see ourselves as pioneers of world civilization, of religious and worldview pluralism, or critical freedom? If the critical international pluralism which is presupposed by the very sinews of education is a worldview theme at least, then why not adopt it as our civil religion? No doubt we can find many resources in our own history to back up this theme? Britain has not been wanting in the voices of pluralism, universal humanity and critical freedom. In brief, if now we have the watery Christianity and partial democracy which serves as the worldview underpinning our tribal identities, why not equally switch to a more robust and universal individualism? Anyone who wishes to follow Christ can still do so.

Second, critical individualism is not in the long run against the interests of the State, so long as the State is concerned with the economic welfare of the citizenry. For the individualism and pluralism which I have been advocating are themselves vital ingredients in the development of modern technological capitalism. If there is a lesson to be learned by the contemporary economic state of the world it is to be found in the vital character of open education. In some ways British education is better than that found in California, but Californian education is having more punch in the development of new forms of high technology, and the reason I believe is that the young of California are more daring, ambitious and wide ranging in their interests. It is a heady brew of pluralistic living, with possibilities of exploiting new ideas. So we have in California a simultaneous revolution in ideas and living. It is not a coincidence that there are so many new lifestyles in California: the culture breeds both experimentation in living and in thinking. So it actually helps the State of California to broaden and deepen its tax base, this adventurous quality. For all its profoundly civilized merits, British education tends more towards conformism, of doing things thus because tradition tells us that things are indeed done thus. And because innovation is not widely spread the true inventions of Britain are not rapidly exploited, or their patents are sold in America and maybe in Japan. In brief, an open education may in fact be seen by rulers as in conformity with the interests of the State.

Third, the internationalist aspect of education fits with the growing facts of global life. We are increasingly in the world dominated by the transnationals, and governments themselves often function as agents and facilitators of the transnational companies. This being so, knowledge of the wider world is often a great advantage. If American education is weak in this respect, it is so far compensated for by two things – one is the relative, though by no means absolute, dominance of American-based transnationals; and the other is the fact that America contains still enough people who have come from anywhere you care to mention to provide a pool of talent and knowledge related to that region of the world. Even so, some educators in the United States are beginning to worry about the parochialism of Americn education, and it is indeed a factor in various errors and misjudgments in US political and commercial policy in the wider world.

So an open internationalist education is not without its attractions to our rulers. It represents a worldview-theme that can be built into our sense of national identity. But to do it effectively we need to drop the cant of establishment, the pretence that ours is a 'Christian country', the notion that we have some monopoly of common-sense and rationality. We need to defy the implicit claims both of theology and philosophy. It is perhaps a propitious time to cast off some of our traditional ways of thinking about education, for the crisis which afflicts so much of higher education in Britain and elsewhere means that we need new thinking to reshape our goals with the relatively limited resources we now have and to begin a push for recognition of the benefits both of economics and of the spirit that might arise from new freedoms.

But the revolution which we need, overthrowing the mental

controls which States tend to impose upon citizens, cannot simply be a revolution in one country. There is a final set of thoughts which the vision of openness generates and which maybe I can set briefly before you.

The revolution towards individualism and a tolerant openness does ultimately need to be universal in scope. Ultimately it is not much good if it is only citizens of the northern democracies who have equal rights, protection against the State and a reasonable standard of living. If the citizens of Cuba, Angola, Ethiopia, Chile, Peru, Algeria, Romania and so on are neither free nor prosperous, how can the free people of the North be happy? The logic of open education and a plural regard for others is that all human beings are our community. Patriotism erodes, save as the principle that we have a set of nations like families, nurturers of identity, but not having ultimate calls upon citizens. Yet there is so much in today's world which builds in the concept of the sovereignty of nation-States. It is assumed that though cruelties occur in this country or that the governments in question have at least a prima facie right to inflict them. Only in a few cases of flagrant villainy would others think of interfering. The case of Kampuchea is chilling. For policy reasons certain major states, notably the US, Britain and China, still recognize the Khmer Rouge succession against the Vietnamese-imposed regime. The latter is no paragon of virtue, but the former was relatively the most homicidal regime in the bloody history of the Twentieth Century.

It therefore seems reasonable for us to ask to whom is our ultimate allegiance? Which is our community of ultimate concern? For many, it remains the nation-State. Your ultimate duty is to your own ethnie. By 'ultimate' duty I mean: Who would you die for? To whom do you assign the power of life and death? It is for most people no longer the family or the clan.

There is as yet no world Government. Nevertheless, it is the teaching of many great religions, and it is in the logic of the present enquiry, that the ultimate community is or ought to be the human race. If we still have special bonds to our ethnic or national group, this is in itself no harm, provided a kind of utilitarianism prevails: we do not want everyone to be taking in each other's washing, and the division of the earth's surface among nations has a convenience to it that we should go along with. It is better for me to police my region and for Swedes to police theirs. But ultimately we are to be considered human beings. Basically we are persons, and secondarily Italians, Catholics and what have you.

For this reason, freedom of migration itself becomes a very important matter: it means that you are not tied down to being Soviet or American or British but can have the choice of lives and of nationalities. But the complex events of the half-century or more since the Nazis seized power in Europe mean that we are now perhaps sated with migrants and refugees. Maybe so: but the principle remains vital.

Fortunately the symbolisms of our world are making it easier for us to conceive of and indeed feel ourselves as part of a universal human group. Thus in the *Los Angeles Times* of 4 February 1985 we read:

> Sophisticated remote sensing devices in space, coupled with super computers that can process staggering amounts of information, have made it possible for scientists to plan a project that is so ambitious and complex that it would have been out of reach just a few years ago.
>
> The technology should be available within the next few years to permit scientists from a wide range of disciplines to study the Earth as a single ecosystem, increasing the odds that the planet will continue to support life in the future.

The item went on to describe a meeting in Pasadena lately to plan an international and interdisciplinary 'mission to planet Earth' – a project for answering questions about the earth as a total life-support system. Already such a project trails a large number of symbolic values. Already those pictures of the earth from half way to the moon give us a symbolic feel for such transnational plans, and make being a Russian or a Scot or a Ghanaian less significant. No longer is the human habitat something indefinite 'the wide, wide world': it is a beautiful green, blue and white ball, small against the infinite spaces which once frightened Pascal.

All this reinforces the need for education to help with the process of generating a sense of historical identity. We need, as I have repeated more than once, to teach world history, and to emphasize the multiplicity of cultural pasts to which this planet is heir.

46   *Religion and the Western Mind*

Out of all this a new world culture is beginning to emerge. We shall not escape backlashes as the acids of individualism erose some aspects of existing cultures. We shall all have to live in mingled ways with mingled worldview themes, and because this is uneasy for many people there will be small nationalisms and fervid demands for ethnic independence. The bomb and the bullet will still express the hardness of fanaticism, and will still serve those who recognize that the new pluralism does indeed soften older identities at the edges.

A federalism of tolerance gives more scope for difference than any of the homegenies: if ours represents a worldview-theme, it at least allows individuals and groups great freedoms to choose the worldviews that they will live by. Most people will get 80 per cent of what they might wish for, and that is a great advance on some getting everything and others virtually nothing. For power too has to be distributed among individuals and groups. Within the vast mosaic of human experiments in living there may be places where as yet individuals have little freedom. But with good fortune the time will come when indeed we can choose how to live. Those countries such as America and Britain which turn towards an open pluralism can pride themselves on being at the forefront of a movement when the Earth will be our only country, and diversity our watchword.

Notes

1. See Robert N. Bellah and Phillip Hammond, *Varieties of Civil Religion* (San Francisco: Harper & Row, 1980).
2. See David Martin, *A General Theory of Secularization* (Oxford: Blackwell, 1978).
3. *A Theory of Religious and Ideological Change: Illustrated from Modern South Asian and Other Religious Nationalisms* (Tempe: Department of Religious Studies, Arizona State University, 1984).
4. Willy Brandt, *Independent Commission on International Development Issues: Common Crisis North-South*(Cambridge, Mass.: MIT Press, 1983).
5. Karl Popper, *The Open Society and Its Enemies*, 5th edn rev. (Princeton University Press, 1966).

VI

RELIGIOUS ETHICS

CHAPTER 24

Gods, Bliss and Morality

I WISH here to review rather generally the relations between religious and moral discourse. At first sight, such an enterprise might seem odd or objectionable on a number of counts. First, some might think that there is no real distinction between the two; for is not such a commandment as ' Love thy neighbour as thyself' an integral part of spiritual discourse? Yet it is at least doubtful whether any moral principles or rules are entailed by specifically religious doctrines, except trivially (*e.g.*, where we have ' God's Will is . . . ' and ' One ought to conform to God's Will ': therefore ' One ought to . . . '). One does not require religious insight to see that lying or stealing is wrong; or, to put it a little more formally, one can justify such pronouncements without asserting anything which refers to a religious entity, *etc.* It is therefore convenient to make a rough distinction between specifically religious utterances and those which are specifically moral: thus ' God created the world' would fall into the former class, ' Adultery is wrong' into the latter. Perhaps, however, it will be questioned whether there is any clearly discernible field of discourse to be described as ' moral language'. For though moral philosophers have traditionally addressed themselves to such problems as the justification of social rules and the nature of (so-called) moral judgment, it is by no means clear which practical affairs are to count as falling under the aegis of morality and which judgments about people are to count as ' moral'. Is to commend someone as gay to make a moral pronouncement? And while most folk would say that the Wolfenden report is about morals, what pigeon-hole would a report on pensions fit into? Nevertheless, though it is unclear what the limits of morality are,

60   R. N. SMART.

and though within the area there is great variegation in kinds of assertion, a rough indication of the sort of discourse which we can call moral is possible: those assertions (*etc.*) which concern the dispositions and conduct to be cultivated by individuals so that their and their neighbours' lives will benefit or at least not avoidably suffer—these would hold a pretty central place in this sphere of language. Next, some may complain on the other side: ' It is foolish to talk about religious language—there is Christian, there is Buddhist, there is Hindu—very different sorts.' True; and it is grossly mistaken for philosophers (as they have so frequently done) to pretend to discuss something called ' religion ' when they have merely been speaking about Christianity or Judaism.[1] Nevertheless, there is at least a family resemblance between religions, and phenomenologists of religion have not been utterly frustrated in their attempts to adduce similarities: thus one does not always have to speak with incurable particularity. And though in this paper I shall confine attention largely to examples drawn from Western religions, some of the remarks will have a wider relevance. Finally—and this is the most powerful objection to my project: since both fields display much subtlety and variety, it would seem shockingly crude, in so short a space, to try to characterise the relations between the two. But I think that it does no harm to try to present a rather general picture, which can function as a kind of plan if one wishes to deal with individual and knotty problems in this area. Thus the intention of this paper is to provide certain preliminaries to the investigation in more detail of problems (*e.g.*, those clustering about *grace* and analogous concepts) which arise on the boundary between ethics and the philosophy of religion. As such, I wish to give something like a *description* of the relation between religious and

---

[1] A possible reply: Philosophers do not base their enlightened comments (on the nature of scientific explanation, *etc.*) upon discredited theories, though they may use these as a warning; why should not the philosopher similarly concentrate on examining the true religion? But criteria of truth here are so misty that it is presumptuous to pay exclusive attention to one faith.

moral concepts: I shall not therefore be indulging in philosophical *arguments*. These, perhaps, come later.

My task requires the exposition of certain points about religion which I shall have to state somewhat dogmatically. To this I now proceed.

a.

A striking aspect of spiritual discourse is its variegation. However hard it may be to translate into a foreign tongue common words for colours, shapes, objects, feelings, *etc.*, the difficulty is small in comparison with that which besets attempts to give the meaning of key expressions occurring in the discourse of an alien faith. This is mainly because each religion has a doctrinal system—or *scheme*, a word I prefer because it is less rigour-suggesting—and the propositions thereof have, so to speak, a mutual effect, such that not merely does one have to understand a proposition by reference to its neighbours, but the comprehension of a key expression requires the exposition of a number of central propositions at least. But further, even within a faith, the language is far from homogeneous. For example, in Christianity certain assertions are made about a Creator God Who is, so to say, beyond or behind the visible world; while others concern a divine human being Who lived within the world. Again, some propositions in Buddhism concern nirvāna, which is neither God nor man nor both. Already, therefore, we have three types of doctrinal proposition: those dealing with invisible and mysterious objects of worship, those concerning incarnate deities and those which deal with a mystical path and goal. These types of propositions (and it is sufficient for our purposes here to consider these three varieties) I propose to call respectively the *numinous*, the *incarnation* and the *mystical* strands of spiritual discourse.[2] And some doctrinal schemes are woven together from different strands and so are in a

---

[2] As in some cases and respects an incarnate deity is a limiting form of the saintly prophet, the range of propositions of this strand is wider than here indicated; but it is convenient to focus attention on the extreme cases.

62   R. N. SMART.

special way complex. But further, not all propositions in
a strand are of the same logical sort: *e.g.*, those about
nirvāna are sometimes expressions of its joys, sometimes
recommendations on how to attain it, and so forth.

An illustration of the weaving together of strands into a
complex doctrinal scheme is to be found in Brahmanism.
Here two disparate concepts are identified: Brahman, the
Sacred Power lying behind the visible world, and the Ātman
or Self, lying within man and attainable through mystical
endeavour. Again, in Christianity, Jesus, the sinless human
Teacher, is identified with the Father in heaven. These
points prompt such questions as: Why should the mystical
goal and the object of worship be one? Why should a
certain human be one with the Creator?

The first of these questions may be put in a sharper way
by asking why the Christian mystic should consider his
nirvāna-like state to be union with God while the agnostic
Buddhist does not so speak?[3] An account which covers
both the similarity between some of the things said by
Buddhist and by Christian contemplatives and their
doctrinal differences is this: that there are certain loose
resemblances between the mystical state and the object of
worship—both are timeless, glorious, transcendent, liberating and imperceptible.[4] Again an incarnate deity may
have likenesses to the Creator—He has the power to save
(by teaching and performatively through self-sacrifice); is
miracle-working (a sign of omnipotence); has deep spiritual
insight (a sign of omniscience); is good—and so forth.
The moral here is that the similarities justifying identifica-
tions in religion are looser than those criteria which would

---

[3] It is not just that each has been brought up in a certain doctrinal tradition,
so that the Christian mystic for instance ' reads into ' his experience Christian
doctrines: there appears to be an inner plausibility in the theistic account of
these matters—though I do not wish to imply by this that it is correct (nor by
this that it is *in*-correct).

[4] These predicates are applicable in often peculiar and diverse senses:
e.g., the mystical attainment is timeless and banishes the fear of death, while
God is immortal; it is transcendent because it is unworldly, while God is in
another world, *etc.* A proper exposition of these important and interesting
points is, however, impossible here.

justify a mundane claim that A and B are identical (consequently, while there may be a case for asserting a given identity in religion, it is not absurd to deny it). And, briefly, a complex doctrinal scheme has a certain artistic composition, so to speak, which makes the disparate elements hang together.

This point is relevant to the way moral propositions are incorporated into the fabric of spiritual discourse. That is, moral discourse, in the context of religion, functions like one of the strands of specifically religious discourse mentioned above. Thus (i) the justification for integrating moral and religious discourse lies in a somewhat loose agreement between certain moral concepts and certain specifically religious ones, an agreement which I wish to illustrate here; and (ii) the moral strand and the others have, as do the latter reciprocally, an effect on each other: crudely, the moral attitudes, *etc.*, of the religious man differ in flavour from those of the secular, while religion itself is moralised. It may be thought that the first of these points is hardly relevant to a descriptive project such as this; but it is often hard to penetrate to the meaning of an utterance without considering the sort of backing it would have. Actually, however, I shall be dealing not so much with the explicit justifications ordinary men might give for such claims as that morality in some sense presupposes religious doctrine,[5] as with the reasons why the integration has such convincingness as it may possess; though it is not to be thought that the considerations I shall describe have no place in explicit religious arguments. (Unfortunately, religious language itself is bedevilled in at least two ways: first, through having been mixed up with philosophical metaphysics, and secondly, because the logical status of religious concepts has been far from clear even to their

---

[5] These are often confused, and in any case may be formulated in language where the integration of morality and religion is already taken for granted. Further, in some circles only the ghost of an argument would be permitted— where there is fundamentalist appeal to the authority of the scriptures, for example (and this is not quite like someone's being irrational in purely non-religious matters).

64   R. N. SMART.

employers—so that, for instance, certain spiritual doctrines have been inappropriately taken as straightforward empirical pronouncements.)

b.

A central activity for one who is the adherent of a numinous faith is worship. For a God is by definition to be worshipped.[6] That is, the recognition of X as a God is a recognition that X is to be worshipped. An object of worship is holy and the adherent conversely unclean and sinful; and he expresses this profanity of his in awe-struck abasement, which is given ritual shape in formal worship. However, we discover that the notion of worship is considerably extended, so that the service of God in everyday life, through being virtuous and charitable, counts as a kind of worship. Thus it is written:

> Pure religion and undefiled before God and the Father is this, to visit the fatherless and widows in their affliction, and to keep himself unspotted from the world.[7]

And in a somewhat similar vein:

> Take my life, and let it be
> Consecrated, Lord, to Thee.
> Take my moments and my days
> Let them flow in ceaseless praise.[8]

But this kind of worship can only count as such if there is worship in the primary sense (*i.e.*, the religious ritual): otherwise we cannot know what it means to say that it is actions performed *in the right spirit* that count as worship. It may be objected that even if we had lost the notion and institution of ritual worship, there might still be a use for the word ' worship '—as in, *e.g.*, ' the worship of the State '.

---

[6] Though there are queer cases: *e.g.*, what are we to make of the attitude of Ivan in *The Brothers Karamazov* ? or of devil worship?
[7] *James*, i. 27.
[8] Hymn 256, Church of Scotland Hymnary.

But the important example here is: suppose we still spoke of ' worshipping God ', but all that would count as this would be visiting the fatherless, *etc.* It seems to me extremely doubtful whether we could understand this as a religious concept, nor could we easily comprehend the sense of the word ' God ' as used here. It would doubtless have the same status as ' ether ' in such locutions as ' The programme came over the ether '—a mere element in a stereotyped phrase: and so ' Visiting the fatherless is a way of worshipping God ' would be equivalent in import to ' Visiting the fatherless is a way of doing good '. But it would hardly have the same sense as it would in a *serious* religious context.

But though the existence of formal worship would be a necessary condition for counting daily conduct seriously as a form of worship, it is hardly a sufficient one. What would make the extension of the concept plausible?

(i) In any case, the concept *worship* is extended within the sphere of the specifically religious, so that more than a public ritual performance counts as worship. Private devotions of a certain pattern—these count as a kind of worship: it being seen that the so-called ' external ' performances without proper humility before God are useless, even though this humility is taught in part *through* the rituals. But further, in a monotheistic faith, God is given the most exalted value, is infinitely to be praised—so that it is insufficient to worship Him on fixed occasions (more will be said below on this).

(ii) More vitally, humility is an important moral disposition, since the common tendency among humans towards pride is liable to issue in conflict and suffering, while conversely humility involves a comparatively high prizing of others and so brings greater interest in their welfare. Personal abasement, then, before the All-Holy fits in with the disposition of humility which is important in moral conduct. The solidarity between the two is enhanced in monotheistic faiths by the above-mentioned infinite praiseworthiness of God. His utter transcendence

66   R. N. SMART.

is expressed by saying: We never sufficiently praise Him.
But at least we can increase the quantity and intensity of
our praise when daily actions performed in the right spirit
count as worship. In speaking of 'quantity' and 'intensity'
here I am formulating crudely two aspects of expressive
speech. For in the non-expressive giving of plain information, for example, repetition only has a marginal use—to
drum facts into the obtuse or hard of hearing, say; and
intensity of manner and verbal expression has no obvious
function here. On the other hand, in the expressing of
gratitude, for instance, repetition and intensity do count
for something: to repeat one's thanks is not otiose, and to
say seriously and sincerely ' My *immense* gratitude ' is to
express more, *ceteris paribus*, than is done by ' My gratitude '.
A further point: *sincerity* is what may be termed a ' pattern
concept ', for though it may be applied to particular actions
(*etc.*), the criteria for its application spread over a much
wider area; and to say that an action is sincere is to imply
(roughly) that it fits consistently into a pattern of actions.
Consequently, once the notion of worship is extended to
cover daily actions performed in the right spirit, the idea of
intensity in worship is affected: fervent praise will not be
thought to be truly so if it fails to fit into a pattern of
worshipful behaviour.

The performance of duties and services in a humble
spirit can, then, be presented as a form of worship. By
consequence, moral blemishes and inadequacies are to be
regarded not merely as failings, but as sins. The latter
notion is, indeed, incomplete without reference to some
numinous entity. Thus the Psalmist can say:

> Wash me throughly from mine iniquity, and
> cleanse me from my sin. For I acknowledge my
> transgressions; and my sin is ever before me. Against
> thee, thee only, have I sinned.[9]

Sin, then, is here moralised, inasmuch as it is not merely
the uncleanness of a profane creature before the All-Holy,

---

[9] Psalm 51.

but covers his moral wickedness (and this becomes a sort of uncleanness). Both *worship* and *sin* are thus given extended scope, beyond their specifically religious applications.

Another example of the way in which religious concepts (in the numinous strand) and moral ones exhibit a certain solidarity is as follows. Sacrifice is a religious ritual which is fairly closely linked, for a number of reasons, with worship. But, like other rituals, it can become mechanical and indelicate; so that, by way of protest, it is said:

The sacrifices of the Lord are a broken spirit.[10]

Here already there is a wide extension of the concept beyond its specifically religious use, leading to the notion that good conduct, or at least the dispositions leading thereto, are a kind of sacrifice. Now although sacrifices have often been offered to the gods in order to buy them off, much as one might give presents to the powerful to sweeten them, the deeper spiritual point of sacrifice is that it is a gesture of expiation, and the object sacrificed a token. (In speaking of a deeper spiritual point, I am aware that herein lies a value-judgment, and there are many objections to using valuations when one is engaged on a descriptive task; but the deeper point mentioned does exist, and it is not entirely unphilosophical to be charitable in matters of interpretation.) Sacrifice is a gesture of expiation, for words alone are not sufficient to express properly man's abasement before the numinous and the sincerity of his worship. This idea of something's 'going beyond mere words' is interesting to investigate, and is connected with what was said above about repetition and intensity. For whereas it might well be deemed absurd to speak of some factual matter as inexpressible, as eluding description—since language defines, so to speak, the realm of the possible[11]—when we come to

---

[10] Psalm 51.
[11] Though: (*a*) certain things may be very hard to describe, *e.g.*, a complicated piece of machinery; for the uninitiate it is too complex and unfamiliar to describe. This is contingent indescribability. (*b*) There may be 'facts' no-one can describe, because science has not yet given us the conceptual framework.

expressive (and some other) modes of speech, it is by no means suspect. For here the notion of something's being ' too much to express ' has a use, for already we are in an area where quantitative expressions have (in a peculiar way) application. Nor, since here speech is often in a narrower sense a way of doing something, is it absurd to speak of non-linguistic performances as transcending speech. Thus a gesture, for instance, is a manner of transcending language when there is, say, a felt necessity to render a situation morally tolerable. If A saves the life of B's child, B can only make the situation tolerable by performing a gesture as a pledge of his continuing and overwhelming gratitude: for instance, he can invite A's children on a long summer holiday. But what counts as an appropriate gesture is governed by the most delicate rules—many such gestures seem gross and unfeeling, as with the rich man who repays kindnesses by gifts of money.[12] Hence indeed the Psalmist's protest. For though by giving up a prized possession—a ram or a bullock—one performs a gesture of expiation, it may not be a good one. But a broken spirit? How is this a sacrifice? What plausibility is there in holding that a moral disposition counts as an expiatory gesture?

Nothing is a sacrifice unless something is being given up; and holy conduct is a sort of giving up for the following reasons: (i) There are many occasions on which the performance of duty conflicts with self-interest. Indeed, if it were not so there would hardly be a practical use for the word ' duty ' and its cousins—a point which is probably responsible for the idea that nothing counts as a duty *unless* it so conflicts. (Though also this idea is in line with the ascetic outlook of Puritanism: on asceticism, see below.) And failing to attain one's interests is a sort of loss, even if not always of the sort we call ' tangible '. (One might

---

[12] There are of course other uses of ' gesture ' besides cases where the balance between two or more people is upset: *e.g.*, the Hungarian who shakes his fist at a Soviet tank—a gesture of defiance (not, however, entirely unconnected in type from the unbalance cases). Also obviously, the behavioural sense. Incidentally, speech-transcending actions are clearly relevant to a discussion of religious ineffability.

draw a distinction between tangible and intangible sacrifices: and compare visible and invisible exports—the latter need not be ' ex- ' and cannot be ported, but it is still useful to have the word.)   (ii) Ascetic training—the giving up of certain pleasures—is sometimes thought to conduce to virtue, inasmuch as dispositions are created which facilitate the correct decision in the event of a conflict of interest and duty.   Although asceticism plays a more prominent spiritual rôle in mystical rather than numinous religion, it has a part to play in the latter, both as a way of atoning for sins and as a method of directing our thoughts and inclinations away from the world towards the things of God.   (iii) Self-indulgence, it is often thought, leads to unhappiness, both first- and second-order, *i.e.*, the unhappiness directly occasioned by indulgence and that which accrues upon recognition of one's own wickedness and weakness.   In such ways, then, moral conduct aimed at the production of others' and one's own happiness is considered to involve some degree of giving up.   Thus is the path open for an extension of the notion of sacrifice so that a man's life or stream of conduct can count as a holy and living sacrifice to the Lord.   And so he can do something to expiate his sinfulness and moral unworthiness.   (Note that even in the quotation with which we started, which might be used out of context to show that religion is simply or mainly a matter of doing good, there is the requirement not merely that we should visit the fatherless and widows but also that we should ' keep ourselves unspotted from the world '.)

I have given two instances of the superimposition of religious upon other concepts.   The effects are often subtle and difficult briefly to explicate.   But one point worth mentioning is that, though there is an independent application for the notion of happiness, the major goal of life is thought to be salvation.   (Here, by the way, the conflation of morality and numinous religion results in disputes about faith versus works as being necessary or sufficient or both conditions for salvation.)   Further, specifically religious duties remain, so to speak, at the centre of life; and in themselves constitute the chief difference in content between secular and religious morality. Often, by consequence, a believer's path will diverge widely from that of the non-believer—as when a man dies for his faith. Another effect is that since a supremely Holy entity is regarded as being the source, in some way, of all that is holy, holy conduct has as its source God, Who is held to grant grace to His devotees. And it is not just that God is supposed to have the power to release the worshipper from his religious uncleanness, but given that sin comprises moral unworthiness as well, He can give him grace to do good and avoid evil. (And it is a good indication of the difficulties besetting analysis of this notion that grace is connected with a numinous object of worship, whose status, so to speak, is already obscure.) Two further points. (i) The superimposition of religious upon moral concepts as illustrated above gives the latter a different flavour: (*a*) because a moral action will have a double significance (not mere kindness, but consecrated kindness; not mere self-control, but a sacrifice, *etc.*); (*b*) because the solemnity of moral utterances becomes considerably increased: it is not merely that murder is wrong, but that life is *sacred*; a bad action is *sinful* and *impious*; discrimination against black folk in South Africa is not merely a great injustice, but it is (to quote a Churchman's recent pronouncement) *blasphemy*; marriage is more than a fine institution, it is a *sacrament*. (ii) The presentation of morality as part of numinous religion involves it in the conservatism of the latter (which is due to two main factors: first, the inexcogitability of revelation means that the ordinary man is discouraged from formulating his own beliefs and so must take doctrines on authority; and secondly, there are social causes for the entrenchment of religious organisations.) Hence, although there are ways and means of reforming the moral teaching of a faith in accordance with scientific, technical and social changes, there is much greater difficulty here than where moral beliefs are thought not to have divine sanction.

Finally, two general remarks on the preceding. First,

it might be objected that when one ' does all to the glory of God ' one is performing many actions which lie outside the area of morals—for instance, in doing one's daily work ' to the glory of God ' one is not performing works of charity, *etc.* Are not discussions of humility and asceticism beside the point here? A brief answer: roughly, we tend to regard the spirit of what we do (of whatever sort this is) as falling within the purview of moral judgment and training. Thus, we praise a man for playing a game fairly and enthusiastically, and this is a kind of moral praise: though the rules of the game could not be thought to be *moral* rules, and success in the game is not thought to be, in normal circumstances, morally praiseworthy.[13] Second, the foregoing illustrations of the extension of religious concepts should not lead one to suppose that the performance of duties, *etc.*, in the right spirit is simply to be justified as being religious acts. The good is not good because it is the Will of God, but because it is good. On the other hand, the good is not the Will of God just because it is good, but because it has divine qualities. Much of the structure of independent moral discourse remains, even though morality is integrated with religion; just as much of the characteristic language of mysticism remains even when it is woven into discourse about God.

c.

Because of its convenience and familiarity I shall use the Christian doctrine of the Incarnation to illustrate briefly the relation which this sort of belief bears to morality. (i) The doctrine involves a deepening of the points already made about humility and sacrifice. For the teaching here is that only the self-sacrifice of God could be enough to expiate the enormous weight of sin upon mankind and to bring about atonement.[14] But God could only achieve this

---

[13] As a commemorative plaque in the Wanderers ground in Johannesburg has it: ' And when the one great Scorer comes to write against your name, He writes not how you won or lost, but how you played the game.'

[14] Christ is not a sacrifice the way a lamb might be or the way Isaac was intended, in that His death on the Cross was voluntary. He was not offered by others as a sacrifice, nor is God wicked in providing a human sacrifice.

in a state of solidarity with mankind: hence the obstinate rejection by the Church of any form of docetism—it must insist on the humanity of Christ as well as on His divinity. This seeming paradox that Christ is both God and man[15] brings new light to the religious 'demand for humility. Christ himself seems to exhibit the most profound humility; and He is, because divine (and uniquely so among humans) the central model for imitation. We too must take up our Cross. (ii) The abasement and suffering of Christ is on behalf of mankind: our most luminous evidence that God is Love (a point foreshadowed in doctrines of grace; and one which finds some, though ambiguous, backing in the claim that God is Creator.) Hence there accrues a tighter knitting together of the moral demand ' Love thy neighbour as thyself' and the spiritual one ' Love God '. (iii) As mentioned above, the belief that a human is divine, and uniquely so, implies that there is one supreme life to model our conduct on (models are one main method of inculcating moral insight). This, incidentally, has both an advantage and a defect: for while it harnesses the resources of worship and meditation to the task of self-improvement, a single main model is likely to be hard to apply to the varied circumstances of many lives. Note also that the life to be imitated is a religious one (though the religion of Christ might be thought to differ in certain particulars from that expected of the ordinary adherent) and this serves to cement the moral and religious requirements in the faith. (iv) The Teacher founded a Church, membership of which is thought necessary or conducive to salvation: this creates special loyalties and obligations for the faithful. These are given supernatural expression in such notions as ' fellowship in Christ '. (v) Finally, certain concepts concerning Christ are given application to individual lives. Thus:

---

[15] It is doubtful whether the God-manhood of Christ is a strict contradiction, *e.g.*, Christ was for a time in Galilee while God is from eternity in Heaven, and Christ is God: does this constitute a contradiction? Only if Heaven and Galilee are both places in the same sense of ' place '.

> Like as Christ was raised up from the dead by the glory of the Father, so we also should walk in newness of life.[16]

Christ's resurrection, though claimed to be a physical fact, has a significance beyond the marvel of a man's rising from the dead. It is a demonstration that Christ has overcome death, though this is a peculiar sort of victory (and a peculiar sense of ' death '). For the victory is so described partly at least because Christ has saved mankind. But this saving is only hypothetical: if such-and-such conditions are fulfilled you will be saved (not: you are saved in any case). And one of the conditions is a change of heart: you must repent and believe. This conversion is a ' new birth '. What might at first glance appear a merely metaphorical use of a phrase can hardly be considered as such in view of the ramified nexus of analogical expressions connected with this one (the converted die unto sin; this also through grace, wherefore Christ is life—which is borne out, so it is said, in the spiritual life: for me to live is Christ.)[17]

Again:

> And they that are Christians have crucified the flesh.[18]

The notion ' crucifixion of the flesh ' is applicable to expiatory asceticism in virtue of the extension of the concept *sacrifice* as explicated above and of the history of the divine model's career.

In such ways, then, certain spiritual concepts prominently instantiated in Christ's life are applied also to individual lives.

Briefly, then, while the main point of Christ's career is his specifically religious rôle as Saviour of men, his words

---

[16] *Romans*, vi. 4.

[17] Unfortunately it is hard to see any dividing line between analogical uses of expressions in religion (*i.e.*, non-literal but indispensable ones) and mere metaphors and allegories, *etc.* But one rough test is to consider how closely related a locution is to central doctrines. Some expressions in religious discourse are not, of course, non-literally used, *e.g.*, ' god '.

[18] *Gal.* v. 24.

74   R. N. SMART.

and conduct illustrate in a profound manner the way numinous religion and morality hang together.

d.

Mysticism is usually or always associated with some degree of ascetic training. Through such endeavour (known variously as ' the Path ', ' the Way ', *etc.*) one attains a blissful goal (in this life). The purest form of this goal—inasmuch as there is no theistic complication of doctrine—is the Buddhist aim of nirvāna. This is given such epithets as ' The Other Shore ', ' Peace ', ' The Immortal ', ' The Unshakeable ', *etc.* For in gaining bliss we go beyond the impermanent and painful world, attain calm and detachment, lose the fear of death, *etc.* These epithets serve to indicate, perhaps, that there is (as claimed earlier) a pattern of loose resemblances between nirvāna and an object of worship; but it is not of course a God. It is this principally that makes agnostic Buddhism so unlike Christianity, Judaism and Islam—the faiths we have the greatest acquaintance with in the West. And even the traditional gods of Indian religion are assigned the status merely of somewhat remarkable items in the furniture of the impermanent universe. These facts account for the disinclination felt by some to calling Buddhism a religion. Nevertheless, the mystical quest occurs also in theistic faiths, and there are certain other resemblances we can point to; and so we are justified in giving it the title of a spiritual system. There are two aspects of agnostic Buddhism which I wish to draw attention to, since they throw light on two general points about mystical religion.

First: the *anicca* doctrine, that all things are impermanent, is a mild form of those idealistic doctrines commonly associated with mysticism in which the world is declared to be unreal or not fully real.[19] At first sight, we might wish to dismiss such doctrines as being, metaphysics-wise, vacuous through

---

[19] The use of ' fully ' and other such adverbs is significant here.

lack of contrast (all life, surely, cannot be a dream, for the concept *dream* gains its force from the contrast of dreaming and waking.) But such criticism would pass the mystic by, for there is, so to speak, an *inner* life which is real. The world is illusory or impermanent: but not the Ātman, not nirvāṇa. And a sense can be given to ' inner ' here (whether or not a sense can be given to the rather different philosophical inner-outer distinction enshrined in such phrases as ' the external world '), because a method of training is laid down as conducive to spiritual well-being, and this involves the rejection of ordinary interests and pleasures: it is, roughly, this range of enjoyments that delimits the ' external world '. This mystical ascetic training has, incidentally, a likeness to the abnegation practised by worshippers to atone for their sins, and is peripherally one of the considerations making the identification of the numinous object with the mystical goal convincing. It may be mentioned also that a full-blown mystical idealism fits easily into the theistic picture: the inner state is outside the web of unreality, and so is God—the one on the hither, the other on the farther side, so to speak; and this may help to explain the moderate idealism of early Buddhism, for indeed the extreme Mahāyānist idealists paved the way for theistic forms of the faith. Briefly then, the idealistic beliefs function as a picture advertising the mystical quest. Normally, therefore, since many moral issues concern the so-called outer world, a mystical faith will tend to pay little attention to these, and will be quietistic. On the other hand, this tendency is mitigated by three factors: (*a*) idealistic doctrines are not likely to affect the content of ordinary moral rules to any great degree, since practical affairs nearly all fall within the orbit of the illusory world, and there is no special reason to abandon ordinary moral distinctions within that sphere—any more than there is to abandon colour-contrasts. (And certain mystical theologians make a contrast between higher and lower knowledge: thus Śaṅkara distinguishes between the two in a manner which corresponds with his distinction between the

76   R. N. SMART.

higher and lower Brahman—the former being without attributes (nirguṇam), the latter with attributes (saguṇam); the latter is the Lord and object of worship, and the performance of moral duties goes with the ceremonial worship, *etc.*, due to Him: in such ways characteristically theistic doctrines and practices have a place even though ' in the highest truth ' the world is illusory.)   (*b*) Belief in rebirth takes an edge off the rigorous demands of mystical religion, since the ordinary adherent who does not tread the monk's path can hope to raise himself in a future existence to within striking distance of the supreme spiritual goal.   (*c*) It is generally considered that no-one can attain the goal who is not morally good: the cultivation of benevolent dispositions and others is part of the spiritual training.   This indeed is the second aspect of agnostic Buddhism I wished to draw attention to: that moral training is built into the Noble Eightfold Path.[20]   This is understandable in two ways.   First, the mystical goal is, after all, merely a very peculiar *summum bonum*: herein, it is claimed, lies the highest joy, and therefore the truly wise man will tread the Path.   So a moral code containing a recommendation of this as the right aim would not differ in structure, one would expect, from that with more mundane goals: one aims at happiness (of whatever quality) in accordance with virtue.   Secondly, the dispositions to be cultivated as morally important are in line with the ascetic requirements of the mystic, though the latter involve more rigour (hence the difference in rules laid down for the layman and the *bhikku* respectively in Buddhism).   In addition, detachment from worldly interests is assisted by the cultivation of impartiality.[21] Finally, the picture of the saintly *arhat* who has attained nirvāṇa is that of one who has undergone a transfiguration of character, and the calm and radiant peacefulness

---

[20] The third, fourth and fifth stages are: right speech, right conduct and right mode of livelihood.

[21] An important segment of Buddhist spiritual exercises is concerned with the cultivation of dispositions such as universal compassion (*Visuddhimagga*, ch. iv).

of such a man is presented as a glorious example to follow.[22]

e.

The outline that I have given will, I hope, help to throw light on the peculiarities of such passages as the following (written by a theistic mystic):

> You must understand that, as Saint Gregory says, there are two ways of life in Holy Church through which Christians may reach salvation; one is called active and the other contemplative. One or other of these is necessary to salvation. The active life consists in love and charity shown outwardly in good works, in obedience to God's Commandments, and performing the seven corporal and spiritual works of mercy for the benefit of our fellow-Christians ... Another requirement of the active life is the disciplining of our bodies through fasting, vigils and other severe forms of penance. For the body must be chastised with discretion to atone for our past misdoings, to restrain its desires and inclinations to sin, and to render it obedient to obey the spirit. Provided that they are used with discretion, these practices, although active in form, greatly assist and dispose a person in the early stages of the spiritual life to approach the contemplative life.[23]

Gestures of atonement, the cultivation of good character and mystical asceticism can plausibly be thought to hang together. Probably it is the convincingness of the pattern of doctrine and moral teaching that would tend to justify those who loosely assert that morality presupposes religion, rather than any dry arguments about the objectivity of ethics or the evolution of conscience. In any case I hope to have given enough description to have shown (what is

---

[22] Though the picture lost much of its appeal: one of the main motives in the development of Mahāyāna Buddhism was the feeling that the Hinayāna aim was too self-centred.

[23] William Hilton, *The Ladder of Perfection*, trans. L. Sherley-Price, London (1957).

78   R. N. SMART.

perhaps obvious) that an analysis of religious moral language requires an investigation of such concepts as *atonement, worship, sacrifice, sin, grace, holiness,* and so on: it is not just that religious people, while sharing principles, have different factual or metaphysical beliefs. There may, however, be those who would be indifferent to such investigations because of a prior rejection of religious beliefs. Yet these enquiries ought to have some interest even for them. For instance, if my cursory attempt at sketching some of the relations between spiritual and moral concepts is in any degree accurate, it may help to show the kind of absurdity which (on their view) characterises religious morality.

CHAPTER 25

The Ethics of Chinese Communism

[This item has been re-keyed. Page numbers in square brackets have been inserted to indicate the format of the original.]

The ethical dimension of Chinese Communism and of the thought of Mao Zedong is partly shaped by the logic of Chinese reconstruction. In order to act as normative inspiration for individuals collectively engaged on building a new China it has needed to have both a continuity and a discontinuity with the Confucian past. That there will be discontinuity is of course guaranteed by the fact that we are after all dealing with Marxist morality, even if Maoism diverges markedly in some respects from Soviet and other Western interpretations of the tradition. It has a different class basis from the old ethic.

But we can look more deeply at its contribution to reconstruction. Let me sketch a few features of China's situation in the period before and during the transition to the Communist Party's victory. First, China was a particular case of the general dislocation caused to non-European culture brought about by the impact of Western empire, trade and penetration. China, like other major cultures faced with the challenge, needed to work out, in the hot muddle of historical changes, how far her traditional heritage, Confucian, Taoist and Buddhist, could be harnessed to the goals of dignity and independence. Unlike India, which for various reasons found in a neo-Hindu ideology an admirable vehicle for reshaping Indian values and exploiting the weaknesses of British imperial rule, the Chinese tradition for its own reasons was unequal to the modernizing task. Buddhism, admirable and subtle as it might be, was too pacific and otherworldly to give backbone to the flesh of a new nationalism. Taoist magic was not in temper with the scientific and technological genie which had been released from the Western bottle, and its anarchistic passions were at variance with a newly demanded centralism, if China were to restore her old power. Confucianism suffered from too close an integration with the old hierarchical administration which had already crumbled; its educational ideals were no longer relevant; and its ethic lost its meaning in the chaos and poverty of the warring years between the two world wars.

Second, a damaged society is in some respects like an individual in trouble. The way forward out of despair lies with internal change, with inner reform, a kind of conversion. A condition of China's success in expelling both Japanese imperialists and the internal incubus of a corrupt Guomindang was the supplying of a vision of a new China. The revolutionary character of Marxism was a vital inspiration because of the very sharpness of its demands for a quite new structure for Chinese society.

Marxism, moreover, had some other helpful properties. It claimed to be scientific and so it had for China a modern air. It stressed the solidarity of theory and practice, a solidarity much in consonance with China's Neo-Confucian past, and so it promised that science would not just stay at the refined level of theory but would reach deep down as a magic to replace the sacrifices and incense of the old peasant culture. If India took its own heritage and gave it a Western form, some other cultures have done the opposite – taking a Western ideology and giving it indigenous meaning: this is precisely the achievement of Mao Zedong. Moreover, Marxism had this inestimable attraction: while Western and so 'modern' (such is the ideology of the times), it was anti-Western, because anti-capitalist, and so anti-imperialist, and so anti- the forces of Europe, America and Japan whose marauding and trading had weakened the very fabric of Chinese culture and society. [90]

Marxism too supplied a mythic sense of destiny. To young Chinese of the twenties onwards it made sense of China's historical predicament. The Russian revolution was the sign and signal for a quite new turn in world processes. The dialectic of history, made concrete in October 1917, the May 4th Movement of 1919, the struggles in Kiangsi, the Long March above all and in the Liberation, provided a pattern of ongoing meaning and the material for faith: faith which was necessary as an engine of revolutionary success and powerful reconstruction

The evangelical character of Maoism, as it came to be used in the new China, was reinforced by the fact that its materialism was not just materialist, to put the matter paradoxically. What I have in mind is two features of Marxist attitudes in general and Chinese Marxist ones in particular. First, and this is of course much stressed in the writings of Mao, the spiritual or human factor is vitally important: power may grow out of the barrel of the gun, but it is the eye and brain behind the sights which determine its effectiveness. The so-called voluntarism of Mao's thought can be exaggerated, but yet it is there, and the correct analysis of the 'objective' situation is a crucial factor in its transformation. Thus Marxist materialism turns out to be, from the practical point of view, itself a means of transforming consciousness which in turn helps to determine material events. Second, material existence comes to be invested with a high symbolic content. The visitor who is given so many statistics of new production – hectares and kilowatts and yuan – and shown the new fruits of the revolutionary harvest – dams, brick houses, pigs, pigiron, homegrown tractors, school rooms, noodles and cucumbers – is of course involved in a kind of celebration. These material facts are important because they have symbolic weight, a kind of spiritual glow. Why? Because the houses and dams, the noodles and the cucumbers mean dignity for folk once trodden down; the tractors and steel plants mean a new China, still poor but with energy and nobility showing its prowess to its old enemies and its new friends. The pigs have haloes, and the newly planted walnut trees put out meaningful leaves. In brief, matter is more than matter, and the materialism of Maoism is what may be described as 'symbolic materialism'.

Because Marxism was the key to the reconstruction of China and because Maoism, in espousing guerrilla warfare and peasant revolution, gave a needed Asian twist to Marxist analysis, it had to have both an international and a national significance. It had to be universal truth to stand up to the universals of the invading West; but it had also to be strongly national. As Mao wrote in 1941:

> For a hundred years the finest sons of the disaster-ridden Chinese nation fought and sacrificed their lives, one stepping into the breach as another fell, in quest of the truth that would save the country and the people. This moves us to song and tears. But it was only after World War I and the October Revolution in Russia that we found Marxist-Leninism, the best of truths, the best of weapons for liberating our nation.[1]

And for the evangelical purpose of social reconstruction it was good that the analysis upon which the ethics depended could be seen as universal, while the nationalism inherent in Mao's whole struggle provided a general framework of identity which could give fire and substance to the material efforts of the people.

Incidentally, there is an obvious and often overlooked point about the very idea of 'the people' or 'the masses'. They are defined – as 'the Chinese people', and so on – in the modern world by national identity. Inevitably, Marxism becomes entangled in nationalism, which is of course the most powerful ideological force in twentieth-century history.

Some of these points can be illustrated by the moral examples which have been held up to the Chinese – for ethics are taught not merely by the deduction of action from principles, but also by the example of heroes and the telling of parables. [91]

First, the internationalism and so universality of the ethic is illustrated in the life of the Canadian doctor Norman Bethune. As Mao wrote:

> Comrade Bethune's spirit, his utter devotion to others without any thought of self, was shown in his boundless sense of responsibility in his work and his boundless warm-heartedness towards all comrades and the people. Every Communist must learn from him.[2]

This passage is reproduced in the so-called Little Red Book.[3]

The evangelical emphasis on faith is expressed in the well-known parable of 'Mr Foolish', Yu Küng, who was able to move mountains. The two mountains to be removed are, it will be recalled, those of imperialism and feudalism. If, Mao says, we persevere and work without ceasing, we will touch God's heart. 'Our God is none other than the masses of the Chinese people. If they stand up and dig together with us, why can't these two mountains be cleared away?'[4]

The symbolic materialism can be illustrated by the case of Chin Hsun-hua, discussed by Frederic Wakeman Jr. in his deep and excellent *History and Will*.[5] This young man, a Red Guard, somewhat typically of the heroes cited at that time, kept a diary which was to prove an inspiration to others. But above all he died in moving circumstances: he drowned in the Hsun river, then flooding, while trying to save some pieces of state property. In fact, the items in question were two electric light poles. A trivial cause for which to die? Not at all, for they were themselves expressions of the material transformation of China. Chin's death symbolizes that selfless heroism which is inculcated in those who are dedicated to the reconstruction of their country and who offer their loyal hearts to Chairman Mao.

Mao himself, eschewing a cult of personality, nevertheless himself becomes part of the fabric of his own symbolic materialism.

What then could be said to be the main strands in the new ethic? We have noted the necessity for the unity between theory and practice: this is in its own way an interpretation of the virtue of sincerity. Then there is the stress on continued struggle, the continued need strenuously to deal with contradictions that are inherent in the changing world. Such continued struggle implies self-improvement and self-criticism, a kind of Marxist humility. This can be translated into the humiliation of others of course: the ritual of the dunce's cap and of struggle sessions are methods of reform (for the fragile dignity of the individual is preserved in the rites of solidarity and courtesy: their deliberate reversal is a terrible thing – and it is not, incidentally, a matter of brainwashing as if it is the *brain* that is somehow taken in hand; rather it is the spirit that is broken and perhaps resurrected through the gestures of rejection and holding out of hope of reform). There is, then, a strong strand of self- and other- reform through the use of ethically-weighted rituals.

In tune with Marxism, the ethic involves also the proletarian line. The proletarian virtues are symbolized by puritanism in clothing and behaviour and the relative unostentation of China's leaders, and they consist in selflessness, class loyalty and putting the good of society above personal ambition. But though there must be collectivism, there is also need for individual courage and self-reliance. This indeed is the essence of Maoist evangelical ethics: the reform of the individual, leading to faith in the future, Marxist loyalty and patriotic selflessness, is that which so to speak supplies the new glue of society. The ethical individual exudes, so to speak, a moral gum by which he and all other good members of society stick together. Because the old glue no longer works, because individuals have not imbibed 'naturally' the values which of yore held society together, a powerful inner motivation has to be created through the celebrations and propaganda of the new heroic age. And doubtless we are in process of seeing the new Maoist ethic becoming 'naturalized' in the new (now not so new) China, as the generations slide onwards and away from the memory of the old, bad order. [92]

In all this we can see that the Maoist ethic functions analogously to the old ethic, but in the main there is a reversal of content.[6] In regard to function, the old Confucian ethic supplied the norms weaving together the fabric of Empire – the hierarchy from Heaven through Emperor to the civil service and the gentry down to the people clustered in clans and families. Its reciprocities were layered: elder–younger, father–son, husband–wife and so on. Its courtesies and sacred ceremonies were rituals for expressing and reinforcing the order, an order extending to ancestors and the gods. Its source-books were the Classics; its heroes scholarly gentlemen.

The function of supplying norms, but now in a revolutionary context, remains in the new China, but the reversals and transpositions are striking. As to transpositions: now Heaven is replaced as we saw by the masses, by the Chinese people. Indeed, in Mao's thinking, this is fairly explicit. But the people, a metaphysical whole, is mediated to individuals by the Party under the Chairmanship of Mao (and his successor). The civil service is the ganbu now, the cadres. The populace now are clustered still in families, but the clans have become brigades and communes. And the reversals? Now the reciprocity is not, in principle, layered: all men and women are equal, in a kind of fraternity (or sorority), but one in which the deference of younger brother to older is missing. To redress the balance, it is often the young who are the vanguard and the respected heroes, rather than the old men. Instead of ancestors, there is the celebration of the historical dialectic, and above all the heroes of the revolution who have fallen. Instead of an ancient golden age there is a future one. The *ta t'ung* or Great Harmony of the coming age is seen now in communist perspective. Instead of the interplay of *yin* and *yang* there is the dialectic – the engine of contradictions within matter and history which drive them onwards. Instead of the old Classics, there are the works of scientific Marxism, and in lieu of the old scholarship there is a new practicality in which the students' hands have to become dirty with engine-grease as well as ink, and work with millet as well as paper. Instead of the old deferential courtesies and ceremoniousness there is a new highly charged ritual of proletarian and peasant solidarity.

Something of the militant, selfless puritanism of the new ethic can be gleaned from the following list of topics lying at the heart of the *Quotations from Chairman Maotsetung*: serving the people, patriotism and internationalism, revolutionary heroism, building our country through diligence and frugality, self-reliance and arduous struggle, methods of thinking and methods of work, investigation and study, correcting mistaken ideas, unity, discipline, criticism and self-criticism.

Though the new ethic contains the weakness which is evident in the contradictory nature of democratic centralism (for Mao himself really never solved the problem of reconciling a kind of dictatorship with the demands of spontaneity), it nevertheless has proved impressive as the binding agent of a new society. Doubtless, three decades after the Liberation, and with new forces at work in cross-cultural exchange, something of the old zeal will fade, and it may well be that social changes will come less from inside, as was the case in the time of Mao, especially during the Cultural Revolution, than from outside. But there can be little doubt that Maoist morality has been a striking response to that slogan of the Cultural Revolution of May 4th 1919: 'Down with the Old Ethics and up with the New...'.

1. 'Reform our Study', *Selected Works*, III, 17.
2. 'In Memory of Norman Bethune', *Selected Works*, II, 337–8.
3. *Quotations from Chairman Maotsetung* (English edition), 171.
4. *Selected Works*, III, 32.
5. University of California Press, paperback 1975, 25.
6. For a fuller discussion see my *Mao*, Collins, 1974, ch.10.

CHAPTER 26

Clarity and Imagination as Buddhist Means to Virtue

THIS PAPER IS NOT INTENDED as an analytic or descriptive one. In it I wish to commend certain ideas drawn from the Buddhist tradition and freely adapted to a global view of ethics. The comparative study of cultures is important from a number of points of view: one of them is that denizens of differing cultures can learn from one another. I am sure that the Western tradition of ethics can learn much from the Buddhist tradition, partly because its assumptions are so very diverse from those of most of the West. Of course, the distinctions between cultures are beginning to melt as we move into a new global civilization. It could be a vastly rich period of human cultivation.

A first important observation about Buddhist ethics is that it contains various more or less detailed accounts of what virtue has to overcome. These obstacles are most simply described as greed (*rāga*), hatred (*dosa*), and delusion (*moha*). While the list of the deadly sins in Christianity covers varieties of the first two problems, it does not include delusion as such. Yet Buddhism has consistently considered lack of insight, ignorance, delusion, etc., as being crucial to the human condition. In fact the chain of dependent origination ends as the root cause of our being immersed unsatisfactorily and even painfully in the round of existence in ignorance (*avijjā*).

As we shall see, the kind of knowledge which replaces ignorance is not merely intellectual; it is a kind of knowledge involving experience and a kind of vision. It is more like *gnosis* than *epistēmē*; so I like to call it "gnowing"! But it is not without its intellectual side. So clear-headedness is important. For example,

126   Teaching Virtue in Different Cultures

treating all human beings equally, and not discriminating against any one group, is something which arises from the observation that all humans belong to the same species. Moreover humans have the freedom to be better or worse and therefore have the same chance to attain spiritual enlightenment. Such intellectual arguments are not, then, irrelevant to the right attitude of looking upon all humans as equals. Hence the Buddha rejected the moral importance of the division into four classes which was customary in the society of his day, and which formed the structure of what was to develop into the caste system of classical and modern Hinduism.

This links up to an observation about Buddhist philosophy. The insight that everything is impermanent, for instance, has both an intellectual and a practical significance. We can note that the idea of a permanent substance has no real purchase on the changing world, since what is permanent or unchanging cannot account for change. That is because if S unchangingly underlies the transition from E1 to E2 it cannot be the reason for the transition. Such and other intellectual thoughts might convince one of the truth of the statement that everything is impermanent. But the statement has a practical impact too: it helps to dispel egoism, since there is no permanent soul to safeguard and pamper; and it implies the brevity of satisfactions. And so in general Buddhist doctrines have their rational basis, but they are also expected to have existential impact. One needs too to be convinced of them in a kind of experiential way, as happened to the Buddha, of course, under the Bodhi tree. From the perspective, then, of overcoming delusion, one of the three "deadly conditions," Buddhism sees conceptual clarity as being vital to virtue.

Another general feature of Buddhist ethics which for the most part distinguishes it from the Western tradition is the use made of meditation to help strengthen virtues. There is a very practical approach to self-cultivation. Thus to promote benevolence or *mettā*, which is one of the sublime states or cardinal virtues (*brahma-vihāras*), one may in imagination exercise it toward some respected person, then toward a neutral person, and finally toward a hostile person. Such modes of meditation, which I shall come back to, frequently involve the use of our imagination.

Another aspect of Buddhist methods is the emphasis upon self-awareness or *sati*. It is a vital element in the Eightfold Path.

We are constantly called upon to become self-aware and thus to clarify and then purify our motives. For instance, I may read something in the paper and feel pleased. I should pause to notice the quality of my pleasure and to ask myself what gives rise to it. Say it is the demise of still another Marxist state. It satisfies me in part, of course, because I believe that Marxism is a deluded system, built on unnecessary hatreds. But is that all? Maybe I am glad to see Western Marxists further depressed; and maybe I am thinking of some foolish academics who have slighted me in a certain way, or perhaps have scorned my field. This reveals a deeper element in my motivation. My field is *mine*, and I identify with it. In scorning it Marxists have scorned me. Now the tables are beginning to be turned. So a small sliver at least of my satisfaction with the event I read of in the paper is egoism. I should, in thinking about my feelings, be able to see this. This exercise of *sati* may enable me to begin to banish egoism in that connection, and satisfaction based on the hatred of others, even if they be Marxists.

This, then, is another aspect of the clarity which can be a means to virtue in the Buddhist perspective. I wish to explore these means of intellectual analysis, imaginative meditation, and active self-awareness in relation to the four sublime virtues in particular and to the development of moral education more generally.

It will be recalled that the four *brahmaviharās* are *mettā* ("love" or "benevolence"), *karuṇā* ("compassion"), *mudita* ("sympathetic joy"), and *upekkhā* ("equanimity"). The name for these four is peculiar, for it means "holy abodes" or "abodes at the Brahma level"— or again, "heavenly abodes." The point is that the one who practices them attains the moral level of God, though God is not at all an ultimate in the Buddhist schema. The word reflects a Buddhist ploy, of moralizing the whole system of concepts involving Brahmins (those who have *brahma*-power or substance), divine power, and so on. The true Brahmin is not one who is a hereditary priest but the genuinely virtuous person. It is part of the way in which early Buddhism took the ritual and sacramental religion of the Brahmins and hollowed it out within.

Because of the centrality of compassion in the Mahāyāna, there has been a tendency for Western scholars to underrate the other three holy virtues. It is, so to speak, the melancholy analogue to *mudita*, which is that sympathetic joy a person ought to feel at the joy of others. Perhaps we naturally feel this in contemplating, let us say, the birth of a baby to friends. But often we do not feel unmixed joy at the successes of others, having an element of envy in our nature. The truly self-confident person will have achieved equanimity or *upekkhā*. This is not supposed to be indifference. That is easily achieved by locking ourselves up in a circle of family and friends, and remaining indifferent to those beyond the circle. Equanimity should make us treat others equally and in a positive way, because such equanimity is controlled by love or *mettā*. While the Buddha was keen to emphasize the virtues of the household life and the benefits of friendship he was also keen that his followers should press their moral concerns outward from their social circles to embrace all humans, and beyond that all living beings. The classical definitions of the holy virtues are in *Visuddhimagga* 318, and I have drawn on Buddhaghosa's explanations.

The process of universalizing virtues is assisted by various meditations — for instance, suffusing the differing quarters of the world with love, compassion, and so on. It is important to overcome hostilities and prejudices which we may harbor. Often, though, a meditation starts with the easier tasks, such as suffusing friends and compatriots with love. But one should train oneself to feel compassion for all. In up-to-date terms it means that we should think of "hate" figures and bathe them in love: Adolf Hitler, Joseph Stalin, Saddam Hussein, Idi Amin, and so forth. One should reflect that they too are human, have or have had freedom, and are heirs to the consequences of their acts. We see in such practices the development of imagination. One should reflect that anything which hate might dictate should happen to such people ("May they rot in hell," we might think) could happen to oneself. As one should not wish pain and disaster on oneself, so one should not wish it upon another. There are many references to such an imaginative use of reciprocity, or the Golden Rule, especially applied negatively.

The meditations which develop the virtues lead to a state of mind which is limitless (*appamaññā*) and well developed (*subhāvita*), rather than narrow or constricted and undeveloped. So the meditations are seen as a way of improving character. As a *Jātaka* verse has it:

When a person with a mind of love
Feels compassion for the whole world,
Above and below and across,
Everywhere unbounded

Filled with unlimited kindness,
Complete and developed,
Any limited actions one may have done
Do not remain loitering in the mind.
                        (*Jātakas*, 37–38)

A person who has cruel dispositions should perform meditations based on compassion in order to reform his nature.

Both the meditations regarding the holy virtues and the use of the principle of reciprocity imply something about the imagination: it is to be used constructively to widen and deepen compassion. It was a marked feature of the accounts of the life of the Buddha that he was ascribed considerable psychological insight into the motives and feelings of others. Later this was to be woven into accounting for his skill in means or *upāya*. He could adapt his teachings to the conditions of the hearers. This doctrine was to give Buddhism quite a lot of cultural flexibility in its expansion through much of Asia. Similarly, then, the development of meditation and the virtues could give his followers something of that psychological, and therefore therapeutic, insight. There are, by the way, some modern analogues in academic studies, which I shall come to later.

While I have illustrated something of the relationship between imagination and the holy virtues, what about the conceptual clarity and intellectual insight with which I began? For there is one feature of the Buddha's teaching which has often seemed to those raised in the tangle of Western presuppositions to be in some tension with virtues such as *muditā* and *karuṇā*. This is the doctrine of non-self. Does the intellect not look upon other human (and, more widely, all living) beings as empty shells, without egos, as it were, holding them together? Can an egoless being have rights? And can I have reverence for a hollow animal? How does the doctrine fit with the whole pattern of Buddhist ethics?

In a way the non-self doctrine leaves everything in place,

130   Teaching Virtue in Different Cultures

though under a different description. A person still has feelings, perceptions, dispositions, states of consciousness, etc. The person is still a bundle of *khandhas*. Nevertheless, meditation on the elements of one's existence should lead to a new view of oneself as individual, and this occurs from two points of view. First, as meditation gives a strong sense of the impersonal and instantaneous nature of psychic and bodily events, the idea of a self which possesses anything disappears. The notion that one has no substantial locus as an ego becomes lively and real; this is the function of meditation, deepening reflection. And so in a genuine way the metaphysical doctrine of *anattā* becomes transformed into a moral attitude. Another mode of understanding oneself is as a bunch of ongoing, causatively connected events. One thus begins to see the connections between this bunch of events and neighboring bunches (that is, other people). Second, in dissolving one's own ego one in effect dissolves the boundary between oneself and others. Meditation helps to strengthen the sense of connectedness of differing beings in the universe.

      There is maybe a certain paradox anyway in our modes for understanding ourselves and others. The idea of the human soul, of that divine spark which resides in each one of us, is excellent in underlying such notions as the human rights of others. Exalting humans is morally good from this angle. But in regard to ourselves, is it so good? It might be held to encourage egoism, to celebrate one's own eternal soul. From this perspective it might be best to think that I have no soul but all others do. Such an asymmetry of the imagination does not work, however. Similarly, in regard to freedom, it is important that I should recognize my own freedom, but determinism in others would conduce to a more forgiving and understanding attitude. Again the imaginative asymmetry does not work.

      In looking upon oneself as a complex chain of events, or rather a mass of chains, both parallel and intertwined, one is encouraged imaginatively to see oneself in the total pattern of interdependent origination (*paṭiccasamuppāda*). The most striking image of this interconnectedness was to await the Mahāyāna, through the picture of Indra's jewel net, in which every jewel in the net reflects every other one. This was of course splendidly worked out in the Chinese tradition through the Hua-yen philosophy.

Clarity and Imagination as Buddhist Means to Virtue   131

Positions in Buddhism can be expressed both negatively and positively. Negatively every entity is relative to others and so lacks its "own-existence" or *svabhāva*. The doctrine of dependent or relative origination can testify to that negative appraisal. But positively this means that ultimately every event is connected to every other, as in the great jewel net of Indra.

This position is not emphasized in the Theravāda in ontological terms, but rather through the practice of meditation. Meditation on relativity connects one to other living beings and so one sees oneself as inevitably enmeshed in the lives of other living beings. The imagination is thus directed outward to all those other bundles of causation and impermanence which are the loci of living biographies. Essentially the only difference between my actions and those of others is that this stream of causation here has more effects on my future than do other streams. But in fact other streams do enter powerfully into my stream: my mother and father, friends, enemies, and so on all have some effects upon my stream. The person of perfect equanimity will thus take other streams as seriously as her own. We note in this a rather different attitude from that of Kant, who advised us to treat another never merely as a means but always at the same time as an end-in-herself.

This Buddhist understanding of non-self relates to the ideal of *nibbāna* or nirvana. It is notable that the Buddha treated the notion of the self in a functional way. That is, in so far as the notion has any use at all it somehow seems to guarantee liberation. The liberated soul is one which exists beyond the usual round of rebirth. This was to be the function of the *puruṣa* in Samkhya-Yoga. The ultimate salvation of the *puruṣa* was to exist in splendid isolation. But the Buddha considered that one did not need to have a substance to perform this role. Why not substitute for the soul the possibility of liberation? That liberation would have to be austerely described or indicated, of course; there is no being there. It is a transcendental event or non-event supervening upon the previous chains of events. Psychologically it can look like annihilation, though it is annihilation with a kind of heavenly glow. It is not surprising that annihilationism should have been a Buddhist heresy. But if we find the ideal of nirvana very disappointing, since it seems to signify the loss of individuality, then that attitude only shows how far we are from attaining to it. It is because we are still entangled in selfish desires that we find nirvana off-putting. Had we reached pure equanimity, then we would desire neither to continue to exist nor not to continue. Both immortality and suicide would be unattractive. Nirvana does also mean the cessation of suffering or illfare (*dukkha*), since there is no more rebirth. This gives us a picture, then, of the Buddha's substitution: he saw egoless rebirth plus the possibility of transcendental liberation as functionally the equivalent of postulating a permanent self (*puruṣa* or *ātman*). The self, to sum up, had three disadvantages. First, it was superfluous as a means of explaining liberation. Second, it was a useless substance, for in being unchanging it could not even begin to enter into the description of change. Third, it conduced to egoism.

As well as these more abstract uses of imagination, to understand egolessness and causation, there is also the imaginative use of the idea of rebirth, and of other exercises, such as looking back on the conduct of the Buddha. So in order to look upon an enemy positively, one might try to still one's anger at him by reflecting that his bad conduct will bring him to be reborn in a horrid purgatory (and such Buddhist hells are most vividly described). Alternatively one may reflect that another person may have been — or indeed very likely was — one's mother or father or brother or sister or son or daughter in some previous life. So one can mobilize attitudes through reflecting that the other, as mother, "removed from me without disgust as if it were yellow sandalwood my urine, excrement, spittle, snot, etc., and played with me in her lap" (Buddhaghosa *Visuddhimagga* pp. 305–7).

There is running through Buddhist teachings a strong idealism, if I may call it that. Strictly speaking there is a continuum from bodily events to pure conscious events, and while the texts certainly differentiate body and mind in some sense (that is, *sarīra* and *citta*) the cosmos is basically woven out of the same kind of stuff, which occurs in denser and more subtle forms. Still, there is a strong emphasis upon the mental component of reality as being formative. This is what makes contemplation so important in the Buddhist scheme of things: the purification of consciousness resolves the problem of suffering. Likewise ultimately social reform must arise from mental factors, for each sort of society is a mental creation, a projection of the values and ideas of the people who belong to a given society. Of course the texts are well aware of the importance of material factors, for instance in the drive for private property in early society. Nevertheless, Buddhism essentially teaches that it is by purifying mental factors that we reform the world and achieve ultimate liberation. The cosmos disappears in nirvana, even though it may survive the liberation of any one individual.

It is perhaps useful to consider what the Buddhist attitude, at least in the Theravāda, does not include. It is contrasted to theistic morality in a number of ways. First, the rules or precepts are not considered to be commandments. Even the Buddha's teachings have to be tested in experience and so assimilated by the individual. Second, and connectedly, ethics is not something whose nature is revealed, as in theistic revelation. On the whole, the ethical injunctions are looked on naturalistically. For instance, the person who genuinely practices love can not only reflect on the nature of other beings, in some of the ways we have described, but can also benefit here and now from rewards. They are eleven in number, according to the *Anguttara Nikāya* (v. 142): he will sleep in comfort: he will not have bad dreams; he will be dear to others; he is dear to nonhumans; he is looked after by deities; fire, poison, and weapons do not affect him; his mind is easily concentrated; the expression on his face will be serene; he will die without confusion; and he will be reborn at least in the Brahma world (or, as we might say, in heaven).

A third difference from the theistic context is that there is in the Theravāda little room for grace or supernatural help. It is true that the teaching of the Buddha will open up new vistas for the individual. Without the intervention of the Buddha in the world the upward trend of new spiritual life would not have occurred. But the lack of the idea of grace has notable advantages: the Christian message is often clothed in too much emotion without proper attention to self-cultivation. The idea is sometimes abroad that because God does the work of sanctifying we ourselves are not also engaged in that same work: God works, in Christian orthodoxy, through us and from within us. It is striking, though, how much more there is in the Buddhist canon of detailed practical advice. As I have hinted, there is no incompatibility between such practicality and theistic belief. This is where Western religious traditions could do well to take on board some Buddhist advice.

Fourth, we may note that the Theravāda, and a lot of the

Buddhist tradition, is remarkably unsacramental; we do not have such attitudes as that marriage is a sacrament. This lack of concern with the sacramental aspects of ritual translates in a pragmatic and psychological defense of Buddhist rituals, such as they are (modes of honoring the Buddha, for instance). It is also connected to the lack of the active concept of substance. Ritual is often seen as transforming or conveying substance, but not in the Theravāda. In fact Buddhist unsubstantialism accords much more closely with modern science than the substance-loaded philosophies which have often dominated the Christian tradition. Again, it is possible to have a nonsubstantialist cosmology within the ambit of theism (a cosmos perhaps sustained and created by a personal divine, though changing, substance).

We also may note that Theravādin ethics, while generally speaking predicated upon a utilitarian schema, differs from its typical Western counterparts in its conception of happiness and the means of getting there. Thus alcohol and drugs are banned because not only do they lead to quarreling and strife, but they cloud the mind; and this is particularly important because of the · role played by insight and self-awareness in the Buddhist schema. But most significantly, the Buddhist view has a conception of the highest happiness (*sukha*) which is spiritual in nature. We can learn from this, because the Theravādin vision involves a critical attitude towards common-sense values, and a doctrine of humans as having a transcendental goal. We may call it therefore a critical, transcendentalist utilitarianism.

While the rebirth doctrine does not distinguish Buddhism from some kinds of theism, for instance that of Rāmānuja in the Hindu tradition, it does distinguish it from the framework of most Western ethics. Because the notions of *kamma* and rebirth enter into the calculation of the possibilities of attaining liberation, they also affect the utilitarian judgements. Obviously, too, the whole structure of thought gives Buddhism different potentialities of the use of moral imagination, using for instance, the wonderful *Jātaka* stories of previous lives of the Buddha to educate people in right conduct. Perhaps Westerners could adopt a version of rebirth doctrine which makes it merely metaphorical (though one might ask what this does to nirvana); such a doctrine would at least challenge us to think carefully about what promotes the highest human welfare.

Let me conclude by considering the relevance of some of these Buddhist ideas to academic life. I have long held that if we were to cultivate the virtues which arise from the whole enterprise of pursuing the truth, we would have a splendid ethic to present to our students and even the outside world. To this "ethic of truth" the Buddhist example has much relevance. First, it is obvious in the human and social sciences that we need among other things empathetic imagination (*anukampa*) to enter into the lives of other people and other times. Such empathy does not mean acceptance of others' values, but at least the possibility of understanding them. Thus, we would need it to enter into the thought world of Hitler. In such endeavors we suspend our judgments and use what some have called *epoche*. The Buddhist ethos in its advice on how to calm our feelings, both negative and positive, toward others is relevant to this concern. Maybe we can invent new methods of contemplation to enhance our ability to understand other people and cultures.

Second, the Buddhist ethos is critical and in a broad sense empirical. We of course acknowledge the critical character of enquiry and education in the West. But we do not necessarily cultivate the dispositions that have to go with it. We have to expect, for instance, critical reviews of books we write. But how well prepared are we to accept such criticism? The student is somewhat inured to criticism from teachers, and by creating a caste system wherein the two levels of academic society are differentiated the pain of professors' criticism can be made more bearable. But faculty easily become slightly paranoid, because so much subject to peer review. The pursuit of truth requires two values often lacking: one is equanimity, the fourth of the *brahmavihāras*. The other is recognition of the altruistic nature of our enterprise. This recognition would discourage the tendency to pursue knowledge egoistically, where my theories become my intellectual property.

The recognition of the impersonal character of truth might help to reinforce something arising from the *brahmavihāras*, namely, the extension of our imagination to the whole human race. It is especially for this reason that any form of groupism (racism, nationalism, sexism, etc.) is inappropriate in an academic setting. But this is not something which is abolished just by saying that it is wrong. Buddhist methods of using our imaginations could be invoked to better our attitudes towards others, and to lessen

136   Teaching Virtue in Different Cultures

the groupism which is endemic, in one form or another, in global society.

These virtues — empathetic imagination, equanimity, love of all human (and other living) beings — are intrinsic to the proper pursuit of truth, and they represent a high ideal.

I have argued that clarity and imagination are vital as means to virtue in the Buddhist ethos, particularly as represented in the Theravāda. I have tried to indicate something of the divergence of atmosphere from much of the Western ethical tradition, both theistic and nontheistic. I have also suggested that in a global society we can borrow one another's insights. There is much to borrow from the Buddhist tradition.

BIBLIOGRAPHICAL NOTE

In writing this paper I have made use of ideas expressed in my *Beyond Ideology* (San Francisco: Harper and Row, 1981). I have benefited from Gunapala Dharmasiri, *Fundamentals of Buddhist Ethics* (Singapore: Buddhist Research Society, 1986); J. Dhirasekara, ed., *The Encyclopedia of Buddhism*, vol. 4 (Colombo: Government of Sri Lanka, 1984), article on "Compassion"; and Rune Johansson, *Dynamic Psychology of Early Buddhism* (Oxford: Curzon Press, 1979).

CHAPTER 27

Religious Values and the University

It is for me a great honour to have been asked to give this address. I am also proud that it is a former doctoral student of mine, Professor M. M. J. Marasinghe, who now so excellently leads this University.

I wish to explore with you the relations between religious, and in particular Buddhist, values and the life of higher learning. The reason for my wishing to do this is that I have devoted most of my career to promoting the academic study of religion and religions. Both in Britain and in America I have striven for a plural or crosscultural approach in the field. At one time we had a flourish and eminent group of citizens of Sri Lanka studying for the doctorate: I used to say that the University should be renamed Sri Lankaster! For me it was among other things a vital symobl of our commitment to cultural pluralism.

For a University should be both a rooted and a universal institution. It should be rooted in the culture where it is placed; but it should also have an outreach to the whole of human experience and indeed, through the sciences, to the whole of the cosmos. As the astronomer reaches out beyond the solar system to the galaxy and beyond to the myriad of other galaxies, so the humanist or social scientist reaches out to the human community as a multicultural phenomenon. But it happens that in the past the study of religon has tended to be confined by and to traditions. Christians studied Christianity, Jews studied Judaism, Buddhists Buddhism, Hindus Hinduism, Muslims Islam and so on. But it is important for us to go beyond such confinement.

More imporatnt in a way is that the academic study of religion should inculcate certain values which themselves relate in an interesting way to certain religious values. Let me explain. There is a major need in studying religions to exercise a kind of warm detachment. In studying the values of a culture or tradition different from our own we need to be as objective as we can be. Indeed we need the same objectivity with our own tradition. But since in dealing with human affairs we are necessarily concerned with sentient beings with a high degree of cultural and linguistic determination it is necessary, in order to be objective, to be in a certain way, subjective as well. That is, we are not here dealing with rocks or electrons where the point of view of the individual rock or electron does not exist: we are dealing with beings who have an inward as weas well as an outward side. It is therefore important for us to use our imaginations in entering other people's points of view and feelings. There is a fine Native American proverb which bears on this: "Never judge a person till you have walked a mile in his moccasins". Imagining what it is like to be another person or what it is like to be in another culture is a vital activity in understanding. It is of course not everything. To exercise such informed empathy does not necessarily mean that questions about why people do what they do are settled. But it is at least a vital step in the process of human or social knowledge. This informed empathy is what I also called warm detachment earlier. It is a necessary ingredient in the academic life. Now, this bears some relation, as it happens, to some Buddhist values.

Thus one of the great virtues or *brahmavihāras* of Buddhism is that of equanimity or *upekkhā*. That equanimity is itself conducive to objectivity. Moreover, two of the other virtues concern entering into other people's experience: rejoicing with those who rejoice and sorrowing with those who sorrow. I am not suggesting that the academic exercise of empathizing is precisely the same as *muditā* and *karunā*. But the same imagination enters into both the academic empathy and the ethical concerns expressed in these virtues.

But also it may be noted that many scholars have thought of the correct approach in the crosscultural or comparative study of religion involves the use of *epoche*. This is the suspension of belief. A Buddhist who wants to understand Islam needs to forget for the moment that he or she is a Buddhist. It is not much good interpreting Muslim texts and behaviour from a Buddhist angle. Nor should the Buddhist explorer of Islam be full of judgements while he is studying Islam. As a Theravadin Buddhist he may not believe in a Creator or think that daily worship of God is important. He may not think that Islamic virtues are quite right. He may

20

think that the Buddha is a better model to follow than the Prophet. But to enter into the thought and feeling world of Islam he needs to suspend all those beliefs and attitudes and commitments. That suspension in the West is often called *epoche*—a Greek word. A friend of mine in South Africa who was teaching a class of Muslim students about Indian religions discovered that they felt threatened by learning about Buddhism and Hinduism. But he managed to persuade them to take these religious traditions seriously by suggesting that they only had to imagine what it was like to be a Buddhist or a Hindu for fifty minutes at a time, when they were in class. He did not want them to give up their Muslim faith but just to understand other faiths. On that temporary basis they were satisfied. So *epoche* is a suspension, not an abandonment, of belief.

Now this idea has an interesting connection with the Buddhist practice of *sati*. If we are to try to be objective about other human values we need to know what our own feelings and attitudes really are. Though there is in some traditional forms of Christianity some emphasis on such self-knowledge it is much more prominent and clearly presented in Buddhism. True self-awareness reveals to the individual his or her feelings and prejudices. So there is a kind of academic *sati* too which we ought to cultivate. We are not always good at this. I have known some Oriental scholars in the West who have eccentric attitudes to other cultures, even when they are very learned about them. The late Edward Conze, a fine explorer of the *Prajnaparamita* literature, nevertheless never visited Buddhist countries. I do not know what he feared about them, but there was something in him perhaps of the attitudes which Edward Said has castigated in his book *Orientalism*. John Brough, though a fine Sanskritist, did not, amazingly, like Indian culture as a whole. It is important if we are to be balanced students to put prejudices behind us and for this the practice of *sati* is important.

I realize that for many of you the events of the past decade have caused sorrow and grief, and from these may spring hatreds, because of the differing aspects of civil war which have manifested themselves in Sri Lanka. It is a noble task of the university, with its search for empathy and objectivity, to do something to heal such wounds. It was notable in Europe, after World War II, where hatreds were very severe, that it was university people who probably first took to repairing them, by the exchange between British and German universities. So the virtues of equanimity can floursih in our academic communities.

To sum up what I have tried to say so far : though Buddhist values such as the great *brahmaviharas* are primarily aimed at the cultivation of fine and upright individuals and to help them in the process of spiritual betterment, they also are relevant to the creation of objectivity and empathy in the scholarly community. I think the true student of the humanities and the social sciences in particular should value equanimity and the practice of *sati*. This is where there is a bonding between religious values and the pursuit of higher education.

Another religious value which importantly relates to the pursuit of truth is to do with the universal character of certain traditions. Truth, as is said, is no respecter of persons. That is why in many places a university is in the forefront of struggle for equality and fairness. For instance such universities as that of Cape Town have played a noble part in the struggle against the injustices of the apartheid system. Now there is an intrinsic bond between liberal ideas and the pursuit of knowledge, for various reasons. First, the origin of ideas and theories does not matter : what matters is whether they work and survive testing. Second, it is necessary for the testing of ideas that there should be an open society. Where people are inhibited from expressing their ideas, then the testing of theories withers. Even science, despite the degree which it can benefit from monetary support from the State, can decline when the State demands conformity. Most totalitarian regimes inevitably become parasitical upon open societies where science and technology are openly and critically practised. For instance, even the Soviet Union, though it became militarily advanced, did not produce great scientific results in general despite its great size and relatively scienti-fically—educated population. Hitler's Germany lost a great deal because it drove out many of its geniuses, including Einstein. Third, a university should follow where logic takes it. Its logic leads it towards all cultures, in the long run. It leads it towards a sense of universal humanity, and beyond that to the concerned interest in all living beings. Indeed I would say that this latter point is

22

insufficiently attested in the West and is something for universities in such countries as Sri Lanka, with its Buddhist heritage, to promote. But at least the logic of studying such things as philosophy, religion, social science, literature and history should lead us to world philosophy, world religions, world societies, world literature and world history. That does not block off more particular histories and so on. But it should take us outwards to embrace all humanity. This logic has not of course been followed in the past, and there is not a single university any-where which has a thoroughly global perspective. But the logic of exploration leads there. In brief, there are several reasons why we have to be internationalists. And several of the great religious traditions stress the same thing, at least part of the time. Buddhist compassion is not reserved only for practising Buddhists. Christian love for one's neighbour does not ask whether the neighbour be Jew or Christian, Hindu or Buddhist, atheist or theist, pious or not pious. Suffice it that he or she should be your neighbour. The brotherhood and sisterhood of all humanity is vital : and it responds also to the logic of the university.

Another religious value which we in universities ought to ponder is connected both to the suspension of belief and the universalism of the open society. It has to do with the possibility of liberating human beings from *avijja* or ignorance, liberating them from *moha* or delusion. It is a vital notion in the Buddhist tradition, as well as in the Hindu and in the Advaita Vedantin tradition in particular, that so many of our problems, perhaps all of them in ultimate origin, can be traced back to ignorance and confusion. In referring to ignorance the Buddhist tradition does not of course mean infor-mational ignorance, like not knowing where Irkutsk is or who Ramanuja was or what the electron is. It is much deeper : it is a kind of existential confusion. Anyone can know in an informa-tional sense that some people go to hospital or get killed in war or car accidents: but knowing the nature of suffering or *dukkha* is something much deeper. You can know something by being told, but something deeper by actually experiencing it. It was something of this latter and deeper knowledge that Gnostics in the world of the Roman Empire conveyed with the word *gnosis*. This is related to terms such as *nana* in the Pali tradition. The importance of insightful knowledge or *panna* is not to be underestimated. It is a kind of wisdom and clarity, and lack of it is confusion and ignorance. We in universities need to think about this. Often the pursuit of knowledge and its teaching are obscured by the fact that, necessarily as human beings, we tend to conceptual confusion. The very categories we use, whether in the sciences or in the humanities, are often confused, and they keep us in a state of ignorance. It is often that science makes leaps forwards through conceptual revolutions. It was through such reshapings of ideas that Galileo critiqued Aristotleian physics, Newton synthesized various previous astronomical advances by his theory of gravitation, Einstein went further with his theories of relativity, and Dirac produced another revolution through quantum theory. We can point to other such advances in biology (for instance Darwin's presentation of evolution by natural selection), in psychology and so on. And although the deeper kind of ignorance and the deeper kind of insight differ from those simply at the conceptual level, there is some connection. For often it is our moral qualities which hold us back from the conceptual revolutions. Often traditionalism or sloth holds us back from new insights, and the insecurity from the overthrow of old ideas, and so on. We are often in thrall to old *ditthis*. To miantain an open, creative and scientific attitude we need to be better human beings, not just clever people.

I have stressed among other things our openness to humanity as a whole. It is important that science is a total human enterprise. Our work in the social sciences and humanities should be crosscultural and transnational. But there is a danger in all this which I feel I can allude to freely because it is a Western peril, and that was my original culture. I refer to the danger of continued Western domination of global culture. World culture ought to be *world* culture. Though Buddhism, for instance, is a universal religion with a message for everyone, it also has a certain rootage, for instance in Sinhala culture. Hinduism has its rootage in Tamil and other forms of Indian and Sri Lankan culture. Islam has some rootage too here in Sri Lanka; and Christianity. The universalism of knowledge should not lead to an uncritical abandonment of particular forms of tradition, custom, language, music, art and so on. There are perils in modernity that the plural character of the globe will be elbowed aside, primarily by Western chauvinism. To take one example which engages me at the moment: philosophy. Generally speaking the West has come to dominate global organizations. For much of the time the word "philosophy" just means Western philosophy, from Thales to Wittgenstein and from Socrates to Derrida. I am currently writing a history of world philosophies as an antidote to this Western hegemonism. I of course appreciate the great achievements and continued vitality of Western thinkers : but I wish to surround them with a sense of perspective. The intricacies and splendours of Buddhist and more generally Indian philosophy, the subtle ethical and other contributions of Chinese philosphy, the fertility of Korean Neoconfucianism, modern Japanese syntheses, Islamic metaphysics, African ideas, Latin American thought—all these are important. A global philosophy needs to have give and take, a dialogue between East and West, North and South. And so it is more generally. I would think that one main vocation of this University is keeping alive some of the great cultural heritages of Sri Lanka and more widely South Asia, in the face of Western cultural imperialism. And so we are led to the question of how we can be both particular in our heritage and yet universal in our thoughts, feelings and theories.

Part of the answer lies in attitudes: we must treasure our own cultural riches, but at the same time must be open to those of others. It is this lack of openness which often leads to Western cultural imperialism, a kind of broader tribalism. We have to be self-critical about our feelings. So much of modern education is inward-looking.

To sum up all I have said. First, I have drawn attention to the need for informed empathy in our studies, and this I noted fits with the great Buddhist virtues and with the practice of self-critical awareness or *sati*. Second, I have drawn attention to the need for the suspension of belief, if we are to understand another tradition or culture. Third, I have noted that many of the great religions stress universalism, their concern with all of humankind (and beyond that the whole of the living world). But fourth, I have also noted a danger in universalism, for it can too easily be hijacked by western ways of looking at and interpreting reality. Ours should be a genuinely plural world. This is in line with some contemporary religious thinkers. All in all the study of religions links in with the values of the modern university and the modern world. So it is of course that we should be open to all religious and philosophical traditions and should therefore foster religious and other worldviews as having something important to contribute to the academic enterprise.

But all this implies too that the modern university has to be universal, but without losing its cultural identity. I bid you all in Kelaniya the best in your endeavours. I am honoured to be part of this University. Buddhist values course through my veins as well as Christian and liberal ones !

Ninian Smart,
University of California Santa Barbara
and University of Lancaster England.

26

CHAPTER 28

Sacred Civilities

WE HAVE A fairly narrow conception of what counts as a moral issue or a moral rule in Western society. Killing a person or committing adultery is usually considered morally wrong; yet there is a wide area adjoining morality which counts as civility. And that shades off into etiquette. Perhaps virtues extend further in scope than moral behavior, but they again fade into other aspects of character.

Civility covers certain dispositions in humans such as gentleness, which is not precisely listed among the virtues but seems to be adjacent to humility, which is more obviously counted as one. But a gentle disposition is seen as a generally good thing to possess. And what about cheerfulness?. Or humorousness? These are desirable. But are they virtues?

Civility is important partly because it includes treating other individuals in a way which regards them as persons. From one point of view the rights of a person can be seen in the manner in which they are to be treated. Many traditional religions seem not to have an explicit concept of human rights, but still demand toward human beings and animal life a certain kind of ritual behavior.

Religions tend to treat morals by examples—saints, heroes, and so on. Thus in Islam the *hadith* provides a fountain of stories which paint a rounded picture of the Prophet, and he then becomes a model to follow in life. It is peculiarly detailed, and there probably is not elsewhere so dense a collection of tales. The Buddha has many stories gathered about him, but generally he does not furnish us with so many clear human examples. (The *Jatakas*, of course, give us numerous examples, but chiefly of animals; so the examples do not have the warm human detail as provided by the Prophet.) There is the call in Christianity to imitate Christ, but it is often by analogy and rather abstract; consequently we have many detailed stories of the saints. Some are dear to Christians, such as Saint Francis, and provide a source of inspiration. In the days of the Great Proletarian Revolution especially, Chairman Mao was held as an ideal, and many of his pattern-forming exploits were recorded, as were those of others who caught his attention and were commended by him.

It is also noteworthy that ethics in religious contexts overlaps with the ritual demands of the faith. But ritual contains in it many forms of politeness and proper human interaction. In the original Confucian tradition this was valued as part of education, both as a proper aspect of it and as a way of molding it. *Li* or propriety was a vital part of Confucian training. It incorporates respect for others as part of its practice. It therefore overlaps seriously with what we would regard as morality.

Consider the various aspects of ritual and polite behavior which enter into a wedding occasion in modern times, in a Christian church. Not all of the customs enshrined come under moral rules, though they relate to them. The ritual contains a promise to be faithful sexually for the two partners. The clothing of the couple is related to this (especially because the bride's unusual gown, if worn, symbolizes such purity and faithfulness). The whole ceremony, including the banquet, involves a cheerfulness and a politeness which imply great good wishes and friendship which help to send the couple on their way. Maybe here and there some hypocrisy is present. But it has to be concealed; it is something for after and doubtless in private. Publicly it would mar the occasion: it would disrupt and render partly ineffective the ritual. Togetherness of the congregation and the families is reinforced by the touches of bawdiness that may come into the speeches. A joking relation is not to be fostered by overt enemies but by friends (or at least pretended friends). All the proper moves have to be made in the auspicious service and its aftermath. It is seen as a duty to perform the occasion properly, but it is not laid down in a commandment. Maybe Orthodox Jews or Hindus might have a religious handbook. But the detail of the religious law may not quite rate the depth of morality that their more serious elements warrant.

Of course a piously Christian person may see her actions as occurring in praise of God. This is where praise is superimposed upon moral, civil, or polite action to give it a deeper sense. But this does not subtract from its other meanings.

Consider by contrast what may be done to a person to humiliate him, for instance through prison and torture. He is deprived of his dignity, by having exiguous clothes, a filthy lavatory, a bad cell, revolting food, little drink. The warders who come in contact with him use foul language, calling him all sorts of names, swearing at him. And then they torture him. They love to kick his private parts, and in other ways to cause him excruciating pain. In all these ways they help to lower his self-esteem and make him look belittled in the eyes of others. Apart from the actual pain that they may cause him, much of the other acts are ritual in character and have a symbolic character. What can he do to counter them?

Well, if he is a pious Christian he can see himself as identifying with the suffering of Christ. He can dedicate his pain to God. This imports into it a new meaning, positive in its way. And so he does not seek delicacies or luxuries. He does not hate the guards. Indeed, he loves them or tries to. He is sorry for them; they must need to be cruel out of some obscure lack of self-esteem. And if he has to die he will thank his Lord who has clasped him to his eternal Self. That is how he will try to behave in his great misery and privation, which he sees only as an opportunity to follow his God. Once again we see an individual superimposing meaning on his actions, to perceive them as following Christ. It does not subtract from the pain, but it gives it a different meaning.

And so in all this there is something which goes well beyond the rules of morality as usually laid out. The ritual and symbolic character of action takes us into the realm of civility and incivility.

Perhaps it is in the Confucian tradition that we have the most vital fusing of the notions of the ethical and civility. This is through the ideas of *jen* and *li*. The idea of virtue in a human being is summed up in the former character; it was translated as benevolence by the famous translator of Chinese, James Legge. The reason is that morality is at root framed in relation to other people. The person who has *jen* is other-regarding. It also has a natural manifestation, in the way in which we respond to others. On the other hand, *li* originates, as the character implies, from ritual used in a religious act. But it spreads far beyond its narrower use, even extending to etiquette. The rules of propriety are the condition of a well-ordered society. Confucius' emphasis on education was intended to produce a harmonious social life, a kind of paradise on earth. It was a vision born of much strife and chaos in existing social relations. By the time and example of Hsun-tzu (Third Century BCE) it had become more or less secularized. But it might still have had a sacred aura—much as politicians nowadays may refer to sacrifices as sacred, especially in war.

Sacred Civilities **225**

To approach the topic from a different direction: why did Confucius think music was so vital in education? First, of course, we need to rid ourselves of the modern tendency to treat education almost wholly in terms of knowledge and technical skills. His education was conceived more as spiritual, but with strong ethical concerns. So it was a question of "how to bring up" a good offspring. But again, the West looks on education as a thing chiefly for the young, while for Confucius it should last all a person's life. I think, by the way, that both forms of education are important, and should complement one another. We now return to the question of: why music? Clearly because music plays so strongly upon the emotions. How does something so complex in genesis come to have this impact? The assumption is that some forms of music can encourage good feelings (and others by contrast bad feelings), and presumably this wells from deep springs in our nature. A similar appeal to the power of music and its *ethos* was found in Plato. I think he would be distressed by much of our popular music, some of which expresses hatred, rebellion, violence, and aspects of vulgar sexuality.

For the Confucian tradition a knowledge both of music and of sacred *li* could nurture good and just behavior in society. Again, however, we must look on knowledge as more than book knowledge, or laboratory knowledge. It is more that existential, in-experience knowledge which I like to call *gnowledge*. The word *gnowing* descends as it were from the Greek *gnosis*. It is knowing what love is, or genuine loving conduct. It is part of what existential education teaches. It does not despise factual or theoretical knowledge; and in the arts and literature it overlaps with it. The aesthetic is not even absent in scientific and mathematical discoveries.

But we live in a different world from that of Confucius or Mencius or Hsun-tzu. For one thing, the nisus of our world is towards democracy. Even our tyrannies claim to work for the people. For another thing, it is capitalist and often in a rather harsh market form. But old China was somewhat hierarchical, with an elite on top. Admittedly the elite was not a crude, powerful one but somewhat refined. The moral and political system depended on a ruler and an oligarchy. The emperor could, if necessary, of course call on armed force. But he was surrounded by dense rituals, which were much more effective, day in and day out, in controlling the country. Behind the ritual, notably in the relations between the scholarly elite and the lesser orders, there were a philosophical attitude and relevant forms of "gnowing."

We have vestiges of an elitism even in the modern world, but the more important forces are driven by the market. Our civil service and system of administering things is driven by a mass of bureaucrats, who are not especially admired or rated for moral or spiritual excellence. Nor are politicians greatly admired for their moral standing. But there is nevertheless in our society a large role played by politeness and civility to one another, largely because of the democratization of the elite. Let me expand on this.

Having an elite can encourage positive virtues. The elite can be used to elevate manners. The fact that a member of a certain class can be counted a gentleman (and in effect created as such by a certain ritual, namely, a kind of address) can lead to a transformation of the social order by democratization. After certain phases of social revolution, everyone becomes a gentleman or a lady. All are addressed as "Sir" or "Madam," and so on, in various languages and societies. And so manners spread out from the elite and become entrenched in social relations. The waiter who addresses the customer as "Sir" exchanges his uniform for other clothes and dresses for a dinner in a restaurant where a waiter addresses *him* as "Sir." And in this way everyone is equally respected, at least as a person and a human being. Courtesy becomes the way a person gains human dignity.

In the Confucian ethos there are different relations appropriate between different sorts of people, but generally these differing classes of folk are treated without the superimposition of religious meanings. The sage and the ruler are described as such. Similarly, in Theravadin Buddhism there are straight descriptions of social entities, such as the wife or the farmer. But something else occurs to titles sometimes in religious contexts. For a person is not just a person, for example, in Christianity, but also a son or daughter of God and a brother or sister in Christ. Here a way of looking on people gives them in principle a deeper social dignity, and one more deeply egalitarian. Accordingly, it may be held alongside social class distinctions. Naturally this situation lends itself to hypocrisy, but where a religious meaning is superimposed, it produces a kind of sacred civility.

Civility is related to human rights because of the secular ritual involved in treating other persons with dignity. There has sometimes been a somewhat negative reaction to a Western insistence on human rights, as though this vocabulary is the only one to use. From a Confucian perspective the individual has an obligation to *jen* and with it the

Sacred Civilities 227

associated proper behavior. From a Buddhist viewpoint there is the unfortunate aspect of rights as a possession. We may sometimes admire a person for standing up for her rights, but it is more admirable when others out of benevolence and compassion can stand up for them on her behalf. Even though the language of rights has emerged out of a Christian civilization, there is an uneasiness as to how we can square the demand for our rights with unselfishness and humility, which are Christian virtues in the path of following Christ. But Christians nevertheless have no difficulty with the idea that the person is sacred, which means in effect that the concept of a person is a performative one.

Consider the following example. If I were walking in a wood and found various logs lying there, I might hop on them in walking across them happily enough. But suppose I found two or three people lying there. I would normally carefully avoid stepping on them. If I did trample on their faces, it would be a deliberate and heartlessly cruel act. In civilized behavior I would avoid them so as not to cause pain. But even if perchance they were anesthetized I still think I would avoid stepping on them, out of respect. A person is something toward which certain kinds of behavior are to be avoided. This is what I mean by calling it a partly performative concept. And in calling a person sacred, say, in a theistic context, I am linking the appropriate behavior to that of worship. She is seen to reflect the divine nature. It is as though a person has a sort of charisma, as part of her basic endowments. The adjective *charismatic* implies that the person to whom it is applied exudes a kind of power and attraction, for whom deference is the appropriate reaction. It may be noted that my performative analysis here differs from Buber's "I-Thou" account, though it is compatible with it. It also calls on the behavior of others, rather than making the person in herself the bearer of rights. The concept of rights is a social construct. But in a theistic framework, we note that the society is comprised of persons, not just humans. For it includes the supreme Person, who has conferred personhood on individuals.

But in a nontheistic framework such as in Buddhism, does the performative aspect of the person have the same force—especially in view of the *anatta* doctrine? It is true that in Mahayana Buddhism the notion of the Buddha-nature evolved, which assigned a quasi-transcendent nature—a capacity for liberation—to each individual. Therefore Buddhahood became a sort of substitute for the eternal soul and carried with it the idea of a resemblance in each individual to the Buddha. Still, Theravada Buddhism scarcely included this notion, or only dimly. The rights of the individual could only spring from the suffering which might attract the compassion of others. In addition, perhaps, there was the demand for *mudita* or joy in the joy of others, which could be an invitation to courtesy.

We may note that there is some emphasis on courtesy in the depiction of people's responsibilities. For instance, in order to honor teachers a person should rise in salutation at their coming, should attend upon them in various ways, and so on. Students should show an eagerness to learn, which boosts the morale of teachers. Again, a husband should respect his wife and be courteous toward her. He should supply her with adornments, and so forth. In such advice (notably in the *Sigalovada Sutta*) we notice how there is a duty to adhere to good manners. This stems from the *brahmaviharas* or holy virtues. One would suppose that if people adhered to the Buddhist ethic, human rights would be respected, but the emphasis upon them is stronger elsewhere.

My brief survey of some traditions and some aspects of civility would conclude that civil behavior is continuous with ethics and is part of education. The Confucian ethos of continuing that education through life is important. Self-improvement should have a continuous place in the spiritual life. The Christian concept of the sacred person who reflects the nature of God helps us to see how performatively the person may induce proper behavior in others. Buddhism does not give much sacred significance to the individual, but in its practical advice emphasizes courtesy and respect for persons.

CHAPTER 29

A Global Ethic Arising from the Epistemology of Religious and Similar Value-Systems

Since the time of the Enlightenment we in the West have got used to the idea of the autonomy of morals, yet of course this very idea could be thought to depend upon a worldview of a certain sort. On the other hand not only are there behavioural requirements which must be observed on the whole if society is not to break down, but also behind them are typical ideal attitudes (love towards all, compassion, a sense of brotherhood, the golden rule) which are found widely expressed in world literature and social teachings. All this justifies us in speaking of a 'moral strand' which is a component of religious and other worldviews. But, and this is the point of my remark about the autonomy of morals, the moral strand is woven differently into the fabrics of differing worldviews and is variously affected by them. Sometimes, for instance, what in the West count as moral commands are embedded in a system of divine or sacred law; sometimes the right is what is commanded by God; sometimes good behaviour is seen as conformity with a cosmic pattern, such as the Tao or the Dharma; and sometimes moral rules are justified by a secularly stated utilitarianism; and so on. It is thus a useful model to think of a moral ingredient consisting of a relatively stable set of ideas, precepts and attitudes which both affects and is affected by the worldview contexts of the varied traditions and subtraditions. I want to discuss some implications of this model for the possibility of a global ethic. I shall argue that the model implies a soft non-relativism which in turn implies certain values: in brief that a higher-order situation has lower-order implications. I shall also

A Global Ethic 121

consider what the presuppositions are not just of the over-lappingly plural character of ethical systems as we find them in the world, but also of our very study. The comparative or corsscultural study of religions and worldviews, if conducted in a descriptive and critical manner, yields values which may be in conflict with the methods and attitudes of lower-order systems. Thus: taking seriously some beliefs, such as those of the Bahai, may conflict with the zeal and religious epistemology of many Muslims. Where scripture or learned authority is committed to some thesis in the history of religions it is liable to collide with the findings of modern studies in the field. Sometimes these collisions are profound, and open up to us some deep issues about the very possibility of a global ethics.

It may be useful, before coming directly to these points to look at some of the major alternative worldvews in the world today. Such a sketch enables to bear in mind the actualities with which any global ethics proposals have to deal. To try to categorize the lifeways of a myriad societies is foolhardy: but it may have some virtue in the focusing of our thought. Many of these outlooks and moral systems are in fact syncretisms, to complicate matters: syncretisms between secular ideologies or ideological themes, such as liberalism and nationalism, and traditional beliefs, or between Marxist socialism and nationalism, and so on. Generally, because of this, traditions as they emerge into today's world, take differing forms – as premodern ways of life persisting obliviously into the present time; as tradition mixed with liberalism and modernity; as reactive tradition – neoconservatism, mingling, typically, technological modernity, a reinterpreted tradition (neo-foundational, or neoclassical, etc., often lumped together as 'fundamentalist') often having nationalist overtones. Thus the SLFP variety of Buddhism in Sri Lanka tends to be neoclassical rein-terpreted Theravada Buddhism, shown to be compatible with scientific modernity, and nationalist in tone. The moral majority is a similar Protestant movement, but neofoundational and yet rejecting modernity in relation to historical scholarship but not in regard to technology, and likewise nationalistic. By contrast ecumenical Christianity tends to be liberal and internationalist. To complicate matters it is possible to take different stances, or blends thereof, in regard to the differing dimensions of religion: being perhaps institutionally traditionalist, ritually modernistic, doctrinally neofoundationalist, ethically liberal, experientially syncretic and mythically modernistic – consider a modern Catholic, defending and maintaining the ecclesiastical institutions rather conservatively, reaffirming the first creeds, taking a progressive line in moral teachings, absorbing the pentecostalist tradition of ecstatic experience into Church life, and reading salvation history in secularist terms. All these complications of the emerging forms of traditions are laid on top of the various layers of regional and denominational variegation of the past as transmitted to us.

So doubly do we have an obligation to speak of Christianities, Islams and so on in the plural. For all their plural character, perhaps because of it, the religious traditions retain great power, but alongside and blending with some major ideological traditions and motifs: liberal humanism (or humanisms), Marxism, and nationalism. Some traditions, having lost their main habitat, such as Confucianism, are perhaps most important as resources for humankind to draw upon: in general of course we live in a syncretic, pragmatic age in which a novel eclecticism is possible. A special problem is seen among relatively small-scale traditions, those particularly that are identified with particular ethnic or tribal cultures chiefly in the Third World. They have to make adaptation to the powerful incoming forces of Christianity (and Islam), modernity, liberalism, etc., but typically without a strong enough classical indigenous base. One solution is to move towards a more universal regionalism – hence such concepts as African religion and Native American religion have been created; another solution is to move towards a federal theory of religions – that each has something to offer within the wider whole. Thus tradition can be maintained, no doubt with modifications, and at the same time one's spiritual heritage becomes a *resource* for humanity. An example is how Native American attitudes and concepts are used to reinforce a universal environmentalism.

This leads to the thought that one consequence of mutual awareness of cultures will be a rich global eclecticism: and doubtless such an ethical collage could be justified by the thought that different cultures are so many experiments in living and so should together supply the matter for a wise ethic. However, such an eclecticism would itself be in part consequence of some new worldview, and I would rather now persist with the question of what happens given our present range of worldviews, both religious and otherwise.

In line with my preliminary remarks I shall assume that there are some oppositions of religious imperatives (and secular imperatives), e.g. over abortion, marriage, the logic and nature of punishment, war, etc. as between different traditions and sub-traditions. Such oppositions are to be distinguished from alternatives. For instance, it is forbidden for orthopractic Jews to eat pork. A Christian has no such inhibition: but a situation in which the Christians and the Jew allow each other to practice their own way in this matter does not represent a contradiction. Alternatives can thus become a set of tolerated customary options. But behind such toleration there typically lurks a theory ('Such externals are not important', 'God laid this command on us but not on them', etc.)

As well as oppositions of imperatives there are differing emphases which might lead to divergent conduct, and these can arise both from basic attitudes and from differing models in history and myth. The theme of martyrdom is emphasized in Shi'i Islam but not in Theravada Buddhism; self-analysis is much more prominent in the latter than the former tradition, etc. These divergences in part derive from and in part are summed up in the differing focal figures such as Ali and Buddha.

The derivation of differing rules and emphases from the world-views is hardly strict: one can imagine a Catholicism without a ban on abortion and an Islam without martyrdom, even a Judaism without the ban on pork. But typically the ethical items get worked into an authoritative tradition – at its hardest a sacred scripture. It is here that the derivation can become subjectively certain. The item is seen by the believer as absolute and binding in so far as the canon has this quality (canon whether oral or written, etc.). Though notoriously the interpretations of authoritative traditions come to vary, nevertheless the insider – formed already by the variant interpretation – sees the preferred interpretation as authoritative, and often as quite certain (even if religion often goes with underlying doubts).

So a common, though not universal, aspect of worldviews is a 'hard' epistemology: an item is in the Canon, so it certainly must be binding: or it is the ruling of those in authority, so it certainly must be binding. The major question posed by the comparative study of religions (and worldview analysis) is how such oppositions of hard epistemologies can be resolved. For it inevitably turns out that crosscultural or crosstraditional arguments on behalf of my hard epistemology over yours are soft. Thus to argue for the Qur'an on the basis that it is wonderfully beautiful, resonant, awe-inspiring in its style – and how could an illiterate fellow have produced such a masterpiece? – is a soft argument depending first· on esthetic judgments (wonderfully beautiful, etc.) and second on an alleged empirical impossibility (but who could have thought. Mozart possible, before the event?). Actually, the arguments for hard epistemologies are doubly soft: they are soft in themselves, and they have to overcome the hurdles constituted by different worldviews, which not only are often institutionally entrenched, but also filter the arguments through different conceptual lenses. Concretely: if I am embedded in the Episcopal Church and see the world through Western Christian cosmopolitan eyes, the esthetic arguments about the Qur'an have a lot of inertial scepticism to overcome. And so we come to the following conclusive reasoning: the epistemology of a worldview is either hard or soft; but if it is hard it itself has to argue against conflicting epistemologies and the arguments it uses are bound to be soft; so the net result is that a worldview epistemology is soft. For soft arguments for the validity of a hard proof render the proof soft.

This is not a conclusion that is congenial to many religious or similar worldview believers. Their phenomenological certainty of faith collides with the outer judgment of uncertainty. This seems disagreeable and upsetting. The good news I suppose is that often we can be inwardly sure of things which we cannot prove or even persuade others about. We can contrast inner certitude and public certainty. They by no means go together. Even so, the conclusion is unsettling, for it licenses alternative and opposing views. It reflects the truth that the only proof in religion is internal to a system or tradition, and that is not enough. To put it another way, faith cannot produce external guarantees of its correctness. So how can it legitmately deny alternative ways and formulations of faith?

It will be replied that this is not how the situation is perceived in conservative seminaries and prestigious mosques, nor in sacred temples or totalitarian academies. I am not presenting these conclusions as a piece of phenomenology, but only as arising from the logic of the situation. We should note however that logic (in this loose sense) creates its own pressures. Those who resist the softness argument have to create more and more ingenious ways of keeping the situation concealed. The logic of the one world will have its slow effects, despite frontiers and visas of the mind.

But softness is not relativism: lack of proof in these matters does not imply that all positions are equal. For one thing a position which does not recognize epistemological softness is in that respect inferior to one which does. There are other tests of worldview – consonance with science, richness of relevant experience, capacity to bear fruits, etc. These are sometimes spiral (not circular but with an element of circularity) – e.g. the fruits: What if one faith produces persimmons and another oranges, because of a difference of value-emphasis?

The position I have sketched emphasizes the softness of epistemology, but does not go on to draw the conclusion of relativism, for there are soft reasons at least that can be deployed pro and contra differing worldviews. Soft non-relativism does not rob people of the quest for truth, but it does deprive them of the rights that pertain to being legitimately certain. There is no right therefore to teach your own worldview as though it alone could be true. Much, ethically and politically, flows from this.

First, it follows that we should be tolerant and understanding of the varied worldviews. Even if we are convinced of the absurdity of someone else's position we should remember that there are phases and forms of our own tradition or position which can likewise seem absurd, to ourselves or others or both.

Second, there is a Popperian argument from worldview-epistemology to politics as there is from science to politics. The open society which allows differing forms of belief and opinion is the best. At the level of doctrine, this pluralism is not hard to describe: the ways of allowing freedom of speech are well known. But what of customary oppositions? What about differing ethical and ritual practices? And what if a group decides it needs authoritarian arrangements internally in order to preserve its ethos and way of life?

As for customary oppositions, e.g. over abortions, then there is no question of stopping legitimate agitation and argument: obviously freedom of belief implies freedom of expression thereof. But this has something important to say about the question of authoritarian structures. It implies that if a group wants an authority figure it needs to set it up on a voluntary basis, for if people are free to criticise then only voluntarily can they suspend their freedom to criticize an authoritarian leader. That of course

126   *The Western World and Global Change*

involves a seachange in many authoritarian groups: once they become voluntary the Leader in a strange way is elected.

But to be realistic: though we think of most such ethical and social questions as arising within a society – which for all practical purposes is a nation-State – a global ethic has to deal with a citizenship far beyond that milieu. Indeed, the soft non-relativist position is subversive of the nation-State in certain ways. I shall proceed to a discussion of the pressures of the argument in a moment. But let me first add a second main reason for us, in the context of comparative religious ethics, to espouse the open society. It is that opposition to knowledge about alternative world-views to the official one is the norm in worldview-closed societies (such as 18th-century Sweden or 20th-century East Germany). Often such studies are only possible in such monistic societies on condition that what is studied does not look like a live alternative option. Programmes in comparative religion tend to be exiguous in Marxist, Islamic and traditional Catholic countries; and in many other countries there is sometimes opposition from another direction – scientific–utilitarian humanism, as the dominant philosophy of the educated technocrat. The very attempt at a plural, descriptive comparative ethics is somewhat foreign to the totalitarian and authoritarian State. In any event, we are part, in this enterprise, of the open humanities and social sciences, whose flourishing presupposes a pluralistic politics.

Yet there is a paradox here. For – and this brings us back to the earlier discussion – our study concentrates on traditions of which Western liberalism is a major solvent, for it ends up with a disintegrative individualism. Are we then by our presuppositions, committed to the disappearance of what we study? There is no contradiction as such in this, but it is to say the least an eccentric pursuit to do this –. though let it be remembered that the huntsman admires the fox, and the fisherperson the trout.

I slipped in the word 'Western' just above. Does the open and plural society need to be *Western*? There is nothing in my previous arguments to identify the open society with the West. On the contrary, it may be that in some respects other societies have a better understanding of pluralism than some typical Western democracies. For individualism as practised can, by majority pressure, paradoxically produce great conformism. The tendency of Western capitalism is to homogenize, so that gradually cultural differences are being eliminated. But be that as it may, the argument that openness is a precondition of our very subject adds an extra force to the argument from soft non-relativism. I now turn back to the question of a global as distinguished from a social, that is to say a national, ethic; and we can ask how non-relativism relates to this wider field.

It is perhaps wise to think of several factors relevant to the global milieu. When we use the world 'global' we are assuming that in some manner the life of humanity forms something of a system. That is now true. Especially since World War II this global system has become manifest. First, the period saw the rough completion of the process of distributing the land surface of the world among independent nation-States (and State-nations). Theoretically this international order is guaranteed by the United Nations Charter. In practice, it entrenches States' rights over against minorities' and individuals' rights, despite the Universal Declaration on Human Rights. Second, modern means of communication and transport have speeded up the process of the formation of a single global economic community – basically as capitalist order incorporating regions of socialism as part of the system, and dominated by a few hundred powerful multinational corporations. Third, travel and the media have created the framework for a world cultural superstructure, so that certain events like the Olympics have become phenomenologically world events. We are getting nearer de Chardin's noosphere as a unitary medium. At the moment it is embodied in an international set of overlapping elites: a kind of aristosphere. Fourth, there are a number of transnational agencies which help to bind the globe together or at least to mitigate the fragmentation represented by the system of nations. Among important transnationals are the aforementioned corporations; also there are intergovernment entities such as UNO, FAO and so on; there are global learned societies, consultative groups and the like; last but not least are the ecumenical religions, notably Christianity, Buddhism and Islam. In these, then, and other ways we can rightly think of ourselves as entering into a One World System; but an unstable one, not only because there can be crises in global capitalism, but more importantly because of the real possibility of the war to end wars.

In this global situation the role of the religions can be paradoxical. On the one hand the major faiths are transnational, and even those that are ethnically based (either because a religion is definitional of an ethnie or because it is an aspect of the ethnie's culture) can only persist on the tacit understanding that there is as it were a federal spirituality of which the ethnic religions are differing expressions. On the other hand the religions represent a problem of particularism, since they have in part rival views of right and wrong and of ultimate human happiness, etc., and these views affect social institutions. It seems to me that religious ethics are to be interpreted in the light of real possible global and troubles and disasters, such as the following:

> violent conflict between religions;
> war, including global war;
> widespread destruction of the natural environment;
> poverty and attendant evils, such as illiteracy, poor health, etc.;
> the oppression of minorities;
> the oppression of individuals;
> the painful destruction of traditions;
> widespread spiritual emptiness and lack of meaning.

There are other evils, of course, but these seem to be major ones. What does their treatment suggest about religious ethics?

First, even if we cannot attain unanimity on the contents of moral and political action, we can at least find in the moral strand overlapping beliefs in universal values. So a positive accentuation of these inter-religious overlaps conduces to a more unitary approach to human problems.

Second, soft non-relativism's drive towards toleration implies that it cannot be right to spread alternative views by force, save in so far as minimization of violence may itself be an issue (to which I come).

Third, as a corollary to the preceding, engagement in alternative modes of persuasion presupposes the validity of the proverb 'Never judge a man till you have walked a mile in his moccasins', i.e. the positive attempt to understand phenomenologically other people's viewpoints and values is always a correct endeavour.

Fourth, attention to the preceding three points implies that the rights of minorities within societies (i.e. nations) are something which the transnational and other religions ought to protect, within the limits of the minimization of violence.

Fifth, questions about the distribution of goods relate to the whole world, not just to the poor within a given society: so the religions need to promote a sense of universal sisterhood and citizenship in the kingdom of the dharma. In brief, religion is in principle internationalist, even when highly particularist. Likewise the environment is something held in trust for all citizens of the planet.

Sixth, in so far as the group of ultimate concern must be humanity (plus somewhat other living beings), and not the nation or ethnie or even the religious community of the elect, the rights of individuals become paramount – i.e. the right of a person simply because she is a member of the human race.

Seventh, the religions (and serious secular worldviews) should attempt to conserve or enhance meaning, partly by modernizing without violent ruptures, where possible, of the traditions which help to provide a framework of meaning, and partly by combating the trivialization of experience made possible with today's technological affluence.

Eighth, both because of soft non-relativism's implication of toleration and the use of means such as argument and example to spread one's ideas and values, and because of other considerations (compassion, etc.) the ecumenical and other religions ought to be or could agree at least on the principle of the minimization of violence. This is not to say that violence may never be justified: that depends in part with your worldview. But even the use of war should be conducted in the spirit of applying the least violence. This is a common, if oten hypocritically applied, defence of war.

Now to these remarks it may be replied that they are in part political imperatives. It is hard to separate politics from ethics; and it is obvious that many regimes would reject one or other of these theses I have been putting forward. But let me at least attempt to transpose these imperatives explicitly into personal terms, that is into the language of virtues rather than imperatives. What virtues do the theses imply? And how do they connect with traditional religious virtue? It seems to me that the virtues can be listed as follows:

> generosity of spirit towards those holding other worldviews;
> spiritual self-confidence;
> the cultivation of imaginative empathy;
> tenderness towards minorities;

the sense of universal brotherhood and justice;
reverence towards all as individuals;
the love of human meaning;
the attitude of non-violence.

Some of these are clearly covered by such traditional religious notions as that one should love one's neighbour/enemy; the *brahma-vihāras*; the Sufi notion of *jihad* as a spiritual struggle; the Islamic ideal of the brotherhood of humanity, etc.

It is of course clear that there are militant versions of religious and other worldviews which would only accept some of these putative virtues. Often wounded identity, a common collective condition in the modern age for various reasons, issues in vehemence of commitment; and 'realistic' politics suggests that one would become soft in the face of evil empires and the like were one to adopt these virtues. To this let me just add a few ripostes.

What makes an evil empire evil? Repression of minorities and individuals, the use of the propoganda of hate, threatening international behaviour. It is conceivable that in order to combat such it is necessary to use repression, hate and threats. But the justification for opposing evil then disappears. Even if some degree of threat of violence is needed to restrain violence, this would be justified as the minimization of violence which needs to be underpinned by attitudes of non-violence and universal brotherhood, etc. Moreover effective restraint of the other if violent requires an understanding of the other, and that implies imaginative empathy. So the virtues listed are not merely not inimicable to true *realpolitik* but are presupposed by it, if, that is, the *realpolitik* is on the side of the angels. If not, so what? We are after all discussing *ethics*, not self-interest.

However, there are thorny issues which these implications of soft non-relativism leave unresolved, and which I have skated round. They are issues concerned with not just freedom to express spiritual positions but to practice according to diverse systems of religious and other law. Should a Muslim in the United States be permitted to practice polygamy? Should Native Americans or the Amish have privileges in regard to the waiving of religion-State separation in the schools? Can pluralism in other words extend to intra-societal legal and ethical structures?

It may be noted that if the principles of individual and group freedom are applied – and these seem to be a consequence *inter alia* of soft non-relativism – customs can be practised privately on a voluntary basis: e.g. a widower and a widow can marry in Italy in Church but not register it as a civil wedding, which would lead to loss of certain pension rights. But the implication of our position is that pluralism does imply a voluntary basis for adherence to alternative and so different customary modes of living. There are moreover historical precedents which might if suitably adapted be made use of: the Ottoman millet system, the caste system (so far as it can be stated and implemented non-hierarchically), the cantonal system, etc. Even in the days of *cuius regio eius religio* there was usually freedom of migration if you did not wish to embrace your ruler's religion. It seems singularly inappropriate, other things being equal, that the majority's law should be forced upon a minority group (e.g. Islamic law being applied in the Christian and so-called 'animist' South Sudan). Even if some minority custom is offensive or repugnant to the majority there is room for discretion: and the majority in accordance with the virtues I have outlined might ask themselves whether their repugnance does not stem from a lack of imaginative empathy and of a sense of brotherhood, a lack of tenderness towards minorities, etc. Even if they be hard absolutists they may find echoes of these virtues in their traditional authoritative sources.

My total argument is from epistemology and global plurality. To rehearse its essence: some moral values are common and represent the primary thread in the moral strand. Others diverge because of differences of worldviews. Thus, since worldviews are not susceptible of proof and at best can only produce internal proofs of ethical rules, etc. the divergences between systems are not resolvable by proofs. The reasoning is soft, and the appropriate position to adopt is soft non-relativism. But this implies tolerant attitudes, which in world perspective imply certain religious attitudes, and certain virtues, notably those conducing to imaginative empathy, the minimization of violence and a sense of universal world citizenship.

Additional Publications by Ninian Smart

Virtually all of the items listed below have been published, and full details are available in the Ninian Smart Bibliography in Appendix 2 of Volume 2: [A] books; [B] papers in edited books; [C] papers in journals or published as pamphlets. (The bibliography is also available on the Ashgate website.) A few, though, are to be found only in typescript in the Ninian Smart Archive located in Lancaster University Library. These are referred to according to their location as listed in the Archive Catalogue, which is available on-line on the website of the Department of Religious Studies at Lancaster University. The entries are grouped by section.

I Autobiographical

Fragments of a Life in Academe (1974-1977) [E4]
SOAS at a Strange Time (1997) [E4]
Fifty Years in Ivory Towers: From Hitler to Beyond the Cold War (Archive F4)
Smart Ivory (Archive, Appendix)

II Religious Experience and the Logic of Religious Discourse

Reasons and Faiths: An Investigation of Religious Discourse, Christian and Non-Christian (1958)
The Concept of Worship (1972)
The Criteria of Religious Identity (1958) [C]
The Transcendence of Doctrines (1959) [C]
Paradox in Religion (1959) [C]
Social Anthropology and the Philosophy of Religion (1963) [C]
Religious Experience (1976) [B]
Our Experience of the Ultimate (1984) [C]
Ultimate Non-Existence Revisited (1985) [B]

III Mystical Experience

Mystical Experience (1962) [C]
Mystical Experience, with Rejoinders (1967) [B]

The Exploration of Mysticism (1977) [B]
Interpretations of Mysticism (1972) [Archive F4]

IV Comparative Studies

A Dialogue of Religions (1960)
East-West Encounters in Philosophy and Religion (1996)
Buddhism and Religious Belief (1961) [C]
Attitudes Towards Death in Eastern Religions (1968) [B]
Consciousness: Permanent or Fleeting? Reflections on Indian Views of Consciousness
    and Self (1989) [B]
Western Society and Buddhism (1989) [C]
'Transcendence in a Pluralistic Context' (1997) [B]
The Nature of Religion: Multiple Dimensions of Meaning (2000) [B]
Is Hinduism an Offshoot of Buddhism? [with Knut Jacobsen] (2006) [B]

V Religious Studies and Religious Education: Method and Theory in the Study of Religion

The Teacher and Christian Belief (1966)
Secular Education and the Logic of Religion (1968)
The Phenomenon of Religion (1973, second edition 1978)
The Science of Religion and the Sociology of Knowledge: Some Methodological Questions (1973)
New Movements in Religious Education (1975)
Religion and the Western Mind (1987) [chapters 1-3]
The Nature of Religion (1964) [E1]
Theology (1966) [B]
A New Look at Religious Studies: The Lancaster Idea (1967) [C]
The Comparative Study of Religion in Schools (1969) [C]
The Principles and Meaning of the Study of Religion (1970) [C]
What is Truth in RE? (1970) [C]
Religion as a Subject (1970) [C]
Religious Studies at Lancaster, England (1971) [C]
Philosophy and Religion: Conversation with Ninian Smart (1971) [B]
Comparative Hermeneutics: An Epilogue about the Future (1973) [B]
The Exploration of Religion and Education (1975) [C]
Exploring Religion in a Plural Society (1976) [C]
Beyond Eliade: The Future of Theory in Religion (1978) [C]
History of Religions (1979) [C]
Towards a Dialogue at the Level of the Science of Religion: A Reply to Ren Jiyu (1979) [C]
The Exploration of Religion in Public Education, I and II (1979 and 1980) [C]

The Philosophy of Worldviews, or the Philosophy of Religion Transformed (1981) [C]
A Curricular Paradigm for Religious Education (1981) [B]
Threat to Religion on the Campus (1981) [C]
Religious Studies and South Africa (1982) [C]
Worldview Analysis: A Way of Looking At Our Field (1982) [C]
Scientific Phenomenology and Wilfred Cantwell Smith's Misgivings (1984) [B]
The Scientific Study of Religion in its Plurality (1984) [B]
The History of Religions and Its Conversation Partners (1985) [B]
From Rome to Sydney: Reflections on the Study of Religions (1985) [C]
Identity and a Dynamic Phenomenology of Religion (1985) [C]
Foreword [to G. van der Leeuw, *Religion in Essence and Manifestation*] (1986) [B]
Methods and Disciplines in the Study of Religion (1986) [B]
Towards an Agreed Place for Religious Studies in Higher Education (1986) [B]
The Study of Religion: Where Are We Going? (1987) [C]
Comparative-Historical Method (1987) [B]
Religious Studies in the United Kingdom (1988) [C]
Graduate Education: Some Practical Issues (1988) [C]
Religious Studies, Worldview Analysis and Business Education (1989) [C]
Concluding Reflections: Religious Studies in Global Perspective (1990) [B]
Religious Studies and Religious Education: Challenges for a New South Africa (1991) [C]
Teaching Religion and Religions: The "World Religions" Course (1991) [B]
The Pros and Cons of Thinking of Religion as Tradition (1991) [B]
Secular Ideologies: How Do They Figure in Religious Studies Courses? (1991) [B]
The Introductory Course: A Balanced Approach (1991) [B]
Retrospect and Prospect: The History of Religions (1994) [B]
The Values of Religious Studies (1995) [C]
Some Thoughts on the Science of Religion (1996) [B]
Freedom, Authority and the Study of Religion in the United States (1996) [B]
Religious Studies and Theology (1997) [C]
Does the Philosophy of Religion Rest on Two Mistakes? (1997) [C]
Foreword [to P. Connelly, ed., *Approaches to the Study of Religion*] (1999) [B]
The Future of the Academy (2001) [C]
Religious Education (Archive F4)
The University, the Ocean of Empathy and the Way to the Truth (Archive F4)
What Most Needs to be Done in the Study of Religion (Archive F6)
The Birth of Religious Studies in the U.K. and the U.S.A. (Archive F6)
Comparative Religion and the Social Sciences (Archive F6)

VI Religious Ethics

The Perfect Good (1955) [C]
Omnipotence, Evil and Supermen (1961) [C]

Ethics and Linguistic Philosophy (1965) [C]
What is Happiness? (1980) [B]
Spiritual Diversity and the Planet in the 21st Century (1993) [B]
Friendship and Enmity Among Nations (1994) [B]
Marriage in the World's Religions (1995) [C]

Table of Contents for Volume 2

III: Christian Theology of Religions and Interfaith Dialogue

20 'Revelation, Reason and Religions', in Ian Ramsey (ed.), *Prospect for Metaphysics: Essays of Metaphysical Exploration*, London: George Allen and Unwin, 1961, pp. 80–92

21 The Relation Between Christianity and the Other Great Religions', in A. R. Vidler (ed.), *Soundings: Essays Concerning Christian Understanding*, Cambridge: Cambridge University Press, 1962, pp. 103–121

22 'God's Body', *Union Seminary Quarterly Review*, **37** (1 and 2) (1981–2): 51–59

23 'Soft Natural Theology', in Eugene Thomas Long (ed.), *Prospects for Natural Theology*, Studies in Philosophy and the History of Philosophy, Vol. 25, Washington, DC: The Catholic University of America Press, 1992, pp. 198–206

IV: Plurality of Religions: Religious Interpretations

24 'The Convergence of Religions', in Purusottama Bilimoria and Peter Fenner (eds), *Religious and Comparative Thought*, Delhi: Indian Books Centre, 1988, pp. 247–256

25 'A Contemplation of Absolutes', in Arvind Sharma (ed.), *God, Truth and Reality: Essays in Honour of John Hick*, London: Macmillan; New York: St. Martin's Press, 1993, pp. 176–188

26 'Models for Understanding the Relations Between Religions', in J. Kellenberger (ed.), *Inter-Religious Models and Criteria*, London: Macmillan; New York: St. Martin's Press, 1993, pp. 58–67

27 'Pluralism', in Donald W. Musser and Joseph L. Price (eds), *A New Handbook of Christian Theology*, Nashville, TN: Abingdon Press, 1992, pp. 360–364

V: Plurality of Religions: Ethico-Political Implications

28 'On Knowing What is Uncertain', in Leroy S. Rouner (ed.), *Knowing Religiously*, Boston University Studies in Philosophy and Religion, Vol. 7, Notre Dame, IN: University of Notre Dame Press, 1985, pp. 76–86

29 'The Epistemology of Pluralism: The Basis of Liberal Philosophy', *Philosophy and Social Action* (New Delhi), **16** (2) (1990): 5–14

30 'Does a Universal Standard of Value Need to be Higher-Order?', in *Science and Absolute Values*, Vol. 1, Proceedings of the Third International Conference on the Unity of the Sciences, London; New York: International Cultural Foundation, 1974, pp. 589–597

31 'Worldview-Pluralism: An Important Paradox and Its Possible Solution', *Journal of Religious Pluralism*, **1** (1991): 21–43

VI: Conclusion

Name Index